Seafaring Labour

Seafaring Labour

The Merchant Marine of Atlantic Canada, 1820–1914

ERIC W. SAGER

McGill-Queen's University Press
Kingston, Montreal, London

© McGill-Queen's University Press 1989
ISBN 0-7735-0670-5

Legal deposit first quarter 1989
Bibliothèque nationale du Québec

Printed in Canada on acid-free paper

This book has been published with the help of a
grant from the Social Science Federation of Canada,
using funds provided by the Social Sciences and
Humanities Research Council of Canada.

Canadian Cataloguing in Publication Data

Sager, Eric W., 1946–
    Seafaring labour : the merchant marine of
    Atlantic Canada, 1820–1914–
    Includes bibliographical references and an index.
    ISBN 0-7735-0670-5
    1. Merchant seamen—Maritime Provinces—History
    —19th century. 2. Merchant seamen—Newfound-
    land—History—19th century. 3. Merchant
    marine—Maritime Provinces—History—19th
    century. 4. Merchant marine— Newfoundland—
    History—19th century.
    I. Title.
    HD8039.S42C35 1989   305′.93875′09715   C88-090341-4

In memory of Keith Matthews

Contents

Illustrations xix

Abbreviations viii

Illustrative Material ix

Acknowledgments xv

Introduction 3

1 A Pre-Industrial Workplace 13

2 Working the Small Craft 44

3 A Workplace in Transition 74

4 Working the Deep-Sea Ship 104

5 Recruitment 136

6 Struggles for Protection and Control 164

7 Capital, Labour, and Wages 201

8 Home to the Sea 222

9 An Industrial Workplace 245

Notes 267

Index 317

Abbreviations

MHA	Maritime History Archive, Memorial University of Newfoundland, St John's (until 1986 the Archive of the Maritime History Group)
MHG	Maritime History Group, Memorial University of Newfoundland, St John's
NBM	New Brunswick Museum, Saint John
NMM	National Maritime Museum, Greenwich, England
NSM	Nova Scotia Museum, Halifax
PANS	Public Archives of Nova Scotia, Halifax
PAPEI	Provincial Archives of Prince Edward Island, Charlottetown

Illustrative Material

FIGURES

1 Gaff Mainsail: An Example of Fore-and-Aft Rig   27
2 The Square Sail and Its Running Rigging   32
3 Vessel Rigs, 1860s and 1870s   33
4 Sail Plan of a Three-Masted Ship   36
5 Principal Elements of a Ship's Standing Rigging   124
6 Foremast: Principal Elements of a Ship's Running Rigging   125

GRAPHS

1 Small Vessels on Registry, Major Nova Scotia Ports, 1825-1914   37
2 Small Vessels on Registry, Saint John and Miramichi, 1825-1914   38
3 Small Vessels on Registry, Prince Edward Island, 1826-1914   39
4 Small Vessels on Registry, Newfoundland, 1826-1914   40
5 Tonnage Employed in Canadian Coasting Trades, 1876-1914   41
6 Tonnage and Values in Newfoundland's External Trade, 1850-99   68

7 Index of Sugar Freight Rates, Havana–New York, 1865–89 69

8 Larger Vessels on Registry in Four Major Ports, 1826–1914 76

9 Estimated Total Mid-Summer Employment in Vessels Registered in Atlantic Canada, 1830–1914 77

10 Tramp Shipping Freights and Selected North Atlantic Sailing Ship Freights, 1855–99 165

11 Discharge Reasons by Year, Saint John Fleet, 1863–1910 189

12 Man-Ton Ratios, Saint John Fleet, 1863–1900 203

13 Monthly Wages of ABs, Saint John Fleet, 1863–1903 216

14 Average Monthly Wages of All Crew Members by Rank, Windsor Fleet, 1863–1904 217

15 Tonnage At Sea, Labour Inputs, and Total Wage Payments, Saint John Fleet, 1863–1900 219

16 Man-Ton Ratios in British Sailing Vessels and Steamers, 1863–1913 251

17 Average Wages of Sailors in British Ships, 1863–1908 258

MAPS

1 Eastern Coastal Waters 17

2 The Sailing Ship's North Atlantic 19

3 Nova Scotia Tonnage Clearing for Halifax, 1839 22

4 Newfoundland-Owned Tonnage Clearing St John's, 1839–44 23

5 Nova Scotia Tonnage Clearing Halifax, 1873 25

6 Mid-July Locations, Vessels and Men of Four Fleets, 1863 118

7 Mid-July Locations, Vessels and Men of Four Fleets, 1890 119

8 Birthplaces of Officers and Crew Members, Nova Scotia Fleets, 1863-1914 148

9 Birthplaces of Officers and Crew Members, Saint John Fleet, 1863-1914 149

10 Birthplaces of Sailors from the Maritimes Serving in Four Fleets, 1863-1914 151

11 Birthplaces of Sailors in British Sailing and Steam Vessels, 1863-1914 255

TABLES

1 Sailing Vessels Clearing Port in Canadian Coastal Trades, 1900 42

2 Birthplaces of Sailors Signing on Yarmouth-Registered Ocean-Going Vessels, 1846-7 53

3 Wages of Nova Scotia-Born ABs in Yarmouth Vessels, 1846-7 55

4 Tonnage and Crew Size, Newfoundland Vessels, 1860-99 67

5 Ranks of Sailors Signing on at Departure, St John's-Registered Sailing Vessels, 1863-99 107

6 Distribution by Rank, Saint John Fleet, 1863-1914 109

7 Age of Sailors in Four Fleets, 1863-1912 139

8 Birthplaces of Masters in Four Fleets, 1863-1914 142

9 Birthplaces of Masters, Four Fleets, 1863-1914 143

10 Birthplaces of Officers, 1863-1914 146

11 Age of Officers, Four Fleets, 1863-1914 147

12 Crew Participation Rates, 1863-1914 150

13 Birthplaces of Crew Members (Excluding Masters) Departing British Isles in British and Four Canadian Sailing Fleets, 1863–1914   152

14 Age of Deckhands, Four Fleets, 1863–1914   154

15 Literacy of Crew, Four Fleets, 1863–1912   159

16 Census and Crew Literacy, 1871–91   160

17 Literacy in Selected Countries, 1863–1900   161

18 Reasons for Refusal to Proceed in Vessels Leaving British Ports, 1870–2   172

19 Discharge Reasons by Rank, Four Fleets, 1863–1914   190

20 Discharge Reasons by Trade Route, Four Fleets, 1863–1914   191

21 Desertions, North Atlantic Voyages, Saint John Fleets, 1880s   193

22 North American High-Desertion Ports, 1863–1914   195

23 Wage Levels and Discharges of ABs Entering Selected North American Ports, 1863–1914   197

24 Marine Disasters, Saint John Fleet, 1860–99   206

25 Number of Men by Tonnage Class and Rig, Saint John Fleet, 1863-1914   208

26 Man-Ton Ratios, Saint John Fleet, 1863–1914   213

27 Man-Ton Ratios in Sailing Vessels of Britain and of Yarmouth, 1860–99   215

28 Annual Growth Rates of Tonnage at Sea and Labour Inputs, Saint John Fleet, 1863–99   220

29 Causes of Death of Sailors as Reported to the Board of Trade, 1875–7   225

30 Average Monthly Wages of Sailors in Saint John Steamers and Auxiliary Steamers, 1863–1914   247

31 Distribution of Sailors by Rank, British
   Sailing Vessels and Steamers,
   1863–1914   252–3
32 Age Distribution of Crew Members in
   British Vessels, 1863–1914   254
33 Average Days of Service per Voyage by ABs
   in British Ships, 1860–1914   256
34 Reasons for Leaving Vessels in Canadian
   and British Fleets, 1863–1914   257

Acknowledgments

Robert Albion once wrote that maritime history consists of crossing sailors' yarns with customs records. I have tried such a mixture in what follows, and it will be readily obvious that I could have done little of it had I worked alone. The interpretation and the mistakes are mine, but this book is also the product of a collaborative research effort involving many people and several institutions.

The first debt, as is so often the case in Canada, is to those institutions that make scholarly research possible. The Atlantic Canada Shipping Project (1976–82), whose members and employees compiled much of the data used in this book, was funded initially by the Canada Council and subsequently by the Social Sciences and Humanities Research Council of Canada. The granting agencies bestowed upon us not only funds but also generous measures of time, confidence, and advice. They created a collaborative research project that became the envy of maritime historians around the world. They gave me a unique research opportunity at a time when no other academic job was available.

The project was supported also by Memorial University of Newfoundland, and we owe a great deal to two presidents of that university, Dr. M.O. Morgan and Dr. Leslie Harris. Without their unyielding commitment to research in their university this project would not have existed. Members of the History Department at Memorial University supported us, befriended us, attended our conferences, and gave us counsel and good cheer. James A. Tague looked after the accounts and much more, and James K. Hiller was a sound rudder in many a squall.

The Maritime History Group was the home for all this, and many of the data were collected by its research assistants and staff and are now housed in its archive at Memorial. Doris Pike has a special place in our hearts. Roberta Thomas, B.A. (Sandy) Balcom, Olga Prentice (Olga Ilich), Janet Bartlett, Heather Wareham, and Terry Bishop (Terry Sterling) were part of the team, and one could not wish for a better group of research assistants. Much of the clerical work was done by a hard-working staff: Ivy Dodge, Rose Slaney, Paula Marshall, Doris King, Alyson Carter, Hilary Rifkin, Lorraine Rogers, Irene Whitfield, Geraldine Starkes, Catherine Brennan, Mary Walsh, June Knight, Rita O'Keefe, and Barbara Chapman. Skip Fischer, Rosemary Ommer, and Gerald Panting were colleagues and fellow pioneers in the enterprise. These were the friends who did so much of the work from which I now benefit.

Those who came to the Maritime History Group in those years and looked in awe at that great archive seldom knew the extent of our debt to Newfoundland and Labrador Computer Services and the Computing Services at Memorial University. Without their skill and understanding we would have dabbled in the archive but never penetrated its holdings. T.W. Bussey was the principal architect of the data entry system. Gregg Bennett and Craig Slaney did much of the programming. Ruth Cornish introduced me to SPSS and helped with the statistics. We learned a great deal from Jake Knoppers, who was then at McGill University. At the University of Victoria Michael Keating introduced me to a new computing facility.

We were scolded out of our ignorance by the many participants in the conferences of the Atlantic Canada Shipping Project. Robin Craig told me where answers lay and gave unstintingly of his time, understanding, and hospitality. Niels Jannasch tried valiantly to educate a landsman and read the whole of the first version of this book. Judith Fingard saved me from many errors, sent me to many sources, and read the book in first draft. Douglass C. North did not discuss seafaring labour with us, but his arresting critique in 1981 compelled me to think again. I learned a great deal from Conrad Dixon, Peter Davies, Sarah Palmer, David Williams, Richard Rice, Richard Goss, Campbell McMurray, Helge Nordvik, Peter McClelland, Phil Buckner, Stuart Pierson, and many others who came to those exciting workshops.

I have spent many happy hours in the New Brunswick Museum, and I am grateful to Carol Rosevear and her colleagues. In Halifax Charles Armour guided me through his archive at Dalhousie University and offered many useful suggestions. The archivists at the Public Archives of Nova Scotia were cheerful and eager to assist. David Flemming of the Maritime Museum of the Atlantic offered assistance and hospitality. In Charlottetown I was welcomed by Nicolas De Jong and his staff at the Public Archives of Prince Edward Island. In St John's I was assisted by David Davis and the staff of the Provincial Archives of Newfoundland and Labrador. In Greenwich the staff of the National Maritime Museum was very helpful, and I am especially indebted to David Proctor.

In Toronto Suzanne Zeller and John Noble gave valuable assistance, and Erindale College granted me a year's leave to return to Memorial and continue with related work. Many others helped the inquisitive landsman, and I wish to thank Ivor and Frances Jefferies of Saint John, Raymond Simpson of Merigomish, Eric Ruff of Yarmouth, and, in Victoria, the Sail and Life Training Society, the crew of the *Robertson II*, and the Maritime Museum of British Columbia. Bent G. Sivertz of Nanoose Bay, BC, offered valuable insights which appear in the text. Tony Lane of the University of Liverpool gave critical last-minute advice and saved me from a serious error. The anonymous readers who assessed the manuscript for the publisher spurred me on to further revisions.

The Social Sciences and Humanities Research Council did not give up on me and shortened the distance between Victoria and the Atlantic. The Social Sciences Federation gave the grant that made publication possible. Stuart Daniel of Victoria did the cartography and graphs. The University of Victoria offered a spiritual home and a lively intellectual environment: I owe much to my colleagues and more than they realize to our past and present graduate students. The University of Victoria granted a half-year study leave that allowed me to complete the final revisions. June Bull, Dinah Dickie, Gloria Orr, Laurel Barnes, and Joyce Gutensohn patiently typed and retyped a changing manuscript. John Parry of Toronto did the copy-editing and cleansed the muddy prose.

I am grateful to the following for kindly granting permission to use various material: Oxford University Press, for illustrations of sailing ships from Peter Kemp, *Oxford Companion to Ships and the Sea* (1976); Laurence Pollinger Ltd. and the Estate of Alan Villiers, for the map of the North Atlantic from Villiers's *The Way of a Ship* (London: Hodder and Stoughton, 1954); *The Canadian Encyclopedia* for the map of eastern coastal waters; and Jesperson Press, St John's, for selections from *On the High Seas: The Diary of Capt. John W. Froude* (1983), with Froude's original spelling and format.

This book was finished in Victoria, but it began in Newfoundland. The project that preceded the book was the creation of, above all, Gerry Panting, David Alexander, and Keith Matthews. David died when the project was still young, but the debt is great and the sense of loss still keen, and another book, now being written, will continue the acknowledgment to him.

Keith Matthews, chairman and co-founder of the Maritime History Group, died in 1984 before I began writing this book. He might not have liked all that I have written, but none of it would have surprised him, because all of what follows, and much more about sailors, he already knew, such was his acuity and sensitivity as historian. He was the remarkable, sometimes exasperating, but very dear friend who began all this.

There are very few photographs of sailors at work in wooden sailing vessels in Atlantic Canada. This leaves an author with a difficult choice: to omit photographs, to commission drawings from an artist, or to include photographs from non-Canadian ships. Specialists will note that some of the photographs included here are of iron-hulled sailing ships. They do, however, show something of the work that men did in sailing vessels in the late nineteenth and early twentieth centuries and of the general experiences that those in Atlantic Canadian vessels shared.

At the wheel (F.W. Wallace Collection [FWW], Maritime Museum of the
Atlantic, Halifax)

Working the capstan (FWW)

Stowing the jib (FWW)

Nova Scotia ship masters in Newcastle, NSW, Australia, 1904.
Left to right: standing: Farnham Doty, of Yarmouth; Oscar Henderson,
Halifax; seated: Everett MacDougall, Maitland; Henry Nickerson, Shelburne;
Percy Crosby, Yarmouth (Maritime Museum of the Atlantic, Halifax)

Going aloft in a schooner (FWW)

Work about the sails continued even in port. (The vessel is British comparable photos of Canadian sailing ships do not exist.) (FWW)

Master's cabin, *Abyssinia* (1,127 tons), built Saint John, 1885 (Yarmouth County Historical Society)

Seafaring Labour

Introduction

Several years have passed since David Alexander suggested that sailors might be "working men who got wet."[1] We have only begun to grasp the implications of his suggestion, which he offered not as a firm conclusion but as a challenge to those who might continue his work. Our portrait of the merchant sailor remains very much as Alexander found it a decade ago. His point was not simply that the sailor is too often perceived as a drunken and violent ruffian from "the dregs of society." The deeper point was that sailors as an occupational group were portrayed as misfits living in a world of their own, separated from landward society. Sailors were "a breed apart," and much of the literature of the nineteenth and twentieth centuries reinforces the impression: "He is like the inhabitants of some undiscovered country whereinto none of the latter-day adjuncts of civilization had penetrated."[2] The full implication of Alexander's suggestion was this: sailors were not beyond the pale of the civilization that sent them to sea.

In Britain and in the United States a few scholars have sought to discover the seafarers and the historical context of seafaring labour.[3] In Canada professional historians have entered the field only recently. Historians and sociologists have told us more about those who worked in fishing vessels than about deep-sea sailors. Labour historians have given us valuable studies of mid-twentieth-century sailors and their trade unions. Military historians have written about naval seafarers, and there are many specialized studies of exploration, whaling, sealing, and other maritime activities. At Memorial University of Newfoundland between 1979 and 1982 members of the Atlantic Canada Shipping Project assembled a large data base relating to ships and sailors and offered preliminary essays on those employed in the deep-sea vessels of Atlantic Canada.[4] For deep-water sailors we have Judith Fingard's *Jack in Port*, which is a "largely descriptive" investigation of the labour market, the application of the law, the work of crimps and reformers, and other aspects of the shoreside environment of the "sailortown." Intelligent and provocative suggestions appear in Richard Rice's hostile review of Fingard's book, but nobody has taken up Rice's gauntlet and attempted to study labour at sea in the transition to industrial capitalism.[5] Professional historians have not neglected the Canadian seafarer, but much of what we know has come from popular historians, journalists, and diarists. Their success is a measure of popular interest in Canadian maritime history and in the history of working people in Canada.

To learn about the sailing ships that were inherited from Europe we must read histories of the technology by non-university historians. Perhaps the finest of these works is John Harland's *Seamanship in the Age of Sail*. Written by an amateur historian living in Kelowna, British Columbia, this book is perhaps the most lucid and scholarly study of sailing-ship technology ever written, at least in the English language. To learn something about seafaring in Canadian ships we must read Frederick William Wallace, Stanley Spicer, John P. Parker, Claude Darrach, and Cassie Brown, to name only a few.[6] To learn more about the sailor and his work we must read the small but growing body of published memoirs of seafarers themselves. In the published diary of John W. Froude of Twillingate, cited often in what follows, the stereotype of the sailor is comprehensively demolished, and no more useful work has been published in Canada on the subject of the merchant seafarer.[7] Valuable as such works may be, the broader historical context is still missing. And the popular historians tell us more about the "wooden ships" than the "iron men." Their discussion of sailors often assumes that readers will be interested only in the sensational and unusual, the "true gripping stories of men and ships." And so we read about shipwrecks, tragedies, "greed and guilt on the high seas," and "dastardly mutiny."[8] Sometimes unwittingly the popular historian reflects the attitudes and bias of the shipowner or shipmaster, and this is particularly evident in the writings of Frederick William Wallace.[9] The sailors of our past have suffered not so much from neglect as from condescension: helpless victims of landward predators, or victims of their own moral and economic weakness, sailors are deprived of choice and autonomy in their lives. It is hardly fair to blame the popular historian if the stereotype remains. It is the task of the professional historian to uncover the historical context of working people in the past and to set their work and experience in the frame of time. This we have yet to do.

In maritime history the popular and the academic historians sometimes meet and learn from each other, and the exchange is not merely useful but essential.[10] This is particularly true for the professional historian who is also a landsman. Vast though the documentation on ships and sailors may be, there is much in the past experience of seafaring that the documents do not record. The historian uses many techniques, but among these is intuitive perception, the faculty that allows us, with varying degrees of success, to recreate in the mind experiences from the past that are otherwise irrecoverable. In studying those who worked in sailing ships we are fortunate that many of these ships still survive, and the historian who has never set a foot on ratlines and climbed to the yard above is at a disadvantage in understanding the experience of seafaring labour. The problem is faced by any historian who wishes to study labour and workplaces in the past: how can we understand workers, their relationships with each other, with employers, and with technology, when so little remains? We cannot eat their food, nor see with their eyes, nor sleep in the bunks of their forecastle. Only rarely may we see the machinery that was central to their working lives and relationships, and to see this machinery scarcely helps, for they knew it with all five senses, with hands and muscles, for days and months on end. The visceral understanding eludes us, and perhaps we must make room for what my colleague Morris Berman calls "somatic empathy," the reconstruction of psychic and corporal experience through imaginative introspection.[11] Certainly it is not enough to read technical manuals, although this too is essential.

The popular historian, the memorialist, and the novelist are often helpful guides, because they set out to recreate in our imagination the sense of past experience. They are helpful not merely to the historian interested in achieving verisimilitude in descriptive exercises of an antiquarian kind. They can help our analysis as well. To give merely one instance from the history of seafaring: it is reasonable to ask what was the structure of authority between masters, mates, and deckhands and to ask why sailors accepted that structure while protesting against abuses of authority. In answering such a question the psychic and visceral map of the master mariner offered in Conrad's *Mirror of the Sea* is, I believe, not only useful but essential. This does not mean that the historian should forgo the necessary detachment from sources or repeat uncritically the "romance of the sea." In the exchange with popular history and with the younger members of Conrad's fraternity, there is in fact a greater danger than romanticism. The greater danger comes from the tireless insistence of sailors that their calling was unique and that their sailing ships were beyond the ken of "benighted landsmen," as Conrad called us. Depressed by our ignorance of the complexity of ships and their peculiar ways, the landsman-historian is easily seduced by Conrad's prose and the eloquent testimony of his fellow seafarers into believing that the sailing ship and its inhabitants must lie beyond all normal experience, and hence beyond the compass of our models and social theories.

Men and women are the servants of their creations, we are told, and the sailing ship was a tyrannical mistress. These were "tender creatures," these barques and ships, whose idiosyncracies must be understood and indulged by faithful human servants.[12] Is there another industry whose chroniclers so tempt the historian into technological determinism? Of course the complex working parts of sailing ships demanded specific and recurring actions on the part of workers if the vessels were to move through water. But this does not mean that the ship dictated all working relationships. Still less does it mean that the particular structure of ranks and authority in nineteenth-century sailing vessels were dictated by those ships. Among seafarers it is a commonplace assumption that a ship is necessarily a type of dictatorship, whether benevolent or otherwise, and that a rigid authoritarian system is essential in a complex workplace which trespasses into the dangerous elements of wind and sea. To many naval and merchant mariners the idea that forms of industrial democracy or workers' control could be compatible with sailing ships is an unthinkable absurdity, or a far greater romanticism than any committed by Frederick William Wallace.

This book suggests that the structure of authority in a ship was part of the social relations of production in an industry. These relationships were social artefacts created by men and not by ships. To prove that this is so we need only contrast the inherited workplace relationships of the nineteenth century with an alternative set of relationships. Consider, for instance, a fleet in which the authority of the master depended upon the consent of his crew. Authority and command existed, but these were delegated to the captain by ship's articles, an employment contract that the sailors wrote themselves. This employment contract allocated authority, set rules of behaviour, and determined the distribution of material rewards. The captain was elected by his crew. Important decisions about work and trade routes were decided by majority vote in a council that included all crew. The crew consisted not of wage labourers but of risk-sharing partners. Shares in the proceeds of voyages were allocated by contract in such a way as to reduce income disparities: the master received one and a half or two shares; petty officers such as the bosun received one and a half; the rest of the crew one share each. There was no such thing as desertion, since nobody was required to stay against his will. Those who did stay but transgressed the agreed rules could be expelled or even executed. This was a social world in which workers had, as one of them put it, "the choice in themselves." This fleet is not the creation of romantic fiction – it existed, and historians have written a great deal about it. Nor was it the product of an ancient or remote civilization: it was the work of Anglo-Americans in the era of merchant capitalism. These ships were also modestly successful: they carried perhaps five thousand men, and their earnings "were exceptional in both volume and value." Of course this egalitarian system did not survive, but that does not weaken my case. The system died out, not because its creators defied the ineluctable constraints of technology, but because they were systematically hunted and destroyed by the world's largest navies. They were, of course, pirates.[13] Their social world suggests how far workplace relationships may depart from those that the dominant Anglo-American culture regarded as normal and tolerable.

The rise of the steamship brought changes in workplace relationships, but the steamship did not by itself determine those changes. Consider a 45,000-ton freighter in which the social divisions between officers and crew been reduced to the point where they eat, drink, and play together. A division of labour remains, but deckhands perform a range of tasks and officers can be seen doing simple manual labour. Deckhands receive training in the use of technology in the ship, and the workplace is also a kind of school. Supervision of labour is minimized, and the office of bosun is sometimes eliminated in order to encourage worker discretion and autonomy. This is a modern Norwegian freighter, and although industrial democracy at sea remains the subject of debate, it suggests a social world very different from that of the Canadian tramp steamer in our century.[14] There are technological constraints upon work, but workplace relationships are highly variable and not graven in machinery.

Since technology does not dictate relationships, it follows that technology alone does not determine the level of skill attained by those who occupy specific ranks or jobs. Skill is also a social artefact, and it is the subject of a considerable scholarly literature.[15] Since much of this book is about skill a few definitions are necessary. At the simplest level, and in common parlance, skill refers to manual facility, or the co-ordination of perception and muscles that allows one to perform complex actions. While such a definition may be adequate in everyday speech, it leaves problems if we are to distinguish between skilled and unskilled workers. Obviously all types of manual work require some quantity of skill so defined. So what quantity or level separates the skilled from the unskilled? Skill implies more than manual facility: it means that the worker possesses knowledge of materials and processes that makes possible complex actions in a process of production. It follows that a high level of skill means a combination of qualities that come only after training, and some would argue that length of training is one measure of skill levels. Length of training is often difficult to measure, of course, because the acquisition of knowledge may occur without formal schooling and even prior to formal apprenticeship.

Once we accept knowledge and training as parts of skill, other things necessarily follow that relate the subject of skill to larger issues. If a worker possesses the knowledge necessary to execute a set of tasks, then the worker is presumably using that knowledge to plan those tasks and to organize tools and materials in space and time. This, therefore, is another necessary component of skill: the opportunity to plan work and to make decisions, sometimes referred to as discretion or discretion content. Alan Fox has defined discretion and pursued its meaning: "Performance of the discretionary content requires, not trained obedience to specific external controls, but the exercise of wisdom, judgment, expertise. The control comes from within – it is, in the literal sense, self-control. The occupant of the role must himself choose, judge, feel, sense, consider, conclude what would be the best thing to do in the circumstances, the best way of going about what he is doing."[16] Discretion implies a degree of control over the work process, and it is at this point that the presence of skill may be affected very critically by historical and social forces. Industrial capital and its management systems may separate discretion and control from manual labour, and conception from execution, in an increasing division of labour. Conception is often allocated to planning departments, and decisions may even be incorporated into the design and operation of machines.[17] It is possible then to conceive of skill as a complex social creation, and, this being so, it is possible to conceive of a process of de-skilling.

Work may comprise more than skill, of course, and Alan Fox adds that work roles may vary in the range of tasks set for each role.[18] Task range may be a component of skill: where a craftsman, manager, or professional person performs a range of tasks, each of which requires special knowledge and judgment, then such occupational elasticity may be another part of a worker's skill. It is sometimes easier to prove that a range of tasks exists than to prove that discretion exists, however. Task range cannot by itself be a sufficient condition of skill: it is possible, for instance, for a general labourer to perform many different tasks, each of which requires little knowledge and little discretion, and we should not consider such a worker skilled. Nevertheless, where other defining characteristics of skill are present, then task range may be a part of skill: there are, for instance, machinists and mechanics who possess the knowledge required to build, repair, and operate many different kinds of machinery, and the range of their tasks and abilities is certainly a part of their skill. In twentieth-century seafaring there are precise examples in the role of bosun and, sometimes, the role of pipe fitter: here one may find the "real machinist" who will "do anything."[19]

In shipping, labour is applied to transportation and communication, and the product of labour is not a material commodity but a service. This rather obvious fact does not affect the discussion of skill or diminish the likelihood of its presence. It is necessary to state the obvious because all too often we equate economic activity with the production of physical goods and assume that service-sector activity constitutes exchange rather than production. Sailoring thus becomes "non-productive labour."[20] It must follow that the sailor cannot be a craftsman because he produces nothing. Such reasoning is fallacious, in both economic and historical analysis. Value may be added to commodities, and surplus value created, through the labour performed in transport. Marx himself insisted that the laws of commodity production held for transportation as for any other industry.[21] In neo-classical economics production refers to the output of services as well as goods, and output in shipping is a function of inputs, such as labour and capital. The point is that the sailor is part of a process of production, just as much as the factory worker on land. The word "craftsman" must be allowed to embrace the master mariner as well as the carpenter and the shoemaker.

In the nineteenth century the process of production at sea was changing as never before. The sailor was part of the transition to industrial capitalism, as capital transformed work and production on land and at sea. Many "maritime historians" will be reluctant to accept this thesis and its implications. "Maritime history," I would argue, is not a discrete thalassic realm of human experience. It is the study of historical conjunctures in which landward society interacts with the sea and its resources. This study is flawed and incomplete if events at sea are abstracted from their landward context. The point will seem self-evident to labour historians, but it is necessary to be explicit, as one reader of this book proved when he inferred that it was my purpose to draw an "analogy" between merchant seafaring and industrialization and wondered why I had ignored the analogy with naval and military traditions.

There is no analogy in what follows. The argument is that merchant seafaring was a particular part of a larger process, transcending both sea and land and national boundaries. Changes occurring in merchant seafaring were not analogous to a parallel process occurring on land; these changes *were* industrialization as it occurred at sea. In the chapters that follow I attempt to trace the industrial transition, from the small craft of the early nineteenth century to the industrial workplace a century later. In passing we must examine the ships themselves (chapters 1, 2, and 3) and the sailors – their work (chapter 4), their origins (chapter 5), their conflict with authority (chapter 6), their wages (chapter 7), and their community at sea (chapter 8) – for these things all bear witness to the transition to industrial capitalism.

This book is about craft, a single word that encompasses both vessel and skill, and it is about the fate of craft, its survival and its extinction in the age of industry. Although the story transcends national boundaries and takes us at the end to vessels owned far beyond Atlantic Canada, nevertheless this book is about Atlantic Canadian craft. The point needs emphasizing. Some of the vessels and many of the workers appearing in this book never got near the shores of Atlantic Canada.[22] They tell us nonetheless about an industry of this region. In our ongoing search for the roots of regional underdevelopment, and in our awareness of the richness of local culture and identity in Canada, it is well to remember that the sources of much of our historical experience lay beyond the region and even beyond the nation. Of course there were local and regional variations in the industrial transformation of seafaring, and these are not ignored here.

But we inherited our shipping technology and seafaring traditions from other shores, after all. Ships and sailors were extraordinarily mobile: they were vehicles of technology and culture as well as carriers of cargo, and they remind us that regional identities were shaped in a fluid environment in which transnational borrowing was very easy. In the nineteenth century Canadian shipping was at many levels a subset of British shipping, but this is not to relegate maritime Canada to the margins of empire and the periphery of historical developments. Still less does it follow, as landbound Canadians sometimes infer, that maritime Canada was "insular" or "parochial." The words do not apply to places that were open and accessible to the sea and hence the first landfall of transatlantic peoples and their influences. Atlantic colonists were at the centre of developments that transcended region and nation and fully part of the great social transformation of the nineteenth century. Here the popular historians do have a point, in their insistence on the particular quality of seafaring life: the mariner was a man of the world, who had more in common with his fellow seafarers from other lands than with many of his own fellow countrymen.[23]

There is a lesson, I believe, in the unromantic story of these seafaring workers. The heritage from other shores was often a baneful one. The workplace at sea was often cruel, and it was certainly a place of exploitation. But these things were not inevitable, even if the sea itself was a dangerous place for humankind. The social relationships of this industry were not historical necessities or technological imperatives. Implicit in the community of men and women at sea there was always an alternative. At the heart of that community and in its collective skill lay the possibility of recovering "the choice in themselves" and "the control that comes from within." But the sailor said it best, as he stood at the helm of his ship, musing over his full if momentary mastery of his great machine: "I did not sense a sternness in my ship that morning, as at times I seemed to do. At my least touch she'd shift her long lean shape, swift-answering me." In that swift answer Bill Adams knew his "calling," and it was that of a craftsman: "The dream the soldier knows, thinking he has a holy cause ... The dream that makes the tailor cut with eyes contented, shearing his finest woollen goods to shape."[24] The sailor's dream was not romance but reality, and it is the real legacy of the working men and women who got wet.

CHAPTER ONE

A Pre-Industrial Workplace

The wooden sailing vessel was a pre-industrial transportation tech-nology that survived the industrial revolution. Early in the nine-teenth century men first used steam-power in water transportation, but they confronted serious technical problems, and in this indus-try, as in others, industrialization was less a revolution than a slow evolution occurring over a century and a half. Until the 1890s most of the world's ocean commerce was carried by sailing vessels. Even after the 1890s wooden-hulled sailing vessels survived in the waters of industrial Europe and North America. In Canadian waters such vessels were still engaged in commercial interprise in the mid-twentieth century.[1]

The slow technological evolution in shipping meant that many types of vessel shared the same harbours at the same time. From Cape Breton came the steam-powered collier carrying coal to Montreal and the little "pinky" schooner which fishermen had used since the eighteenth century. In Halifax and St John's, a century after the first steam-powered vessel appeared in Britain, the wooden-hulled schooner slipped past the iron coastal steamer 20 times its size, while in nearby Atlantic waters stood the steel-hulled passenger liner, 30 times as large as the coastal steamer, propelled by 3 million turbine blades and consuming a thousand tons of coal a day.[2] In landward transportation, horse-drawn carts sometimes shared adjacent berths with the steam locomotive and with the wheeled lorry powered by an internal combustion engine, but not for a century or more. The analogy is dramatic, but in one respect it is misleading: the wooden schooner of the early twentieth cen-tury was no horse-drawn cart, but a highly complex piece of machinery for all its pre-industrial lineage. If there is a point to the contrast between landward and seaward transportation, it is this: the technological transition at sea was slow, and a pre-industrial technology co-existed for a century and a half with its successors. In the modern history of shipping there can be no neat temporal division to the stages of industrialization.

There is a deeper problem here than the absence of neat temporal divisions. The ship was a peculiar machine in the context of European merchant capitalism, because of the way labour was organized in combination with the rope, wood, metal, and canvas in a ship. In certain important respects the seventeenth-century sailing ship anticipated the nineteenth-century factory. "Long before the Industrial Revolution of the early nineteenth century which ushered in the factory system," writes E.P. Hohman, "the seamen had been working under many of the same characteristic features which have now become so well known in connection with factory production; and even though their settings were so different as to obscure or to hide the likeness, in essentials they were the same."[3] These features included the high ratio of capital to labour, constant repetition of specific tasks, very close supervision of workers, division of labour, and removal of work from home. Noticing these parallels, Peter Linebaugh has even suggested that by the late seventeenth century ships may be a distinct mode of production in themselves.[4] While much of this is open to question and will be rejected in what follows, there is a useful reminder here that the large sailing ship of the seventeenth and eighteenth centuries was a complex workplace with traditions and patterns of work that could easily survive into the age of industrial capitalism and be subsumed into the seafaring workplace of the nineteenth century. There is also a useful reminder that the industrial revolution in shipping was much more than the introduction of iron and steam. But the eighteenth-century sailing ship, proto-factory as it was in certain respects, is only the beginning of our story, for the long transition to industrial capitalism was only beginning. In Atlantic Canada particularly the transition had not begun in the era of Hohman's proto-factories, because even in the late eighteenth century the colonial shipping industry meant small coastal vessels, of which the schooner may be the best representative.

The schooner was a pre-industrial craft, a small workplace where a few men applied their skill and labour to the manual art of setting sails to the wind. The etymology of "craft" is evident: the schooner was a "vessel of small craft," where craft referred to the nets, lines, and hooks of fishermen *and* the art of using these tools. Between this small coastal schooner and the iron steamships that a few Maritimers were purchasing a century later lay a social and technological transformation. The tramp steamer was no craft but an artefact of industrial capitalism, its labour force a complex hierarchy of rank, skill, and wage differentials. Between these very different workplaces lay many that shared attributes of both, and even the wind-propelled schooner changed with the impact of the industrial revolution. Gradual as it was, this evolution from pre-industrial craft to twentieth-century factory ship was the critical influence upon the lives of seafaring men and women. Joseph Conrad, that wise if rhapsodic observer of seafaring men, knew all this long ago when he wrote about the difference between the "fine art" of seafaring and the "taking of a modern steamship around the world": "And therein I think I can lay my finger upon the difference between the seamen of yesterday, who are still with us, and the seamen of tomorrow, already entered upon the possession of their inheritance."[5]

The evolution of seafaring labour was not simply the result of changes in the technology of vessel construction and operation, but it is appropriate to begin by describing the vessels of the Atlantic colonies and the marine environment in which they operated. The vessels and their environment were, after all, the setting in which the industrial evolution occurred and in which labour was applied to the process of production. These were, in short, the workplace. The sailing ships owned and worked by British North Americans were not a distinct technology but rather the product of centuries of evolution in sailing ship design, adapted and sometimes modified for use in particular markets and environments. British shipbuilding expertise had been carried across the Atlantic and modified by North American experience to serve the great staple trades – the export of fish and timber and agricultural products and the import of manufactured and other goods for colonial consumption. Until the nineteenth century most of the freights between Britain and its northern colonies could be handled by a plentiful supply of tonnage from the mother country. The colonists specialized in the building and owning of small craft designed primarily for coastal and West Indian trading or for fishing. What the colonists required were vessels capable of successful manoeuvre along sharply indented coastlines and in highly variable wind and weather. They required vessels that performed well to windward, not only in order to escape pursuit in wartime, but also to perform well when sailing on a tack to windward against prevailing wester-lies. Colonists also required vessels that minimized capital invest-ment. These were the conditions that produced the small and versatile coastal vessels of the early nineteenth century.

These were also the conditions of work for coastal mariners and fishermen. Pre-industrial work was always deeply influenced by the seasons and by weather, but nowhere more intimately than in ship-ping. Vessels and men were adapted to a particular climate and specified seas, and they worked with and against particular weather systems. The North Atlantic was a difficult environment, more turbulent and unpredictable even than the South Atlantic. Seafaring began much later in the North Atlantic than in the In-dian Ocean, for instance, where clearly defined seasons brought more predictable winds and currents.[6] The North Atlantic is hemmed in by vast land masses and surrounded by inland seas that pour huge quantities of fresh water and ice into the ocean. Its ocean currents are strong, and they are strongest on the west side of the ocean. The westen Atlantic currents begin in the Caribbean, where the Caribbean current and the currents from the Gulf of Mexico emerge through the straits between Florida and Cuba, to form the Florida Current. Off the US coast this current joins the northward currents of the Atlantic itself to form the Gulf Stream, a boon to vessels on the homeward run from the West Indies, but often an obstacle to vessels moving south. The Gulf Stream is separated from the North American coast by colder water, and at the latitudes of New England and Nova Scotia this colder water is fed by a southwest drift, moving in the opposite direction to the Gulf Stream. Off Halifax the northern edge of the Gulf Stream may be 250 miles away or even as far as 500 miles. To the southwest of Newfoundland, off the Grand Banks, the Gulf Stream meets the southward-flowing polar water of the Labrador Current (Map 1). This means that sailors venturing south or east from Atlantic Canada face an area of mixed and turbulent waters as treacherous as any in the Atlantic.

MAP 1
Eastern Coastal Waters

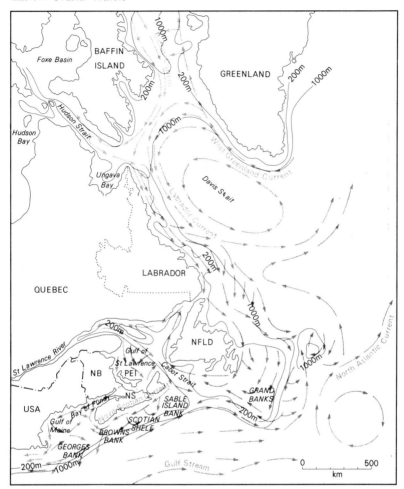

Source: The Canadian Encyclopedia (Edmonton: Hurtig Publishers, 1985)

The Labrador Current brings not only cold water and cold air
but also ice, not the least of the many hazards to shipping off
Atlantic Canada. Much of the Gulf of St Lawrence and the coasts
of Newfoundland and Labrador may be covered in ice in February
and March. But drifting pancake ice and icebergs flow into the
North Atlantic, south and east of Newfoundland and Nova Scotia,
where they may threaten shipping well into spring and summer.

The meeting of warm and moist air from the south with the cold waters of the Labrador Current produces fog, which makes drifting ice even more dangerous. The sea fog is particularly frequent on the Grand Banks in spring and summer.

The story of the working environment of Canadian sailors is even more complex, for that environment results also from the interaction of wind and water. The differences in atmospheric temperature between the North Atlantic and its adjacent land masses can be very great; sharp differences in temperature and air pressure over the ocean itself often occur within small areas. The result is that within a general pattern of atmospheric circulation sudden changes regularly occur, and unexpected gales may appear at any time of year. There are prevailing winds, however. Very important for the seamen of the North Atlantic were the northeast trade winds, which appear from about 30 degrees north latitude to about 10 degrees north (see Map 2). Although prevailing winds in this area are from the northeast, brisk winds may blow from any quarter of the compass. But the regularity of the winds is more impressive than their uncertain direction, and many sailing ships crossing from Europe to the eastern United States went "south about," in a long southerly semi-circle, rather than face the westerlies on a more direct course. Crucial for Canadian sailors were the westerlies, which begin off the American coast with winds from the southwest. These westerlies, stronger in winter than in summer, confronted the vessel heading south toward the United States or the Caribbean.

To the east of Newfoundland the westerlies meet the polar air currents moving south, producing some of the more disturbed atmospheric conditions on earth. In winter particularly winds of Beaufort force seven and higher are very frequent in the western Atlantic between 40 degrees and 60 degrees north. In mid-Atlantic, between Newfoundland and the British Isles, the frequency of such winds in January is between 30 and 40 per cent.[7] The force of the wind exerted on the surface of water puts the sea in motion and results in waves which, although not so high or so long as elsewhere, are nevertheless violent and irregular. The effect of the northern air currents is also to lower the temperatures of both sea surface and air in areas adjacent to eastern Canada. In waters off Nova Scotia and Newfoundland the average air temperature in January is below freezing. Even summer temperatures in

MAP 2
The Sailing Ship's North Atlantic

Source: Alan Villiers, *The Way of a Ship* (London: Hodder and Stoughton, 1954)

these waters are, on average, 10 to 20 degrees Fahrenheit below mean temperatures at the latitude of New York. The confluence of warm air from the south and cold air from the north also produces precipitation, in winter more frequent in the northwest Atlantic than anywhere else in this ocean. Precipitation, although not cloud, is much less frequent by summer, but by July sea fog occurs as often as anywhere in the world.[8]

Such was the environment in which seafarers from the Atlantic colonies worked. In the first half of the nineteenth century most sailors employed in the fleets of the Atlantic colonies worked in coastal waters, in the North Atlantic, and in waters between British North America and the West Indian islands; it is difficult to be more precise about voyage patterns. After 1860, records for locally owned vessels are more complete. Sources for earlier decades, such as tables of trade and navigation in the Colonial Office's Blue Books, do not separate local vessels from those owned and registered in Britain or elsewhere.[9] However, a few sources allow a partial portrait of voyage patterns and confirm that most local vessels were working north of 40 degrees latitude. A collection of crew lists for the late 1840s and early 1850s tells us something about the voyages of vessels that moved regularly *outside* British North American coastal trades. Crew lists indicate that these small ocean-going vessels were employed most often in passages between British North America and the British Isles. In fact no less than 53 per cent of all passages were either westward or eastward between British North America and Britain. Maritime and British ports together accounted for 77 per cent of all entrances into port (Liverpool alone for 26 per cent).[10] Workers in the brigs and barques of Atlantic Canada knew this North Atlantic passage better than any other and knew very well the ports of Liverpool, Saint John, and Halifax.

In the first half of the century a majority of sailors working in British North American vessels would be found in waters close to the eastern coasts of North America or on the more extended coastal passages to and from the West Indies. Even the crews employed in passages to and from Britain would not outnumber those in the coastal and West Indies trades. In 1827 the *Nova Scotian* reported 1,060 entrances and clearances at the port of Halifax, the major entrepôt in Nova Scotia. Only 8 per cent of these were to or from ports in the British Isles or Europe; a third

were entrances to or from British North America, and this understates the importance of North American coastal passages, since
very few passages to and from Nova Scotian outports were included. Twenty-nine per cent of entrances and clearances were to
or from the West Indies, and another 23 per cent were to or from
the United States (although most of these were by American vessels). Although the vessels employed in passages across the Atlantic
were larger, the relative importance of coastal and West Indies
trades is confirmed. Unfortunately newspapers do not distinguish
between locally owned and other vessels. What about vessels owned
or registered in the Maritime colonies? Another Halifax source –
the Sambro Light Duty Records – confirms that Halifax-owned
vessels were heavily committed to trades from their home port and
that coastal and West Indies trades were major employers of tonnage and men.[11] In 1839 about 41,000 Nova Scotia-owned tons
entered Halifax; about 40 per cent of the tonnage, and a similar
proportion of the men employed, entered from the West Indies.
About a third were from Nova Scotian outports. Coastal and West
Indies passages accounted for over 85 per cent of all tonnage entering (Map 3).

The story was different in Saint John, of course. There a majority of local tonnage was employed in the runs to and from Britain.[12]
But the Saint John fleet, large as it was, was untypical of the shipping industry as a whole, at least in the first half of the nineteenth
century. By 1850 over 56 per cent of all tonnage in nine major
ports of registry was accounted for by small vessels – under 250
tons.[13] Although these small vessels occasionally crossed the Atlantic, they were used mainly in coastal trading. When we add the
large coastal fleet of Newfoundland to the small-vessel fleets of
Nova Scotia, it is clear that small vessels predominated and that a
majority of sailors in the industry spent most of their time in coastal
waters. The evidence for Newfoundland's fleet is incomplete, but
an estimate of locally owned tonnage clearing St John's between
1839 and 1844 has been prepared from one of the few sources that
allows such analysis, and the data are summarized in Map 4.[14] A
majority of the Newfoundland-owned tonnage was employed in
Newfoundland's coastal waters. Less than 10 per cent of tonnage
was employed in passages to Britain.

Voyage patterns changed dramatically in the last half of the century, when the great ocean-going fleets of the Maritime provinces
were launched from local shipyards. But the many small vessels of

MAP 3
Nova Scotia Tonnage Clearing for Halifax, 1839

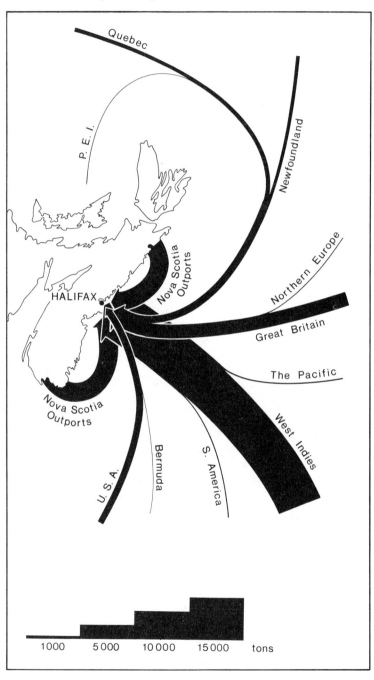

MAP 4
Newfoundland-Owned Tonnage Clearing St John's, 1839-44

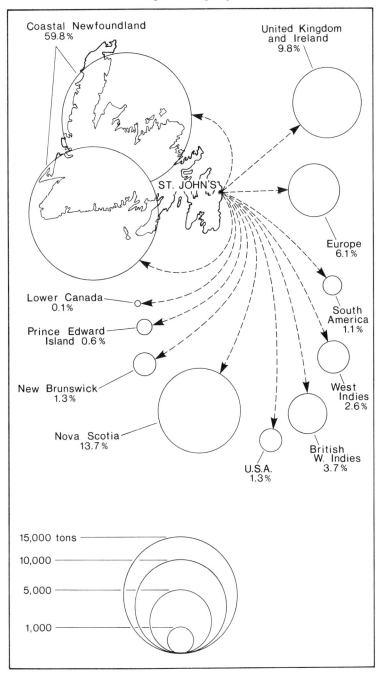

Coastal Newfoundland
59.8%

United Kingdom
and Ireland
9.8%

ST. JOHN'S

Europe
6.1%

Lower Canada
0.1%

South
America
1.1%

Prince Edward
Island 0.6%

New Brunswick
1.3%

West
Indies
2.6%

Nova Scotia
13.7%

British
W. Indies
3.7%

U.S.A.
1.3%

15,000 tons

10,000

5,000

1,000

Nova Scotia and Newfoundland remained within the same general trading patterns established early in the century. Map 5 indicates the movement of Nova Scotian tonnage from Halifax in 1873, from one of the few sources that does record the port of registry of vessels entering and clearing a local port. Most of the vessels were under 200 tons, and only sailing vessels are included. The large barques and ships of the age of sail, which by this time dominated even the Halifax fleet, did not appear often in their home port – they were employed in more distant waters. But the great fleet of small vessels remained, still setting sail for Nova Scotian outports, for the United States, or for the West Indies. The small pre-industrial workplace remained much as it had been in the early nineteenth century, employing more men than ever before in the western waters of the North Atlantic, from Trinidad to the Gulf of St Lawrence and to Newfoundland.

The seafarers of Atlantic Canada learned their craft in a hard school. A fisherman from Newfoundland named John Froude, crossing the Atlantic for the first time in 1887, found nothing to dismay him in more temperate latitudes:

as the winds are increasing and the sky looking dark and the seas rolling over our ship
but I was not disapointed or very much alarmed as I had gone threw the thing before
on our coast and grand bank and far away down the bradore[15]

He was accustomed to the quixotic power of ice:

we got down about 60 miles ENE from the grey islands when we ran her into another block of ice which split the vessel in two we took everything out on the ice and she went to the bottom of the atlantic ocean[16]

He feared the savage power of a squall and knew the result of a small delay taking in sail: "The captain then gave orders to shorten sail. We began with the flying jib and spanker, and before we had them secured the rest of the sails were blown away, nothing remaining but the rope of our mainsail, foresail, jib, and jumbo."[17] He was used to hauling on frozen rope and chipping ice from wheel

MAP 5
Nova Scotia Tonnage Clearing Halifax, 1873

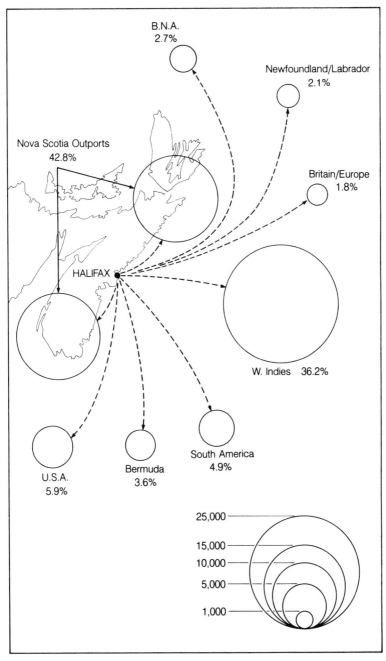

and blocks; he cherished the warmth of the small stove below decks, until it too froze:

> now we are all wet and frozen I am now going under the canvas
> to lie down and die may god pity and have mercy on my
> soul.[18]

The seafarer acquired a deeply intimate relationship with his vessel, the craft that kept him from a watery grave, until the vessel took on a life of its own, and in the language of sailors the behaviour of vessels, always feminine in gender, acquired human complexity. The craftsman reared in North Atlantic waters learned above all to fear and to respect the sea, until it too acquired human characteristics: "The sea is tameless: as it was in the beginning, it is now, and shall ever be – mighty, savage, dread, infinitely treacherous and hateful, yielding only that which is wrested from it, snarling, raging, snatching lives, spoiling souls of their graces."[19] Terrible as it was, this sea was his place of work and his temporary home.

Both vessels and men were adapted to this North Atlantic environment, and the vessels represented a host of compromises with the perilous necessity of softwood hulls. The plentiful local supply of spruce and pine allowed relatively inexpensive construction, but such vessels were easily crushed, torn apart, or simply frozen into immobility in local waters. The search for structural strength and durability was a constant preoccupation. Coastal vessels, particularly those in Newfoundland, were squat and cumbersome, with thick beams and planking, like "a box rounded off at the ends."[20] Built for strength and stability rather than speed, they were unlike the fast, narrow-hulled racing schooners of the *Bluenose* era. The working environment also gave the advantage to the fore and aft sail – the sail suspended behind the mast on gaffs and booms (Figure 1). This sail could be shifted quickly, and either side of it might take the wind. Since it could be worked from the deck and shifted close to the wind, vessels were manoeuvrable and handy to windward. The schooner, which carried fore and aft sails on her two or more masts, became the most common coastal vessel in North American waters in the nineteenth century.

The pre-industrial craft was not a single entity, and even the schooner was part of a continuing technological evolution. In the

FIGURE 1

Gaff Mainsail: An Example of Fore-and-Aft-Rig

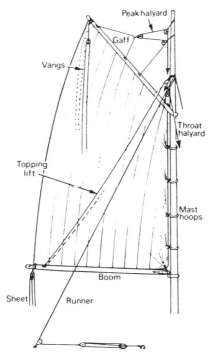

Source: Oxford Companion to Ships and the Sea by Peter Kemp. Published by Oxford University Press 1976 © Oxford University Press 1976.

eighteenth century fishing and coastal trading required small, easily built craft which travelled short distances within inshore waters. The open boat with one or two masts was common. Behind the masts there might be only one sail, which might be "loose-footed" – not attached to a boom. In such small craft, running rigging was of the simplest kind: one or two ropes were sufficient to raise and lower a sail. A few men shared small working spaces, and there was no provision for long passages. The sloop, still common in the early nineteenth century, was such a short-haul coastal craft. Many could be worked by two men. The sloop had only one mast, which carried fore and aft sails, and there might be one or more headsails (sails suspended between mast and bowsprit). In the nineteenth-century Halifax fleet sloops had a capacity of only 15 tons on average.[21]

The shallop was slightly more complex, and more often than the sloop it combined both living and working spaces. The shallop was a two-masted vessel, like the schooner, but it was without a deck, or half-decked. On the mainsail there was more likely to be a boom, and there would be two halyards, ropes used to raise and lower the sail. Shallops were still being built and registered after 1820, but the two-masted schooner with a full deck had long since become the preferred vessel in coastal trading. The decked vessel meant greater carrying capacity, and it extended the range of the vessel by allowing for better overnight accommodation. At first there appears to have been a single cabin or "cuddy" under the raised quarterdeck aft of the mainmast. The crew, including the master, lived in this shared space. The cabin acquired a fireplace of loose bricks, and smoke escaped through either an open cabin hatch or a wooden smokestack. A boy was hired as cook and extra hand, and all men shared meals in the cabin. In larger schooners there was a forecastle, a triangular cabin under the raised deck in the forward end of the vessel. In the nineteenth century this was the living space for the crew. But in many small schooners in the early nineteenth century both master and man slept in the aft cabin, while the forecastle was used for storing gear or provisions. The physical separation of master and men had scarcely begun in these early schooners. [22]

The schooner remained a wide-beamed vessel; her shallow draught allowed entry to shallow and rocky harbours where knowledge of coastal navigation and pilotage was elementary. There was as yet little specialization by function, and it was not until the late nineteenth century that several distinct differences between fishing and coasting vessels appeared. But for longer coastal voyages, or passages to the West Indies, the shallow vessel with fore and aft sails had disadvantages, for she was unhandy in big seas and relatively inefficient in long runs to leeward (with the wind from the stern). To compensate, the coastal schooner in British North America often employed one or more square sails, suspended on yardarms fitted at right angles to the line of the hull. [23] In schooners square sails were topsails, above the fore and aft sail on the foremast, although square topsails occasionally appeared on the mainmast as well. The square sail could not be shifted so close to an approaching wind as the fore and aft sails, but it gave additional driving power in longer North Atlantic or West Indies passages. With or without this square sail, the schooner was numerically preponderant, even in ports of registry specializing in deepsea tonnage, such as Saint John. Among Maritime-owned nineteenth-century fleets, more than 55 per cent of all vessels were rigged as schooners. In Newfoundland, 83 per cent of all vessels newly registered between 1820 and 1936 were rigged as schooners.[24]

As the schooner evolved into a larger and more versatile craft, sails and crew increased in number. Accustomed to longer passages between port and living together at sea for several weeks, the crew found semi-permanent accommodation in the craft. Master and men had separate living spaces: the forecastle was fitted with a stove, an iron chimney, lockers, bunks, and a triangular table on which the men took their meals. Separate living spaces were delineated not only by distance but also by the two cabin trunks fore and aft, above the master's cabin and above the forecastle. Cabin trunks were the upper housing of the cabins, rising above the deck, which had become flush as the sudden rise and fall in the deck (the "break") disappeared. The gradual separation of master and crew also occurred in Newfoundland sealing vessels, as J.B. Jukes reported in 1842: "The generality of vessels going to the ice are schooners and brigs from 80 to 150 tons, manned by a stout crew of rough fishermen, with a skipper at their head of their own stamp. Crew and skipper all live and lie together in a narrow dark cabin of the smallest possible dimensions, and the fewest possible conveniences, everything being common ... There are, however, one or two masters of ships of superior description who reserve the after cabin to themselves and keep the crew in the forecastle."[25]

By the late nineteenth century the forecastle in coastal schooners had often become a separate cabin house erected on the deck, allowing more cargo space below deck. But the separate cabins of master and men remained close to each other: while the average schooner of the early nineteenth century was less than 50 feet in length, by the 1880s schooners in Atlantic Canada were still between 60 and 70 feet in length on average. Master and men were a few steps from each other: to call his crew on deck the master had only to walk to the hatch fitted into the companionway leading down to the forecastle. In calm weather his voice could be heard from any part of the vessel. Between the living spaces lay the galley, usually aft of the forecastle, and the cook was a wage-paid specialist even in fishing vessels.[26] The cook's domain was less a barrier than a link between master and men, for they could often take meals together. In fishing vessels with larger crews there would be two sittings at meals, and the master could eat with one "half" and he might even be found in the forecastle with the crew "passing the bottle around," in the days before many skippers became tee-totallers.[27]

The sailor entered his forecastle by descending the six or seven steps of the steeply sloping ladder of the forward companionway. The sliding hatch was perhaps the only source of light and air for the small triangular space below. Yet it was not the darkness that first caught the attention of the novice, but the "unforgettable fo'c'sle fug"–the dank odour of coal or paraffin, old boots, tar, salt fish, and the bilge water swishing under the floors. The landsman, even where a larger vessel allowed him an adjacent cabin, felt the air of the forecastle: "Last night as I turned in and the hot stifling and rotten air of the hole of the ship poured through crack and crevice and filled my lungs I thought I would never survive 'til morning, but I have nerved myself to bear many things hitherto unknown to me."[28] Sometimes the only light within the forecastle came from old fat poured over wool in a tin and called a "bully light." There might be a small table, and on either side were bunks or, in earlier times, canvas hammocks slung from bulkheads or beams. Oilskins and other gear cluttered the sloping sides of the forecastle and the small wedge-shaped table in the centre, with its bench seats on either side. At the bottom of the ladder stood a small iron stove, burning coal taken from a nearby store, perhaps under the forecastle floor. Sanitary arrangements might consist of nothing more than a bucket in the corner of the forecastle, but by the late nineteenth century the "head" was a separate wooden com-partment aft of the forecastle or on deck.

In these small vessels the seaman came to know his fellow workers very well. Living spaces were crowded and often noisy. Even with heavy planking and bulkheads around the forecastle one was very close to the sea - much closer than the sailor in the large square-rigged ship - and close to the sound of the sea on the hull. "One shouted in speaking, for the forecastle reverberated like a drum to the crashing seas."[29] Even before the vessel put to sea the sailor might meet other occupants of the forecastle, apart from the crew: "Did not sleep any first night - felt something biting me ... At day I caught one. Horror upon Horrors! the ship is discovered to be infested with these vermin."[30] This was a landsman's reaction, in a small brig in the 1870s. The seaman was more laconic. The fore-castle, said one, was "where you can lay back and smoke your pipe calmly and watch the cockroaches climbing up the bulkhead, and enjoy the pleasant sensation of a score of hungry bed-bugs holding a survey on you."[31] A more serious preoccupation was damp, and a great deal of time was spent drying clothes.

The industrial revolution added new gear and hardware but did not transform working relations. The increasing use of iron, for instance, eased many tasks and allowed the schooner to increase in both size and range without proportionate increases in crew size. The windlass, used to raise the anchor, was at first little more than a barrel rotated with wooden handspikes. The introduction of patent windlasses facilitated the handling of anchors.[32] By the late nineteenth century there were iron pumps, iron-strapped blocks, iron water tanks, and even wire standing rigging to replace hemp in the holding of masts in place. Steering was done at the wheel rather than by pushing a simple wooden tiller. The blocks (pulleys) – the most important labour-saving device in sail-handling – had increased in number and in quality; by the 1880s a schooner of 150 tons might use as many as 50 single blocks and 25 double blocks.[33]

The Canadian schooner remained a squat and beamy vessel. After mid-century the ratio of length to breadth actually fell in some ports, and vessels became deeper and more seaworthy in offshore seas and heavy weather.[34] Gradually the multiple square topsails gave way to fore and aft topsails, which were easier to handle, and sails became lighter. The offshore fishing schooners of the turn of the century remained relatively small vessels, but the 100-foot craft might carry eight thousand square feet of sail and was so seaworthy that she could be thrown over on her beam, with masts flat along the water, and still right herself if the hatches were tight and the stone ballast properly stowed. In such vessels even winter fishing on the banks was possible.[35]

The schooner was not the only pre-industrial workplace in marine transportation. Among small vessels it was most numerous, but in British North America, as elsewhere, there was a long history of experimentation with sail plans, and local builders and owners applied ideas borrowed from their British and American contemporaries. Perhaps most important was the adoption of the square sail in conjunction with the fore and aft sails (Figure 2). Builders and owners had to calculate the relative advantages of these two types of sail, and every rigging reflected a set of decisions about seaworthiness, carrying capacity, hull size and shape, speed,

FIGURE 2

The Square Sail and Its Running Rigging

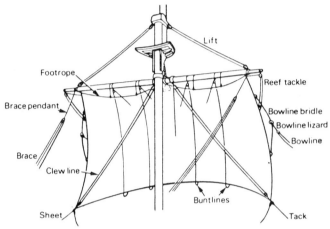

Source: Oxford Companion to Ships and the Sea by Peter Kemp. Published by Oxford University Press 1976 © Oxford University Press 1976.

trade routes, and labour requirements and costs. Vessel owners wished to maximize carrying capacity and seaworthiness without increasing labour costs. The square sail was advantageous in long-distance ocean passages, and in vessels above a certain size square sail was usually essential. Eventually the fore and aft sail could by itself drive vessels 300 feet in length of a thousand tons or more, but such giant schooners were mainly late-nineteenth-century American creations.[36] In British North America vessels of a hundred feet and more usually required at least one square sail, but the square sail could not swing so freely as the fore and aft sail, because standing rigging impeded the movement of yardarms. Further, when the sail was suspended from a yardarm fitted horizontally across the mast, members of the crew usually had to ascend the mast to set the sail or to furl it. Thus the square sail increased propulsive force, at the cost of an increase in labour.

Closest to the schooner in sail plan and in historical evolution was the brigantine, a two-masted vessel carrying square sails on the foremast, a fore and aft sail on the mainmast, a number of staysails between the two masts, and one or more jib sails suspended between jibboom and foremast (Figure 3). There were relatively few brigantines in British North American ports before the 1830s. But

FIGURE 3
Vessel Rigs, 1860s and 1870s

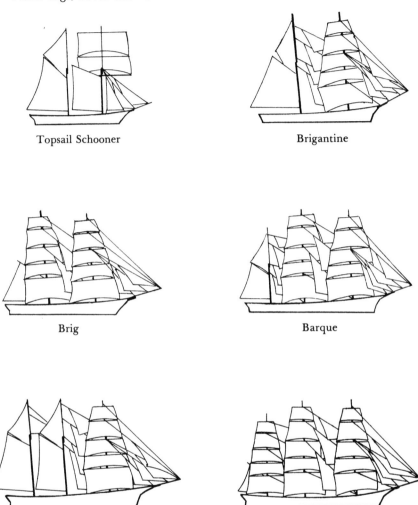

Topsail Schooner

Brigantine

Brig

Barque

Barquentine

Ship

the distinction between schooner and brigantine was not always made clear by contemporaries; it was easy to re-rig a schooner as a brigantine, and one suspects that there were more brigantines than vessel registries indicate. Brigantines were built for long-distance coastal trading, and in Newfoundland, for the seal hunt and the Labrador fishery. This rig was accordingly most common where schooners were most numerous: in Halifax and in Newfoundland.[37] The addition of the square sail required increased labour: in Newfoundland, for instance, schooners of 100 to 149 tons sailed with seven men on average in the later nineteenth century; the brigantine of similar capacity required eight men.[38] The square sail was particularly difficult to operate in winter: "'Tis the frost that makes the coasting navigation so difficult, and almost impracticable to ships. The running ropes freeze in the blocks, the sails are stiff like sheets of tin, and the men cannot expose their hands long enough to the cold to do their duty aloft; so that topsails are not easily handled, however sloops and schooners, where the men stand on the deck and do all their work, succeed well enough."[39] For these reasons the brigantine and other vessels carrying several square sails remained less popular than the schooner in the coastal trades of British North America.

Larger vessels crossing the Atlantic with the wind to leeward or on the quarter required the driving power of the square sail, and the resulting seaworthiness more than compensated for the additional labour cost. Above two hundred tons most vessels carried square sail on both fore and main masts. Most common was the brig, the two-masted vessel designed particularly for ocean passages, in which fore and aft canvas was reduced to a minimum. The brig often carried four square sails on the mainmast and four on the foremast, as well as jibs and a spanker. By the 1860s fore and aft canvas had been increased by the addition of two or more staysails, but three-quarters of the total canvas still consisted of square sail. In the brig a major reduction in canvas required workers to ascend the rigging to furl the sail and make it fast to the yardarm.

The brig was usually larger than the brigantine (mean tonnage of brigs in the Saint John fleet was 218 tons), and greater hull size and length increased labour requirement. As more driving power was required, a common solution was to increase the height of the masts, and so the total area of square canvas. Larger sails were more difficult to handle, and with four sails on each mast the effort and the risk were measurably greater than in a brigantine. The mast itself was rarely a single timber, but three or four masts joined (or "fidded") to each other by heavy brackets. Often the separately fidded masts could be taken down to reduce windage aloft, but several men were required to perform this task.[40]

For these reasons the brig often required more men than vessels of comparable size that were rigged as schooners or brigantines. In the Newfoundland fleet, for instance, the brig of 150 to 199 tons usually required nine men; the brigantine of similar tonnage only eight.[41] In the Halifax fleet in the later nineteenth century the brigantine of a hundred to two hundred tons carried eight men on average; brigs of similar size, 8½.[42] However, the brig remained more popular than the brigantine in Atlantic Canada in the first half of the century. In Halifax and Saint John almost 16 per cent of new vessels before 1850 were rigged as brigs.[43]

The majority of small vessels were rigged as schooners, brigantines, or brigs, but these were not the only rigs purchased by colonial shipowners in the first half of the nineteenth century. The industrial revolution in Britain, the Napoleonic Wars, and the demand for colonial staples transformed international shipping markets and created a demand for new types of vessel from builders in the colonies. Gradually more vessels from Atlantic Canada were being pulled into transatlantic passages. As vessels were built to carry timber across the Atlantic, the structure of hulls and rigging changed again. Despite their reputation for being short-lived, colonial vessels improved in quality and seaworthiness. Diagonal metal strapping in hulls, introduced from the 1830s, and the increasing use of iron knees produced stronger hulls. Total sail area increased relative to hull size, as shipowners sought fast passages with bulky cargoes. The "search for speed under sail" long preceded the fast Cape Horn clippers of mid-century and reflected colonial shipowners' desire to maximize returns from a short-lived asset. The qualities of hull design that tended toward speed were already well known and included a long hull, narrow at the bow, whose sheer lines reduced wave-making resistance.[44] Vessels built in Atlantic Canada lengthened significantly between the 1820s and the 1850s. The length-breadth ratio in vessels of 100 to 249 tons increased from 3.43 to 4.05; in vessels of 250 to 499 tons from 3.77 to 4.72, up 25 per cent.[45] These were not really clipper ships, but the hull configuration was still substantially changed.

Even more dramatic was the search for increased carrying capacity. Improved construction techniques allowed longer hulls, and builders began to discover limits to the efficiency of the two-masted vessel, whatever its combination of sails. One could increase the

FIGURE 4

Sail Plan of a Three-Masted Ship

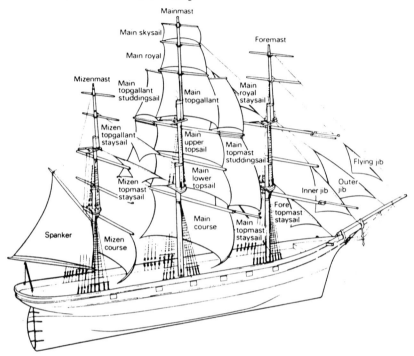

Source: Oxford Companion to Ships and the Sea by Peter Kemp. Published by Oxford University Press 1976 © Oxford University Press 1976.

height of masts and the size of sails only so far, before the two-masted sail plan became cumbersome and the vessel unseaworthy. The solution was a third mast, the mizzen mast. In the 1820s this mast usually carried fore and aft sail, and the vessel of this type was the barque - not a new invention at all, but increasingly popular in Atlantic Canada early in the century. The barque rig served to redistribute the brig's sail area onto three masts: each mast could be shorter in relation to vessel length than in a brig, and the sails could be smaller and hence easier to manage.[46] The additional fore and aft sail on the mizzen could be operated from the deck by the same number of men as handled the square sails on the fore and main. There could be an increase in propulsive power and sea-worthiness, with no increase in labour requirement. In Saint John and Halifax 63 new barques were registered in the 1820s. In Saint

GRAPH 1

Small Vessels on Registry, Major Nova Scotia Ports, 1825–1914

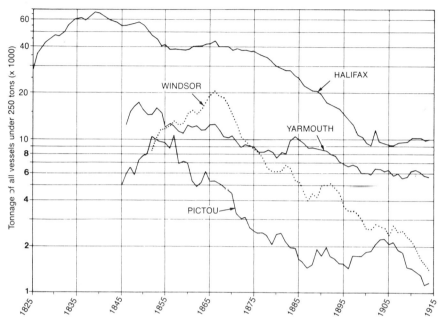

Source: Board of Trade series 107/108 vessel registries.

John by the 1830s barques were already more popular than brigs. Vessels of 200 tons, with a length of around one hundred feet, might be rigged either as brigs or as barques, but above 250 tons and 120 feet the preference was for three masts.[47]

An alternative to the barque was the three-masted ship (Figure 4), which carried a square sail on all three masts, as well as jibs, spanker, and one or more staysails. This rig, while less common than the barque in Atlantic Canada before 1850, was increasingly used in larger vessels owned in Saint John and employed in the timber trade. One would expect that three or four square sails on the mizzen mast would increase labour required, compared to the fore and aft sails common in the barque. In fact ships did not always carry more men than barques, if we compare vessels of similar tonnage in the 300-to-500-ton range.[48] Rig was only one factor influencing crew size, and the passage between New Brunswick and Liverpool, where most of the ships were employed, could be undertaken with fewer men than were required in many other trades.[49]

GRAPH 2

Small Vessels on Registry, Saint John and Miramichi, 1825-1914

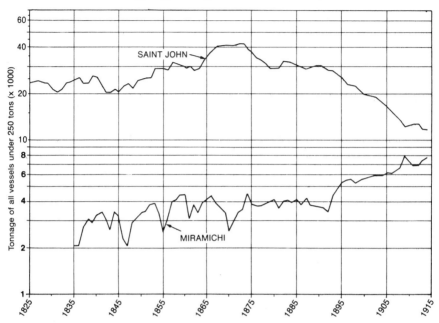

Source: Board of Trade series 107/108 vessel registries.

Nevertheless ship and barque possessed common advantages: more efficient distribution of canvas and increased propulsive power without a commensurate rise in labour requirement. Between the 1820s and 1840s three-masted vessels replaced two-masted craft as the most common *ocean-going* vessels in Atlantic Canada. Three masts allowed the average size of vessels to increase, and in Saint John, for instance, the average tonnage of new vessels almost trebled between the 1820s and the 1850s. The ratio of capital to labour was increasing, at a rate unprecedented in the history of North Atlantic shipping.

The industrial revolution affected colonial shipping, but the technological and social transformation in the ships themselves had scarcely begun. Shipping was unusual among pre-industrial trades in its capital-intensity and in the sophistication of the machinery employed. But before 1850 the pre-industrial craft, represented by small wooden vessels of 250 tons and less, accounted for the major-

GRAPH 3
Small Vessels on Registry, Prince Edward Island, 1826-1914

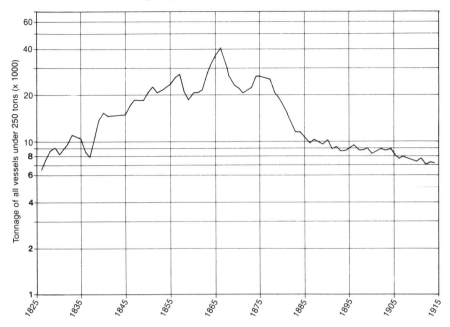

Source: Board of Trade series 107/108 vessel registries.

ity of British North American tonnage. Even after mid-century the fleets of small vessels grew (Graphs 1-4). In Nova Scotia, despite the beginnings of decline in major ports, the peak in small vessel tonnage was not reached until the 1860s, if we take the sum of small-vessel tonnage in all ports. In New Brunswick the peak occurred in the 1870s. In Newfoundland the fleet of small wooden vessels continued to grow in the twentieth century, peaking in 1919.

For small vessel fleets in the region as a whole, total tonnage of vessels under 250 tons was greater in 1914 than in 1830. Graph 5 suggests why so many small sailing vessels remained in use: while demand for them in ocean trades had long since been dwindling, it remained fairly constant in coastal trades into the twentieth century. The measure of coastal tonnage here is far from ideal, since total tonnage entering and clearing ports does not reflect vessel utilization or freight carried. But the graph indicates demand for steam tonnage and sailing tonnage in Canada's coastal waters.

GRAPH 4

Small Vessels on Registry, Newfoundland, 1826–1914

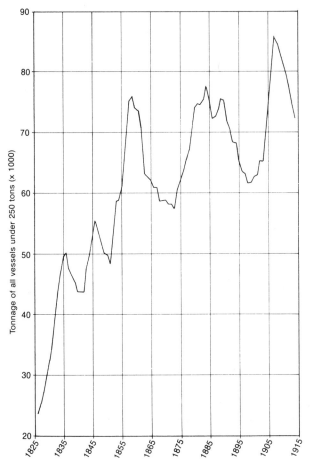

Sources: Board of Trade series 107/108 vessel registries; vessel registries for St John's, National Archives of Canada.

Demand for steam tonnage increased rapidly, but there was still substantial demand for small sailing vessels, particularly in small outports served neither by steamship nor by railway. Sailing vessels remained much smaller than steamers: by 1914 the average tonnage of the sailing vessel entering and clearing port was a mere 179 tons. We do not know the number of vessels coasting at any one time, since vessels could shift from one trade to another, and registrars of shipping did not define them by the nature of their employment.

GRAPH 5

Tonnage Employed in Canadian Coasting Trades, 1876–1914

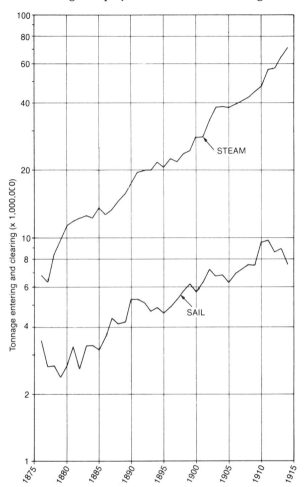

Source: Canada *Sessional Papers*, 1915, vol. L, 82–3.

Nevertheless we do know the type of sailing vessel employed in Canadian waters. As Table 1 suggests, the preferred vessel was still the small schooner, which accounted for almost 58 per cent of all clearances by sailing tonnage in 1900. An increasing share of coasting activity was conducted by barges of various kinds (often converted hulks of old sailing vessels). But the schooner was still pre-eminent, and demand for it had more than doubled since 1876.[50]

TABLE 1

Sailing Vessels Clearing Port in Canadian Coastal Trades, 1900

Vessel Type	Tonnage of All Clearances	% of Total	Average Tonnage
Ship	10,192	0.4	1,699
Barque	28,611	1.0	734
Barquentine	8,593	0.3	409
Brig	800	0.0	200
Brigantine	11,339	0.4	110
Schooner	1,627,051	57.5	61
Sloop	43,264	1.5	34
Barges, canal boats, etc.	1,097,821	38.8	288
Total	2,827,671		

Source: Canada, Sessional Papers, 1901, vol. XXXV, no. 5, p. 857.

These small craft shared many characteristics of pre-industrial crafts and workshops on land. There was little iron in the wooden coastal vessel, and motive power was supplied by wind and by human labour. The average number of workers in each vessel was small: in the first half of the century, and in wooden coastal vessels throughout the century, most sailors shared their workplace with fewer than ten others. In landward trades, the workplace was often in close proximity to the workers' residence. In shipping, master and men shared physical spaces during work and leisure: the workplace was the temporary domicile of workers and master. Neither was there any distinction between the place of work and the machinery to which labour was applied. Machinery, workplace, and bunkhouse were combined in one.

Pre-industrial work often depended upon energy supplied by the action of wind and water and frequently changed with the seasons. Nowhere more than in seafaring did workers depend on the direct action of natural elements, and work was highly seasonal. In St John's, in Halifax, and in most other ports in Atlantic Canada entrances and clearances fell sharply during the winter: in St John's in the late 1830s, for instance, shipping activity in the four winter months was less than a third of its volume for the rest of the year.[51] Vessels avoided the North Atlantic and the Grand Banks in winter, and in many ports ice halted all clearances for several weeks in winter. Of necessity seafaring was a seasonal occupation for those who remained in coastal and fishing vessels.

The real difference between the small wooden vessel and other pre-industrial workplaces was that at sea the work was not stationary, but a craft moving through wind and water, elements constantly in motion. In his "floating habitation," said John Froude, the sailor lives on a "watery plain," "all his life a bitter conflict with the sea thats never still."[52] In this floating workplace men applied a variety of mechanical skills and manual arts to wood and rope and canvas, working together in small spaces on waters dangerous to both vessels and men. This was a pre-industrial workplace, but very different from any known to landsmen.

CHAPTER TWO

Working the Small Craft

However far from land they took their seafaring craft, sailors did not escape the influence of social relations created on land. In the seaboard colonies of British North America these relations were part of merchant capitalism and its evolution on a resource-based frontier. Merchant profits came primarily from control of the processes of circulation and exchange, and particularly from imports and exports. The staples that merchants exported were produced in village and outport communities which merchants dominated mainly by controlling supplies, price mechanisms, and certain forms of capital, such as ships. The organization of production was left very much to planters, farmers, and fishermen, who employed labour largely within master-servant contracts and relationships.

Although the master-servant nexus was not always transferred directly into ships, relations at sea were dictated not simply by the peculiar exigencies of sailing ship technology but also by the paternalism of the master-servant relationship on land and in fishing. The organization of work was left to the workers, even when sailors were property-less wage labourers and merchants owned the means of production. In these ways the small coastal vessel remained a pre-industrial craft: not a factory, where the owner of capital controlled and managed every stage of production, but the domain of a craftsman, a worker who possessed "the accumulated knowledge of materials and processes by which production was accomplished in the craft."[1]

In the late eighteenth century, in Newfoundland and Nova Scotia, the term *master* was applied to a number of different occupations. The fishing master could be hired by a merchant in England to employ labour in the seasonal migratory fishery. The master might be a resident "planter" or bye-boat keeper, who hired servants by contract, trading their output to local or even distant merchants. The term might also refer to a master mariner, a man who specialized in operating vessels rather than boats, hiring workers to assist in shipping goods coast-wise, or even as far as the markets in the West Indies and elsewhere. Obviously these different roles were not mutually exclusive, and individual masters could move from one to another. Common to all, however, was their control of means of production and their hiring of wage labour. Many masters owned means of production – boats, flakes, stages, fishing gear, and even small vessels – and could describe themselves as "traders," aspiring even to the status and functions of a small merchant. Others, particularly the master mariner, were themselves wage labourers, hired to operate vessels owned by their merchant-employer. The smaller fishing master or planter often laboured beside his employees. Whether or not they owned vessels or boats, the planters, boatkeepers, and ship masters were usually middlemen or agents of larger merchant firms located in Britain or, increasingly, in the colonies.[2]

If these masters were in a transitional stage, with some destined to enter the ranks of merchant capitalists and others to descend into the ranks of wage labour or the family-based fishery, the transition was a long one indeed. The Newfoundland historian will point, of course, to the undermining of the planter-middlemen in the Newfoundland fishery through manipulation of the legal and political system between the 1820s and the 1840s. The complex process resulting in the rise of the truck system, the restriction of the wage system, and the rise of the household-based inshore fishery was a critical stage in the social and economic development of Newfoundland.[3] But these developments should not obscure the fact that the independent master mariner and the fishing master did not disappear but survived into the twentieth century, sometimes bearing the title of "planter."

While many of these men operated vessels or boats owned by merchants, their independent ownership of property in vessels was extensive. Of all shareholdings in schooners newly registered in Newfoundland between 1820 and 1936, 26 per cent were held by "planters." A further 19 per cent were held by traders, mariners, or fishermen. In the 1820s planters owned almost a third of all new tonnage registered in Newfoundland; while their share of new investment fell thereafter, their aggregate new investment did not peak until the 1870s. At the end of the nineteenth century the small property owner (trader, planter, mariner, or fisherman) was still responsible for over a fifth of all new shipping investments in Newfoundland, and a much larger share of new investment in schooners.[4] In Nova Scotia the small vessel owner also survived into the twentieth century and dominated coastal trading. In Halifax and Yarmouth, the major ports of registry, two-thirds of all share-holdings in small vessels (new vessels under 250 tons) belonged to master mariners, farmers, or fishermen, and the master mariners were by far the most important of these three.[5] Although most fishermen did not own schooners or any other form of vessel tonnage, nevertheless the small master-owner, who still controlled the organization of production in his vessel, remained a major employer in coastal shipping.

Where a large proportion of schooner tonnage was owned by merchants, as in Newfoundland, the master-employee was still relatively independent of merchant domination in the workplace. The merchant relied upon his ability to dismiss masters or to withhold wages to ensure loyalty and good service. But the ship master, like the fishing skipper, could not be supervised or controlled directly. He was in control of everything in the schooner, in port and at sea. "In most instances, I was my own boss. In all the schooners and boats I sailed, I was skipper ... Also working on the fleet of schooners [i.e. in maintenance], I was my own boss."[6] The skipper's knowledge limited his subordination to the merchant, as one Newfoundland merchant discovered when his schooner lost part of her stem, stern-post, and planking:

"What am I going to do to get her repaired?"

I said, "I don't know what you're going to do. If she were my schooner, I'd know what I'd do ..."

He nearly threw a fit.

"Suit yourself if you want me to do the job on the schooner, take it or leave it," I said.

He cooled down after a while and said, "You got me over a barrel."

I said, "I've been waiting for a long time."[7]

There was, as some theorists would say, a formal subordination of labour here, but not the real subordination that occurs in the industrial workplace.[8]

The pattern of employment in coastal craft was set very largely by that in the fisheries. When the Newfoundland planter hired servants, he did so for the fishing season in their "capacity of Fisherman, Seaman, or otherwise for the good of the Voyage." The indenture was referred to as a "shipping paper," and any servant in Newfoundland was said to be "shipped."[9] The term was apt, even if a master lived in Newfoundland rather than England, because labour might be required not only in the inshore boat fishery but also in the planter's "ship" or vessel, particularly if the planter were engaged in the Labrador fishery or in sealing. We even hear of farm-servants in Newfoundland being "shipped" for the seal hunt. Under such contracts the relationship was not a simple wage-labour exchange. It was "diffuse and paternalistic": the servant committed his whole person, or so it was assumed, and did not perform only a few specified tasks but committed himself to the needs of the entire seasonal enterprise.[10] The master expected his worker "to do everything in his power for my interest."[11] In return the master paid wages and offered food and drink on customary holidays. If the worker did not serve "faithfully and honestly" the master might enforce obedience through corporal punishment or the withholding of wages.

This describes employment relationships not only in the eighteenth-century fishery but also in coastal schooners, and the assumptions lying behind this employment even in the twentieth century. Even where the relationship was increasingly reduced to a wage-labour exchange, old assumptions persisted easily where the master and worker lived and worked together and where the master was obliged to feed and accommodate his workers. The notion that the sailor committed his entire self to the voyage and gave "service" to his master persisted, as did the practice of corporal punishment or the withholding of wages or of food and drink in order to exact obedience. In the seventeenth century, notes Christopher Hill, government of a family was likened "to that of a ship, a corporate town or a State."[12] The model was in fact that of the family or the household as the basis of orderly society, and the ship was a type of working household with the master at its head.

The rise of the family-based fishery in Newfoundland, and the somewhat different role of the household as a unit of production in the Nova Scotia fishery, strengthened the association of ship and family. And domestic commodity production added another strand to the traditions that influenced shipboard relations: out of the family fishery emerged an egalitarianism that resolved paternalism into something more like fraternalism, which was also a natural extension of family relationships. "Fisher families controlled their own social relations of work, built and owned their productive equipment, and wove the various threads of this self-determination within the fabric of social life, alongside and crossing the strands of imposed poverty and need," writes Gerald Sider.[13] The result in the boat fishery was an "ethic of egalitarian relations" in which the fishing skipper was merely a man of seniority and experience working with close relations, usually patrikin, and decisions about how, where, and when to fish depended very much upon consensus within the group rather than the skipper's imposed authority. So strong was this egalitarian ethic that boats have even been caught in storms when no one wanted to make a decision to come back in.[14] This egalitarianism was often reinforced by the presence of brothers and other male kin in the same boat, where subordination of one to another was difficult to establish. Such working relationships were easily transferred to the fishing schooners of the Labrador and Bank fisheries, especially since kin and crew often overlapped there too.

The result was that "every Bank fishing schooner was a sort of seafaring democracy."[15] Although the crew was usually divided into two working groups, or "watches," this division was often ignored and all hands were called when only one watch was required: "By doing this, no favourites are made and no one can complain that he is being imposed upon." The master was the immediate employer, whether or not he owned the vessel, but his crew knew him by the fraternal honorific "skipper." The fishing skipper "tried to make his orders sound like requests," and decisions about the timing and pace of work, as well as control over the fishing gear, were largely in the hands of the fisherman themselves.[16] The fishermen also chose whether or not to fish on Sunday.[17]

Relations between skipper and men were also influenced by the "share system," the most common method of payment in both Nova Scotia and Newfoundland, although it had many variants. Very often the only wage-paid member of the crew was the cook. The rest were "sharemen." In Nova Scotia in the late nineteenth century it was not uncommon for half of the gross catch to go to the vessel. The master took a percentage of the rest (one Halifax merchant was paying 5 per cent in the 1880s), and then the crew divided the remainder equally.[18] Occasionally Nova Scotian fish merchants sold their fishing masters a share of the schooners in which they worked. But the share system was the most common means of ensuring effort and loyalty. It minimized the merchant's risk by spreading the impact of a poor season and eliminating the need to pay wages when few fish had been caught. It also ensured that each worker had a vested interest in the efforts of his fellows: the fishermen became self-supervising when they worked on a "co-operative basis." The skipper was part of the co-operative effort, since he too was paid a share of the total catch.

The share system varied with time and place, and sometimes the crew was paid "by the count": each dory crew was paid in proportion to the number of fish that it caught. Payment "by the count" was another means of controlling effort at a distance, and it was sometimes used when the skipper had "a crowd of strangers whose abilities as fishermen were unknown."[19] The fishing schooner was not quite a democracy, of course, but the share system tended to minimize distinctions of rank and seniority, and in a crew of 20 the master who was paid 5 per cent of the gross might earn only slightly more than his men. The master was the master seaman, the navigator, and the most experienced "fish-killer." His authority rested on these qualities rather than on the kinds of sanctions available to industrial employers. The fishing skipper could not easily withhold wages or dismiss an employee on the spot.

The cargo-carrying coastal schooner was a rather different workplace, but it shared something of the fraternal egalitarianism of the fishing schooner. However, in the coastal passage, wage payment was normal. A master mariner, working for a merchant or on his own account, purchased the manual labour of deckhands in return for a monthly wage. Sometimes the wage payment would go to the worker in the form of goods, especially if he was also a fisherman working for a merchant on credit. Service in a schooner passage could even be a means of paying a debt to the merchant after a poor fishing season.[20] The wage-labour exchange was usually defined by contract, and coastal crew agreements became common in the last half of the nineteenth century. The wage system did not mean that the coastal skipper had left the social world of the fishing village. Sometimes the fishing vessel itself became a coastal trader, worked by part of the fishing crew. And the coaster made relatively short passages to and from the home port of its master or owner, and so the crew was very often hired in that home port.

On most coastal passages many seamen knew each other and knew the master before joining the vessel. This could occur even in vessels from such large ports as Saint John. Department of Transport records exist for seamen hired in Saint John for coastal passages in the 1880s.[21] Most of the vessels were registered in Saint John and were under 150 tons. Of 781 crew members filling positions in these vessels in 1883-4, no less than 42 per cent stated Saint John to be their home. A further 32.3 per cent were from elsewhere in New Brunswick. There were not 781 individuals in this sample, since many appear more than once in the same vessel (in all of the analysis that follows individuals may be counted more than once, but this does not weaken the analysis: we are interested in the labour force filling all available crew positions, and so the occupant of the berth, rather than the individual, is the appropriate unit of analysis).

Almost three in every four men working in these vessels was from New Brunswick, even though Saint John was a port frequented by sailors from many countries. The contrast with crews hired in ocean-going vessels in Saint John at the same time is startling: only 12.2 per cent in ocean-going vessels were Saint John residents, and only 36.7 per cent were from the Atlantic region (over 88 per cent in coastal vessels were from the region).[22] Coastal seamen were not a completely distinct group in the seafaring labour force, but familiarity and cohesion in the workplace undoubtedly resulted from the common home and the shared language and dialect. Continuity of service was also a characteristic of the coastal labour force: 21 per cent of those listed in the engagement books had previously served in the same vessel.

We know less about the masters of these vessels, but they too appear to have been local men, and probably they knew many of their crew before the voyage. In 19 of the 30 vessels, at least one member of the crew had the same surname as the master, and masters were probably hiring brothers or sons or other relations. Harris Barnes of Halifax, working in a Nova Scotian coastal schooner in the 1860s, noted the paternal and even fraternal relationships that could follow: "Captain Broderick, however, was a fine old gentleman and seemed more like a father to all of his crew, as indeed he was to all except myself. His sons for some years previous had been playmates of mine, and there was between us something more than an ordinary friendship, which time increased in intensity."[23] Although there were no women in the Saint John sample discussed here, occasionally women did appear on the decks of coastal vessels, where the craft was a family venture. Frederick William Wallace remembered such a vessel: "The most astonishing sight of all was a dirty little coasting schooner, with ill-stayed masts and stained and badly-fitted sails, simply ghosting along past the whole lot of us ... As her skipper went about the work of sail trimming, his wife took the wheel."[24]

But paternalism was more common than actual kinship, not least because the majority of crews were very young men. Crew members in these Saint John coasters were even younger than seamen in Saint John ocean-going vessels in the 1870s and 1880s. Almost 16 per cent were teenagers, and 75 per cent were under the age of 30. It was not unusual for a master to take charge of a crew of men aged between 17 and 22. This did not mean that his workers were inexperienced, however. Only 3.3 per cent of the 781 crew positions were held by men on their first voyage. In no vessel do we find more than two sailors on their first voyage. If masters were choosing young men, they were also finding experienced workers.

The pattern of paternalism reinforced by kinship and community was even more marked in Newfoundland. Records for crews on coastal passages are scarce, but crew agreements exist for 353 longer voyages by Newfoundland vessels between 1860 and 1900.[25] Most of the voyages were by small vessels, 250 tons or less, and most were rigged as schooners, brigantines, or brigs. Almost half the crew members were born in Newfoundland (47.5 per cent), and a majority of the masters were Newfoundlanders. These surviving records include a disproportionate number of passages between Newfoundland and the United Kingdom; under-represented are the very common passages by Newfoundland's "fish boxes" to and from the West Indies, South America, and southern Europe, in which the proportion of Newfoundlanders, hired in their home ports for the return voyage, was even higher. The small vessels clearing from St John's in the 1840s were sailed by men born in

Newfoundland, England, or Ireland, and most very likely resided in Newfoundland.[26]

The independent master mariners who owned their own schooners had a large share of coastal trading, but they were not the only owners of small vessels in Atlantic Canada. Although still small vessels, brigantines and brigs were larger than the average schooner and were better adapted for long-distance coastal voyages and transatlantic passages – in the timber trade, for instance. The larger the vessel, the greater the initial capital investment, and the more likely that the owners were merchants. In the 1830s and 1840s these vessels were the immediate predecessors of the great ocean-going fleets owned in Atlantic Canada after 1850. The social relations of production were somewhat different from those in the small coastal schooner: the element of fraternalism remains, but critical was the paternalism stemming from mercantile domination of society and the economy in the ports of Atlantic Canada.

There is no better representative source of these relationships than the little town of Yarmouth, Nova Scotia, in the first half of the nineteenth century. There fishing and coasting schooners stood beside the small timber-carrying brigs and West Indies traders. There shipowning was the business of a small number of merchant families in a town of a few thousand people. In their various commercial dealings, merchants depended on a network of personal and family contacts and alliances strengthened by judicious marriages. Merchants preferred to deal with men whom they knew. In hiring shipmasters they usually hired men whom they must have known and seen about their town for several years. Of 50 master positions in voyages of Yarmouth vessels in 1846–7, no less than 39 were filled by men born in Yarmouth town, which had a population of about 3,500 by mid-century.[27] Many of the masters were young members of shipowning families: Aaron Goudey (aged 30), Amasa Durkee (32), George Ryerson (31), Lyman Cann (22), Lyman J. Durkee (24), George Killam (24), John K. Ryerson (22), and Thomas B. Cann (29). At this time or in later years the Durkees, Ryersons, and Canns were all related to the Killams as a result of marriages among the town's élite families.[28] Employment at the rank of master was the result of personal and family connections, and often the young master was receiving his informal apprenticeship in the family business.

TABLE 2
Birthplaces of Sailors Signing on Yarmouth-Registered Ocean-Going Vessels, 1846-7

Place of Birth	Number	% of Total
Yarmouth	259	49.1
Other Nova Scotia	48	9.1
New Brunswick	22	4.2
Newfoundland	4	0.7
Prince Edward Island	1	0.2
Total BNA	(334)	(63.3)
England	62	11.7
Scotland	35	6.6
Ireland	39	7.4
Wales	5	0.9
United States	8	1.5
Scandinavia	11	2.1
Western Europe	11	2.1
West Indies	9	1.7
Other/Unknown	14	2.7
Total	528	100.0

Source: Board of Trade series 98, Crew Lists, Yarmouth, NS.

The paternalism of the family business extended even further into the workplace. Even at other ranks almost half of the workers were men born in Yarmouth (Table 2). The names Cann, Ryerson, Killam, and Lovitt appear below the rank of master, and masters often had family relations among the crew. Where so many came from a town that had only about seven hundred adult males, it is likely that many in the crew were known to each other before they put to sea. Further, crew members were mostly of the same generation: 41 per cent were between the ages of 20 and 24, and a further 20 per cent between 25 and 29. There were many more teenagers (17 per cent) than older men; most of the teenagers were 17, 18, or 19. On every Yarmouth vessel there were young men who had homes ashore, in the same small town where as boys they had played together and watched their fathers and uncles put to sea.

These small-town sailors of the 1840s differed from their successors, the deepsea sailors a generation later, who may have had no home other than boarding-houses and ships and met their shipmates for the first time as they signed the crew articles. And unlike the sailors a generation later, these Yarmouth seamen spoke the same language: out of every hundred sailors no less than 93 spoke English as their native tongue.

Where the master was son or brother in the family firm, the ship's business would often be in the hands of the master. But if a trusted family member were not in command the merchant appointed a supercargo, an agent responsible for all transactions relating to the cargo.[29] This was particularly necessary when these vessels were still "trading vessels" carrying goods purchased by the owner of the vessel (later in the century large sailing vessels tended to be "general cargo carriers," carrying goods on charter, and the owner of the cargo was less often the owner of the vessel).[30] With the "trading vessel" the shipowner was seeking a profit from the margin between purchase price in one port and selling price in another. Commodity trading was left to the shipowner or the supercargo; the master was responsible mainly for the speedy passage and the safety of his vessel. Although he was responsible for expenditures relating to the vessel (wages, port charges, victualling), the master was still an employee, not a business partner. He remained close to his workers because of shared tasks, physical proximity, and the shared status of wage-paid employee. And in Yarmouth vessels, masters were usually young men, like their crew: most were in their twenties or early thirties.

The master knew his men well, and his finely judged assessment of their ability as seamen is reflected in the wages that he agreed to pay each able seaman (AB). The average monthly wage paid to Nova Scotia-born ABs in the Yarmouth fleet in 1846-7 was £3-13-0. The deviation around this mean was substantial (see Table 3). In British and American ports in the 1840s, and in all ports in subsequent decades, masters would have no choice but to pay the prevailing wage, and all ABs signing on in the same place would usually be paid the same wage. But Nova Scotians who joined Yarmouth vessels, whether in Yarmouth or Saint John, were paid at different rates, and the variation certainly represents the master's assessment of experience and ability, since other factors (such as port) do not explain much of the variation in wage.

TABLE 3

Wages of Nova Scotia-Born ABs in Yarmouth Vessels, 1846-7

Monthly Wage (£)	Number of Men	Cumulative %
2-0-0	1	
2-5-0	1	
2-10-0	5	
2-12-0	1	
2-15-0	3	12.1
3-0-0	11	
3-5-0	6	
3-7-6	1	
3-10-0	15	
3-12-6	1	
3-15-0	1	56.0
4-0-0	18	
4-5-0	2	
4-10-0	4	
4-15-0	1	
5-0-0	15	
Total	91	

Source: Board of Trade series 98, Crew Agreements.

Note: Signing on in Yarmouth or Saint John only.

Younger men usually received lower wages, but not always. On board the 168-ton *Rover* in 1846 were four able seamen, the youngest of whom, aged only 16, was paid the highest wage (£3-5-0) while another Yarmouth 16-year-old was paid only £2-15-0.[31] The range of wages paid to Yarmouth ABs could be extreme: in the 324-ton *Caroline* in 1847, monthly wages ranged from £2-0-0 to £4-5-0 for ABs signing on in Yarmouth. If the master were convinced that his recruit lacked experience or ability, he could sign him on as an ordinary seaman or a "boy" at an average wage of £2-8-0, but less than 2 per cent of Yarmouth crews were signed on at these lowly ranks.

Of course the Yarmouth master could have hired more men in the British ports that his vessel frequented, and thereby cut a pound or more from the seaman's average wage, at least on the westward passage. But the frequent return to home port gave the master an opportunity to hire men whom he knew, and this alternative was both available and preferred: the local man was better known and less likely to desert than was the sailor hired in a low-wage British port for a passage to high-wage North American ports.[32]

The Yarmouth ships and crews had not severed contact with their home port. Seafarers still had a home on land, where the influence of their employer could soon be reasserted directly. Paternalism was reinforced by short passages and proximity to home, and an element of informal trust endured as it did not in larger vessels a generation later. Before embarking, sailors signed crew agreements which lack the detail and much of the content of later contracts. But the agreements of the 1840s do contain occasional evidence on the critically important matter of victualling. In coasting vessels, because of their closeness to shore and because of sailor's knowledge of fishing, diet was not necessarily worse than on land merely because one was at sea, and often it was better. Sometimes "the people in the harbours that we visited would supply us with fresh fish and in the summer they would supply us with cabbage and an odd meal of potatoes without charging us."[33] Victualling on a longer passage was a different matter, and in the late 1840s the law did not yet require that the scale of provisions be noted on all crew agreements. The sailor merely accepted a master's verbal promise or asked nothing and took his chances.

In the Yarmouth vessels, however, paternalism and proximity to home may have operated to ensure an adequate diet, since there is evidence that victualling was better than in most British vessels at the same time, and better than in many Canadian vessels a generation later. There appear to be few, if any, instances where a master was obliged to demote or dismiss a cook. In smaller vessels - 200 tons or less - many cooks (about half) were teenagers. There were very few apprentices on British North American vessels - teenagers served more often as ordinary seamen or as cooks, and cooking for seven or eight men appears to have been a substitute for apprenticeship and an opportunity for a boy to work while learning something about seafaring. The young cook was easily replaced and as easily terrorized by the older men with whom he worked.[34] Since few were replaced while at sea (the crew lists would record a change in capacity), either they performed well or the "grub" available was adequate.

The provision scales sometimes included in the crew lists of the 1840s suggest that victuals may indeed have been adequate. There was no guarantee that the men got what was stated, but such scales as the following were not untypical: 1½ pounds beef or pork per day; 1 pound peameal per week; ½ pound peas per week; potatoes daily; 1 pound rice per week; 1 pound bread per day; 1 pound sugar per week; 1 gallon water per day; coffee and tea daily. This diet is certainly better than that of the seamen in most British merchant vessels of the 1830s and 1840s.[35]

The inclusion of vegetables, rice, and sugar makes the diet closer to the Board of Trade scale of 1868 – itself only recommended rather than compulsory. Some vessels even mention both potatoes and dried fruit on a daily basis. If such provisions were common, then scurvy was probably unknown, although the short passage would also help to reduce the incidence of that disease. In Yarmouth vessels, only two men were discharged because of illness in 1846 and 1847, which indicates much less illness than in later times.[36] Sometimes, instead of a daily or weekly scale of provisions, there appear the words: "as much as they can eat."[37] While this says nothing about the quantity or quality of food, it suggests a degree of trust that did not exist a generation later, when such words from a master would surely have invited contemptuous disbelief.

The evidence about victualling is suggestive, but not conclusive. A more reliable indicator of conditions at sea is the record of discharge from service. Beside most workers' names the master recorded the termination or renewal of the contract. "Discharge by mutual consent" was the common form for an honourable discharge (although sometimes this form was used when disputes had occurred and the master was glad to see the last of the seaman). The proportion of sailors who were discharged by mutual consent or "remained" on board at the end of the voyage is remarkably high: 97 per cent in Yarmouth vessels in 1846 and 1847. This figure is so high as to invite disbelief – but desertions *were* recorded in these vessels, and desertion was the sailors' most obvious statement of dissatisfaction with wages, victualling, or other conditions of work. Only 1.8 per cent of actions upon termination of voyages were desertions.[38] As a proportion of all man-entrances into port, or individual desertion opportunities, desertions were insignificant (of nine deserters, only one was Yarmouth-born). In no other fleet for which we have such information is the desertion rate so low. This does not mean that exploitation and dissatisfaction were absent. We may conclude, however, that working relationships in this fleet were relatively harmonious and stable.

It is possible to observe these working relations more closely. To do so, we must rely on evidence from the late nineteenth and early twentieth centuries, but it is unlikely that the patterns of work in the small schooner had changed significantly since the early nineteenth century. Observing the master and his crew putting to sea, it is difficult to know precisely when work has begun, for the work was task-oriented and wholly lacking in temporal pattern. It is almost impossible to separate work from non-work, or leisure. Although by the end of the nineteenth century some skippers were teetotallers, the rule of "no grog allowed" did not apply, and one former mariner remembers that "no crafty skipper ever sailed on a trading voyage without ample supply of good old Demerara rum and pipe tobacco, solely for entertaining purposes."[39] Work, therefore, might well begin with a very fraternal exchange between master and crew: "Charlie he was skipper and I was cook. 'Now,' he said, 'we wants some dinner.' [He was] getting a few drinks in now, he was. He said he bought a dozen eggs and three pound of halibut. 'Go aboard now,' he said, 'and cook that ...' We had to get a piece of rope under Albert's arms to get him aboard. Got Charlie aboard ... They never ate their dinner. That was alright."[40] The point is not that insobriety was common but that the voyage can begin with such fraternal intimacy: the deckhands have carried their master aboard.

Whether or not all voyages begin in precisely this way, the fraternalism continues as the vessel gets under way. When embarking from a wharf, the schooner is hauled around by her mooring lines until headed into the stream, if she is not already pointed that way.[41] In a small vessel, without the large numbers of men available to the fishing skipper, the master is likely to lay hands on the lines himself and to haul with the others. "All right for'ard, slip them bowlines," is the next order, and again the master is likely to move to one of the mooring lines, flip the turns off the bit-post, and deftly coil the four-inch manila rope. "Trim that fore sheet in and hoist mainsail." The master might have chosen to hoist the jumbo and the jib first - that decision lay with him, not with the crew, of course. All hands jump to the halyards (originally haul-yards), the ropes used to hoist and lower sails, some on the throat halyards and some on the peak halyards: "Heave, ugh ... Heave, ugh ... Heave, ugh" – men and blocks groan as the spar and un-furling sail inch skyward up the mast.

As likely as not the master has taken the wheel: he has not delegated this task to a trusted subordinate, but turns the wheel to put the vessel on her course, his actions co-ordinated with the labour of his men as the mainsail takes the wind. The men move to raise the headsails, lighter and quicker work after the heavy main-sail and its great main gaff, and together master and men hear the old familiar sounds of hemp and manila ropes creaking and groan-ing in time with the motion of the waves.

Making headway out of the harbour, the vessel may have to be brought about on a different tack, if the master is to find his desired course. Tacking – bringing the vessel directly into the wind and across it, so that the sails will take the wind from the opposite side – requires another series of co-ordinated actions following from a few short commands. "Ready about!," and the master puts the wheel hard down, spoke by spoke and hand over hand, and as the vessel turns into the wind every sail flaps loudly except the jib, the triangular headsail which the deckhands hold to windward. If they sheet the jib across too soon or too late its driving power is lost and it will flap about uselessly. As the manoeuvre is completed the sails fill again, but the mainsail must be trimmed to take the wind to best advantage: the boom is hauled over and the main sheet secured so that the sail fills and the rudder can return almost to midships. " 'Well, Mate, she's all yours now,' he said ..., 'if yer vision is not too heavily oiled, east by south by the compass.' 'East by south by the compass,' came the reply."[42]

The apparent ease with which the schooner has put to sea may deceive the landsman into believing that the process was very simple. In fact a series of decisions have been taken about the number of sails to be set, the order in which to set them, the turn of the rudder, the trim of sails, and the vessel's bearing. Each decision depended on the master's understanding of the way the vessel was lying, the speed and direction of the wind, the strength and direc-tion of the tide, and the nature of the harbour.[43] But the master's knowledge was much deeper than this: his work had begun long before he gave orders to set sail, and he knew much more than the appropriate procedures in the handling of rigging, sails, and rudder.

The master was responsible for maintenance of his machinery. This meant that he knew something about the condition of timbers and planking, of the vessel's bottom, and of the ground tackle, pumps, davits, dories, and much else. The prudent master would occasionally beach his vessel and inspect hull, rudder, caulking, and fastenings. And then there was the rigging itself: the standing rigging that held the masts and yards in place, and the running rigging, the ropes used in hoisting, lowering, and trimming sails. All ropes must be inspected for wear or chafe, and chafing gear renewed where necessary. The blocks must all be running smoothly: their cheeks must be inspected for splits and their pins for wear. Masts, spars, mast hoops, gaff jaws, parrals, and shackles must all be checked, and the sails too, for sails may have mildew, pulled stitches, worn bolt ropes or cringles, or the small tears that can explode the sail into shreds.[44]

The schooner master knew something about stowage, and how his vessel reacted to cargo in the holds or on deck. He knew how to secure a deck load of lumber, which might be six or seven feet in height, and how to relocate sheet blocks and halyards and other running gear so that the deck load did not impede the working of the running rigging. He knew how to stow ballast of stone or iron, for the stability of the schooner depended on proper ballasting.

The coastal master had some knowledge of pilotage, the work of navigating coast-wise when land is near and the water shallow. Whereas large vessels putting into harbour hired pilots, the coastal master was his own pilot. He acquired an extensive knowledge of the locations of channels and shoals and their landmarks and seamarks. He knew local tides, currents, and weather patterns, which in Atlantic Canada could vary considerably from one bay to the next. "His brain is a compass card divided into 360 degrees or 32 points. His sense of location, of tidal and current sets, of wind, is guided by compass indications. Coupled with this continual mental plotting of courses and fixing of positions, is his intimate knowledge of what is underneath the ocean surface in depth of water and character of bottom."[45] Even if he possessed quadrant or sextant, the coastal master had his own methods of estimating his position under cloudy northern skies. He navigated by dead reckoning, by his knowledge of the sea bottom and his use of the lead line, by the flight paths of birds, and sometimes by a few figures scratched on the rusty pipe of the cabin stove.[46] In the early nineteenth century, and even later, coastal masters worked without the aid of charts. There were occasions when the captain of a large Atlantic liner, unable to make a celestial observation and uncertain of his position in thick fog, was relieved to meet a coastal or fishing schooner and get his position from her master.[47]

This is only the beginning of the accumulated knowledge of the coastal master. Sails, ropes, hull, rudder, anchor, wind, currents, and tides were part of a complex mechanical process. The number of moving parts in this process was very great; each part could affect the movement of all others. Control of this process required skill of an unusually high order in pre-industrial work. Consider, for instance, the problem of taking a vessel into a wharf, when the wind is blowing heavily landward with a force that could throw the vessel onto the rocks. The vessel must be taken into the wharf in such a way that she may be put quickly to sea again – against the wind. Such a situation was not uncommon where landward gales occurred frequently. The master orders all sails to be furled in sequence, and this process might be completed a quarter-mile off the wharf. The helm is put hard over so that the vessel briefly takes the waves broadside. The next event is the letting go of the anchor – to the simple order, "Let go!" The anchor must fall clear while the vessel is pitching and rolling, and it must fall straight at this first attempt, to a secure hold on the rocks below. The bow of the vessel turns seaward, the anchor chain falls, and the vessel backs slowly over the length of the cable toward the long, narrow pier jutting out into the waves. When the vessel slides alongside the pier her bow is seaward, and getting her away from the pier is then a matter of hauling in the anchor chain.[48]

At one level this procedure is mechanical; it is the operation of a machine. It is also a supreme act of craftsmanship, whereby the pre-industrial worker combines machinery and natural forces to fashion a specific result in a process of production. The number of calculations in this sequence of actions defy estimation. The precise position of the vessel at the moment when the anchor is let go is the result of a mental image in which each part of the entire machine has its place: vessel, wind, current, waves, and tides. The life of the vessel depends upon the master's calculation of the correct point in space and in time when the words "Let go" are spoken; if the calculation is wrong, the vessel may smash into the wharf or onto the shore. The seamanship described here was not the work of a single master, but the result of an accumulation of experience and skills passed through generations. While the decisions were taken by the master, the level of skill in each seaman was also high, for the entire operation followed from the most cryptic of directions – a few words of command would be enough to complete the entire process. Each seaman would have a partial image of the total procedure and working knowledge of every rope and sail in the vessel and of the anchor.

Masters were often specialists, of course, since there were different kinds of coastal seafaring. The work of the sealing schooner was different from that of the coaster, and different again from that of the bank shcooner. Taking a sealing schooner through loose icepans and fog was specialized work. Managing the sails required brute force, when both sails and rigging froze. Vessels carried poles, ice saws, and axes which the crew used to pry the pans away from the bow. Most feared of all was a northeast gale, which could drive the ice floes toward land and crush the vessel as the ice jammed. In 1852 more than forty of Newfoundland's sealing vessels were crushed by such ice, and others were set on fire when stoves overturned.[49] The master knew how to stow a large cargo of greasy seal pelts in the hold and on deck: incorrect stowage could capsize the vessel. The sealing master knew how to manoeuvre in the narrow spaces between ice, and he knew the peculiar weather and wind conditions off the Labrador coast.

The art of navigating bank schooners was different again. Even in the twentieth century masters were navigating without sextants, and in the nineteenth they often did so without charts, knowing by experience the locations of depressions in the ocean floor, for instance. The bank skipper navigated in fog – not only finding directions at sea but also avoiding drift ice and other vessels (the risk of collision increased as steamers began to cross the banks on transatlantic passages). Winter fishing on the banks brought increased risk of sudden shifts in wind speed and direction; sail and rigging could freeze completely in a sudden gale, and if the sail were not taken in quickly before it froze the vessel could lose mast or spars or be forced to run helplessly before the wind.[50] Many crews must have found themselves with oilskins and sou'westers so coated with ice that the ice itself protected them from the wind, as they struggled to keep the compass face visible and hammered ice from the spokes of the wheel. In better weather, with dories strung out along a particular course, the master had to return along that course in order to recover his dories and their crews, and he must set the dories in such a way that they may be recovered even if visibility were reduced to zero.

Coastal navigation around the shores of Nova Scotia and New Brunswick in spring and summer might seem relatively simple, when compared to the work of the bank schooner. Once again, however, a commonplace event can remind the modern reader of the level of skill required and the knowledge embedded in that skill. The route from Canso to Halifax was covered by small vessels many hundreds of times in each year in the later nineteenth century. The distance over a direct course would be about 130 miles. In spring, however, the vessel was likely to be facing southwest winds, in which case she must tack to windward, and her course could not be straight. The actual distance covered might be 160 miles or more.

As the vessel left Cranberry Island, the master might set a south-easterly course, directly out into the Atlantic, even though Halifax lay to his southwest. He must allow a few degrees of compass bearing for leeway, the distance the vessel would shift to leeward of her course because of wind or tide. After a certain distance the master tacks ship, taking her bows across the wind until she sets a south-westerly course and is close-hauled on the port tack. Again the master adjusts his compass bearing for leeway. The course is maintained until the vessel is again in sight of land, and the master must recognize his landmarks.

So skillful in coastal navigation were some masters that they could estimate course and tacking precisely enough to make three predetermined landfalls. The apex of the onshore angles would take them to lighthouses or fog horns at three places: Country Harbour, Beaver Island, and Sambro. They could make these landfalls without reference to charts, even in the thick fog of spring, their visibility less than a hundred yards.[51] Such skill was not something that one master learned unaided in a single career. It resided in accumulated tradition and in inherited experience passed from fathers to sons, attaining, by its mastery of natural elements, the type of effect that Joseph Conrad argued persuasively to be not merely technique but art.[52]

The knowledge possessed by the master was not always shared by his employees. But the master was not the sole possessor of the knowledge invested in the work process, and sailors did not merely execute manually their master's design. At any point in time, very few coastal sailors were working their first passage. Even if they were, they already knew something of ships and sailhandling. For small boys in village outports of the Atlantic provinces, the sailing ship and her crew were sources of wonder and fascination. Very often the crew were men of the village and might invite the boys on board. "Every day of the ship's stay," remembers one Newfoundlander, "I would be on board, 'helping' with the painting, going in the longboat with the men for water and learning how to climb the rigging, or, in nautical language, how to go aloft."[53] Even in a schooner the worker required an extensive technical vocabulary.

The names of ropes and sails, their location, and the ways of hauling and belaying rope may all have been learned in childhood at the feet of the old master. "Skipper Sam ... liked to sit on a strong carpet stool on his quarterdeck in the sunshine and, between puffs of his pipe ... he would catechize me on nautical words and terms, so I soon acquired a large vocabulary, and such words as martingale, taffrail, binnacle, deadeye, ratlines, throat halliards and a dozen or more sailing commands came readily to my youthful lips."[54] The total confusion of a landsman who had not lived in a seaport and attempted this work for the first time is a useful reminder of the deckhand's accumulated knowledge. "I had been pushed here and there and told to pull this rope and that one, then rushed from place to place, tripping over coils of rope, until in a daze I stopped and looked at the white billowing sails above me and began to feel the rolling movement of the ship under my feet. We were under way."[55]

After a few voyages, the coastal sailor possessed still more extensive knowledge. The nineteenth-century coastal mariner probably, like the modern yachtsman, worked with a knowledge of eight or nine knots, bends, or hitches. He could tie or untie these, right-handed or left-handed, in any weather and in total darkness. He learned how to make seizings (lashings to hold two ropes firmly side by side) and splices (the joining of two ropes by interlacing the strands). He learned how to set up various kinds of tackle or purchase, in which two or more blocks were used to multiply the force exerted on rope. He probably knew how to repair and to sew sails. He knew about caulking and he may have helped build a vessel during the winter.

The deckhand's knowledge of navigation and pilotage might be rudimentary, but he would know how to steer, for every sailor would take his turn at the wheel. In fine weather it was relatively easy to maintain a compass bearing or to steer to a landmark. In heavy weather, or where currents and tide affected the bearing of the vessel, the task was not so easy, and maintaining one's bearing required concentration and practice. The helmsman would know how and when to luff, or put the helm down and bring the vessel closer to the wind, in order perhaps to take a particularly steep sea on the bow rather than on the beam. When running before a freshening gale and a heavy sea, the vessel became less easy to steer. The vessel lifted and surged as the sea approached the stern, and as the stern lifted to the crest of the wave she might broach-to, or turn broad-side to the wind and the sea, and the helmsman would have to find his course again while the master decided whether to reduce sail.[56]

The deckhand had a feel for the wind and an ability to distinguish between different winds by their feel around his neck and ears. He knew, for instance, the difference between true and apparent wind (the latter being the sensation of wind resulting from the forward motion of the vessel, rather than the movement of the air itself). He could *see* a zephyr, before it reached him, by its effect of the surface of the water. He was able to feel a sudden shift of the wind, and it was part of his job to inform the master or mate if such change might require a change in sail or compass bearing. In heavy weather, of course, the master was likely to take the wheel himself. Whatever the weather, the deckhand's turn at the wheel required skill and concentration.

The masters and officers of the schooner had not appropriated knowledge as their exclusive possession. An experienced man, serving as mate or even cook on one voyage, could show up as master on the next and often did.[57] The fraternal egalitarianism of the schooner crew reflected landward pre-industrial relationships, reinforced by the diffusion of knowledge among the crew. The effect may be heard even in the conversations between master and men at sea, particularly in heavy weather: not only terse commands hollered above the wind, but a nervous exchange of views between men who respect each other, and a master who called to his "boys" in the forecastle: "Look, come up on deck, don't know what's going to happen." They are carrying coal from Sydney when the gale strikes, and as the storm hits them the decisions fall to the group, the narrator uses the first person plural, and we can no longer tell which voice is the master's:

And we decided to see what she could do lyin' to, she couldn't run. So we laid her to ... Gale from the westward. And we were down in the cabin – Wils Trowbridge, Ab Warren and Jack Hapgood he was cook – we were down in the cabin when the sea fell down on her ... Abby said, "she's gone, b'y." I said, "I don't know. She's not gone yet." "Well," Abby said, "what are we gonna do?" I said, "We're not goin' to give it up, b'y." We said first thing we're gonna do was get that canvas chopped away if we can and let her come up what she will. So me and Wils got a piece of new manila rope ... I got a axe and he got a big bait chopper and we used to go down underwater and hack and chop as long as we could stop down.[58]

For 22 hours they run before the wind, the vessel's rail in the water because the coal has shifted, and the next morning they find themselves lost in a heavy snowfall. Then comes the final demonstration of knowledge being diffused. The master consults his "chartsman": "I said, 'Abby, where have you got her to?' He said, 'If I'm right,' he said, 'we're on the eastern part of St. Pierre bank in forty one fathom o' water.' I said, 'Jack, let's see what we get.' We got forty two fathoms. Now talk about. Not many navigators could do that ... He was right, that's where we were to." The chartsman was illiterate. His chart was his own creation, bearing his own signs and marks, the fruits of his long experience as fisherman and sailor.

Such were the relations of coastal sailors from outport villages. Fraternal relationships endured in part because independent commodity production in agriculture and fishing persisted through the nineteenth century in Atlantic Canada. The survival of the family boat and the small family farm, of the share system in fishing, and of petty enterprise on land preserved fraternal relationships at sea.

We must not exaggerate the independence of coastal seafarers, however. They did not control the wider conditions of their employment, which were set by an economy in which the old staple trades were under increasing pressure. By the 1880s and 1890s, coastal shipping, like other parts of the staple-based economy, was a form of handicraft production in decline. Under-employed labourers often had to choose between migration and starvation. In these circumstances one might expect the labour force in coasting to have expanded and wages to fall. But an expanding labour market afforded merchants new opportunities to exercise

TABLE 4

Tonnage and Crew Size, Newfoundland Vessels, 1860-99

Years	Average Tons/ Voyage	Average Crew/ Voyage	Man-Ton Ratio
1860-4	158	9.0	5.73
1865-9	156	8.3	5.34
1870-4	220	11.2	5.07
1875-9	186	8.7	4.66
1880-4	194	8.9	4.58
1885-9	193	8.8	4.57
1890-4	190	9.0	4.73
1895-9	180	7.5	4.18

Source: Crew Lists, St John's-registered vessels, 1860-99, MHA.

indirect control and cut costs: wages fell, but so also did manning levels. Shipowners merely hired fewer men for the same work. As one Newfoundland master discovered, when offered a good wage in a trading schooner, "there was a catch. I had to operate the schooner with only one man except myself, with the understanding he would give me a hardy boy in the fall. W.W. expected me to do the same work as if we had three men."[59]

Table 4 suggests that this experience was widespread in the vessels of later-nineteenth-century Newfoundland. Newfoundland-registered vessels in the North Atlantic and in the cod trades increased in size only slightly in the period, while the number of men in each vessel remained constant. There is a standard measure of the ratio of labour to capital in shipping: the man-ton ratio, usually expressed as the number of men per hundred gross tons. The higher the ratio, the more men employed per ton, and the more labour-intensive the industry. In the later nineteenth century a ratio of four men or more per hundred tons was high. As the table indicates, the ratio remained high in Newfoundland's small wooden vessels.[60]

By the standards of ocean-going shipping throughout these decades, this was a relatively labour-intensive fleet. But by the 1890s four men were doing the amount of work done by five or more in the 1860s. Technological changes in small vessels may have assisted this process, but the Newfoundland schooner had not

GRAPH 6

Tonnage and Values in Newfoundland's External Trade, 1850–99

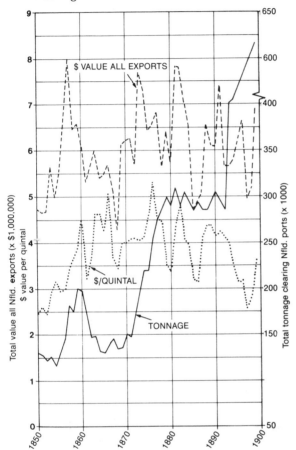

Sources: Tonnage and export figures from Customs Returns in Newfoundland, *Journals of the House of Assembly*, Appendices; prices from Shannon Ryan, "The Newfoundland Cod Fishery in the Nineteenth Century" (MA thesis, Memorial University of Newfoundland, 1971), 269–70.

changed much over these decades. In Canadian coastal trades as a whole there was also a marked decline in man-ton ratios for sailing vessels, even before the introduction of gasoline and other motors. Employers were cutting costs by shedding labour, and sailors who remained had to work harder.

The pressure to cut costs was coming from changes far beyond the control of coastal mariners. Regular steamship service in

GRAPH 7
Index of Sugar Freight Rates, Havana–New York, 1865–89

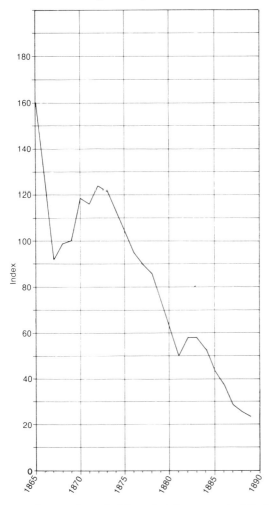

Source: Compiled from freight reports in *Mitchell's Maritime Register* and the *New York Maritime Register.*
Note: 1869 = 100.

coasting was introduced earlier but developed rapidly in the 1880s and 1890s, and after 1900 the coastal service in Newfoundland also expanded rapidly. Sailors often preferred to work in coastal steamers; those who remained in sailing vessels had lower wages and diminished bargaining power. Schooners and brigantines were still used in passages to and from Britain and in the cod trades but were increasingly marginalized. Growing numbers of larger sailing vessels and steamers in these trades, and government subsidies to steamers in certain trades, depressed freight rates and net returns to sailing ship operators.[61]

There remained the old business of carrying fish to markets in the West Indies, Brazil, and the Mediterranean, but here too pressure to cut operating costs and labour costs must have been considerable.[62] Returns depended ultimately on the price received for the cod when landed. The price received for Newfoundland's fish exports always fluctuated sharply, but the trend was stable through the 1860s and early 1870s, and thereafter prices fell until the end of the century (Graph 6). There was a similar decline in returns from Nova Scotia fish exports between 1870 and 1900. Graph 6 also indicates that the volume of tonnage clearing Newfoundland was increasing much faster than were total exports. The small Newfoundland schooners were operating in an increasingly difficult market, and the growing proportion of tonnage clearing in ballast by the 1890s is further evidence of this trend.[63]

One other factor contributed to the pressure on the small West Indies trader, whether from Newfoundland or Nova Scotia: the small vessel in the fish trades often depended on return cargoes of sugar or molasses, either to Newfoundland, the United States, or Europe. The sugar trade to Europe declined in the later nineteenth century because of competition from beet sugar.[64] There was still substantial trade in sugar, rum, and molasses to the United States and Canada, much of it in small vessels. But here too freight rates and gross returns were falling rapidly: the rates for sugar from Havana to New York are one measure of this trend (Graph 7). Even in trades traditionally the domain of small wooden vessels, the increasing supply of tonnage in the freight markets put pressure on gross revenues. Many of the little "fish boxes" from Newfoundland and Nova Scotia were deprived altogether of return cargoes.[65]

While the small craft was experiencing these pressures, the labour supply, at least in Newfoundland, was increasing. Diversification of the Newfoundland economy was never completed in the later nineteenth century, the fishery proved unable to absorb growing numbers in the workforce, and emigration began.[66] Men were willing to sign on ocean voyages for the few pounds a month such work might bring. Thus, for instance, the young John Froude turned from fishing to seafaring in the depressed 1880s:

> as I have had a fair trile in the fishing line now I was 3 summers fishing out from home 2 summers on the french shore and 4 summers on the labradore and 1 summer on the grand bank and was not very successful in all my undertakings so I thought it was time to leave it off and try something else for my money[67]

The effect of depression on employment in shipping may be seen in the numbers of men on vessels clearing from Newfoundland. From the 1870s to the late 1880s the man-ton ratio on all vessels rose from an average of 5.2 men per hundred tons to almost six men per hundred tons (the source does not distinguish vessels by port of registry, but most were likely to be British vessels). On some routes men must have been queueing for berths and offering to sign on for little if any pay: in the 1880s the man-ton ratio on vessels clearing for the United States was no less than 10.2 men per hundred tons![68] In these circumstances seafaring was clearly either an alternative or a prelude to emigration.

Certainly the great coastal fleet of Newfoundland did not lack sailors, and even in the longer voyages represented in the crew list sample (Table 4) we can see the proportion of Newfoundland-born sailors increasing. Newfoundlanders were 39.4 per cent of the total in the 1860s; by the 1890s, 63.8 per cent of the total.[69] The effect was to depress average wages throughout the Newfoundland fleet. Average monthly wages for an able seaman were £3-0-0 in the late 1860s (much lower than the average of £3-13-0 for Nova Scotians in the Yarmouth fleet in the 1840s). Wages rose to £3-8-0 on average in the early 1870s.

This increase was in step with changes in wages in other fleets at the time, but wages were always substantially lower in the Newfoundland fleet than in the ocean-going fleets of the Maritimes in the same years. More voyages originated in the United Kingdom or in Newfoundland itself, where wages were always lower than in other British North American or US ports. By the 1880s wages of able seamen in the Newfoundland fleet had fallen below £3-0-0 – a consequence of falling wages paid to those signing on in Newfoundland. A good time series for wages in coastal schooners does not exist, but wages there were probably even lower. Whatever protection paternalism may have offered now meant little. The small wooden craft was subject to falling rates of return in markets increasingly dominated by large, industrialized production.

Earlier in the century similar pressure on profit margins in the timber trade had led to the over-working of the small timber vessels and their crews in the North Atlantic. The British select committee that examined the shipwrecks of timber ships reported in 1839 that wrecks were not caused by the age or exceptional frailty of the vessels themselves. The primary cause was "the improper over-stowage of the ships, by carrying heavy loads of timber on deck," especially in heavy weather and in winter. The deck loads strained the vessel and its fastenings and impeded work: "The crew cannot so easily perform their duty; they cannot go so quickly from one end of the ship to the other as they would if their deck was clear." The testimony of timber merchants made clear that heavy deck loads and winter passages were the result of competition between merchants and pressure on masters. Masters carried deck loads because of "their eagerness to earn as much by the ship they command for the owners as possible; accounts were kept of each voyage, and each captain or mate endeavours to do as well as the preceding one." Because of the risk and additional labour, the crews of timber ships often had higher wages than crews in other trades, but still they "grumble a good deal and complain about deck loads."[70]

There is nothing romantic about the nineteenth-century coastal schooner or timber ship. Diverse task-oriented labour may have offered little satisfaction to men whose time was not their own but was appropriated to the service of their master and his will. Paternalism was no consolation to the sailor in an undermanned schooner, wrestling with its mainsail in winter: "We found it hard getting underway as she was supposed to have a larger crew than three men."[71] The fraternalism of the fishing schooner had a bitter meaning for Howard Blackburn of Nova Scotia, rowing his dory 60 miles until the flesh was gone from his fingers, the frozen corpse of his dory-mate at his side.[72] Control of the work process was little help to the crew of a timber ship with a ten-foot deck load in a winter storm. Fraternalism was a gruesome reality for the crew of the timber vessel *Francis Spaight*, who were 15 days without food or water in mid-Atlantic when they drew lots to decide whose flesh would be eaten so that the others might live.[73]

Yet these men had forms of protection lacking in the great ocean vessels of the later nineteenth century. First, the sailor knew some of the men with whom he would work, and he often knew the vessel and her reputation before he risked his life in her service. Having signed on, he could be fairly certain that the vessel would return to her home port, and to his home, at the conclusion of the voyage. The voyage was likely to last months rather than years. Seafaring was a part-time occupation in an economy characterized by occupational pluralism. Although highly mobile, this part-time seafarer could have a wife and family to whom he might return regularly. Such was the life of John Froude in his later years – fisherman, boat-builder, carpenter, coastal trader, "owner of thirty seven Schooners and boats" – but always he returned home late in the year and "Sittled down for the winter as usual."[74]

Industrial capital influenced these small vessels but did not transform relationships within the workplace. Master and men shared a common language and common origins. They shared many tasks in their vessels, and they shared knowledge and skills. A master often stayed with the same vessel for many voyages: "His officers and crew usually stayed with him, so they looked upon the ship, not only as their home, but almost as their own private property."[75] Relations were personal, even familial, governed less by formal contract than by custom and by the vagaries of wind and weather. There were the beginnings of a division of labour, but work was not dissolved into discrete components, and each worker had a share in most tasks. There was a range of tasks in the maintenance and operation of the vessel and, on the part of workers, not simply trained obedience to external commands but the exercise of judgment, experience, and knowledge. In the ship's routine, said Joseph Conrad, there is health and peace and satisfaction in the accomplished round of tasks.[76] There may have been little satisfaction in the harsh conditions of work in the pre-industrial craft of Atlantic Canada, but master and men could share a clay pipe and a glass of rum in their cabin, at the end of the completed passage that was their work, and theirs alone.

CHAPTER THREE

A Workplace In Transition

In the third quarter of the nineteenth century, sailing craft co-existed with steam-powered vessels in Atlantic waters, and the industrial revolution transformed the shipping industry and the labour of men and women at sea. The coexistence of sail and steam often appears in the literature as a mythic struggle between old and new, wherein the forces of industrial progress defeat the cherished mistress of the seas. The seafarer's tendency to anthro-pomorphize enters the historical record, and two technologies become women locked in combat: they are "tramps and ladies," the latter refined in beauty and of long ancestry, the other sullied by power and brutal necessity.[1] "She served Man and she appealed to men ... She sailed with quiet grace and she could be beautiful," but the "smoke-belching steamship" moved inexorably into her trades.[2] A century and more after the events, the historian must penetrate beyond the romantic saga and rediscover the workplace in transition. There were not two types of vessel, nor two places of work, but a gradual evolution of pre-industrial craft and industrial technology. Along this evolutionary continuum lay the large wooden-hulled sailing vessels of Atlantic Canada.

The change in technology was also a change in social relations, beginning with those between shipowners and masters and extending to masters and crew. The transition to industrial capitalism brought new methods of supervision and control, a more precisely defined division of labour, and the increasing division of knowledge between master and crew. Many tasks became the exclusive preserve of specialists and even of professionals. Professionalization occurred in part through state regulation, and in this industry, as in so many others, the transition to industrial capitalism brought new forms of state intervention. At the beginning of this social transformation lay the great barques and ships of Atlantic Canada.

The most striking change in the sailing vessel of the last half of the nineteenth century was also the most important: the vessel became much larger. In the carrying of freights greater hull size was just as important as the advantage of regularity afforded by steam. As hull size increased, other operating costs, including wages, did not rise proportionately. The resulting increase in rates of return might be temporary, for greater carrying capacity contributed to the long-term decline in ocean freight rates; the decline in freight rates in turn encouraged the ongoing search for cost-saving economies and innovations.

Part of this process, and directly related to the search for greater carrying capacity, was the introduction of iron hulls. Iron allowed greater carrying capacity: the iron hull could be thinner and longer than the wooden one.[3] For these reasons, and because of the durability of iron hulls, the initial investment could be amortized over several years, and the iron vessel often allowed very substantial profits. This is why the British built so many iron *sailing* vessels in the 1860s and 1870s: 1.7 million tons, a third of all iron tonnage. The iron sailing vessels, almost 950 tons on average by the late 1870s, were much larger than the average iron-hulled steamer and larger than the average wooden-hulled vessel built and registered in Britain.[4]

The iron hull was only one product of the search for greater transport capacity in industrial capitalism; many other changes occurred at sea, even in wooden vessels. Larger hulls and larger cargoes brought changes in masts, spars, sails, standing and running rigging, and the rest of the equipment used to propel the vessel. Some changes were merely refinements in old techniques: square-rigged sailing vessels had been crossing the Atlantic for more than three centuries, after all. But many refinements added up to substantial changes, even in the old technology of wood and sail.

Shipowners in Atlantic Canada purchased very few iron hulls. But they did look for greater carrying capacity and started to industrialize. Several Atlantic shipyards were transformed from small waterfront workshops into large, vertically integrated opera-

GRAPH 8

Larger Vessels on Registry in Four Major Ports, 1826–1914

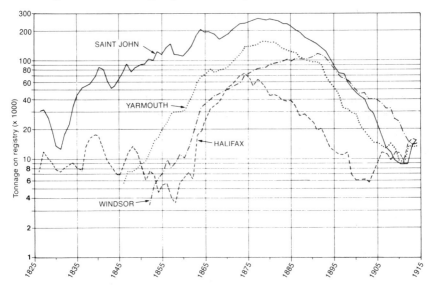

Source: Board of Trade series 107/108 vessel registries.
Note: Vessels of 250 tons and over.

tions employing 100 men or more.[5] Such shipbuilding factories produced vessels structurally similar to the barques and ships of the 1820s but much larger. The barques of the 1820s were about 100 feet in length, on average. By the 1880s the average barque was twice that length.[6] The increase in hull capacity was proportionately greater: in Yarmouth, for instance, the tonnage of new barques increased three and a half times between the 1840s and the 1880s.[7] By the 1880s, vessels rigged as ships were over 1,500 tons on average – almost four times as large as the ships of the 1820s. The search for greater capacity ended the trend toward the narrow "clipper"-like hull formation. After mid-century length-breadth ratios declined: in the fleets of Saint John and Halifax the ratio for all new vessels fell from 4.1 to 3.5 between the 1850s and the 1880s.[8] The great barque of the 1880s was a mobile warehouse in which capacity was not traded for speed.

Most of the large wooden sailing vessels were built and registered between 1850 and 1880. Graph 8 shows the growth of the fleets in four major ports, including only vessels of 250 tons or more. There

GRAPH 9

Estimated Total Mid-Summer Employment in Vessels Registered in
Atlantic Canada, 1830–1914

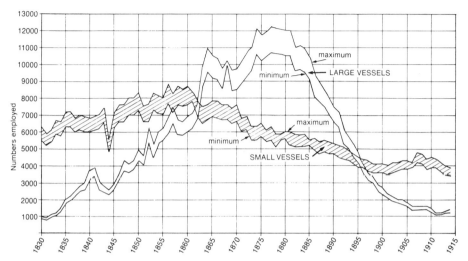

Sources: Tonnage on registry in the Maritimes from British *Parliamentary Papers*,
Canada *Sessional Papers*, and the summary tables in Keith Matthews, "The Shipping Industry of Atlantic Canada: Themes and Problems," in Keith Matthews
and Gerald Panting, eds., *Ships and Shipbuilding in the North Atlantic Region*
(St John's: MHG 1978), Appendix 1; man-ton ratios estimated from Crew Agreements for vessels of Saint John, Yarmouth, Halifax, and Windsor (on the calculation of man-ton ratios see chap. 7).

was never a clear distinction between ocean-going and coastal
vessels, since vessels of any size could cross the Atlantic, and larger
ones could be used in coastal trades. But vessels of 250 tons or more
were designed primarily for use in trades outside the coastal waters
of British North America. By the 1870s these fleets of barques and
ships dwarfed the coastal fleets, and ocean-going bulk carriers
accounted for over 80 per cent of total carrying capacity in the four
fleets.

The rise of the ocean-going fleets increased total employment in
the industry; by the early 1870s probably fifteen thousand people
worked in the fleets of Atlantic Canada. The estimate of total mid-
summer employment contained in Graph 9 is based on official tonnage figures for the three Maritime provinces, reduced by 10 per
cent to allow for overestimates by registrars of shipping, and on
original vessel registries for St John's.[9] Not all vessels were fully

manned, even in mid-summer, because many were in port loading or discharging, and some were being repaired. The lower estimate of total employment assumes that three of every ten vessels were in port and without crew; the upper, one in five vessels without crew.[10]

The estimate rests also on known man-ton ratios for large and small vessels. Total employment grew less rapidly than did total carrying capacity because of the century-long decline in man-ton ratios. Employment in large vessels is not directly proportionate to the share of tonnage in such vessels, because the large vessels were much more capital-intensive. Thus in mid-century the 100-ton vessel carried twice as many men per ton as did the 1,000-ton vessel. For these and other reasons employment in small, mainly coastal vessels remained a significant proportion of total employment. From 1863 to 1895, however, employment in large vessels exceeded that in small vessels. Thus most sailors were employed in larger square-rigged vessels that sailed well beyond the shores of Atlantic Canada.

Although a capital-intensive industry, shipping was a major employer. In 1870 the fleets of Atlantic Canada employed in mid-summer almost as many workers as the entire forest products industries of Nova Scotia and New Brunswick.[11] Shipping employed about three times as many workers as Maritime shipbuilding yards.[12] In winter employment fell, especially in small coastal and fishing vessels (the estimates here do not include inshore fishermen in undecked boats). Although employment in ocean-going vessels also declined in winter, in the later nineteenth century the mid-winter labour force was likely to be 70 per cent of the mid-summer force.[13] Not all sailors were from Atlantic Canada, of course. This was a domestic and even regional industry, but the work-force was not wholly domestic, and in the 1860s and 1870s a growing proportion of employees were not British North American, either by birth or by residence. A man could work in this colonial industry without ever setting foot in Atlantic Canada. Merchant capitalists in Atlantic Canada were employing a labour force that was increasingly remote and foreign.

While the labour force changed, so did the pattern of ownership. Mercantile ownership was far more common with large sailing vessels than with small coastal craft. The rise of the ocean-going fleets in the third quarter of the century therefore increased merchant ownership throughout the shipping industry. The schooner was usually owned by one or two individuals, often an owner-operator or master mariner; the barque or ship more often by several, usually members of family firms engaged in import and export trades and in retailing. In four major ports - Saint John, Halifax, Windsor, and Yarmouth - 74 per cent of all shareholdings in new vessels of 500 tons or more were held by people described as merchants, shipowners, or shipping companies. This under-estimates the total merchant ownership, since merchants tended to have more shares than others. Shares in vessels were divided into 64ths: a merchant would often hold 16 or 32 of the 64 shares in a vessel. Thus the merchants' and shipowners' share in total tonnage purchased was greater than 74 per cent.[14]

Merchant shipowners sought new methods of control over these large vessels. Investment in a wooden sailing vessel meant a sub-stantial risk in an enterprise conducted at great distances from the merchant's residence. The methods of control inherited from the early nineteenth century had to be refined and strengthened. Paternalism, with all its associated rewards and punishments, was still applied, but to it was added the control that comes with man-agement and more formalized contractual relations. Where a ves-sel might be owned by a large number of shareholders, if only as a means of spreading risk, the operation of the vessel had to be dele-gated. Normally one of the shareholders was designated managing owner and looked after the ship's business: he instructed the master on freight rates and cargoes, arranged insurance for the vessel, and issued dividends to the owners after receiving remittances from the master or from their brokers on completion of voyages. Even where the vessel was owned outright by a single family or merchant firm there was a designated managing owner on the employment con-tract (the crew agreement). Working relations in larger sailing vessels began with the managing owner and the control that he sought to exercise.

The managing owner attempted to exercise control through detailed instructions in letters that followed his vessels to their ports of call. Where the vessel carried a supercargo, the owner wrote separately to the master and to the supercargo, and the division of responsibility was clear. The supercargo was the business agent, responsible for arranging the purchase and sale of the cargo, or the delivery of the cargo to is consignees. The master was responsible for the safe and speedy movement of the cargo.

The letters of William Roche of Halifax in the late 1830s and early 1840s clearly define the master's responsibilities: "You will please proceed with the Kate to Demarary and if Mr. Mitchell sells the cargo there use every exertion to get it on shore as soon as possible, and should Mr. M. not deem it for my advantage to proceed farther, you will take in your ballast if no freight offers and return home as speedily as you can."[15] The master also received precise instructions about disbursements, handling of crew, maintenance of the vessel, and even handling of the vessel at sea: "On leaving Demarary bend the old sails, saving the new ones as much as possible for your voyage out in the spring. – after getting through the trades I would advise you to send up your top gallantmast, and get the flying jibboom in ... I trust you will study to be economical with your provisions, and everything you do for the ship."[16]

Roche clearly knew his masters well, but behind his scrupulous personal supervision of his employees lay the wage relationship, with its inherent powers of reward and punishment. In June 1838 Roche wrote to Capt. Hore of the brig *Kate*: "If the voyage be performed in two and half months, without damage to the sails or spars of the vessel & you will receive an addition of one pound p month to your pay for the voyage, if one day less than 3 Month 15/p Month, wishing you health & a prosperous voyage."[17]

This kind of supervision was common practice, of course, well before the growth of ocean-going fleets in mid-century. But important changes were occurring in the third quarter of the century. Ocean-going vessels were now more likely to be chartered to carry goods that the shipowner did not own. Fewer Canadian vessels carried a supercargo. This did not leave the master as an unsupervised business agent, because shipowners had new means of supervision and control. The arrival of telegraph lines in Atlantic Canadian port towns in the 1850s and 1860s allowed much more regular contact between shipowners and their masters, and between shipowners and their brokers in distant ports. Frank Killam of Yarmouth described the effect: "As a general rule our masters have very little discretion in the selection of business. By means of telegraphic communication to all parts of the world and by the shipowners having agents in almost every foreign part, shipowners are enabled to be fully informed before the vessel arrives of the prospect of employment, and the next voyage is not selected by the master but by the owner through his agent."[18]

The most important decisions were taken by the merchant-shipowner, but the work of the shipmaster was expanding, despite closer supervision. Even if the master did not make decisions about voyages, he was more than a mariner. Since he was responsible for the ship's business – its provisions and equipment and disbursements – he was a business agent of the shipowner. As his responsibilities widened, the need and the opportunity for direct communication with his employer increased.

There was no precise parallel in landward industry to the occupation of shipmaster. He was employer and employee, wage-earner and business agent, working man and trustee of capital in his industry. Although his work was different from that of his contemporaries on land, the shipmaster stood at the beginning of broad trends that occurred within the development of industrial capitalism. In the nineteenth century "the immediate employer of many workers was not the large capitalist but the intermediate sub-contractor who was both an employee and in turn a small employer of labour. In fact the skilled worker ... tended to be in some measure a sub-contractor, and in psychology and outlook bore the marks of this status."[19]

The shipmaster was like the subcontractor, and he permitted the shipowner to maintain some control over his capital assets even as they were dispersed across the globe. But in the elevation of the shipmaster there was more than mere subcontracting: there were the beginnings of management itself, the exercise of control over larger numbers of workers gathered under a single roof, by vesting control in a specialized managerial executive. In shipping, even before the arrival of joint stock companies and the modern corporation, there began a separation of ownership and management, whereby "operating control is vested increasingly in a specialized management staff for each enterprise."[20]

As early as 1840 we find a shipowning firm, John Ward and Sons, using the word "management" in a very modern sense when writing to a master: "This being your first voyage in command for us we will make a few leading remarks for your general government. That it is our standing order that no expenses or outlays be incurred above that the Ship can possibly do without, ... and that by the Bills against the Ship while abroad we judge of the Masters management and prudence." Ward also made clear that as trustee of their ship the master was enjoying a "situation of much greater respectability." In return for this elevated status he must consider the property in his care as though it were his own: "Many circumstances may turn up to require the exercise of your own judgment and in these cases by acting for us as you would for yourself under similar circumstances you cannot be far from doing what is right."[21]

Conscious of the master's responsibility for the protection and the productivity of their capital, shipowners engaged in a successful effort to enforce sobriety among masters and to enlarge the social distance between masters and deckhands. "It is truly unfortunate to be concerned in any way with a habitual drunkard, but particularly so in a Ship Master," wrote Ward in 1843. The shipmaster "has at all times so much in his power to do evil and upon [his] sobriety, honesty and capability so much depends ... serving liquor to the crew is sufficiently a thing unknown out of this Port, and must at once be stopped."[22]

By the late nineteenth century the process of selection of shipmasters had brought into their ranks many who shared family connections, investments, and other links with the merchant shipowners who employed them. The published correspondence between Henry and N.B. Lewis of Yarmouth and their masters, Benjamin and Frank Gullison, indicates relations between social equals well known to each other.[23] But other shipowners had also discovered the value of close personal relations with a master: "He may find it necessary to have more done than I thought might be required," wrote a shipowner about his master in 1843, "but at the same time I am sure that his friendship for me will keep her disbursements as low as possible, please therefore do all he wishes."[24]

Yet the relationship was still one between owners and executive employee, as the Lewis-Gullison letters suggest: "Yours obediently" often followed from "Dear Sir"; all transactions were closely monitored; important decisions were left to the head office. The master's first duty on arrival in port was to establish telegraphic communication with his managing owner. When one of his masters failed in this duty, the irascible Robert Quirk of Charlottetown wrote as follows: "Owing to a current report in the streets yesterday that the Isabella was in Halifax I wired you as follows: 'Esson will do your business what do you mean not advising your arrival.' You have been Captain of a vessel long enough to know that immediately on your arrival at a port of destination your first duty is to notify your owners."[25] Unable to exercise direct control over his workplace, the shipowner instead controlled his managerial executive.

The new breed of shipmaster possessed some knowledge of commercial practices and commercial law. His work included the loading and unloading of cargo according to the terms of the "charter party," the contract by which the whole or part of the vessel was hired for freight. Often the master would sign the charter party following a prior decision of his managing owner; occasionally the master could arrange the charter himself. The arrangement of a successful charter required, at the very least, some knowledge of the following: law pertaining to charter parties, rates of freight for commodities and quantities, likely costs on the voyage (pilotage, port charges, insurance), facilities at port of departure and terminal port, likely number of lay days (days in port for loading and discharging), appropriate demurrage rates, and hull capacity given a particular cargo and load line laws.

Having taken charge of the cargo, the master signed and issued to shippers the bill of lading, a receipt for goods being shipped. He also prepared a manifest – a separate list of all articles and quantities being shipped – with other information on the vessel and crew, to be delivered to customs officials. The master must also know the law relating to loss of or damage to cargo. Any damage incurred on the voyage was reported in a protest (a protest against "wind and weather") sworn before a notary or a British consul, and a correct survey was arranged. Expenses and losses incurred in a ship or cargo were adjusted by insurers according to rules of average (in general average, for instance, losses were shared proportionately among all interests affected), and the master must have some knowledge of insurance law and practice. The master must also arrange customs clearance and arrange and supervise all maintenance and repairs of the vessel necessary during a voyage.[26]

As business agent, the master was also responsible for the stowage of cargo, a subject that may be understood today only by referring to volumes of technical literature on the subject.[27] Upon the correct stowage of cargo depended not only the quantity that could be shipped but also the seaworthiness and safety of the vessel.

The correct stowage of cargo or ballast varied from one vessel to another, which complicated the procedure but encouraged ship-owners to keep a master in the same vessel. The arrangement of cargo and ballast affected the centre of gravity of the vessel and hence the rolling of the vessel at sea. The cargo and ballast had to be secured so that they did not shift in heavy weather, when the vessel was thrown on her beam ends (when the vessel was heeled over so far that her deck-beams approached the vertical). Cargo should not be stored flush to the floor of the vessel, so wooden blocks (dunnage) were used to raise the cargo, and the amount of dunnage necessary varied from one type of cargo to another.

The master was a business agent and he was also a navigator and master mariner. The master of a vessel that might cross four oceans in one voyage possessed something of the coastal mariner's skills, but he could no longer rely merely on sextant, chronometer, and instinct. He relied also on charts, the most important of the master's working documents, and by the late nineteenth century Canadian masters had access to charts not only of major ocean passages but also of all bays, anchorages, and approaches that they were likely to encounter around the world.[28] The master used his sextant to calculate the height of the sun above the horizon at noon, and hence to estimate latitude. He estimated the longitudinal position of his vessel by estimating the exact time at the ship from the height of the sun; the vessel's chronometer gave him Greenwich time; he then turned the time difference from Greenwich into an estimate of distance from Greenwich, yielding his estimate of longitude.

But there was much more to navigation than this, and the master who possessed his "ticket," or certificate of competence, had some knowledge of nautical astronomy: he could find latitude from the meridian altitude of a star, for instance; he would be able to observe and compute azimuths, the bearing of a celestial body. The master would have some idea of the effect of iron in his vessel on compass bearing and be able to estimate compass deviation given his latitude and longitude.[29] The shipmaster of the late nineteenth century might well include among his possessions not only charts but also the *Nautical Almanac*, which gave all the information required for working out a vessel's position by celestial navigation. Navigational aids were increasingly sophisticated by that time, and all shipmasters benefited directly or indirectly from the "Wind and Current Chart of the North Atlantic" produced by the American navigator Matthew Fontaine Maury in 1847. Subsequent editions of Maury's maps and his books on sailing directions found their way into the hands of masters and told them the best routes to follow at different times of the year. Where the coastal mariner might learn his craft by observation and experience, accumulating in his memory the knowledge of winds and currents and tides, now the master mariner learned also from the printed record of navigators and hydrographers. The master's craft was a manual art aided more than ever before by applied scientific knowledge.

Much of the craft of seafaring was reserved for the master alone. He had to understand not only navigation but a multitude of techniques in sailhandling. The techniques of tacking and wearing in a large square-rigger fill chapters in seamen's manuals. The approach of a storm, or a sudden squall, required decisions about many parts of the great machine: the choice of sail, the order of taking in sail, the choice of tack, the use of the helm, and much else.

The important art of trimming sail to the wind was much more complicated in a large square-rigger than in a schooner. Masters did not fully understand the principles in physics and aerodynamics underlying the movement of a sailing vessel, but they knew from experience that each sail had an optimal angle to the wind, or trim. It was perhaps not until the early 1900s that most seafarers understood that wind speed is greater aloft than at water line (because of friction between wind and water at sea level), but long before then they knew from experience that sails at different heights could be trimmed differently, to beneficial effect.[30] Sailing close-hauled (as close as possible into the wind), the lower yard would be braced at a sharp angle to the hull, but as one ascended each yard was braced a little more square. Viewed from above or below the yards and sails would appear to be in a spiral. Spiral bracing, for reasons having to do with the greater wind speed aloft, allowed the upper sails to take the wind to best advantage and maximized the collective force of sails upon yards and yards upon hull.[31]

Effective sail trimming involved much more than this, however. Potential forward thrust was greatest when the yard was square to the mast; but the thrust of wind on sail was maximized when the wind hit the sail at right angles. Sail trimming required a delicate compromise between the point where the thrust of yards was maximized and the point where the sail was stretched perpendicular to the wind.

The master had also to minimize the effect of blanketing, which occurred when sails prevented the wind from entering other sails before them. Blanketing helps to explain why vessels did not make their best speed when the wind was directly aft – and why it was sometimes possible to sail faster with fewer sails set.[32] The master learned to trim sail in order to avoid blanketing and a great deal more from observation and from inherited experience about the complex art of sailhandling. Even in port his shiphandling did not end, and there the operation of the great square-rigger required other specialized knowledge: how to come to anchor in a tideway, how to use two anchors to moor a vessel in a tideway, how to set anchors to ride out a storm, and how to approach and get away from mooring of various kinds.[33]

At once business agent, navigator, and master seaman, this wage-paid worker was something else as well – he was an employer of labour and the manager of a labour force. The master was responsible for hiring workers and for keeping them in his ship once he had them, and the master who failed to do this was soon reminded of his duty: "It would have saved all this trouble *if you had only kept those men when you had them*, and we are very much surprised that a man like you who has had so much experience with sailors should lose your men when not laying at a wharf."[34]

In the absence of both shipowners and legal agencies, the master was the trustee at once of capital and of civil authority. He enforced discipline in the workplace, with the backing of both civil and criminal law, and as we shall see the laws that gave him his powers became more extensive and more rigorous as time passed. The master was also responsible for the health of all on board vessel, a consequence of long ocean passages in which workplace and domicile were combined. The master carried a medical manual and a number of medicines specified in successive merchant shipping acts.

The master was also required by the British Merchant Shipping Act of 1854 to carry and to make entries in an official log book supplied by the Board of Trade. In this log he was required to report the names of all crew, punishable offences committed and punishments inflicted, illnesses and injuries, births, deaths, marriages (which he was not empowered in law to perform), discharges, desertions, collisions, and certain other events that might occur at sea. Beside the name of each sailor the master was also required to enter his assessment of conduct. This usually took the form of an abbreviation, such as "VG" for very good or "B" for bad. The intention here was not only to buttress the master's disciplinary powers but to provide the registrar-general of seamen in Britain with a record of the conduct of all seamen, which other masters might use if they wished.[35]

Nova Scotian shipmasters had the thick hands and weathered faces of seamen, but in the old photographs they show no discomfort in their three-piece suits and stiff white collars. They had a reputation, sometimes deserved, for harsh discipline and even brutality. But the surviving log books and other accounts reveal men who strived to preserve a physical distance between themselves and all crew, except mates. When on deck the master occupied the poop deck, usually the weather side. Only in unusual circumstances would he go forward toward the forecastle. He did not always supervise the ordinary routine of sail-handling or other work about the vessel; often he merely issued orders to his chief mate, and left much of the supervision to him. In circumstances that required all hands on deck, he would issue orders directly to crew while standing at the break of the poop.

Masters usually cultivated aloofness, and some intentionally disappeard from sight for the first days of the voyage in order that the authority of the chief mate be established and so that the routine of work should dictate relationships between members of the crew. One result of this aloofness was a common complaint of masters at sea - loneliness. One master confided in a letter: "It is so lonesome & miserable to be always alone like this with no one to talk to."[36] And in mid-Atlantic Capt. I.B. Morris of Harbourville, Nova Scotia, wrote in his diary: "Saturday, April 13 / This day is calm and cloudy. One ship in sight, feeling very lonesome. Lat. 48.30 Lon. 27.10 / Sunday April 14 / Light breeze from the westward. Lonesome and dreary today. No one to associate with. Lat. 41.50 Lon. 23.53."[37]

That this complaint should be heard so frequently in a workplace where numbers of men were crowded into very small spaces is testimony to the physical and social separation that had occurred in the hierarchy of work at sea. Of course the competent master still kept a watchful and solicitous eye on his crew, and official statements recorded in log books cannot conceal the care and kindness that masters sometimes bestowed on their workers, especially when ill. But the relationship between master and able seaman was no longer what it had been in the small vessels of Yarmouth in the 1840s. Rarely was the master personally acquainted with those who served him. Theirs was a relationship between management and labour, carefully circumscribed by tradition and by law. This was still a pre-industrial workplace, but the fraternalism of the schooner master and his crew was disappearing.

The sailing ship itself circumscribed relations between men at sea, and it was designed to do so. The technology purchased by Canadian shipowners was not new, after all: the sailing ship was a machine inherited from centuries of European experience. When they borrowed and adapted this technology, Atlantic Canadians were accepting certain social choices and assumptions that went into the design of the vessel. The sailing ship was never the autonomous creation of shipbuilders aiming to solve merely technical problems. Shipbuilders were also the servants of shipowners, including not only seamen but merchants, governments, and the military agencies of European states. Within each decision about technology lay choices about labour and the organization of work processes.[38] This is all the more true where the machine is also a living space: in designing sailing ships, builders were designing enclosed spaces that would constrain relations between everybody who lived and worked there. The sailing ship, for instance, assumed a division of labour and a social hierarchy. The division of labour in small coastal vessels was embryonic and often overridden by social and familial proximity.

Much of the division of labour in sailing ships reflected the influence of a military division of labour in naval vessels, although historians have paid little attention to this interaction between military models and merchant practices. The division went much further than that between the quarterdeck, the domain of officers, and the forecastle, the domain of seamen. Naval vessels connected specific duties or tasks, groups of men, and distinct spaces, so that one may speak of "duties allocated to the different parts of the ship."[39] There were forecastlemen, foretopmen, maintopmen, mizzentopmen, and quarterdeckmen, each responsible for the working of particular parts of the ship. The division of the crew into watches was also related to working areas, since those in the starboard watch worked the starboard side of the ship, and those in the port watch worked the port side. The execution of tasks in sail-handling was performed by military "drill" and "evolutionary movements." Of course only parts of the naval division of labour were adopted by the merchant marine. The merchant sailing ship was an unusual workplace, however, because it could so easily absorb parts of its social organization and command structure from a military model. In a merchant ship the foremen were "officers"; specialist craftsmen were "petty officers"; the master gave orders, and the crew's work was "duty."

As Atlantic Canadian shipowners invested in larger sailing vessels in the nineteenth century, they accepted an age-old physical separation of master, officers, and crew. The crew lived in the forecastle, which sometimes remained under the forward deck but more often became a separate cabin-house on the forward deck, visible in many paintings of sailing vessels in the later nineteenth century. Removing the sailors' living quarters to this house had the effect of increasing cargo space in the "tween decks": the deck-house, although disliked by some shipowners, was one of many concessions to the search for greater carrying capacity, while preserving the separation between officers and deckhands. The forecastle accommodated only the crew of lower ranks. In larger vessels the deckhouse included separate cabins for apprentices and petty officers. The mate lived aft, a hundred feet away. The fore-castle, in one large sailing vessel, was "fitted up complete with berths, pegs, lockers, table, stove" and with "W.C. and boatswain's locker outside of forecastle."[40] Aft of the living quarters, and sometimes in a separate small deckhouse, was the galley, with a large cooking stove, shelves, coal bunker, pantry, bread lockers, and an array of cooking equipment. The deckhouse also included the carpenter's stores, a small sailroom, and sailmaker's stores. Adjacent to the deckhouse were the water tanks, which might hold two thousand gallons each; each tank had a small copper hand pump. Near the deckhouse were pens for livestock (which might include chickens, pigs, and even sheep), since large vessels often took live animals on long voyages.

Moving aft one passed the main hatch, the largest of the openings in the deck, through which the cargo entered the hold below. Here in the great barque of the 1880s the coamings rose 18 inches above the deck, and the hatch covers were solid pine. Further aft one approached the poop, the raised deck that formed the roof of the main cabin and the master's quarters. Here was "the august place in every vessel."[41] The poop also contained accommodation for the first and second mates. The poop deck itself was a private space reserved for the master and his wife or children. The deck of the *Bowman B. Law* of Yarmouth, as ordered from the builders in 1885, was surrounded by a teak rail supported by iron stanchions, and the deck was a floor of the finest pine. In the deck were skylights and ventilators, allowing light and air to enter the rooms below. Elsewhere on deck was the master's boat, distinguished by its brass rowlocks.

Below the poop deck were a saloon and staterooms with a floor area of six hundred square feet or more. The man who lived in this private domain was no longer simply master, but a businessman, the manager of a branch office of the shipping company, and his cabin was also his office space. The physical appointments were carefully designed to reflect this managerial status:

Saloon. – Sides neatly finished with pannelling of polished maple, teak or other woods. Polished pilaster, cornice, and gilt trusses. Moulding of beams to be gilded ...

Sideboard with marble top and brass guard. Large mirror with neat lever clock set in gilt frame. Polished hardwood table, with guards. Six swing chairs alongside saloon table, and armchair at end of table, stuffed with hair and covered with crimson or other shade of velvet, secured to deck with brass screws. Brass rods in skylight, with large lamp and racks for bottles and glasses. Candle or oil lamp in each room. Neat stove with iron funnel cased in brass. Neat scuttle for coals and set fire-irons. Saloon, staterooms and captain's rooms to have Brussels carpet, with runners. Officers' rooms, pantry, passages, and bath-rooms laid with best wax cloth or coir matting, or linoleum as required.

All staterooms and officers rooms to be neatly finished, with berths, sofas, pegs, wash-basins, soap-boxes, jugs, and receivers, mirrors, bottle, and brush and comb racks, and brass, oil, or candle gimble lamps. Captain's room to have berth to draw out with drawers underneath, rack and bookcase, and chronometer stand, in polished hardwood. First officer's room to have polished hardwood drawers underneath berth, also desk. Waxcloth cover and cloth cover for saloon table. All sofas, settees, chairs and seats in saloon and staterooms to be stuffed with hair, and covered with velvet. Polished medicine chest with ship's name.[42]

In the small schooner the master entertained his guests to a glass of rum, served into plain glass tumblers. In the barque the master, if he were not a teetotaller, served claret or champagne from cut glass decanters, and the vessel carried one dozen claret glasses, two dozen wine glasses, and one dozen champagne glasses. The cook and the steward included in their stores a dozen white table cloths, five dozen towels, ivory table knives, coffeecups with saucers, tea cups with saucers, dinner plates, soup plates, pudding plates, cheese plates, and a further array of kitchenware of a kind never seen in a cookhouse of a New Brunswick lumber camp (although beside this list the future owner of the vessel noted in pencil "reduction to be made here").[43] The vessel carried seven sofas, all under the poop. It is unlikely that many Nova Scotian vessels were as well provisioned as the *Bowman B. Law*, but the original specifications for this vessel indicate how far the master's domain could differ from the spartan cabin of the coastal master. Into this domain the deckhand entered rarely: this was where he might come to receive medical treatment or to witness entries in the official log regarding his behaviour.

The knowledge of navigation that was essential to the operation of the vessel was increasingly the preserve of the master. His appropriation of knowledge is reflected in his personal possession of navigational aids. The master supplied his own sextant, charts, seaman's manuals, telescope, and dividers. The vessel carried several compasses (the *Bowman B. Law* had five), including "compass in binnacle on dolphin stand on poop, with dripping needles and lamps complete." The vessel also carried a barometer and a sympiesometer (another device to measure atmospheric pressure). This equipment was located aft, in the master's domain. It was reserved for the master and his chief mate and was used by others at the master's pleasure.

Every master had his foreman and chief officer, the first mate, who had his own territory in the vessel. He lived under the poop in his own cabin, but his working domain lay forward, and he stood on the forecastle deck to issue orders and to supervise the work. He was "executive supervisor" in the fore part of the ship and the "satrap of that province in the autocratic realm of the ship," Joseph Conrad tells us.[44] The first mate arranged and supervised the daily work of the crew, supervised the stowage of cargo, and made the vessel ready for sea. He inspected the sails and rigging, ensuring that all was in working order. He was in charge of the ship's stores. He usually kept the ship's log (not the official log but the record of the passage and navigational details). Often he made the daily estimates of latitude and longitude. He was usually responsible for the patent log, the device used to estimate the vessel's speed. The extent to which the mate shared in the task of navigation varied from one vessel to another, and there must have been many mates in Canadian vessels who had little knowledge of the subject (some were illiterate).[45]

But the mate was the only person on board who was at all close to the master. He might be the only officer to enter the master's cabin on a regular basis, and in many vessels he would take his meals with the master. In small vessels the mate might do more than issue orders: he might actually assist with the handling of rigging and sails. But in large sailing vessels the mate kept his place on the forecastle deck, observing the work of the crew. In steam vessels the mate often found company and equality with the engineers, but in sail he occupied a solitary position in the hierarchy. As foreman and disciplinarian, he was not one of the crew, nor even first among equals, and the "majority of mates must for a season learn to rely upon themselves for society."[46]

In Canadian sailing vessels there was often a second mate, particularly in vessels over five hundred tons. The second mate was little removed from the deckhands: he went aloft, worked the sails, and helped in trimming the yards.[47] He did not "take the sun" or have anything to do with navigation. The second mate was expected to assist the first mate in supervising the stowing of cargo, and he tallied the cargo entering one hatch while the mate tallied the cargo at the other hatch. Although the British "certificate of competency" for a second mate required that he have some knowledge of arithmetic, be able to use the sextant, and have some basic navigational skills, these must rarely have been used by second mates in Canadian vessels. Five per cent of second mates in Canadian vessels were illiterate.[48] In Canadian vessels the second mate was often an older, more experienced seaman who had been promoted from among the ABs (in the Saint John fleet, for instance, 59 per cent of second mates were aged 30 or over).[49] Among contemporaries, the second mate, if he were a "Bluenoser," had the same reputation for ferocity as did the first mate: he was, said Frank Bullen, "a large man with horny hands and hairy chest" and quite capable of throwing a man overboard for swearing.[50] Although closer to the crew than the chief mate, this officer was also responsible for the enforcing of discipline. And like the first mate he usually had the right to be addressed as Mister.

Behind the physical and social separation of masters and men lay not simply an age-old division of labour but new divisions of knowledge. In the mid-nineteenth century these divisions, and the traditional structures of authority at sea, were reconfirmed and buttressed by merchant shipping legislation. It has often been said that shipping was an industry operating in a very "free" market, closest to the old textbook definitions of laissez-faire.[51] The notion is misleading: although the shipowner did make freighting and financial decisions with little direct reference to statutory regulations, his industry and its workers were subject to detailed legislative provisions.

Certainly no shipowner in the late nineteenth century would have said that he worked in a market-place free of state intervention and regulation. W.S. Lindsay, the British politician and historian of shipping, was hardly the first to note that the British state was engaged in the third quarter of the nineteenth century "in attempting to regulate minute details about shipping" until shipowners complained about "being harassed by over-legislation."[52] The shipowners' opposition does not mean that the legislation worked against the interests of private capital, but it is a reminder that state regulation was an integral part of the development of the industry. Much has been written about British merchant shipping acts, passenger acts, load-line laws, and related legislation. Relatively little has been written about their effect on workplace relations.

Of critical importance in British shipping was the movement toward professionalization of the merchant marine. This movement began when humanitarian concern for seamen coincided with a growing desire to protect property at sea. The rapid growth in demand for vessels and men to freight goods across the North

Atlantic had increased total losses, until by the 1830s about nine hundred men and £2.8 million worth of property were being lost at sea each year.[53] The British Parliament's Select Committee on Shipwrecks (1836) recommended, among other things, that all who held authority in a ship should have to pass examinations designed to test their competence. Nautical schools should be established to provide the necessary training.

The recommendations were not implemented immediately: the powerful shipowners' lobby did not dispute the idea that safety at sea was in their own economic interest, but they did reject the idea that government should regulate the training and certification of seamen. The assumptions of the pre-industrial era of small family firms and small vessels still prevailed in Britain, as they did in British North America. Shipowners argued that they were best able to assess the ability of masters and officers and should choose them personally.[54] This may well have been true of shipowners in such places as Yarmouth, Nova Scotia, where the owner had had experience at sea and knew the local candidates for employment. It was less true in the larger shipping firms trading across oceans, and it is no surprise to find some British shipowners requiring their masters and officers to take company examinations, and other shipowners pressing the Board of Trade for a system of voluntary examinations.

Shipowners' opposition to a compulsory system did not disappear, but their argument for personal control of the hiring process was weakened by repeal of the Navigation Acts, beginning in 1849. When British and colonial shipping was opened to wider competition, government feared that British shipowners might lose freights to foreign fleets if their merchant marine had a reputation for excessive risk-taking and incompetence in officers and masters. The repeal of one form of protection therefore required the institution of another, and the state would now intervene to protect the industry by setting standards of performance and competence. State-regulated examinations and professionalization followed as one instance of protective intervention by the state in the interests of private enterprise.[55]

In 1850 the British Parliament passed An Act for Improving the Condition of Masters, Mates, and Seamen, and Maintaining Discipline in the Merchant Service (13 & 14 Vic. cap 93), known more commonly as the Mercantile Marine Act of 1850. Some of the 124 clauses related to the certification of officers and masters in foreign-going British ships. All officers and masters in such vessels were required to have a certificate of competency awarded after examination by a local marine board. The provision did not apply retrospectively, much to the relief of masters and owners in the colonies. Those who had already been serving as masters and officers were not required to pass examinations but could receive certificates of service enabling them to serve in their existing capacities. Those without certificates of service must, however, apply for certificates of competency.

In proposing certification of masters and mates, British legislators had very clear definitions of "competency." Masters and officers required training in the science of navigation, but this competence could not be separated from the question of authority and discipline in a ship. As Henry Labouchere said, in introducing the 1850 act, "the notorious incompetency and misconduct" of many masters was "closely connected with ... the want of discipline on the part of the crews which prevailed to a fatal extent in many portions of our mercantile marine." The connection between knowledge and power was fully understood, and the masters and mates would, through the examination system, be supplied with both. By introducing examinations Parliament "would promote that kind of knowledge which was of the deepest interest to the mercantile navy – they would elevate both captains and mates in the scale of their profession, arm them with proper power over their crews, and confer many benefits upon all concerned in the navigation of the seas." Proper qualifications would "render masters respectable in the eyes of the crews" and would thereby "strenghten the reins of discipline."[56]

The standards of competence laid down in the 1850 act were high, and many seamen on both sides of the Atlantic did not meet the standards. To qualify as second mate the candidate had to be at least 17 years of age and to have served four years at sea. He must be literate; he must understand the first five rules of arithmetic; he must be able to correct the course steered for variation in the compass bearing, make observations with the sextant, find the latitude from the meridian altitude of the sun, and answer questions about rigging, stowage, the log-line, and the rule of the road for ships.[57]

A candidate for first mate's certificate had to be 19 years of age and to have served at least five years at sea, with one year as second or only mate. In addition to the skills required of a second mate, he must be able to observe and compute azimuths, use chronometers, use and adjust the sextant, calculate the time of high water, understand the methods for shifting sails and yards and masts, manage the vessel in stormy weather, and stow cargo properly. Most mates in colonial vessels were over 19 years of age, but some mates in the crew lists of the 1840s and 1850s were 20 or 21, and probably few of these met all the qualifications in the 1850 act.

The master's qualifications, of course, were the most extensive. He had to be 21 years of age and to have been at sea for six years, with at least one year at the rank of mate. He had to demonstrate an ability to navigate along any coast, by drawing on a chart the courses and distances he would run, with bearings corrected for variation. He had to know the method of determining the effect of iron in a vessel on the ship's compass. He had to know the law regarding hiring, discharge, and management of crew, including all provisions of merchant shipping legislation, and the rules for making entries in the official log. He had to be able to answer questions about charter parties, bills of lading, insurance, and bottomry. There was also a provision for examination at the rank of "extra master," for masters of superior qualifications who wished to serve in sailing vessels and steamers of the first class.[58]

Once again the presence of 20- and 21-year-old masters in crew lists for the late 1840s suggests that there were masters of colonial vessels who did not meet the age and experience requirements. In vessels of Halifax, Saint John, Windsor, and Yarmouth there were masters aged 20 or 21 in every year in the 1860s. In 1871 Peter Mitchell, Canada's minister of marine and fisheries, acknowledged that many masters from New Brunswick and Nova Scotia, "while they are masters of their profession as seamen, have not had opportunities to acquire sufficient knowledge of the science of navigation."[59]

In 1854 the British Parliament passed another Merchant Shipping Act. This was a major consolidation of British shipping laws, and it incorporated among its 548 sections the provisions of the 1850 act on certification of masters and mates. The legislation applied to colonial vessels entering British ports - an incentive to Canadian masters to obtain certificates. There were also serious problems for vessels whose masters did not have certificates and growing demands that the colonies establish their own examination and certification procedures.

A solution did not emerge until the passing of the Merchant Shipping (Colonial) Act in 1869, which granted colonial legislatures the right to establish certification procedures.[60] Provided that the Board of Trade was satisfied that examinations met the appropriate standards, Canadian certificates would have the same validity as certificates issued in the United Kingdom. By 1870 Canada's Department of Marine and Fisheries had arranged for examinations to take place under its supervision, initially at three ports (Quebec, Halifax, and Saint John), and in 1870 the Canadian Parliament passed the "Act Respecting Certificates to Masters and Mates of Ships" (33 Vic. cap 17). The certification system applied only to ocean-going vessels (although it was extended to Canadian vessels on inland waters in 1883), and so it confirmed the distinction between coastal and ocean-going ships and the demand for professional standards in the latter. In supporting the act, Peter Mitchell insisted that it was essential to bring "a sober industrious man" into Canada's merchant marine, to serve not only the nation's commercial interests but also to serve "in time of danger when her shores are threatened by the invading forces of a foreign foe." Certification was intended to promote "sobriety, experience, ability, and general good conduct on board a ship."[61]

Certificates of competency in the colonies were similar to British ones. Canada did not at first offer second mate's certificates, partly because so many Canadian owners and masters preferred not to carry a man at this rank. The standards for first mate and master were modelled directly on British standards. Recognition of service in the coasting trade was given: in applications for a mate's certificate, service in coasting could count toward the required four years' coasting service (in 1871 an amendment required five years' service for mates). In applications for a master's ticket, two years' service at the rank of mate in coasting could count among the six years' experience required. Where an applicant for master had served only in vessels with fore and aft rig, he could obtain a certificate for ocean-going service on which the words "Fore-and-aft-rigged vessel" were to be written. A master with such a certificate was not allowed to command a square-rigged vessel.

Candidates for examination were required to take a six-hour written examination, to which they were not allowed to take books or paper. Candidates were urged to spend their spare time studying, and masters were encouraged to permit officers and others to attend nautical schools, many of which appeared in Canadian ports in the 1860s and 1870s. The legislation also authorized the minister of marine and fisheries to issue colonial certificates of service to masters and mates who provided proof that they had served in their capacity prior to 1870.[62]

Candidates began presenting themselves for Canadian certificates, although of course many masters of Canadian ocean-going vessels would have possessed a British certificate by this time. In 1871 the chairman of the board of examiners reported that 39 candidates had been examined for the rank of master at Saint John and Halifax that year. Twenty per cent had failed, which suggests that the examinations were not perfunctory, even though Marine and Fisheries believed that "the qualifications have been kept as low as possible."[63] In 1872–3 the board was more successful in attracting candidates: 207 certificates of competency for masters were awarded, as well as 372 certificates of service for masters. Thirty-five certificates of competency, and 122 of service, were awarded to mates.[64] By 1884 certificates of service were still being issued, but they were few in number. Although the failure rate in examinations remained high (30 per cent in 1884), suggesting that standards were not relaxed, over two thousand certificates of competency had been awarded since 1871.[65]

Many people criticized the examinations for testing ability to memorize or "cram" rather than practical seamanship. But the higher ranks of the Canadian merchant marine were becoming a professional occupation. The professionalization of seafaring was limited to masters and mates and reinforced and formalized the social distance between poop and forecastle. At the same time it reinforced the differences between service in the coastal sailing vessel and service in the deep-sea merchant marine.

Britain's Merchant Shipping Acts of 1850 and 1854 affected relations at sea in many other ways. While offering specific forms of protection to the deckhand, these acts also laid down a comprehensive code of conduct and a definition of legal misdemeanours at sea, buttressing in law the master's traditional disciplinary powers.

As Conrad Dixon has pointed out, longstanding precedents made the relationship between sailor and employer a contractual arrangement sanctioned in law.[66] From the early eighteenth century, merchant seamen were unlike many civil workers in that their contracts of employment contained substantial penalties in criminal law if the terms were not fulfilled. Desertion was a major area of concern in legislation. After 1729, the penalty for desertion was 30 days' imprisonment, but the law proved difficult to enforce, not least because of wage disparities between British and colonial vessels.

Major legislative changes came after growing concern in the 1830s and 1840s that industrial work-discipline had not been imposed in shipping. The 1836 Select Committee on Shipwrecks noted several reasons for marine disasters, but legislators focused on the conduct of crew. Stories of insobriety among masters, officers, and crew abounded and seemed to be confirmed when the Foreign Office requested and received reports on the merchant marine from British consuls around the world. In 1843 the consuls reported at length on drunkenness, incompetence, carelessness, lechery, illiteracy, and other evils among both masters and crew of British and colonial vessels.[67] These consular reports were published in 1848, and while they aroused considerable protest and objections from owners and masters, they helped to convince both Parliament and shipowners that the legislative backing for discipline at sea must be strengthened.

Offences and punishments were specified in section 243 of the 1854 act. Desertion – withdrawal from the vessel before the term of the contract expired and without an official discharge – was punishable by 12 weeks' imprisonment, with or without hard labour. The deserter was also liable for the loss of his clothes and all other effects left on board and any wages owing to him. He was also liable to forfeit any wages earned in another vessel between his desertion and return to the United Kingdom and also to pay the difference between his own wage and that of a substitute hired to replace him. Refusing to join a ship or to proceed to sea, and absence without leave, were offences punishable by 10 weeks' imprisonment, with or without hard labour, and two days' pay. "Wilful disobedience to any lawful command" was punishable by 4 weeks' imprisonment and the forfeit of two days' pay. Continued wilful disobedience could be punished by 12 weeks' imprisonment and the forfeit of six days' pay for every 24 hours in which disobedience continued. The law also recognized that sailors might act together to disobey the master, and such "combining with any others or others of the crew to disobey lawful commands" or "to neglect duty" or to "impede the progress of the voyage" was a separate offence, punishable by 12 weeks' imprisonment. Assaulting the master or mate, damaging the ship or cargo, and "embezzling" the ship's stores or cargo were also punishable by 12 weeks' imprisonment. These and other provisions of the legislation were summarized and distributed to masters with copies of official logs.[68]

The Board of Trade also issued "Regulations for Maintaining Discipline": a list of offences that could be enforced in a court of law, provided that the master had specified on the crew list that these regulations were in force and had entered the offence in his official log in the correct manner. The offences suggest how far the master's control was being reinforced by statute. The master was given authority to control not only the labour of workers but also time and behaviour even during "watch below." The workplace was also the workers' domicile, but in law this was now a workplace above all else, and work-discipline required control even of leisure time.

Many of the regulations sanctioned by the Board of Trade through the 1860s and 1870s related directly to the contractual obligation to provide labour: thus failure to be on board at the agreed time, sleeping while on look-out, and not returning on board promptly at the expiry of shore leave were offences punishable by loss of one or two days' pay. But other offences related directly to the master's control over time, leisure, and even language. Smoking below, neglecting to air one's bedding, not attending divine service, or interrupting divine service by "indecorous conduct" could be punished by small fines. Failure to be washed and shaved on Sunday, or washing clothes on Sunday, could be punished by fines. Swearing, quarrelling, provoking a quarrel, or carrying a sheath-knife could result in the fine of one days' pay. These provisions were not applied regularly, and it was a brave or foolhardy master who attempted to enforce Sunday observances as strictly as the regulations allowed. Nevertheless, these mid-century regulations were more extensive than any that preceded them. "A ship at sea is in herself a little kingdom," said W.S.

Lindsay, and this was no analogy: the master was civil and criminal authority in his fragment of British society.[69]

Legislators were concerned not only to enforce work-discipline but also to ensure an adequate supply of labour in the industry. Labour must not be deterred from entering this industry by its reputation for danger, brutality, and poor working conditions. For this reason Parliament enacted a long series of provisions designed to protect the worker, or at least to encourage certain minimal standards and conditions of work at sea. Legislation in 1844 and 1845 made the first of many provisions for the recovery of un-paid wages and for the dispensing of lime-juice.[70] The 1850 act specified a minimum amount of space in a forecastle for each sea-man and set a scale of medical stores to be carried in all vessels. All ocean-going vessels were required to carry weights and measures, so that the seaman might be satisfied that victuals specified in the crew list were being given (there was no compulsory victualling scale until 1906). The 1850 act also instructed local marine boards to establish shipping offices, where crew members might be hired without the intermediary services of crimps. After 1855 seamen had the legal right to refuse to serve in an unseaworthy vessel, and after 1864 government surveyors were available to magistrates to solve the problem of proving seaworthiness. Subsequent legislation extended the right to demand surveys and increased the powers of the Board of Trade to detain unseaworthy vessels. In the 1870s oc-curred the campaign over unseaworthy ships associated with Samuel Plimsoll. The Plimsoll Mark, a load line showing the greatest draught to which a ship should be loaded, was made com-pulsory by the 1876 Merchant Shipping Act, but responsibility for fixing the load line remained with the individual shipowner until 1890. There were many other provisions relating to safety and working conditions, but all related, in whole or in part, to parliamentary concern to guarantee the quantity and quality of labour in the industry.[71]

These and other provisions led to the widespread complaint by owners and masters that sailors were the most protected and pampered of workers. The effect, said W.S. Lindsay, was to give seamen, *"at the expense of the community*, what no other class is allowed, easy and ready means of inquiring into their com-plaints."[72] The protection had gone so far as to encourage desertion, to promote insubordination, and "to destroy the confidence which should ever exist between the master and his crew."[73] In Atlantic Canada such complaints were even more vehement. The master of a Windsor vessel expressed his anger in his official log: "We hear of new Laws every day for so called Sailors but protection for Captains Officers, shipowners or Underwriters is a thing of the past."[74] Writing in the 1920s, Frederick William Wallace expressed clearly the view of shipowners and masters in his father's generation: the Merchant Shipping Acts were an unwarranted and unnecessary interference in the relationship between employer and employee.[75]

These responses tell us more about the attitude of employers than about the legislation itself. It was simply not true that "the law as it at present stands, gives him [the master] very little power of punishing a sailor for anything but mutinous conduct."[76] In this industry the law gave the master extensive authority over his workers and penalties in criminal law to enforce his power. Masters and owners responded as they did because they did not see protection as the necessary solution to the problem of labour supply and believed that working relationships were the sole responsibility of owners and masters.

Behind Wallace's objections lay the interests of owners and masters, but also the view that reward and punishment in the workplace must be left entirely to the employer. As Frank Bullen remarked, in a Bluenose vessel "discipline ... is not based upon law, but upon force."[77] This extra-legal authority was what Canadian masters assumed to be traditional and wished to enforce. And behind this attitude was the darker side of a paternalism inherited from pre-industrial times, the belief that workers in one's employ were predisposed by a sinful nature to be "duffers and slackers" or worse. There must therefore be no restrictions upon the power to punish the "lazy, truculent, and incompetent man" for "punishment ... was his just due." The problem, as Wallace put it, was that "the wasters, the bums and hoboes, the sea-lawyers and trouble-makers ... unfortunately made up a considerable percentage of the men before the mast in the days of sail."[78] The master must have the right and the power to punish these men and to use physical force; to limit that right was to invite mutiny. Owners and masters did not question the powers that Merchant

Shipping Acts gave to masters. They assumed that these powers already existed and questioned instead the limits to those powers.

The opposition to merchant shipping legislation reflects the erosion of older fraternal relationships and the presence of new social divisions in the workplace. Owners and masters accepted the assumption behind much of the legislation – that a serious disciplinary problem existed among a deteriorating labour force. There was one set of solutions for masters and officers, another for deckhands. The solution for masters and officers was examination and certification; for deckhands, enforcement of discipline by embedding punishment in the contractual relationship between employer and employee. The merchant ship was coming close to what American sociologist Erving Goffman described as a "total institution" – all-encompassing regulation of the inmate's way of life, reinforced by barriers to intercourse with the outside world.[79] More obviously, law-makers wrote into statutory regulations a set of behavioural norms to distinguish duty from disobedience, and the rough from the respectable. It was not assumed that a more productive work-force might result from compulsory improvements in victualling, manning levels, wages, or working conditions. Legislators aimed, after all, to limit rather than increase the operating costs of shipowners, not least by ensuring a continuing increase in the labour supply. There was now a formal contract between master and worker, and the worker had the right to know in advance the conditions of his service; but the right to bargain over those conditions was constrained in law. Whereas the relationship between master and worker had once been personal and paternal, now it was also governed by contract and by statute. Together with changes in capital and technology, this constituted the industrial revolution that began to transform the social relations of production at sea.

CHAPTER FOUR

Working the Deep-Sea Ship

The three-masted barque was a fragment of the society that created it, and so this great machine reflected the influences of industrial capitalism. Men at sea were part of a machine, a "living appendage" to technology, or so some contemporaries believed: "Each task has its man, and each man its place. A ship contains a set of human machinery in which every man is a part of the whole, a band or a crank, all moving with wonderful regularity and precision to the will of its machinist – the all-powerful Captain."[1] Here, it would seem, was a complete subordination of labour in which a deskilled worker applied manual labour in routine, standardized tasks requiring little or no understanding or discretion.

But the story of work in the large sailing ships is not so simple. The great barque was a fragment of Atlantic Canada, and the landward influences contained all the ambiguity of a society in which the forms and assumptions of paternalism persisted into the age of industrial capital. And the barque was not the end but the beginning of a technological and social transformation; she was proto-industrial, but not yet a factory. In his work the sailor was subject to the dictates of a changing technology, contractual obligations, and statutory regulations, but he was still not a factory worker. Because capital and the state sought all-encompassing control does not mean that they achieved it. The ship was not a neat pyramid of power, but a complex fabric of prohibitions, rules, and traditions to which the sailor also contributed, sometimes giving and sometimes withholding his consent.

In pre-industrial and pre-contractual production, the relationship between master and servant tended to be diffuse and holistic.[2]

The servant committed his entire person to the master's service and performed a range of tasks in that service. With the growth of industrial production came an increasing occupational division of labour, where work is differentiated into a number of separate tasks and each task is allocated to a person who specializes in it. Industrialism expanded impersonal labour and commodity markets, where specific forms of labour, usually defined by contract, were provided in return for a wage. Industrialism narrowed relations between master and worker to the exchange of specified labour and specified wages and so undermined the diffuse mutual obligations of paternalism. To the extent that all these things were occurring in shipping, all relationships and all work were being transformed, because entirely new forms of subordination were being imposed. By the end of the nineteenth century "the employment contract had become a very special sort of contract – in large part a legal device for guaranteeing to management the unilateral power to make rules and exercise discretion."[3] This is a succinct definition of the purposes of the crew agreement, the labour contract in shipping.

Yet there were limits to the subordination that followed from the use of labour contracts in shipping and from the supervision of managing owner and master. No written labour contract can determine all the specific tasks to be performed by the workers over an extended period of time. An employment contract always assumes a degree of diffuseness in the exchange: it is "a continuing implied renewal of contracts," in which the employer hires labour for tasks that may be specified only in general terms.[4] In sailing ships the deckhand agreed by contract to serve in a specific vessel, for a specific voyage, and for a maximum period of time. The nature of that service was not spelled out in greater detail, and probably could not be. The able seaman's work was defined by the interaction of custom, technology, expectations of the master, and even to some extent the sailor's own understanding of his obligations and his rights. Further, however closely the managing owner of a deep-sea ship might attempt to supervise operations, day-to-day supervision fell necessarily to his employee and agent, the master.

At sea the master was, above all else, master mariner and navigator. As the immediate employer of sailors, he must not only supervise but also feed and house his workers, tend to their health if they were ill, and ensure the survival of both men and machine. In these circumstances the diffuse mutual obligations of paternalism could not be undermined. The wage-labour exchange was still suffused with paternalist assumptions, especially where the master came, as so often he did, from the small port towns of Atlantic Canada and from their seafaring traditions. The master expected not only labour in return for wages but personal deference as well; the sailor expected not only wages but also such attention to diet, health, and personal safety as customary practice warranted.

A further limit to subordination came from the technology itself. It was impossible for all discretion, judgment, and control to be appropriated by management, or even by the master. Given the growing variety and complexity of tasks in sailing ships, and given the operation of the machinery in distant places and unforeseeable conditions, the worker could not be a living appendage to the machine. It was possible to remove most decisions to the level of masters and officers, but not to remove all discretion from the worker, by incorporating decisions into the very design and functioning of the machine. In sailing ships workers did not merely respond to the rhythms and exigencies of a technical system over which they exercised no control and no understanding.

There was an increasing division of labour in sailing vessels as time passed and as the great ocean-going fleets expanded.[5] There were, of course, distinct ranks to which the crew were assigned in the small schooners of Atlantic Canada. But the ranks were few in number. In the small vessels of Newfoundland for which crew lists survive, there were no more than 11 ranks: master, first mate, second mate, cook, steward, bosun, carpenter, able seaman, ordinary seaman, boy, and apprentice. There were only two carpenters, two apprentices, five stewards, and twenty-five boys among the 2,177 crew hired at the outset of voyages, so there were only six ranks of any real importance.[6] Half of the positions on these vessels were accounted for by men hired as able seamen (Table 5). There was no formal apprenticeship system, but boys and ordinary seamen were often teenagers who were learning their trade.

There was no rigid differentiation of tasks by rank, because all hands including the master could share in the work of handling sails. On 14 voyages there was no cook; one of the other ranks

TABLE 5

Ranks of Sailors Signing on at Departure, St John's-Registered Sailing Vessels, 1863-99

Rank	Number	% of Total	% of Voyages in Which Rank Filled
Master	262	12.0	100.0
First mate	252	11.6	96.2
Second mate	63	2.9	24.1
Bosun	114	5.2	43.5
Cook	248	11.4	94.7
Steward	5	0.2	1.9
Carpenter	2	0.1	0.8
Able seaman	1,085	49.8	100.0
Ordinary seaman	119	5.5	30.5
Boy	25	1.2	9.2
Apprentice	2	0.1	0.8
Total	2,177	100	

Source: Crew Lists, St John's-registered vessels, MHA.

Note: Vessels under 250 tons.

would perform this vital task. The voyages in this sample were mainly ocean passages or long coastal voyages beyond Newfoundland waters - we may safely assume that the cook was even more often absent on shorter coastal voyages. The relative flexibility of rank and task in the coastal schooner was noted by the astonished mate of a British vessel: "Lying in a Nova Scotia harbour once, loading lumber from a large schooner, I went on board at breakfast time. I found the skipper preparing breakfast for all hands - four of them. They did not muster a cook."[7] On ten voyages there was no mate at all; the mate's duties were assumed probably by the master or by a bosun. The different ranks usually meant something in terms of responsibilities and pay, but they did not constitute a social hierarchy within the workplace.

In the ocean-going vessels of the late nineteenth century there were many more ranks: the code-book used in the data entry process contains over 70 different entries under rank, or capacity. Some of these ranks (engineer, fireman, trimmer) come from the small number of steamers in the Crew List files, but most ranks were those of men and women serving in sailing vessels. Table 6 shows the number of crew in each rank in all voyage starts by vessels in the Saint John crew list file. Where most small schooners put to sea with master, mate, cook, and deckhands (ABs or OSs), the large barques and ships were more likely to carry a second mate, a bosun, a steward, and a carpenter or sailmaker as well as ABs and OSs. While the number of petty officers had increased, nevertheless the proportion of all crew consisting of deckhands (ABs and OSs) had also increased. The larger workplaces meant more specialist positions, but also a larger proportion of workers in lower ranks.

The system of ranks served two related functions: it defined the general nature of the duties for which one was hired, and it was a structure of authority. There was status in each rank. Status derived not only from the legally protected right of masters and mates to issue orders, but also from inherited British traditions of subordination and superordination in seafaring. Rank and its status served to maintain order in ships, as a story about one Nova Scotian second mate suggests. Upon mustering the men in his watch at the beginning of a long voyage, he discovered that they were all "huge negroes" and very likely "a rowdy lot." Instantly he promoted the biggest man to the rank of bosun. " 'Ay, ay, sah,' bellowed the delighted black man, 'I put de b'ys froo sah.' And put them through he did. There was never any trouble from that day."[8] Status was bound up with work, however, for every seaman associated each rank with a set of skills and tasks. The more knowledge and skill required at each rank, the greater the status conferred upon its holder. Discussions of ranks by seamen themselves invariably become ad hominem, but the respect accorded particular individuals derives from the way in which they performed their work.

The division of labour did not necessarily mean that skill and knowledge were diminished at each rank. Even in terms of discretion content, the work done by the occupant of a particular rank might require greater discretion and independent judgment as specialization occurred.[9] This could happen when the range and complexity of tasks in a workplace increased so significantly that a progressive splitting of work did not mean a reduction of skill at

TABLE 6

Distribution by Rank, Saint John Fleet, 1863-1914

Rank	Number	% of Total
Master	2,081	5.9
Mate	2,081	5.9
Second mate	884	2.5
Third mate	75	0.2
Bosun	1,324	3.7
Carpenter	976	2.8
Sailmaker	237	0.7
Cook	804	2.3
Cook/steward	1,245	3.5
Steward/stewardess	955	2.7
Able seaman	19,881	56.1
Ordinary seaman	2,307	6.5
Boy	757	2.1
AB/sailmaker	64	0.2
Bosun/mate	128	0.4
Assistant steward	46	0.1
Stowaway	12	0.0
Carpenter/bosun	25	0.1
Carpenter/AB	151	0.4
Carpenter's mate	11	0.0
Apprentice	352	1.0
Donkeyman	73	0.2
First, second, or third engineer	260	0.7
Fireman or fireman/trimmer	506	1.4
Bosun/trimmer	41	0.1
Other	189	
Total	35,465	100

Source: Saint John Labour File. The total number of crew records in the Saint John Master File is 54,147. But many of these are accounted for by sailors who joined during a voyage. The above table includes only those for whom the variable substitute = 1, meaning that the crew member is an original member of the crew, not a substitute for one who died, deserted, or did not join. Although a few vessels carried a second master or extra master, these have been omitted.

each rank. Thus small coastal vessels did not normally carry a bosun, and his work was done by deckhands in a schooner. But the presence of a bosun in a large barque did not necessarily mean that the skill or task range of either bosun or deckhand was thereby diminished. Certain critical components of skill could still be present at each rank: complexity of tasks performed; training required for each set of tasks; and knowledge invested in each set of tasks. The task range could also increase at each rank, even where all work was split into more divisions and assigned to specialists. Even if this happened, however, it is possible that very little discretion or decison-making was left to the deckhands, because their tasks may have been prescribed, routinized, and thoroughly supervised. Only by examining the work of sailors in more detail can we arrive at conclusions about the real effects of the division of labour.

The division of labour in large sailing ships was related to the range and complexity of tasks to be performed and to the extension of managerial supervision and control. A critical difference between the small schooner and the large barque was the ratio of officers to crew. In the schooner the master and his mate were likely to be two in a company of five to ten men. In barques and ships of 500 tons and more, a master and his two officers were likely to be responsible for a crew of 15 to 30 men. Sharing all tasks in the ship equally between all sailors, and allowing the more experienced to train the less experienced, would have taxed unduly the supervisory abilities of the officers or else required an unacceptable delegation of responsibility to deckhands. Given the inherited traditions of subordination in deep-sea ships, the alternative was unthinkable.

From the point of view of management it made sense to delegate responsibilities to particular individuals holding particular ranks and to reward those individuals with status and modest increments in wages. Most Canadian sailing vessels carried a bosun. In British ships he was "essentially a foreman, a working man who, by reason of his superior qualifications, has risen above his fellow workers, and takes the oversight of them."[10] In Canadian vessels the bosun was not a more experienced man; usually he was a young man who was given a small addition in pay in return for looking after particular parts of the vessel and supervising those parts. He was responsible for the spare cordage, for the maintenance of rope and rigging, and for the smooth operation of capstans and other gear about the vessel. The bosun took orders from the first mate and relieved the mate of the need to supervise constantly all maintenance work. The supervisory role of the bosun is suggested by the fact that in Canadian vessels he very often took the place of the second mate: ocean-going vessels carried bosuns much more often than second mates (Table 6).

Saint John vessels were also more likely to carry a carpenter than a second mate. The ship's carpenter was a specialist craftsman responsible, like the bosun, for particular parts of the ship. He was a petty officer to whom some of the crew would be sent to assist in particular maintenance tasks. His work suggests the extent to which specialization may increase both the range and discretion of work roles. "Chips," as he was invariably called, was assumed to have such knowledge that he required little or no supervision. He was a joiner, a block and spar maker, a caulker, and a blacksmith. It was assumed that he could work with metal as well as with wood, and if work was required about the pumps, or about the iron work aloft (the iron trusses and goose-necks that held the yards to the masts, for instance), it was often the carpenter who was summoned. The carpenter's shop was "sacred to him alone," Frank Bullen tells us. "Under ordinary circumstances the carpenter goes his own way, no man interfering with him, and few knowing what he is employed upon."[11]

Most Saint John vessels did not carry a sailmaker: he was present on about 12 per cent of voyages. The sailmaker was a specialist craftsman whose work required much more than the ability to sew. On a long voyage a vessel carried two or three suits of sails, including a fine-weather suit for regions where winds were light and the weather less stormy. The first task of the sailmaker was to maintain and to repair all sails, and this required some knowledge of the sailmaker's craft and many of the tools of the sailmaker's loft on shore. Preparing sails involved more than merely sewing pieces of canvas together. It required an understanding of the art of cutting sail and the means of stitching boltrope, the ropes sewn along the edges of the sail to give it strength. The sailmaker must work with the cringles, the earings, the robands, and other ropes used to bend the sail to the yard and secure it. Although the sailmaker at sea did not cut and fit entirely new sails, his work could come close to this when a storm had blown a sail to pieces and repairs required the reconstruction of the sail. In such circumstances the sailmaker did not work alone: he worked with deckhands who followed his instructions.[12]

The cook was one petty officer who did not have a supervisory role, unless he had a steward to assist him. And his work required minimal skill, given the materials at his disposal, since it took little time to learn how to boil salt meat, make pea soup and bread, and boil rice. Yet the cook in a large sailing ship did more than this, and he did take supervisory responsibilities that fell more often, in a small schooner, to the master or mate. In a long ocean passage it was essential that the consumption of victuals be planned carefully in order that supplies not run short. The cook must also understand something about the proper means of preserving food. There was also more to the task of cooking than boiling salt meat, since the cook prepared food for masters, officers, and deckhands, and expectations differed. The cook's success depended also on his ability to conceal the poor quality of his provisions or to provide a semblance of variety with limited materials.

The cook was responsible for his own small domain and all its equipment, and a cook who forgot to keep his galley clean was soon compelled to do so. In larger vessels, particularly where there were passengers, the cook was assisted by a steward or stewardess. The steward or stewardess was usually required to tend to the livestock, to clean the linen and chinaware and cutlery in the master's cabin, to serve meals to the crew or passengers, and to help keep the galley clean. The work did not require such levels of skill as other petty officers possessed, but it did have a certain variety, since it combined the role of waiter, domestic servant, and assistant cook. In Canadian vessels the role of cook was often combined with that of steward (see Table 6). This meant that the cook in a large sailing vessel often performed a range of tasks unknown to most cooks on land. Both the variety and the skill were increased by the fact that the cook was also required to help in working the sails, if not regularly, at least when all hands were called.[13]

When a vessel carried all four of these petty officers, as well as a second mate, specialization had not reduced skill or task range. The division of labour, compared to small coastal vessels, merely meant the addition of positions which, although under the command of officers, nevertheless allowed a degree of discretion, task range, and even supervisory responsibility. But what about deckhands? To some extent petty officers had been allocated the skilled tasks of maintenance, repair, and sailmaking which in former times, and especially in small vessels, had been shared among deckhands. The presence of such petty officers, particularly the bosun, limited the discretion and control otherwise falling to deck-hands by ensuring that sailors rarely worked without supervision.

Supervision of deckhands by officers was facilitated by the division of the crew into two groups, the port and the starboard watches. At the beginning of the voyage the crew was assembled and divided, the mate taking the port watch and the second mate taking the starboard watch. The port watch took bunks on the port side of the forecastle, and the starboard watch took the starboard side. In organizing watches, Canadian vessels followed long-established British practice. The same division was used in coastal vessels, but there the separate watches did not always observe a strict schedule of hours on deck and hours at rest.

The term *watch* referred also to the divisions of time that en-sured regular rest periods for the crew. By ancient custom the day was divided into six watches of four hours each, and each watch had its name: from eight in the evening to midnight was first watch; midnight to 4 a.m. was middle watch; 4 a.m. to 8 a.m. was morning watch; 8 a.m. to noon was forenoon watch; and noon to 4 p.m. was afternoon watch. Normally half the crew would be on duty while the other half had "watch below."

The four-hour period from 4 to 8 p.m. was different from the others. If it were treated as a single watch like all the others, then there would have been an even number of watches in a 24-hour day and the men who kept first watch on the first day of the voyage would be keeping first watch on every subsequent day. In order to ensure that this did not happen, the hours between 4 and 8 p.m. were divided into two watches, called first dog watch and second dog watch. This ensured an odd number of watches in a 24-hour day, and each work-group had different four-hour watches on deck on subsequent days.[14]

Work in a sailing vessel was task-oriented, but in large sailing vessels it was also governed by the clock and closely supervised by the officer in charge of one's watch. In ships the clock meant a bell: at 8 p.m. eight bells, to mark the change of watch; at 8.30 one bell, and thereafter one additional bell every half hour until mid-night, when eight bells were rung again. At four bells in the morning watch (6 a.m.) the cook served coffee, after which the watch on deck would begin the daily work (apart from the handling of sails, which could occur at any time). At seven bells (7.30 a.m., but sometimes rung at 7.20 to allow for "coming up") the watch below was called for breakfast. At eight bells (8 a.m.) the watch finishing breakfast went on deck and the watch completing its four hours on deck would have breakfast. Dinner (the midday meal) and supper were similarly at fixed times for each watch. In the second dog watch it was customary for both watches to be on deck – one time that the crew was likely to be on deck together, if the weather were fine, for a common period of leisure.

A pre-industrial division of time and work survived into the late nineteenth century and after: part of the means by which the master enforced work-discipline in a larger and more complex workplace. The division of crew into watches set the relationships between master, officers, and others from the beginning of the voyage. It was a routine that large crews, from various landward backgrounds, could all understand. It served to establish the authority of master and officers from the moment of departure, and it asserted the master's control over time in the workplace. The procedure also ensured that the crew was divided into two groups separated spatially from each other for most of the voyage. The system thus assisted master and mate in maintaining authority over larger crews as vessel size increased. Of course, the division of work and time varied between vessels of different nations, and North American masters were known for their attempts to keep both watches on deck during afternoon watch.[15] Whatever the variations, the system was an essential part of working relationships at sea.

The able seaman was not an unskilled machine-tender, despite the close supervision and regulation of his tasks and his time. In order to understand how skill, including a degree of discretion, may coexist with supervision and prescribed tasks, it is necessary to consider the size and complexity of the workplace. The sailor who joined an ocean-going vessel in the later nineteenth century was part of an expanding wage-paid labour force and part of a larger workplace. When John Froude of Twillingate left the small schooner in which he first crossed the Atlantic and signed on the barques and ships of the 1880s, he found himself in a larger company than ever before.[16] Whereas the coastal mariner worked with five, six, or seven others, the deep-water sailor found himself among a dozen or more. In the vessels of Saint John for which crew lists have been analysed, 36 per cent of all sailors entering port were in a company of 20 or more.[17] The number of fellow workers each sailor would meet in a single voyage would be greater, given the turnover in crew during the voyage. In the Saint John sample of voyages, 80 per cent of which were by vessels rigged as barques or ships, most sailors met at least 22 others during a voyage. On a long voyage one might easily work with 50 or more individuals at different times, if one remained for the duration of the voyage.

If the vessel measured 200 feet in length and 38 feet in width at midships, the total hull capacity might be over 100,000 cubic feet.[18] The vessel was likely to have more than one deck, which so increased the working spaces that total working area was much more than ten times that of the 100-ton schooner. Working spaces also included the masts and spars above the deck. The mainmast might extend 140 feet from deck to truck (the wooden cap at the top of the mast). Foremast and mizzenmast would be slightly shorter (Figure 4). The lower yards would be longer than the hull was wide at midships; a square-rigged ship at mid-century might carry four yards (lower, topmast, topgallant, and royal) on each of its three masts. The bowsprit, projecting over the stem of the vessel, and the jibboom, the further extension of the bowsprit, must also be included among the working areas. In many large vessels the lower yards and the topsail yards carried booms that projected beyond the yardarms, further extending the sail-carrying dimensions of the spars. These booms were called the studdingsail (pronounced stunsail) booms. In a 1,000-ton barque, masts and spars might account for over 1,000 linear feet, excluding the studdingsail booms.[19] Where the small schooner had several hundred feet of canvas in its half-dozen sails, the great barque might carry 20,000 square feet stretched over 20 or more separate sails.

By the 1860s and 1870s the sailing vessel was no longer built of wood and canvas. There was always a certain amount of iron even in small vessels, but by the 1860s iron and copper could account for 20 to 30 per cent of the material costs of a new vessel.[20] In the 1870s, Frank Killam of Yarmouth estimated that a new 1,000-ton ship required about 60 tons of iron.[21] The deckhand was almost as familiar with iron as he was with hemp and manila. The iron knees, bolts and diagonal iron trussing in the hull were perhaps not so obvious; on and above decks he saw iron and chain in many places. The most important change in rigging by mid-century was the introduction of galvanized wire standing rigging, available in Britain in practical form by the 1840s and introduced into Canadian vessels gradually in the following decades.[22] Wire rigging was more durable than hemp, and lighter per fathom.[23] It was also easier to "set up" and maintain in taut position. Throughout the rigging were blocks of various types and sizes: a vessel might carry several hundred blocks, made of wood with iron sheaves and wire stropping. A large vessel might have two capstans and a windlass fitted to iron plates on the fore deck. The capstan was a vertical cylinder, rotated by heaving on wooden bars inserted in the head of the cylinder. Vessels employed patent iron windlasses for raising anchors; the Emerson windlass linked the capstan on deck to a geared windlass below the deck so that when the capstan was turned the windlass below revolved.[24]

The largest anchor in a vessel of 1,000 tons might weigh over 4,000 pounds. Chain cable was commonplace by mid-century, and a hundred fathoms of chain of 2¼-inch diameter links would weigh about 240 hundredweight.[25] With this massive cable came iron chain stoppers, chain hooks, and large iron hawsepipes through which the cable ran. The large vessel would likely carry iron cleats for battening down hatches, iron davits, iron ring bolts for securing boats, and several cast iron or brass pumps. The built wooden masts were encased in iron bands at the masthead, and in some later vessels there were iron or steel yards. The hull, of course, was coppered. Around the decks, set in racks, were belaying pins used to secure or belay running rigging, and some of these pins were iron. On deck there might be two water tanks capable of holding 2,000 gallons each, and each tank had its copper hand-pump. Above the deck and above the deckhouse were ventilators with their iron coamings, providing ventilation to the spaces below.

The deckhand found himself in a workplace of wood and metal, all of which required maintenance and endless cleaning and painting. His vessel carried an array of equipment. A vessel might have 15 lamps for use on deck, brushes, deck scrubbers, fishing lines and nets, and perhaps a harpoon. There were hammers, nails, spikes, screws, grindstone, and a portable forge. There might be several hundred gallons of paint, oils, turpentine, varnish, tar, oakum, and pitch. There would be a dozen or more buckets, casks, and wash-tubs. There was the standard navigational equipment, of course, and there were signal flags and a foghorn. There would be a "fire engine" or pump with a long length of hose. Apart from the extra suit of sails, there were likely to be several hundred fathoms of spare rope of varying sizes.[26]

The differences between the barques of the late nineteenth century and the schooners of previous decades should not be exaggerated. There was no technological revolution here, and many of the changes, such as the introduction of wire rigging, also occurred in schooners. What we are observing is the introduction of greater quantities of iron, multiplication of old techniques, and wider segregation of physical spaces as vessels increased in size. We are also observing increments in the fund of technique and knowledge required to operate a vessel.

The barques and ships of the later nineteenth century differed from their small predecessors and contemporaries not only in scale and detail but also in working environment. The large sailing vessels went far beyond coastal waters, and as time passed greater numbers went beyond the North Atlantic. The sailing ship extended the range of a sailor's knowledge and experience, taking him far beyond his outport home. Maps 6 and 7 offer some indication of the ocean passages undertaken by seamen in the four major fleets of Atlantic Canada (ocean-going vessels registered in Saint John, Yarmouth, Windsor, and Halifax). Map 6 plots the route of vessels in July 1863 (obviously not all vessels were at sea, but where vessels were loading or unloading the route of their prospective or completed passage is plotted).

Although much more detailed analysis of voyages by these fleets has been undertaken elsewhere, these maps allow us to see at a glance where the majority of seamen were working at particular points in time.[27] In 1863 most were within the relatively familiar waters of the North Atlantic. Almost 46 per cent were working a passage between the United Kingdom and British North America. Another 13 per cent were working the passage between a few eastern American ports and the United Kingdom.

The North Atlantic passage could be difficult at any time of year, but the summer passage was familiar to Canadian masters and to most of their crews. It was possible for the seaman to sign on

MAP 6
Mid-July Locations, Vessels and Men of Four Fleets, 1863

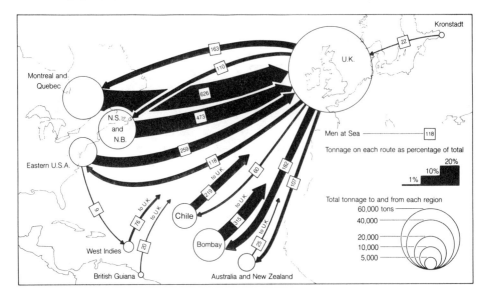

for such voyages and maintain a home in Atlantic Canada, to which he could return on a regular basis. Since coastal vessels frequented the same ports on the Atlantic seaboard from which these ocean vessels departed, the transition from coastal sailing to deep-sea work was not difficult.

But there was something different about the location of vessels and men by 1863, compared to anything we should find for the smaller vessels of Yarmouth discussed in chapter 2. More than a third of sailors in mid-summer 1863 were working passages that took them outside North Atlantic waters. A third of all crews were in the Indian Ocean, the Pacific Ocean, or the South Atlantic, or they were about to enter or leave these oceans. Of every hundred men at sea that summer, about fifteen rounded Cape Horn at least once during the summer or early autumn.

In the decades after 1863 the industrial revolution in shipping altered voyage patterns of sailing ships as steam vessels came to dominate most North Atlantic trades. Sailing vessels had advantages in trades where regularity of service was of little importance and in long-distance trades, which steam vessels entered

MAP 7
Mid-July Locations, Vessels and Men of Four Fleets, 1890

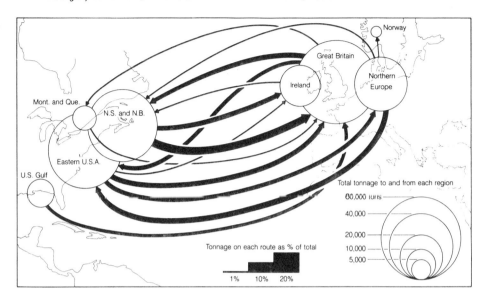

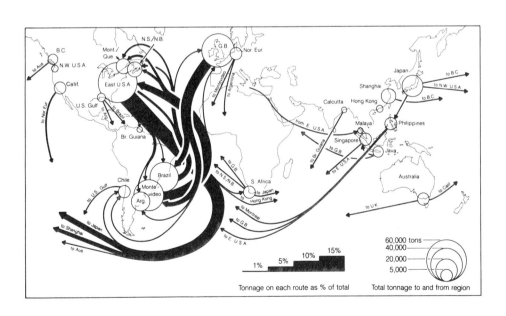

gradually.[28] The general effect of these changes is apparent in Map 7, which shows the trade routes being worked by about 2,600 seamen in mid-summer 1890. The sailors of 1890 found themselves much further removed from their vessels' home ports in Canada. Whereas almost half in 1863 had been working between the British Isles and British North America, by 1890 less than 20 per cent were in those North Atlantic waters. In 1863 most seamen became very familiar with a small number of ports: Saint John, Quebec City, Liverpool, London, Boston, New York, and Philadelphia. By 1890 most sailors entered a wide range of ports, on both sides of the North Atlantic and beyond. Ports in Europe, from Le Havre to Hamburg, saw the arrival of more Canadian sailing ships than in 1863, as did Irish ports and small ports in England and Wales. Sailors entered ports in South America and in the Pacific more often than before. If we count each entry into port by every sailor in the four fleets, we find that about a third of all man-entrances were accounted for by ports outside Europe and the eastern seaboard of North America.

By 1890 sailors could still remain within the major North Atlantic trade routes if they waited for berths in particular vessels. But in mid-summer 1890 the majority in our four major fleets were outside the North Atlantic or in vessels about to leave the North Atlantic. A third were on vessels sailing to or from the South Atlantic, calling at ports in Brazil, Uruguay, or Argentina. A quarter of all crews were in the Pacific or Indian oceans during the summer of 1890. This somewhat static analysis of the distribution of vessels and men does not capture fully the change between 1863 and 1890, which was not merely spatial – it was also temporal. Given the relative distances involved, crews were spending more time outside the North Atlantic than the breakdown of mid-summer locations might suggest. The lines on the map must be seen not only as voyage patterns across the sea but also as very crude approximations of time, or man-hours spent in each ocean. It is impossible to calculate precisely the working hours spent in each part of the world, but in one fleet – that of Windsor – voyage duration has been broken down by major trade routes. The result suggests that by the 1890s less than a quarter of total man-days were spent on voyages wholly within the North Atlantic. Of course a portion of time on voyages to South America and into the Pacific was spent in the North Atlantic. But even when this is taken into account, by the 1890s over 40 per cent of all man-days were spent outside the North Atlantic.[29]

The late-nineteenth-century sailor had a working experience very different from that of his father or grandfather. Not only was his vessel likely to be very much larger and more complex than the vessel of the early nineteenth century, but it had to be worked in a greater variety of conditions and climates, and sailors were in their vessels for longer periods of time. This was, perhaps, the most important difference between the deep-water sailor and the coastal mariner: for the deep-water man, the vessel was not merely a temporary domicile; it was a home for months and even years. At the beginning of each voyage the sailor signed the crew list, and the agreement specified the term of service – the maximum time that the sailor agreed to serve in the vessel. In half of the crew lists for the vessels of Saint John between 1863 and 1914 the term was for one year; in almost 40 per cent, from 18 months to three years.

But actual voyage duration increased over time and with vessel size. In vessels under 250 tons the average voyage was under four months; over 1,500 tons, nine months (of course not all sailors remained for the full duration of the voyage).[30] In some fleets the change in voyage time could be dramatic: the average voyage by Windsor ocean-going vessels lasted five months in the early 1860s; by the first decade of the twentieth century the average voyage was almost 12 months in duration. Of course vessels often put into port during a voyage, and crew might be granted shore leave in some ports – but the deep-sea sailor was accustomed to spending months at sea between ports of call. In the small coastal vessel, passage times between ports were measured in days or (for the vessel sailing to the West Indies) in weeks. Passages by vessels of 250 to 500 tons averaged about 50 days. By the 1890s the average passage for a Saint John vessel of 1,500 tons was over 3½ months.[31]

The great barques and ships of Atlantic Canada incorporated the products of the industrial revolution in their hulls and their rigging, and they shattered the barriers of pre-industrial, localized market-places, just as the industrial revolution did in other economic sectors. The merchant capitalists of Atlantic Canada no longer operated within colonial and West Indies markets for local staple products; now they sold their services in world-wide markets. The barques and ships transformed the relationship between work and time, just as industrialization did in other spheres. The coastal mariner's craft was governed by the seasons rather than the clock, and there was no neat temporal division between work and leisure. In the great ocean-going barque, work was less seasonal. There were fewer departures, or voyage starts, in winter months, but ocean-going vessels did not cease work in winter. If voyage starts were randomly distributed through the year we should expect 25 per cent of them to occur in December, January, or February; in the Saint John fleet 21 per cent of all voyages began in those three months. The Newfoundlander John Froude, accustomed to the seasonal nature of work in his birthplace, commented on the oddity of living in summer almost continuously for 12 months; the deep-sea sailor, he noted, might see no winter for 10 years, "if you Take the right boat to sail in."[32]

In conditions of such variety and complexity the seaman's skill was preserved, even as specialization and new divisions of labour increased. The traditional definition of able seaman was that he could "hand, reef and steer." In fact the able seaman did more than this, and even his basic tasks required an extensive knowledge of the purposes and functions of the working parts of a ship. The able seaman had to know an entire language of work.[33] One of the most common reasons for demotion of an able seaman to ordinary seaman was inability to understand orders. "We are supposed to know The names of the sails and ropes of The ship we an unboard of," writes John Froude. His abbreviated list of sails and ropes includes about a hundred different items. Referring only to the rigging, Froude writes:

Now as these sails are set we need to know all the
Ropes or running gear before we can reef clew
Or furl. Which we has to do if these sails are set
And the names of these ropes are as follows. flying jib
Halliards. jib halliards. troat halliards. peak halliards
Royal halliards. topgallant halliards. royalbraces
Topgallant braces topsail braces. fore and main
Braces. preventer maine braces. after maine braces
Royal lifts. topgallant lifts. topsail lifts. man lifts
Royal sheets. topgallant sheets. topsail sheets
Main sheets. Royal clewling. topgallant clewing
Clewgarnets. fore tack. topsail buntlines. reef burtons

Main bowlines. top bowlings. leech lines. slablines
Spankers brail and outhall. boom topping lift.
Boom sheet. fore topmast stays. halliards
Flying jib downhall. jib downhall fore topmast
Stays. downhal flying jib sheets. jib sheets
Fore topmast stays. sheets. Now there are the
Standing rigging to be named Which is as
Follows. stays. shouds. backstays. bobstays
Bowsprit shrouds. gammoing. futtock shrouds
Lanyards. ratlings. back ropes. jib guys. footropes
Topgallant rigging. royal rigging. sheer poles
After swifters and catch ratlines[34]

There are two main types of equipment in Froude's list. First, the standing rigging supported the masts against fore and aft or athwartships strains (Figure 5). It is called standing rigging because it is made fast, and not hauled upon, although many of the ropes required resetting when they became slack. Stays supported the masts from forward; shrouds and backstays provided lateral support. The bowsprit, although it does not rise from the deck but projects from the bow, is like a mast and has its own stays.

The second category of rigging is the running rigging, the ropes by which yards, booms, and sails are manipulated for trimming sail to the wind or for making or shortening sail (Figure 6). Froude refers to lifts and halyards, ropes used to raise and lower spars and sails. Lifts ran from mast to yards and provided upward support as well as canting the yards in a vertical plane. Froude refers to tacks and sheets, which hold down the lower corners of sails. The braces are ropes used to traverse a yard in a horizontal plane; to "brace up" a yard means to swing it into a more acute angle with the keel. Braces were named for the yard that they controlled and for the side of the vessel on which they were found – port or starboard, or, at sea, "lee" or "weather." The rigging also provided sailors the means of going aloft and laying on the yards to handle sails. Ratlines are the rope steps that form the ladder up the shrouds. Footropes extend from the middle of the yard to its extremities, the yardarms, and sailors stand on the footropes when furling or reefing sail. These are merely the main elements of rigging. It would require a long technical treatise to explain all the ropes that John Froude used and understood.[35]

FIGURE 5   Principal Elements of a Ship's Standing Rigging

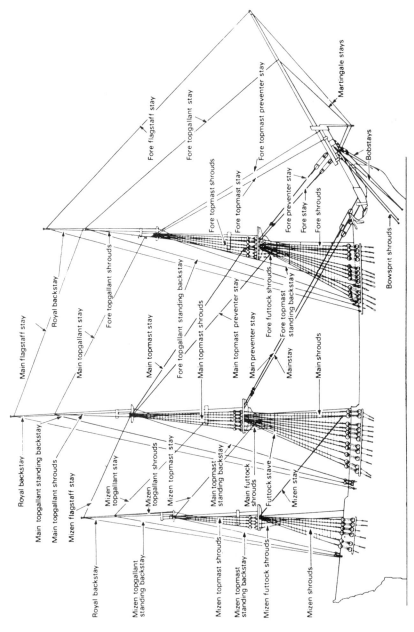

Source: Oxford Companion to Ships and the Sea by Peter Kemp. Published by Oxford University Press 1976 © Oxford University Press 1976.

FIGURE 6

Foremast: Principal Elements of a Ship's Running Rigging

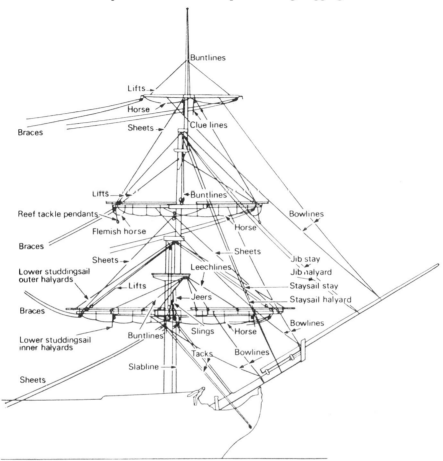

Source: Oxford Companion to Ships and the Sea by Peter Kemp. Published by Oxford University Press 1976 © Oxford University Press 1976.

Froude's list of running gear includes only a part of the equipment used to "hand, reef and steer." The first of these tasks meant the furling of sails, or making the sail fast to its yard, which required not only manual dexterity but knowledge of the various ropes used to take in and secure the sail. Reefing meant reducing a sail's area by taking in a portion of it, and "there is an old saying amongst seamen that any fool can make sail, but it requires a skilful sailor to take it in."[36] Reefing the sail meant securing the sail to its yard by reef-points, short pieces of rope sewn into a band running horizontally across a sail, easily visible in many paintings of nineteenth-century sailing ships.

The task of reefing illustrates particular components of the seaman's skill. Reefing required not only a technical vocabulary and an understanding of the operation of sails and running rigging but also several separate but simultaneous actions by workers, each of whom co-ordinated his labour with that of every other worker, including those on deck. When a topsail was being reefed, the yard was first lowered in order to spill the wind from the sail. With the yard held firm by its braces, the men went out on the yard, standing on the footropes. Reefing was often done in a strengthening wind, and elbows, hands, and feet were all employed to hold one's position and move along the yard.

The work of the men aloft was co-ordinated with the man at the wheel, to make the work both easier and safer. If the sail were full it might billow up over the yard and knock the men backward. The yard was therefore braced, and the wheel turned, so that the sail was taking the wind at an acute angle, the wind lifting the sail very slightly, to assist the men in hauling in the sail. The sailors reached down over the yard to seize the reef-points. The order was given to "haul out" and all pulled to windward. The man at the yardarm "passed the earing" – lashed the outer corner of the sail to the yard-arm (passing the earing was no simple task in itself, and seaman's manuals suggest much variation in the method of passing the rope around the yard). The men then hauled to leeward, so that the man at the other yardarm could pass the lee earing. The men then let go the reef-points and gathered up the sail, first in small folds and then in larger folds, holding each fold tight under the chest while gathering the next. The folds were brought to the upper forward side of the yard, the after reef-points were brought around the yard to meet the forward reef-points, and the two points were reef-knotted. If the job were done properly the folds were tight, there were no bulges or granny knots, and the folded sail would shed water.

The procedure was simplified by its regular pattern and the standardized location of all equipment and rope. The seaman could find the required ropes because they were in roughly the same place in all vessels. But the process of shortening or taking in sail was complicated by the conditions in which the work was done.

Often men working together on a yard had to co-ordinate their actions with each other, and with men on deck, when they could not see each other. Working the sails might be done in high winds and heavy precipitation, and sometimes at night. Sailors developed extraordinary night vision: Richard Henry Dana's model British seaman had "eyes he might have sold to a duchess at the price of diamonds, such was their brilliancy," and those eyes gave him "the sight of a vulture."[37] But sailors also worked without the benefit of sight, when the weather made vision the least useful of human senses. Knowledge of the vessel and its working parts was so deeply ingrained in the experienced seaman as to be part of the unconscious mind. The experienced seaman relied on his sense of touch (one rarely found gloves among a seaman's personal effects) and on a highly developed tactile memory, and these were parts of his knowledge and skill.

There is no better way to perceive the co-ordinated labour of deckhands than to see the work performed, or to hear the sailor's account of it. But deckhands rarely wrote about the ordinary work of sailhandling, and we cannot interview those who worked in Canadian vessels a century ago. Fortunately the techniques of the older wooden ships were briefly preserved in the twentieth century, and the historian of the 1980s may ask other Canadians, who went to sea in the 1920s, about the ordinary working experience that they inherited from the previous generation. Listening to these men, and watching them demonstrate the work of hauling on braces as they did it decades ago, we learn that even the simple task of hauling on rope becomes more complicated than a landsman might expect.

It's a team business ... We had decks awash all the time, slippery as hell ... When they holler 'lee fore braces' the senior man goes to the block, right up to the block on top of the bulwarks, and the others take their places in order of rank – you've all got ranks – and the junior boy goes to the belaying pin, and takes the turns off and holds until they are ready to start pulling, and when the senior man looks over his shoulder and says 'ready there' then ... he's probably waiting for the mate or second mate on the other side, the weather side, to slacken away the weather braces, so he's watching across the deck, and when the second mate says 'haul away' and is slacking the weather braces this fellow says 'hand over hand' to take hand over hand, and now he says 'long pulls' and he says 'hey, hey,

... *hey*vee' and hey, hey, ... *hey*vee' and so you do it in unison with the calls, which are generally spoken of as the hilly-hollying, by the senior man. And you all lay into it like that, and you can't put your two feet together out here, you've got to maintain your balance, and it's slippery.

This work is being done in response to orders, but even the junior boy must understand what is happening and even his work requires training:

The junior boy takes a turn over the belaying pin, usually across the top and once under, not more than that, because he's going to have to take in more slack when the fellows give it to him, and the senior man is watching them, and watching the weather brace and the lee brace, and when he sees it slackening down he gives a shout and everybody pulls again, and the junior boy then takes that in, and God help him if he loses some of it (that's the kind of thing I used to do for the first three months in my first ship, slacken away ten inches of hard won pull, and everybody says aw shit why must we go to sea with stupid young bastards like this). And you want the braces pulled good and tight so the yards don't flop around. So the man at the head end, when the second mate says that's good 'haul tight' and he makes fast the weather brace, your senior man gives one last hilly holly and then he says 'swig it' and everybody turns sideways and pulls straight out like that and they give back in the direction of the belaying pin. So you put tremendous stress on the rope by the swigging effect and you're in not too bad a position to give it all the other way, and the junior boy has to take the turn off and secure it so he doesn't lose any of it, and if he does that you refrain from commenting on his ancestry. You don't say well done, or anything. [38]

The experience of working the braces was so commonplace that it does not enter sailor's memoirs. But in these words lies a world of work and skill that was the heart of the sailor's life at sea. The work is prescribed and repetitive, but it requires training and knowledge. Workers respond to spoken orders, but there is only one officer present, a second mate on the weather side, and the "senior man" is an able seaman. There is supervision, but this is teamwork that includes the officer, and the workers are self-supervising, scolding any of their number who does not co-ordinate his labour with theirs. There is a hierarchy of rank, even among deckhands, but this is communal work in a vessel carrying no extra men, and each man depends on every other.

To haul on rope, one applied muscular strength and several related bits of knowledge: how to place one's feet; how to brace muscles, vertebrae, legs, and arms; and how to apply both gravity and muscular power. "Swigging" was a basic seaman's technique: one secured one's feet on rails or bulwarks at waist height and hauled out and down until the body was horizontal, and the resulting force applied to rope combined the weight of the body with the forces of gravity and muscular action.[39] Such work required more than strength in the hands, but sailors acquired hands that were thick and hard. An old man, long retired from the sea, might remember his own young hands as they once were, and the very different hands of his mate: "I feel for the chain hook which he is handing me, moving my hands, the knuckles of which are broken and bloody, from side to side in the pitchy dark. My hand touches his. There is no warmth in his hand. It is like an iron hand, cold, hard as the iron of the freeing ports."[40] If there is no such tangible record of skill, this does not mean that skill did not exist.

Even if such work took practice and experience, it is possible that one part of skill remains missing. Where workers followed orders and performed prescribed tasks, however difficult, it is possible that there was no room for independent thought or judgment on the part of the able seaman. All decisions about tacking, wearing, furling, and reefing – and about navigation – were taken by the master. But it would be misleading to suggest that the work was robbed of all discretion content. The variety of tasks to be performed, and the very complexity of the vessel, made it impossible to prescribe all work, or to remove all decisions from the worker himself. There is a connection between task range and discretion, and even if the sailor knew nothing of these academic distinctions, his words confirm the point:

A ship is a lot like my forests and paths. Something has happened every time you walk a certain route. Every time you go up this mast, every time you go along this yard, you see something that needs attention. And one of the things that I learned very early, and maintained through all my seafaring days, was the way in which a man would come down from aloft … and he would be told by the second mate, for example, "lay for'ard and take a look at the upper t'gans'l – I think the clip-hooks have lost their mousing" … – Whether he had fixed it or not, the chances are not too remote, in fact it was quite likely, that when he came back to the poop he'd say, "I see that there's a bit of chafing gear lost off the mainstay." And the mate would say, "Jesus ... well, put it back." And this fellow would go for'ard and get some spunyarn or whatever and he'd go up there and put it back. But he would go and report knowing full well that the mate would send him straight back to repair it.[41]

Deckhands watched the many small parts of their great machine not because they were ordered to do so but because they had compelling personal reasons for doing so. An ill-attended ship would make a slower passage and more work, and inattention could mean increased personal risks. The danger inherent in any work may not by itself imply a level of skill, but the recurring dangers in seafaring affected sailors and their relations with each other. Danger increased vigilance and mutual dependence: "And oh, the innumerable occasions! when you'd be slithering about a deck, you know, and a hand'll catch you and pull you up, and something like 'By Christ you were bloody near for it then weren't you?' "[42] And danger could be a challenge to pride and skill. Benjamin Doane of Barrington, Nova Scotia, tells us about an occasion when pride compelled him to ignore the command of his mate and make his own decisions:

We had taken in the mizzen royal, topgallant sail and crossjack course, the main royal and topgallant sail and the fore royal when the fore-topgallant sheet parted and unrove out of the topsail yard. As the clew swung forward, the frazzled end of the sheet flew out and caught around the fore royal stay. We lowered the topgallant sail down but, with the sheer caught, we were unable to haul up the weather clew, which was slatting away out of reach, ready to split any moment. I went up to the royal masthead and got out on the stay. It shook so from the surging of the sail that I was afraid to go down.

Mr. Fields was watching me. Seeing me start down the stay, he yelled, "Come back, Dan, don't go down there – Down on deck with you, I say ... " I pulled out my sheath knife, got my legs around the stay, and slid down. The stay was shaking so that though my teeth were well rooted I had to clench them to keep them in my mouth. The mate kept hailing, "Hold on, boy, hold on." I sawed away with the sheath knife on the rope until it was cut through, and then slid down the stay to the jibboom. When I came in on deck the mate shook me by the shoulders and said, "What a man you are, Dan, I never expected to see you come down alive. Why didn't you come down when I told you to?" "Well," I said, "I was afraid you'd send somebody else up there, and if he did what I didn't dare do, I'd be forever ashamed of myself."[43]

Because of frequent dangers involved in working aloft, or even on deck, working in the lee scuppers with the sea coming over the sides, knowledge was often essential to survival, and the correct decision about hands, feet, body, and machinery could mean life or instant death. As often as men died at sea, more often they were close to death:

We had quite a squall hit us, and the chief mate was on watch ... and he said to me "I'm scared about that royal" and I think it was a weak sail, and I took it as a request that I attend to it myself. I jumped into the rigging and ran up to that royal yard, and I went out on it, and the squall hit us before I got well started, and nobody else was on his way up. I got that yard partly furled when ... the sail just went out in front of me ... and the sail was going just like you were shaking a carpet and the yard was shaking something awful. I didn't think I could stay on it but I took my feet off the footropes, and wrapped my arms around the yard, and I managed to get one arm through under the sail and embraced the yard, lying on it with my legs wrapped as much as I could ... and there I watched what was going on on deck. And I saw the captain himself come off the poop and run to the buntlines of that main royal, and call men in ... And when I stepped onto the deck my friend was there and he said "we thought you were going to come down."[44]

There was discretion here, and much more. A sailor's instinct told him to defy a basic rule of work aloft – keeping one's feet on the footropes. And in the moment of danger orders became requests, and a master left his place on the poop. We witness not trained obedience to external controls, but the co-ordinated exercise of judgment and self-control.

Sailhandling was the major part of the able seaman's skill, but his labour included many other tasks, and there is no doubting the variety of his work. Some tasks required considerable knowledge; others did not. Steering was not one of the simpler tasks, and demotion often followed from inability to steer. The man at the wheel was given a course to steer, in points rather than the modern degrees. Before him was the magnetic compass, mounted in its binnacle. The compass card, marked with the standard 32 points, rotated to the movement of a magnetized needle, and on the forward side of the compass bowl a line, often known as the "lubber's line," indicated the direction of the ship's head. The magnetic compass tended to be sluggish, and the helmsman had to check the vessel's heading in relation to distant clouds, or even the sea.

But the experienced seaman could also judge whether the vessel was coming to or falling off by the feel of the wheel in his hands and by the feel and the sound of the wind. If the vessel's head moved toward the wind, the helm felt heavier and the wind felt stronger. This ability to feel the motion of the vessel was all the more important in a large square-rigged vessel because the vast display of canvas, spread before the helmsman, could limit his vision of sea and sky before him. When working the vessel to windward, the helmsman had to steer "by the wind," keeping the vessel's head as close to the wind as possible without letting the wind fall from the sails, still less allowing the wind to strike the forward side of the sails. Steering required careful observation of the way the wind was entering the sails, as much as observation of the compass. In difficult conditions, or when passing from one tack to another, or when entering port, the helmsman responded to orders given by the master or mate. These orders did not consist merely of compass points. The order might refer to the number of spokes of the wheel to be raised or lowered, and in which direction. But orders could be even more complicated, especially when steering by the wind, and we must add another set of terms to the seaman's vocabulary.[45]

The great barque was often motionless for days on end, while her crew awaited the trade winds. Even when the vessel was motionless there was work, for the vessel had to be maintained and repaired while at sea. In the great ocean-going vessel the majority of time might be spent at tasks other than sailhandling. In a sailing vessel the standing rigging became slack with use, particularly where the rigging was hemp or manila. Setting up the rigging, by ensuring that the shrouds were taut, could occupy a crew for many hours during a passage. Another task involving the rigging was putting on chafing gear: where the rigging was being worn by contact with yards or other ropes, it must be protected by applying yarn or canvas or other gear.

Work with ropes did not end with such tasks, however. Rope can easily rot when it is continuously wet, and so it must be wormed, parcelled, and served. Worming involved passing a small rope spirally around a hemp cable; parcelling followed – small strips of tarred canvas were wound around the wormed rope. In serving, spunyarn was wound around the rope using a serving mallet for maximum tension. Much of the yarn used in the vessel might be made on board. Splicing rope was more than merely joining two pieces of rope in a standard way, because there were many kinds of splices: short splices, long splices, eye splices, grummets, and many more.[46]

A twentieth-century landsman, thrown into such work, tells us something about the importance of rope in the seaman's life: "Three quarters of my waking time is devoted to fondling rope – untying it, tying it up again, pulling it up, pulling it down, heaving it, doing forwards-upwards-sideways-downwards physical jerks with it, or else quoiting it neatly on pegs along the bulwark railing and around the masts ... For the first two weeks of the trip I suffered wretchedly from a rope complex. The thing became a nightmare to me. I used to awake from horrible ropey dreams to find my arms and shoulders twitching as though I were still pulling rope. During the second week I had a horrible physical revulsion for all shapes and sizes of rope."[47]

The sailor worked with rope and metal. Scraping rust and polishing metal were regular tasks. So were painting and varnishing. Scrubbing the decks was not simply a matter of applying a scrubbing brush. The holystone was a piece of sandstone used to scour the deck to a smooth, even surface, before washing it with salt water. If a vessel were to be kept watertight, the crew might undertake some caulking: driving oakum or hot pitch into the seams in the vessel's decks or sides. A well-stocked vessel would carry a supply of oakum, but on a long voyage crew members might be employed picking oakum – picking apart the hemp from old ropes (picking oakum was an old workhouse task in Britain and a punishment in the navy).

Of course a vessel was never completely watertight, and so manning the pumps was another commonplace task. The able seaman knew how to use a palm and needle, the basic tools of the sailmaker. On many voyages one might find the bosun and able seamen repairing and refitting masts, spars, blocks, or other wood-work and ironwork about their vessel. An able seaman might complain of many things, but never of boredom. There might be idle moments, in the dog watches or at night, but even the idle sailor was watchful and alert to the sounds and motion of his craft.

A final point about Canadian vessels confirms the variety of tasks that fell to the able seaman, as well as the limits to supervision and external control. Perhaps the most important conclusion to be drawn from Table 6 is that a majority of vessels had no second mate. Further, while there were many bosuns, sailmakers, and carpenters in the fleets of Atlantic Canada, all three were present only in a minority of voyages. Many of the tasks of these specialists fell to able seamen in Canadian (and American) vessels, and, as Frank Bullen noted, "the business of sailmaking, like carpentry, is in those vessels considered tacitly to be part of the education of a thorough seaman."[48] Shipowners sought to maintain managerial control but also to minimize labour costs. In doing so they helped preserve the task range and skill of the able seaman.

Canadian ships rarely carried apprentices, and there was no parallel to Britain's system. Shipowners saw little advantage in hiring untrained boys, even at low wages, and there was little social or political pressure to train young men for careers as officers in the merchant marine or a domestic navy. Ordinary seamen and boys were hired, but these were a small minority even among deck-hands. Often ordinary seaman was a rank to which an AB was demoted if he were found incapable of steering or working aloft.[49] The OS was a man on probation, and although he was expected to take his "trick" at the wheel, he was also likely to find himself cleaning up plates after dinner and sweeping up the forecastle at the bidding of the ABs. Even a man with experience in coastal schooners was likely to be hired as an OS on his first deep-sea voyage in a square-rigger. He was the novitiate, who tells us not that shipowners were interested in giving men training but that there was a universal understanding that able seamen possessed a definable skill and knowledge to which lesser men must still aspire.

In the large sailing ships that Canadians inherited and acquired, much of the knowledge of seafaring was the exclusive possession of the master. This was a result of inherited traditions, reinforced by statutory regulations and professionalization. To this extent the able seaman was not sharing in the conception of tasks that he executed. One measure of the gulf between master and seaman is this: a vessel suddenly deprived of master and officers was likely to be lost, her crew unable to find their way to land, and there were occasions when this happened.[50] But able seamen were not living appendages to the machine or unthinking subjects to the will of an all-powerful master. The master was a craftsman. His able seamen were skilled mechanics who spoke their own language and took their work and its mystery into the age of iron and steel.

CHAPTER FIVE

Recruitment

"Men go to sea, before they know the unhappiness of that way of life; and when they come to know it, they cannot escape from it, because it is then too late to choose another profession; as indeed is generally the case with men, when they have once engaged in a particular way of life."[1] Dr Johnson expressed a commonplace view of seafaring, and one that much of the literature would seem to confirm. For sailors the horizon of choice was narrow: none but the ignorant or the desperate would surely enter such a workplace. On both sides of the Atlantic in the nineteenth century one heard laments about the deteriorating quality of the merchant sailor: the apprenticeship system was declining, the young and ambitious went into better and safer employment on land, and seafaring attracted either foreigners or the least reliable of the local labour pool.[2]

The plight of the sailor in Canadian vessels would seem to have been particularly serious. Ports on the Atlantic seaboard were high-wage ports, and alternative employment on land was available. Canadian masters had a reputation for brutality and "defiance of law."[3] Little wonder that Frederick William Wallace concluded that many masters "had to take what they could get ... fakers of the Paddy West school, jailbirds anxious to get out of the country, and degenerates whom no master or mate would take for ballast."[4] By their behaviour in port, sailors confirmed the impression that they were the rough, not the respectable working men. A superficial reading of the literature might easily lead to Dr Johnson's conclusion, and to the notion that sailors were trapped in a culture of poverty and moral debility, both by their social backgrounds and by their workplace.

It is difficult, even a century later, to shed assumptions embedded even in the language of historical discourse. Were sailors rough or respectable? Were they unusually prone to socially unacceptable behaviour, perhaps because of the severely confining nature of their workplace? To frame the questions in this way is to accept the terms of the nineteenth-century moral reformer. Respectability, after all, was a normative category that may tell us more about bourgeois values than about working-class behaviour. The distinction between rough and respectable was highly fluid, and social historians have shown that working people could adopt or shed the guise of respectability as it suited them.[5] Such distinctions, moreover, emerged from nineteenth-century urban and industrial society, and they are something of an anachronism when applied to sailors in the merchant marine of Atlantic Canada.

The sailors from British North America, if not those from Britain, came from pre-industrial communities wherein the distinctions of social class were often blurred by the prevalence of petty commodity production. Sailors from these communities were not merely sailors: they were the children of fishermen, coastal mariners, farmers, and village craftsmen. The distintion between rough and respectable dissolves in this context: the men of the forecastle defy such categories, and they defy the condescension of Frederick William Wallace. The old distinctions dissolve, not because we know more today about the sailor but because a massive reconstruction of the evidence, both literary and quantitative, allows us to locate seafaring workers in the framework of community and class. We begin to perceive these workers differently because we may ask not only how they behaved, but who they were, and whence they came.

Did men go to sea because they had no choice? There must have been those who went to sea to escape poverty or a worse fate on land. But there is no reason to believe that such motives would be more important in this industry than in lumbering, for instance. While many sailors refer to poverty or, as in John Froude's case, the difficulty of making a living in fishing, almost all refer to the positive attractions of the seafaring life. Seafaring attracted men with ambition to see the world, to acquire skills, and to share warm comradeship that they saw and envied in sailors:

> when I was a boy between twelve and sixteen
> I used to go unboard of the old english vessels that came in from
> distand lands I took a great delight in sitting around listening
> to the old sailours spinning long yarns and singing their quear
> old songs of mountains green and burning sands
> and the bonny brown girls of riogrand[6]

In Tancook, Nova Scotia, a young blacksmith's apprentice was reading novels that "filled my mind with strange and wonderful ideas of the rest of the world," and he soon left the blacksmith to go to sea.[7] The young man who signed crew articles for the first time in his life thought he "had done just the grand thing."[8] The young George Spicer, born in a farming family along the Bay of Fundy, saw almost every day of his childhood the sailing vessels in nearby waters and signed on a schooner at the age of 12. This was the fulfilment of a childhood ambition, not a desperate escape.[9]

Having gone to sea the worker was not trapped there. Sailors made the transition to work on land, and the skills acquired at sea served them well on land. In London sailors often found work as stevedores and shipworkers in the docks (the more skilled of dock workers), and Charles Booth found ex-sailors in a wide range of occupations.[10] In Canada former sailors, because of their special skills, found work installing telephone poles and wires, or as carpenters, stevedores, or in ropeworks.[11] The age profile of sailors serving in Atlantic Canadian vessels shows that the occupation was that of younger men. There was no typical sailor, but most clearly entered the occupation as young men and left before their late thirties or their forties.

There were other reasons why the sailor could find work on land, apart from his particular skills. The seafarer was already trained to work discipline; he possessed great muscular strength and agility, if he survived; and he was trained to accept order and neatness, since much of his work had been related to maintaining a clean and orderly ship, with "a place for everything and everything in its place."[12] And in the communities from which Canadian sailors came, working people did not assume a single lifetime occupation for themselves. Occupational pluralism extended to seafaring, and sailors such as Benjamin Doane and John Froude leave us with the impression of easy movement between sea and land. Between voyages the young Doane dug potatoes, scythed hay, cut timber,

TABLE 7

Age of Sailors in Four Fleets, 1863–1912

Age	Number	% of Total
1–9	14	0
10–19	16,181	8.9
20–29	100,915	55.7
30–39	42,525	23.5
40–49	17,781	9.8
50–59	3,490	1.9
60 +	328	0.2
Total	181,234	100

Source: Crew lists for vessels registered in Saint
John, Yarmouth, Halifax, and Windsor; MHA.
Number missing: 1,427.

and helped to build ships, working for various members of an
extended family as need arose.[13]

Most of those who served in Atlantic Canadian vessels were men,
and they were men with experience at sea. The occupants of
182,661 berths (excluding masters) in four fleets have been analysed (see Table 7); only 765 of these were women.[14] Almost all of
these sailors, of either sex, appear to have had previous experience
at sea. For 63 per cent of the sample the registry of the sailor's
previous vessel is stated on the crew list. Of these, almost 20 per
cent had previously served in the same vessel; 34 per cent had
served in the same vessel or another vessel from Nova Scotia or New
Brunswick. Another 30 per cent had previously served in vessels
from the United Kingdom or Ireland. Of those for whom a
previous vessel is given, only 2.3 per cent were said to be in their
first vessel.

Even if this last figure understates the proportion of those lacking experience, the overwhelming majority of crew members were
men of experience in their work, even though the majority were
young. There was a high retention rate – one in every five sailors
had chosen to work in the same vessel in which he had worked on
his previous voyage, rather than seek another vessel. Further, one
in every three sailors had previously served in a British North
American vessel. The retention rate indicates a degree of stability

in the labour force that we might not have expected. It also suggests something important about sailors themselves: in the context of easy movement between sea and land and between occupations, they were exercising a degree of choice about the vessels in which they worked.

If no process of selection were at work, then we should expect sailors to have been distributed randomly through all fleets on their previous voyages. The registries of previous vessels would then appear roughly in proportion to each national fleet's share of world tonnage, assuming only that Atlantic Canadian vessels departed from the same ports that other national fleets frequented. The assumption is difficult to test.[15] But the high retention rate cannot be explained by the fact that the vessels in our sample depart regularly from ports dominated by Atlantic Canadian ships, thereby increasing the chances that sailors would have served previously in such vessels. Only 9.2 per cent of all crew members signed articles in British North American ports. The relationship between registry of last ship and place joined (aggregated into countries) is not very strong, and in fact no less than 84 per cent of all crew members signed on in British, European, or US ports, which were frequented by British, European, Scandinavian, American, and other national fleets.[16] If the sailors were randomly distributed among national fleets on their previous voyages, between 4 and 7 per cent of crews would have served on Canadian vessels on their previous voyage.[17] Since a third of them had served in Canadian vessels, we may conclude that there was a bias or preference for Canadian vessels among this sample. Of course this should be no surprise: it says merely that those serving in a Canadian vessel exhibited a preference of some kind for a Canadian vessel, which is self-evident.

The retention rate is of interest for two reasons, however. First, it suggests that masters could and did hire crews with previous experience in British North American or British vessels. Second, their ability to hire crews with previous experience in Canadian vessels increased over time. In the Saint John fleet, for instance, 24.2 per cent of crews between 1863 and 1878 had served previously in a New Brunswick vessel; by the 1891–1914 period this proportion had risen to 28 per cent. The retention rate remained high despite two trends that might have discouraged crew to remain in New Brunswick vessels: first, the pressures on owners and masters of local sailing vessels increased as sailing ship freight rates fell; and second, with the decline in the fleets of Atlantic Canada there was a smaller available pool of workers whose previous vessel had been Canadian.

The retention rate, by this admittedly partial measure, did not have much to do with the sailor's birthplace. One might expect a relationship between the last ship in which a man served and his nationality: that is, Nova Scotians would be more likely to come from Nova Scotian vessels, Americans from American vessels, and so on. The statistical relationship is not very strong.[18] There is evidence, however, that New Brunswickers and Nova Scotians *were* exercising a preference, even if others were not. Using the Saint John crew file only, it was found that New Brunswickers working in a Saint John vessel were very likely to have served previously on a New Brunswick vessel (62.1 per cent, compared to only 23 per cent for other nationalities). Even the Nova Scotians serving in a Saint John vessel were likely to have served previously in the same Saint John vessel or in another New Brunswick vessel (49.5 per cent). Of all British North Americans in the fleet, two thirds had been in a British North American vessel on their previous voyage. The weak statistical relationship between previous ship and nationality is accounted for mainly by the Europeans, Americans, and Scandinavians, who had previously served in vessels of other nationalities as well as their own. Of course there were many possible motives for joining particular vessels, but British North Americans apparently preferred to serve in vessels from their part of the world, if they could.

It is not possible to follow many individual sailors through their careers and to analyse conclusively their choices and their employers'. But some conclusions are certain. The process of hiring crew, whether through government shipping offices or through crimps, often limited choice on both sides. The sailor often knew little about the current condition and seaworthiness of the vessel in which he agreed to serve. Further, the master sometimes knew little about his crew, but took what the shipping office or the crimp gave him.

However, such limits to choice should not be exaggerated. The legal necessity of signing a contract before serving in an ocean-going vessel changed the hiring process and gave both sides the time and opportunity to acquire prior information about the

TABLE 8

Birthplaces of Masters in Four Fleets, 1863-1914

Birthplace	Saint John Vessels (%)	Yarmouth Vessels (%)	Windsor Vessels (%)	Halifax Vessels (%)
(Port of registry)	(14.1)	(80.2)	(29.4)	(9.7)
Total New Brunswick	39.7	1.2	3.2	3.0
Total Nova Scotia	29.8	90.8	84.8	74.0
Other BNA	1.5	0.8	0.9	1.9
United States	2.1	0.6	1.2	1.0
England	9.4	2.0	2.4	8.6
Wales	1.8	0.7	0.3	1.0
Scotland	6.4	0.9	3.8	4.0
Ireland	6.6	1.3	1.8	3.8
Scandinavia	1.7	0.2	0.6	1.0
Other Europe	0.8	1.4	0.5	0.7
Other	0.2	0	0.5	1.0
Total	100	100	100	100
Number	9,518	5,781	3,646	1,838

Source: Crew Lists, MHA. There could be more than one master per voyage; hence the number of masters exceeds the number of voyages in the files for each port.

other. For their part, sailors were informed of the nature of the voyage, the intended destination, and the duration of the voyage prior to signing the articles. They clearly preferred what was familiar, and British or Canadian vessels were familiar. This finding has a direct bearing on the question of labour supply. The labour market had not contracted to the point where choice and preference were eliminated. Wallace's conclusion, that masters "had to take what they could get," may have been true in particular circumstances, but it does not apply to the industry as a whole.

Shipowners and masters also preferred to hire British or British colonial men if such were available. This was a continuation of the old practice, so obvious in the Yarmouth fleet of the 1840s, of hiring local men. The process began at the level of master, as

TABLE 9

Birthplaces of Masters (%), Four Fleets, 1863–1914

Birthplace	1863–78	1879–90	1891–1914
Nova Scotia	56.9	60.0	66.5
New Brunswick	20.2	20.7	19.1
Other BNA	1.3	1.1	1.8
United States	1.8	1.2	0.5
England	7.7	4.6	3.7
Wales	0.9	1.5	1.1
Scotland	5.0	4.1	1.8
Ireland	4.1	4.4	3.5
Scandinavia	1.1	1.2	0.9
Other Europe	0.8	1.0	0.7
Other	0.2	0.2	0.5
Total	10,681	7,597	1,505

Source: Crew Lists, MHA.

Tables 8 and 9 suggest. The preference for local men may be understated here, because we are analysing birthplaces: there were undoubtedly many masters born in Britain, for instance, who resided in Nova Scotia or New Brunswick when they were not at sea. The preference for locally born masters was particularly strong among Yarmouth shipowners, but even in the Saint John fleet almost 70 per cent of masters were born in New Brunswick or Nova Scotia.

The unit of analysis here is the master position, not the individual. Thus the same individual will be counted once for every voyage that he undertakes or for every crew list that he signs. This is the appropriate unit of analysis, since we are interested in a portrait of the serving labour force in the industry as a whole. To analyse individual masters would be useful in other contexts but would ignore the fact that one individual might serve once only, whereas another could be the master on 15 successive voyages.

If a local man were not available, then an English or Scottish master was found even more often than an American. When masters from all four fleets are aggregated, as in Table 9, it is clear that the ability to hire a local master increased over time, until by the 1890s and early 1900s almost 86 per cent of master positions were filled by men born in New Brunswick or Nova Scotia. This trend resulted partly from the decline in the number of vessels in the fleet, which left fewer master positions to be filled, and from the fact that through the 1860s and 1870s an increasing number of young men born in these provinces had acquired deep-sea experience and officer rank.

Although some of these masters were so youthful that they must have lacked experience, this problem disappeared by the 1870s and 1880s. There were several 20- and 21-year-old masters in the 1860s, but only one or two in later decades. The average age of those serving as masters increased from 36 years in the 1860s to 41 years in the 1890s. For 78 per cent of all masters in these four fleets we know something about their previous voyage. For those where information is given, 97 per cent had served as master on their previous voyage. In all fleets the proportion of masters with prior experience as master increased over time. Of the 427 who had not held the rank of master on their previous voyage, 96 per cent had been promoted from the rank of first mate.

But the evidence that masters were men of experience goes further than this. Not only did the overwhelming majority have previous experience as master, but almost all of them knew, from previous experience, the vessel they commanded. We know the previous vessel in which almost all (95.9 per cent) masters had served. Of these, 84.7 per cent had served in the same vessel on their previous voyage and thus possessed a very important combination of experience – in their job and with their vessel.

Shipowners clearly understood the value of keeping a master in the same vessel and were able to do so more frequently as time passed. In the 1860s only 77 per cent of serving masters had worked in the same vessel on their previous voyage; by the 1890s almost 89 per cent had commanded the same vessel on their previous voyage. Certainly the increasing longevity of vessels made it easier to keep master and vessel together for more voyages. But the very high retention rates were also the result of choices on the part of shipowners. Owners did not always have clear alternatives, but at most ports of departure they did (including promotion of the first mate.)[19]

The selection process worked both ways, of course, and staying with the vessel was also the result of choice by the master himself.

Of course the master's alternatives were limited, especially if he had experience in sailing vessels only. He might seek work in other vessels, or with other owners, but such a change involved risks, and a transfer to steam would likely mean employment at a rank below that of master, at least initially.[20] It is no surprise that, at the end of voyages, 85.6 per cent of those who held the rank of master stated that they were remaining with the vessel.

The recruiting of officers was a matter for both shipowner and master, but very often the master had to choose his officers on his own. The decision was important, and masters would sometimes go to considerable trouble to obtain a chief mate whom they liked. In the Yarmouth fleet particularly the master was usually a local Yarmouth man and usually chose another Yarmouth man as first mate. When Capt. B.F. Gullison of the *N.B. Lewis* sent a telegram from New Orleans in 1887, asking that a mate be sent to him all the way from Yarmouth, he was abiding the long tradition of employing the man one knew best. "I telegraphed you on Saturday asking you to send me mate ... I know the cost is considerable from home here but sometimes the dearest article is the cheapest in the end."[21]

Table 10 suggests that Nova Scotians were strongly represented among the mates in the three Nova Scotian fleets. In the Saint John fleet, where local masters were a slightly smaller majority, only a third of the officers were Nova Scotians or New Brunswickers. This fleet also reveals the influence of managing owners: about a quarter of them resided outside New Brunswick (mainly in the United Kingdom) and did not show the same predilection for Canadian officers.

Officers were more likely than other members of crew to have had previous experience in a Canadian vessel. Among first mates, 50 per cent had served in the same vessel on their previous voyage; 61.5 per cent had been in a Canadian vessel on their previous voyage. Officers were also much more likely to remain with the vessel at the end of a voyage (5 per cent, compared to 1.6 per cent for all other ranks apart from master) or to receive an honourable discharge. Officers were usually older than the majority of the crews with whom they worked (compare Tables 11 and 7). There were some young mates, mainly from Nova Scotia or New Brunswick, who were receiving a training in the expectation of

TABLE 10

Birthplaces of Officers (%), 1863–1914

Birthplace	Three Nova Scotia Fleets	Saint John Fleet
Nova Scotia	41.8	16.7
New Brunswick	5.4	15.4
Other BNA	2.3	2.7
United States	9.6	9.0
England	13.1	23.0
Wales	1.8	3.4
Scotland	7.4	8.6
Ireland	7.7	10.9
Scandinavia	4.1	3.8
Other Europe	5.9	5.2
Other	0.9	1.3
Total	9,942	3,793

Source: Crew Lists, MHA.

becoming master. For many that expectation would be realized, since the position was so often reserved for Canadians.

For many others, however, the choice was between returning to land, remaining a first mate in sail, and transferring to steam vessels. Working in sail was clearly a young man's occupation, even for officers, and most who served during their twenties and thirties likely had left the sea to find work on land by their forties. There simply were not enough positions available at the rank of master, at least in Canadian sailing vessels, for the majority of those serving as mates to be promoted to the senior rank, particularly since the number of ocean-going sailing vessels was diminishing rapidly in the 1880s and 1890s. Many officers clearly chose to remain in their occupation through their thirties, forties, and fifties, however, and it was from the ranks of these more experienced seamen that masters were able to choose their officers in the last decades of the century. By the 1880s a majority of officers were over thirty, and after 1890 seven out of ten officers working in these vessels was over thirty. When mates signed the crew articles, in an era when hundreds of their fellows were leaving the sea, they did so by choice, or rather by a series of choices made by owners, masters, and mates.

TABLE 11

Age of Officers (%), Four Fleets, 1863–1914

Age Category	1863–78	1879–90	1891–1914
19 or under	1.2	1.1	0.5
20–29	51.2	42.3	28.5
30–39	35.4	34.2	30.3
40–49	9.6	18.3	26.3
50–59	2.3	3.8	12.7
60 or over	0.2	0.3	1.7
Total	7,307	5,468	1,518

Source: Crew Lists, MHA.

Note: There are fewer officers than masters because only officers were sampled.

The preference for local men and women was also exercised at the level of the petty officers – bosun, carpenter, sailmaker, cook, and steward or stewardess. Of those who served in such ranks, 22.2 per cent were born in British North America. But there was a difference between the petty officers and the officers: as time passed fewer of the petty officers were born in North America. As we move further toward the forecastle, and further ahead in time, we find fewer Canadians.

Maps 8 and 9 show the birthplaces of officers and other ranks by period for the Saint John fleet and for the three Nova Scotian fleets, respectively. The shift away from British North America is clear, particularly among those below the rank of officer. In the first period (1863–78) we know the birthplaces of those occupying 75,473 positions at the rank of petty officer or able seaman or other deckhand: 13.9 per cent were Canadians. Most of the rest were English or Welsh (20.8 per cent), Scottish (8.3 per cent), Irish (10.8 per cent), Scandinavian (13.9 per cent), American (11.8 per cent), or other European (16.9 per cent). The proportion of Canadians fell in the next period (1879–90) to 10.6 per cent, and in the last period (1891–1914) to 7.8 per cent. As the numbers and the proportion of Canadians fell, the proportion of Scandinavians and other Europeans increased. The change over three decades was dramatic, and it reinforced the growing distinction between masters and men: in the first period a majority were British or

MAP 8
Birthplaces of Officers and Crew Members, Nova Scotia Fleets, 1863–1914

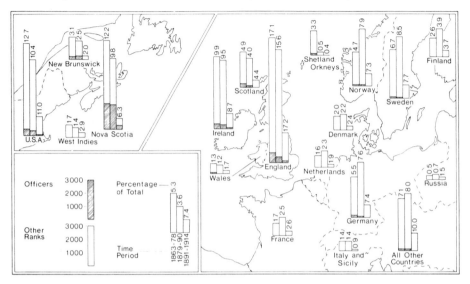

British North American by birth; by the 1890s and early 1900s about half of all deckhands did not speak English as their native language. This, then, is the main evidence for the idea that masters "had to take what they could get": however much they may have preferred men whom they knew, they had to rely increasingly on non-Canadian and even non-British petty officers and crew.

Why did the composition of the labour force change so dramatically? The answer again compels us to reject the idea that seamen were a motiveless herd forced into seafaring by the absence of alternatives. British North American seamen were shunning work at sea because they had a plethora of alternatives available to them on land in the North American economy. Canadian seamen were usually younger than non-Canadians, at least in the 1860s and 1870s.[22] Fewer of them remained at sea in their thirties, and fewer still made seafaring a lifetime occupation. The Canadian census shows a decline in the numbers of "mariners" even at the height of the age of sail.[23] The places of Canadians were taken by men from countries with high rates of emigration and a seafaring tradition or a seaboard population: Norway, Sweden, Finland, Russia, Germany, Austria-Hungary, the West Indies, and a few other European countries. This finding is not inconsistent with Rosemary

MAP 9
Birthplaces of Officers and Crew Members, Saint John Fleet, 1863-1914

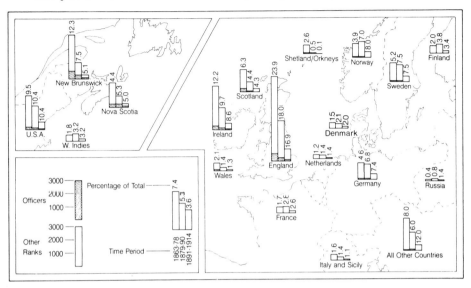

Ommer's explanation for the large number of Shetland and Orkney Islanders among the crews of Windsor vessels, especially in the 1860s: seafaring was an alternative to local employment or to emigration; and when opportunities at home re-emerged, the Islanders returned home to find work.[24]

There is plenty of evidence to suggest that, on both sides, the process of recruitment involved positive choices rather than reluctant entrapment. First, Canadians were still over-represented among petty officers and deckhands. We must take into account not only the proportion of Canadians among these crews, but also the available populations from which the Canadians and others were drawn. It is impossible to derive a perfect measure of the rate of participation of various national populations in the seafaring labour force, and there are many refined tests of hiring preferences that one could apply with knowledge of the fleets and the seafaring populations of other countries.

The simplest measure, however, will suffice: crew positions filled by each nationality per total population from each country. We include only those at the rank of petty officer, able seaman, or

TABLE 12

Crew Participation Rates, 1863–1914

Country	Participation Rate* (Crew per 10,000 Average Pop.)	$LQ = \dfrac{S_i/S}{P_i/P}$
Nova Scotia	255	67
New Brunswick	171	47
Other BNA	19	5
England/Wales	12	3
Scotland	27	7
Ireland	31	9
Scandinavia	33	9
Germany	2	0.6
United States	3	0.9

Source: Population averaged from decadal census returns or nearest equivalent, 1860–1900. World population in labour quotient is total population of Europe, Canada, and the United States. Crew members from all four major fleets were included.

* Officers and masters excluded.

other deckhand. Table 12 also includes a labour quotient of the form

$$\frac{S_i/S}{P_i/P},$$

where S_i is the number of seamen from community i; S is the total number of seamen in the sample (158,670); P_i is the total population in community i, and P is the total "world" population (in this case Europe, the United States, and Canada).

The results suggest that on a per capita basis Nova Scotians and New Brunswickers were far more likely to be hired than were people from any other group. The labour quotients suggest that Nova Scotians were more than seven times as likely to be hired as were Irishmen or Scandinavians, when the relative size of each nationality's total population is taken into account. If we look only at Maritimers below the rank of master, it is also clear that sailors from the four ports of registry (Saint John, Halifax, Yarmouth, and Windsor) were over-represented in these fleets: 50 per cent of Maritimers gave one of these places as their birthplace (Map 10).

MAP 10
Birthplaces of Sailors from the Maritimes Serving in Four Fleets, 1863–1914

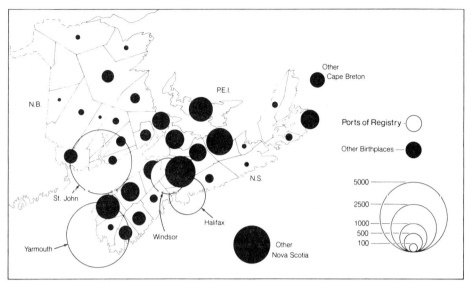

Conclusive proof of selection is possible only if we can observe two national fleets embarking from the same ports at the same time and so drawing from essentially the same labour pool. Fortunately such a comparison is possible. A sample of non-Canadian British crew lists has been analysed; in this sample there were over twenty-two thousand crew positions in sailing vessels in the last four decades of the nineteenth century.[25] All but 4 per cent of these sailing vessels hired crew at the beginning of their voyages in ports in the British Isles. Almost all the managing owners of these British vessels resided in the United Kingdom; all but a few of the masters were born there. It is a simple matter to compare the sailors in these British vessels with crew hired by Canadian vessels in British ports (Table 13).

The proportion of crew members who spoke English as their native language was high in both fleets, but the composition was different. Even when departing from ports in the United Kingdom, Canadian vessels tended to sail with a much larger proportion of North Americans among the crew, especially considering the size of the native population. Almost two-thirds of the crews in British vessels had been born in the United Kingdom. Most of the voyages by British vessels from which this sample was taken occurred in the 1860s and 1870s; in later decades the proportion of British natives

TABLE 13

Birthplaces of Crew Members (Excluding Masters) Departing British Isles in British and Four Canadian Sailing Fleets, 1863–1914

Birthplace	Canadian Vessels		British Vessels	
	% of total	LQ	% of total	LQ
BNA	14.4	26.2	2.3	4.3
England/Wales	23.4	3.8	42.3	6.9
Scotland	8.7	10.0	15.2	17.5
Ireland	12.7	10.7	7.9	6.6
Scandinavia	14.9	7.5	10.9	5.5
Other Europe	13.3	0.2	13.0	0.2
United States	7.2	0.6	3.7	0.3
Other	5.4	–	4.7	–
Total	76,877		20,415	

Source: Crew Lists, MHA.

decreased, and the increasing number of foreign sailors serving in the British merchant marine became a matter of concern in Britain, partly because that country's merchant marine had traditionally relied on native seamen. The labour force in British sailing ships was not truly international. Even in the 1890s a majority were British-born, and over 61 per cent were English-speaking.

In Atlantic Canadian vessels the crews were more international, and Canadian masters had more success in hiring Scandinavians. But the tendency for native-born sailors and Canadian masters to seek each other out is clear enough, even in ports on the other side of the Atlantic.[26] The old pre-industrial tradition of seeking out the familiar and working with people from one's native land persisted into the industrial age, even in an industry that hired its labour force far beyond Atlantic Canada. A strong nativist prejudice occasionally appears in the remarks of ship masters. In 1879 John W. Morris of Windsor rescued the crew of a British ship and found the crew to be "mostly Liverpool Irish men like the most of sailors we get nowadays out of England." Morris, however, had somehow succeeded in exercising preference: "I have but 12 men before the mast and I am shure that six of my crue are worth more than the hole lot of them my men are natives of the Shettelans and Nova Scotia."[27] Jacob K. Hatfield, of the Saint John vessel *Africana*, so disliked shanties sung in foreign languages that "I have forbid them to sing songs of any kind in their own language about the deck."[28] He did not appear to object to their abilities as seamen, however.

Did it matter if an increasing proportion of the deckhands was non-colonial and non-British? Perhaps it is here, among the foreign deckhands, that we find those whom "no master or mate would take for ballast," as Frederick William Wallace put it. Contemporary commentators in Britain were not so worried about the quality of the foreign seaman as they were concerned about the loss of valuable seafaring skills in the domestic population.[29] In Canada there was less worry over this issue. There was even less reason for concern about the quality of the labour force. Even from the perspective of shipowners and masters, there was little reason for complaint about the Scandinavian and European sailors who were taking the place of British and colonial seamen. In the Saint John fleet less than 1 per cent of the Europeans were making their first voyage, compared to almost 4 per cent for Canadians and British. Europeans tended to be older than Canadians, and perhaps also more experienced. Certainly the age profile of deckhands suggests a significant ageing over time: the crews being hired consisted of fewer boys and apprentices and more men for whom seafaring was a lifetime or long-term occupation. The proportion of able seamen and ordinary seamen under 30 fell, until by the period after 1890 about 37 per cent were 30 or over (Table 14).

It was often said in defence of the Scandinavian and other European sailors that they were less likely to reject the authority of the master. As one master put it: "British seamen are far more difficult to manage than foreigners, who are very rarely guilty of either drunkenness or insubordination, the two besetting weaknesses of their British shipmates."[30] There is no way to prove or disprove this claim, since there are no sources that would allow a satisfactory comparison of disciplinary actions against serving sailors by nationality. Even official logs, incomplete as they are, offer a basis only for impressions rather than for estimates.

TABLE 14

Age of Deckhands (%), Four Fleets, 1863–1914

Age Category*	1863–78	1879–90	1891–1914
Under 15	0.6	0.4	0.2
15–19	10.9	9.4	10.9
20–29	62.9	56.7	52.4
30–39	19.0	21.7	22.1
40–49	5.7	10.0	11.6
50–59	0.8	1.6	2.5
60 +	0.1	0.2	0.3
Total	66,127	60,589	17,905

Source: Crew Lists, MHA.

* All ranks below petty officer.

We can, however, analyse desertion and other forms of behaviour that masters and owners most disliked – failure to join the vessel, discharge into jail, discharge due to incompetence, demotion, and the like. For the sake of clarity the latter reasons have been grouped into a "dishonourable discharge" category. We may compare these types of discharge with the more common, and more welcome notations at the conclusion of the seaman's service: remaining with the vessel, and discharge by mutual consent. Europeans and Scandinavians were, in fact, more likely to desert than were Canadian or British sailors. Of all Europeans hired in our four fleets, 31.7 per cent ended their voyages by deserting, compared with 22 per cent for those born in the United Kingdom and only 16 per cent for those born in British North America. But both Scandinavians and other Europeans were *less* prone to dishonourable discharge than were Canadians, British, and particularly Americans. And the statistical relationship between birthplace and reason for discharge is not significant, when we control for capacity or rank. Mates were less likely to desert than ABs, and since a high proportion of mates were Canadian, Canadians were therefore less likely to desert than most others. When we look only at ABs, the differences between nationalities are much less significant.[31] Certainly the Scandinavians and other Europeans were not responsible for any increases in desertion and dishonourable discharges that may have occurred in these fleets over time.

The European and Scandinavian sailors hired in increasing numbers in the later decades of the century were more often hired for long-distance voyages. They were more likely to sign on for voyages outside the North Atlantic than were Canadians, for instance.[32] And they were usually paid less than other sailors, in spite of longer voyages. Here was a major reason why masters hired foreign seamen: the Scandinavians, for instance, were accustomed to relatively low wages in their own national fleets. Recent research on the Norwegian merchant marine suggests that ABs in Norwegian vessels were paid much less than ABs in the Canadian fleets, although the difference narrowed by the 1890s.[33]

As Canadian vessels moved increasingly into European continental ports in the 1870s and 1880s, they found that they could hire crews there at lower wages than elsewhere. If we compare ABs hired at monthly sterling wage rates (the most common form of wage payment), we find that ABs hired in European ports were paid 13 per cent less, on average, than those hired in all other ports. Able seamen hired in continental ports were paid less even than those hired in English ports. The hiring of foreign seamen was one reason why masters were able to keep wages low on long-distance voyages: sterling wages were in fact *less* for ABs on longer voyages (to South America, India, the East Indies, and the Pacific Ocean) than for ABs serving in the North Atlantic.[34] Europe, therefore, offered a relatively cheap labour supply.

Complaints about the quality of seafaring labour coincided with complaints over the total labour supply, as Judith Fingard has pointed out.[35] The two factors might well have reinforced each other: the landsman's image of sailors as uncivilized brutes would deter all but the more desperate from seeking work in the industry; an inadequate labour supply would force masters to "take what they could get." All of this might be true, if the labour market for sailors were a single international market, and if that market were short of labour. Neither condition was true in the later nineteenth century.

The market for labour was in fact a multitude of local markets, each affected by local economic conditions, local wage levels, and local alternative employment opportunities. Wage levels varied enormously from one port to another and from one country to another. Wages for ABs in Liverpool tended to be lower than wages for ABs in other English ports, for instance (over the last decades of the century AB wages from Cardiff were almost 10 per cent higher than from Liverpool). The difference in wage levels between Europe and North America is well known. But even where dollar wages were being paid, the deviation from the mean wage for ABs was very great.[36] In particular North American ports the relative difficulty in hiring crews shows up in the much higher wages being paid to ABs. Masters would sometimes hire crews in one port and transport the men to another port in order to solve the problem of a local labour shortage. Among high-wage American ports were Philadelphia, Charleston, New Orleans, a few other Gulf ports, and ports in the Pacific Northwest. In Canada high-wage ports included Saint John, Quebec, and Montreal.

The very high wages in particular ports do not mean, however, that a labour shortage existed elsewhere. A problem in labour supply would have produced two measurable consequences: an increase in average wages, as owners and masters sought to compete with other industries for labour; and an increase in the overall delay time by vessels in port. Neither of these things occurred. There was a gradual decline in the average wages of deckhands in sailing vessels after the early 1870s.[37] And the time that vessels took to turn around between voyages declined from the 1860s to the 1880s, before increasing again in the 1890s. In the Saint John fleet turn-around averaged 31 days in the 1860s, but less than 27 days in the 1880s. Even in the 1890s the average turn-around (29 days) was still less than in the 1860s.[38]

More interesting, perhaps, is delay time: the time elapsed between the date the voyage was supposed to begin (date of commencement) and the date when the vessel actually left port. Any difficulty in hiring crew would increase delay time. In fact delay times fell slightly, from 2.5 days on average in the 1860s ($n = 1,574$) to 2.4 days in the 1890s ($n = 718$).[39] Thus, in spite of the alternatives available, which included work in the rapidly growing fleets of steamers, men continued to offer their labour to the masters of sailing vessels. There remained a relative scarcity of labour in many North American ports. But there was no labour shortage in most places within the shipping market. We must remember that at this time parents in England were paying a premium (often as much as £60) to shipowners who took their sons as apprentices on sailing vessels.[40]

While in certain North American ports masters might not be able to hire the crews they wanted, in most British and European ports the master was more likely to be able to choose his men more carefully. Frank Bullen tells a story to illustrate the presence of an adequate labour supply in British ports. Bullen offered to serve as first mate in an English brig for £5-15-0 a month; he found himself in competition with a German mate who offered to serve for £3 and another Englishman who offered to work for nothing.[41] This may not have occurred very often, but the story is not incredible, given the value that seamen and owners placed on experience at the rank of mate. And Englishmen were suddenly finding themselves in competition with experienced Europeans who were also hoping for advancement in rank and wage.

Many men who had served in sailing vessels were reluctant to make the change to iron- or steel-hulled steamers, even if the wages were higher. Seamen stuck to what was familiar, and the pride of the craftsman was reflected in a commonplace contempt for those who worked in steam. In the 1880s and 1890s the total number of places available in sailing vessels was declining rapidly, and as a result there were more experienced men available than there were places for them. Masters benefited from this change in the labour market.

If the seamen hired by Canadian masters lived beyond "the latter day adjuncts of civilization," and if they were drawn from the more "brutish" levels of their national populations, then we should expect seafaring to be a non-literate occupation for non-literate workers. Sailors had to sign their name to a crew agreement; they could, and often did, sign an "x." Most of their tasks in the vessel could be learned from experience and observation. What need was there for the skill of literacy, when the only thing an able seaman had to read while on the job was a compass?

While most of the seaman's craft could be learned and performed without the skill of literacy, the occupation did offer both the incentive and the opportunity for reading. By the late nineteenth century masters and their officers had to be literate if they were to obtain certificates. Manuals of instruction for seafarers proliferated, and it was not unusual to find these and other books among the effects of deceased sailors. The image of the seaman as a brutalized and impoverished victim prevents us from seeing the seaman as he often was – sitting on deck in the early evening, if the weather were fair, reading a book. The innocent landsman in Jack London's *Sea Wolf* is surprised to find the brutal schooner captain to be a voracious reader. Similarly we are startled to find an able seaman reading Homer and Shakespeare to his fellows.[42]

Ability to sign one's name is usually considered to be a "middle estimate" of literacy.[43] That is, many people who could sign their names might not be able to read or write fluently; but there were also those who could read to some extent, but not sign their names. If we take ability to sign as a crude measure of literacy, then the majority of the sailors in Atlantic Canadian fleets were literate: more than 76 per cent could sign their names (about 15 per cent with some apparent difficulty).[44] In British sailing vessels in the same decades a similar proportion (78 per cent) could sign.[45] Steamers did not necessarily attract a more literate labour force: of 60,883 crew members serving on British steamers in the same decades, 78.8 per cent signed their names, and 21.2 per cent signed with an "x."

This last figure is somewhat surprising: since 86 per cent of the voyages where crew were hired by steamers occurred after 1880, the literacy of crew in steamers should be compared with the literacy of crew in sailing vessels in the two later periods (Table 15). We must conclude that after 1880, if not before, seamen in sailing vessels were more likely to be literate than those employed in British steamers. Crew members in steamers were slightly older than those in sailing vessels, but the difference is not enough to explain the difference in literacy rates, not least because a larger proportion of the steamer crews were hired at a later time – about half were hired after 1890, whereas most men in the Canadian sailing vessels analysed here were hired before 1890.

Other conclusions follow from the analysis of crew signatures. As David Alexander argued, sailors did not include an unusually large number of illiterates, when compared with the national populations from which they were drawn.[46] As Table 15 suggests, there was a marked increase in the literacy of almost all national groups represented in the sample. Comparisons with national census data on literacy are fraught with problems because of different definitions of literacy and different methods of estimating it. And census estimates are for entire countries rather than for the working class.

TABLE 15

Literacy of Crew (%), Four Fleets, 1863-1912

Birthplace	1863-78	1879-90	1891-1912
Nova Scotia	84.3	89.2	92.3
New Brunswick	76.3	77.2	87.6
Newfoundland	46.6	48.1	52.5
Other BNA	63.7	72.9	91.6
England/Wales	72.5	81.0	89.8
Scotland	79.5	79.8	89.1
Ireland	63.0	70.4	84.4
Scandinavia	69.1	83.7	93.9
Germany	86.4	94.2	97.3
France	61.1	74.1	82.0
Other Europe	59.8	73.3	82.8
United States	65.8	76.6	85.4
All	70.3	79.1	87.3

Source: Crew Lists, MHA.

Note: Literacy = percentage of crew able to sign.

A very rough comparison may be obtained by comparing crew literacy in census years with the literacy of men aged 20-39 in the Canadian decennial census (Table 16). The majority of sailors were in this age category, although the proportion in their thirties increased over time. The comparison requires that we project the appropriate age group in census back to the previous years: thus those who were aged 30-39 in 1891 are treated as the 20-29 age group in 1881. The definitions of literacy are not the same (the census definition is inability to read or write), and so the comparison is inevitably crude, but it does tend to confirm what Alexander discovered. New Brunswick sailors may have been drawn from less-educated strata of their province's population; but Nova Scotian sailors likely were not. The addition of the Saint John crew list sample changes the estimates of literacy for New Brunswick seamen: they are much higher than in the smaller sample that Alexander used in 1980.[47]

A somewhat more satisfactory basis of comparison exists between literacy of seamen and literacy rates in Britain and particu-

TABLE 16

Census and Crew Literacy (%), 1871–91

| Census | Nova Scotia | | New Brunswick | |
	Census	Crew	Census	Crew
1871	86	84	83	76
1881	88	85	84	77
1891	90	90	85	82

Sources: Crew Lists, MHA; Canada, *Census*, 1891.

lar European countries. Here we may refer to signatures of bridegrooms, and the definition of literacy is the same. We may also assume that the age profile of bridegrooms is similar to that of sailors: the majority will be in their twenties or thirties. The comparison is still very rough, but it should serve to confirm the general point: sailors were not unusually illiterate, especially when we consider their social class. Bridegrooms were drawn from all social classes; sailors were working men, and we should expect their literacy rates to be lower for that reason alone.

Table 17 summarizes Carlo Cipolla's data on bridegrooms' signatures, so that comparisons may be made with the figures in Table 15. English, Welsh, and Scottish sailors were slightly below the literacy rates for their countries, but in each case literacy among sailors appears to have increased more rapidly than in the national population (of the crews hired in the last period, from 1891 to 1912, the majority were hired in the 1890s). The improvement in the literacy of Irish sailors is particularly striking. German sailors had the highest literacy rates of all sailors, and they closely approximated the overall German figure. Among other nationalities the literacy of sailors was again slightly lower than for the total population (this applies to American seaman and Scandinavians), but by the last period the gap was narrowing. Certainly there is no evidence here to support the notion that sailors were men who lived "where none of the latter-day adjuncts of civilization had penetrated."[48]

Sailors were not trapped into seafaring by lack of skills or by illiteracy. Insofar as the skill of literacy allowed men to read and learn about opportunities on land, it increased the likelihood that

TABLE 17

Literacy in Selected Countries (%), 1863–1900

Years	England/ Wales	Scotland	Ireland	France	Prussia
1863–78	76–85	89–93	n.a.	72–83	n.a.
1879–90	86–92	93–96	74–80	84–92	95–98
1891–1900	93–96	96–98	80–87	92–95	98–99

Source: Carlo Cipolla, *Literacy and Development in the West* (Harmondsworth: Penguin, 1969), 121–3.

work at sea was a matter of choice rather than an unavoidable act of desperation. It is no surprise to find John Froude, recently an able seaman, employed as assistant secretary to the Twillingate Coal Co.[49] Working at sea, however, was increasingly an occupation for literate men, and level of literacy offers no guide as to whether one would remain at sea into middle age or depart for land. A literate seaman was just as likely to remain at sea as was an illiterate one.

Literate or not, sailors were the most mobile of workers. Their work itself was a recurring migration. Like those other migrants who became immigrants to North America in the nineteenth century, sailors were not bound by a culture of poverty.[50] They were literate and calculating men and the most litigious of workers, who could read their contracts of employment and produce "sea lawyers" from their ranks to argue the rights of those in the forecastle. By virtue of their literacy and the peculiar nature of their craft, they developed skills and resources that they were able to use for adaptation and advantage in new and unfamiliar environments.

The Canadian-born sailors, and likely many of the Europeans as well, brought to their craft not the debility and despair of the poorest of men, but the values of outport fishing and farming communities. The Canadian-born came not simply from the major urban centres of the Atlantic provinces. Three-quarters of them came from outside Saint John and Halifax, and if Map 10 had included those who served in vessels registered in Pictou, Liverpool, Digby, St Martin's, and elsewhere, the outports would be much more heavily represented.

The sons of farmers and fishermen, these sailors were certainly working class, but they brought to sea the ambiguous heritage of the independent producer and small proprietor. Fishing and farming communities experienced a powerful communal solidarity, reinforced by mutual dependence and shared labour. But fishing and farming families also competed against each other and worked for the goal of independent ownership of property: with luck and hard work one might always own one's own boat or schooner. The inshore fishery and the small coastal schooner were constant reminders of the possibility of self-proprietorship.

The "small boat mentality" was a maritime parallel to the "producer ideology" in other parts of Canada. It gave the seafarer his robust pride and independence. It encouraged him to see his grievances as personal rather than collective, and it was certainly a barrier to collective organization.[51]

in battle or buisness whatever the game
in law or in love it is ever the same
in the struggle for power or the scramble for self
let this be your motto rely on yourself
for whether the prize be a ribbon or throne
the victor is he who can go it alone.[52]

The same goal of personal independence sent the sailor into the many formal and informal schools in his community, "where the young men of the neighborhood who were home from sea came to learn mathematics and navigation."[53]

This account of the literate working man may end with two vignettes of life at sea, in which the characters may not be typical (for there was no typical sailor, whatever the legends may say), but wherein the deckhands present the seldom-recorded quality of their life and wherein such distinctions as "rough" and "respectable" have no meaning whatever. In the 947-ton *David* of Saint John, Thomas Manson, the master, engaged in a bitter argument with a 28-year-old Welsh-born deckhand. The sailor, one George Brittain, had been reading a book on deck during his watch. "I asked him if he had not time enough in his watch below to read Books as I did not allow any one to read on deck when they had charge of the deck, he then used some very abusive language towards me." But Brittain was not to be intimidated: he wrote a long letter to Manson, charging that the master had tried to force him "to work all day and keep watch all night" and threatened "to put a bullet through me." And Brittain had a defence against the charge of reading on deck. "When you spoke to me about reading I put the Book away and quietly answered I seen no harm in it, and you abused me with the most disgraceful language man ever used." More important, said Brittain, others read books on deck, with the master's apparent consent: they "were looking at a Book on a Sunday, and your self talking with the parties doing it." In this vessel, where master and men swore at each other, and where the master threatened to use firearms, men also read books together on deck.[54]

The *Magnet* of Saint John, proceeding through the Indian Ocean in September 1866, was no easy ship. There were cases of venereal disease and scurvy, and at least one AB had spent several days in jail in Aden. On 28 September a 21-year-old English AB named John Moule fell overboard and, unable to swim, was drowned. On the next day the master opened Moule's sea chest. He found the wardrobe of a gentleman: among other items, 10 white shirts, 13 pairs of cotton socks, 9 pocket handkerchiefs, 3 silk neckties, 16 shirt collars, shirt studs in a leather case, and an umbrella. He found also a small collection of books: a Bible, a geography text, and no less than 10 books on seamanship and navigation. Such were the possessions of a proud and ambitious working man. But John Moule's possessions are not the most important part of this story. More telling, perhaps, was the auction of his effects at sea on 8 October. While many of his fine clothes went unsold, the deckhands of the *Magnet* purchased every one of his printed books, and his quadrant, for all of which they paid £2-10-0.[55] The men of the *Magnet* disappear from the historical record, as they continue on their passage through the Indian Ocean. But during their watch below, or on deck in the evening light, they may well have spent a few hours with their new possessions.

CHAPTER SIX

Struggles for Protection and Control

The sailor was not trapped within a culture of poverty, but he was constrained by authority and by law. In the third quarter of the nineteenth century the structure of authority in the workplace was confirmed and reinforced by laws that gave some protection to the sailor, but even greater powers to his master. In Britain these laws were intended to protect capital invested in domestic shipping and to maintain a native labour force in seafaring. In Canada, as Judith Fingard has pointed out, neither mercantilist traditions nor the presence of a domestic navy encouraged laws to protect and preserve the seafarer. Instead the interests of efficiency and profit dictated the denial of habeas corpus and the denial of the right of appeal to sailors who broke the law.[1] In Canada little was done to encourage or protect the occupation of seafaring, and merchant shipping legislation differed somewhat from British precedents as a result. At sea, however, British legislation applied in Canadian vessels. The law was being applied not to ignorant, illiterate, and brutal men, but to calculating and literate men who possessed some understanding of their customary and legal rights. In these circumstances paternalism often disappeared. Its passing was hastened when fewer deckhands were known personally to masters or mates and when fewer spoke English as their native tongue. This was a pre-industrial workplace employing skilled mechanics at the onset of industrialization. The conflict that occurred in the workplace must be understood in this context.

It would be tempting, but misleading, to assume that workplace conflict occurred as a direct result of falling rates of return in an obsolescent industry. The steep decline in ocean freight rates after

GRAPH 10

Tramp Shipping Freights and Selected North Atlantic Sailing Ship
Freights, 1855–99

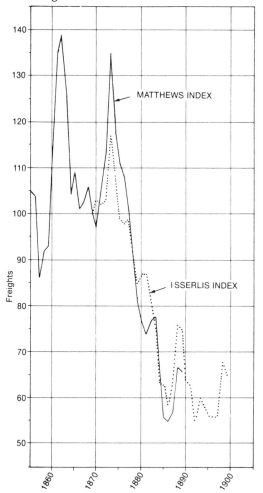

Sources: L. Isserlis, "Tramp Shipping Cargoes and Freights," *Journal of the Royal
Statistical Society* (1938), reprinted in B.R. Mitchell and P. Deane, *Abstract of
British Historical Statistics* (Cambridge, 1962), 224; Keith Matthews's index was
constructed from the following rates given in the *New York Maritime Register*:
cotton, New York–Liverpool; grain, New York–Liverpool; cotton, New Orleans–
Liverpool; deals, Saint John–Liverpool. For each of these the average of monthly
highs and lows was calculated; the annual rate is an unweighted average of the
monthly figures. The index is simply an unweighted average of the annual rates.
The method is crude, but the result is close to the Isserlis index.
Note: 1869 = 100.

the mid-1870s was an obsession to shipowners, and it certainly contributed to severe pressure on profits by the 1880s (see Graph 10). The decline in freight rates was clearly the result not of a short-term trade cycle but of technological changes and an increasing supply of tonnage in a period of relatively slow growth in the volume of international trade. The pressure on masters to overwork vessels and men must have intensified. But to attribute increases in conflict to these conditions alone would be to misunderstand the genesis of discontent in the proto-industrial workplace. Conflict arise from the workplace itself and the structure of authority that governed relations between masters and wage-paid workers. Thus conflict began long before the decline in freight rates.

Although one available measure of conflict, desertion rates, suggests that conflict intensified as freight rates fell, other measures indicate that master-worker conflict was endemic even in the 1860s and early 1870s. Thus dismissal of crew into jail, and other "dishonourable" discharges, did not increase as time passed. It is impossible to derive a satisfactory measure of the frequency of conflict over time, however. Although official logs note disciplinary actions by masters, there is no complete collection of such logs for Canadian vessels. Most available logs were for voyages in the 1860s and early 1870s, and these logs indicate that conflict occurred over many issues, even before the decline in freight rates. More important than falling rates of return was the rise of the large ocean-going square-rigger. There is a striking contrast between the small vessels discussed in chapter 2, or even the small vessels in the later nineteenth century for which crew agreements survive, and the larger ocean-going vessels whose crew agreements and logs are analysed here. In the former, evidence of conflict is relatively scarce; in the latter, the evidence suggests that conflict was endemic.[2]

There was intense pressure on masters even when freight rates were high. The increasing ease of telegraphic communication allowed managing owners to maintain the pressure for speed and economy. Sailing to Argentina in 1871, Annie Butler confided to her diary the anxiety of her husband, the master of a two-masted vessel that was not rigged for speed. Day after day she prayed for favourable winds and lamented the slow progress of the vessel, for fear that the owners would blame her husband: "John is heart sick about this voyage; he knows he will sink so much money but we must try and be patient ... Last evening I felt pretty blue when I thot how matters were and John seemed so bothered. I hope things will turn out all well in the end. John knows he will be found fault with but I wish his owners had to worry through matters as he does every day."[3] Annie's fears were justified: the owners, George and Samuel Ryerson, did not pay John Butler wages owed him after his voyage, and two years later he had still not been paid.

Speed was directly related to economy, especially in port, since the longer a vessel remained in port the higher the disbursements were likely to be. A saving in time could even compensate for a loss in freight rate, as James Duncan of Charlottetown told a master in 1872, when freight rates were high: "Do not lose one hour that can be avoided as we find it is delay which in nearly every instance loses money, and when chartering you must bear in mind that quick dispatch is very important and is worth a small concession in rate of freight."[4] In page after page of correspondence with masters the creed of parsimony is repeated: "Hold things up as cheaply as possible and make all you can of it."[5] Even when freight rates were high, shipowners kept up the pressure: "Some of the richest ship-owners in our city, who have made splendid fortunes out of their ships, were you to judge by their conversation, you would fancy had difficulty in making ends meet, and however high the freights are, you are met with the terrible bug-bear of the heavy expenses."[6]

By the 1880s pressure for speed had often given way to panic: "Shipowning is not what it was in 1870, and things must be worked on a different basis altogether," wrote an enraged managing owner whose master had put back into port in Ireland because of a storm.[7] Speed and economy meant taking risks, as Robert Quirk of Charlottetown was clearly prepared to do. Quirk also argued for increased deck loads and advised his partner to ignore their master's objections: "It will be as well not to listen to the advice of a captain, as I have found out that they begin crying out long before they are hurt."[8] Even in the early 1870s the Moran family of New Brunswick was making severe, if not risky economies. W.H. Moran wrote about the *Crown Prince* in 1871: "I am doing my utmost to keep down disbursements and tending on the ship day & night. I am going to sea this time without many things which are actually necessary such as iron water tanks, plates for forecastle rail, davits, etc., etc. I am doing so to keep down expenses in Liverpool."[9]

Pressure on the master led to pressure on his crew. Of course masters had always driven sailors hard, and of course the threat and the use of force had been part of the master-crew relationship long before the 1860s and 1870s. But merchant shipping legislation now made a critical difference: it had given new legal sanctions to the master's customary use of the force and to the sailor's defence of customary and legal rights. The result was an escalation of conflict and of bargaining through the use of both legal and extra-legal methods. A commonplace instance will suffice to illustrate the change. In 1884 an able seaman in the *Zebina Goudey* of Yarmouth refused to obey the orders of his master on a voyage to the East Indies; the seaman was subdued by force, and on arrival in Sourabaya he spent several days in gaol. In the early nineteenth century the story would have ended there; the dispute might never have involved a gaol sentence at all, for the master might have felt obliged to settle the matter himself. In 1884, however, the master resorted to the police in Sourabaya and deducted the cost of police action and gaol expenses from wages owed to the AB at the end of the voyage. The AB, cognizant of his legal rights, charged the master for non-payment of wages, and the charge was heard in a court in Greenock. The superintendent of mercantile marine in Greenock testified that the entries in the official log were not properly signed and witnessed. The magistrate would not accept the log in evidence and ordered the arrears of wages to be paid.[10] Such appeals to the courts increased in frequency after mid-century, until court and prison officials complained that their premises were filled with seamen.[11] The resolution of disputes was often non-violent, but it was conflict nevertheless, sanctioned and encouraged in law.

The pressure on the master was often reflected in frustration with his crew and with the laws that appeared to protect sailors. George Murray, master of the *J.L. Wickwire* of Windsor, in the North Atlantic in 1870 found himself "nearly broken down from being on deck night and day" and recorded in his official log a protest on behalf of all masters: "For us there is no redress ... The Law will punish us as and brand us as tyrants, take from us our certificates our means of livelihood. if we to protect the property committed to our care drive lazy ignorant impostures to their duties when it is required ... One half of the wrecks in the Western Ocean is the fault of such crews as I have now got."[12]

But hard-pressed masters sought and found means of protecting their interests. One such protection was the provision that a deserter forfeited his claim to unpaid wages, and in the late nineteenth century we read of masters who drove men to desertion in order to make savings in wage costs. "To sail in a Nova Scotian vessel was one of the hardest experiences one could be involved in," remembered a Norwegian sailor. "I sailed in one called the *Grenada*, of Windsor. She was a proper hard case. The captain was proud of the fact that he had not paid off the crew in the course of twenty years. He was a boxer. He came on deck at six o'clock each morning just looking for a chance to get into trouble with one of the men."[13] A simpler method of cutting wage costs was to hire fewer men upon departure. But in the late nineteenth century even that tactic could lead to bargaining and conflict, for sailors could now claim that an undermanned vessel was unseaworthy and seek legal redress.

In the official accounts, undesirable behaviour by sailors often appears to be motiveless, the result of drunkenness, laziness, or the inferior quality of the worker himself. But confrontations with authority, either in the vessel or on shore, were usually purposeful actions designed to effect improvements in working conditions. Long before seamen were organized in trade unions they had learned how to bargain. Their most obvious weapon was withdrawal of labour - a formidable tool at sea, where the employer could not dismiss workers and hire replacements.

Withdrawal of labour took various forms. Sailors could refuse to work, either individually or in groups. In a workplace where labour was usually applied by the co-ordinated action of men working in groups, the co-ordinated withdrawal of labour occurred naturally and frequently. Failing to join a vessel after signing the articles was also a form of withdrawing labour, and a costly one to the vessel if the sailor had been paid an advance. Desertion was also a means of withdrawing labour.

As Judith Fingard has pointed out, the sailor's confrontations with authority in port had more to do with working conditions than with motiveless disorderly behaviour.[14] The use of judicial or criminal records is fraught with problems, and criminal statistics may say more about the activities of police than the activities of sailors. Two conclusions may be drawn, however, from the sources that Fingard used, and from other late-nineteenth-century material:

non-violent withdrawal of labour was far more important than other causes of court appearances by sailors; and withdrawal of labour became relatively more important as time passed. The annual reports of the Quebec and Montreal harbour police report the number of arrests of sailors in each year. This source does not state the port or nationality of vessels in which sailors were working, and so it is not possible to focus on sailors from Atlantic Canadian ships. The source is useful, however, because it states the reasons for arrests on an annual basis. In the five-year period 1870–4, 37 per cent of arrests in Quebec were the consequence of refusals to work (desertion, refusal to proceed, refusal of duty, failing to join a ship).[15] Another 29.8 per cent were for absence without leave – another form of withdrawing labour, and a protest against the master's denial of shore leaves.

At Quebec, as elsewhere, masters often attempted to deny shore leave for fear that sailors might not return. Where shore leave was granted, the hours of leave were fixed in advance, and all too often the master expected his men to return in the early hours of evening. When they did not return they were liable to arrest. The frequency of this crime says something about the vigilance of the police, something about the fears of masters, and a great deal about the concern of masters to retain firm control over their labour force in a high-wage port.

Arrests in Quebec for assault or other types of violence were much less common (10.8 per cent), and arrests of masters and mates for assaults on crew were more frequent (16.6 per cent of crimes of violence) than were arrests of crew for assault on masters or mates (11.9 per cent of crimes of violence). Arrests for drunkenness or for the purpose of "protection for the night" were only 14.6 per cent of all arrests.

It is risky to draw conclusions about changes in crew behaviour over time from these records, since the number of policemen and their methods changed over time. The total number of arrests certainly declined over time: from an annual average of 548 by the Quebec police in the early 1870s to a mere 95 in 1889; from an average of 802 in Montreal in the early 1870s to 610 in 1888.[16] As time passed, arrests for violations of maritime law, or for withdrawal of labour, became relatively more important. Either the police or employers took such activities more seriously, or the withdrawal of labour was becoming relatively more frequent.

In her analysis of sailors' appearances before the magistrates in Quebec in 1854, Fingard found that a third had been charged with desertion or refusal to work; over half with "drunk and disorderly" offences.[17] The Quebec harbour police reports suggest that arrests for desertion or refusal to work increased relatively, to 37 per cent of all arrests by the 1870s and to 38 per cent by 1888. If we include absences without leave, withdrawal-related offences had increased from 41 per cent in 1854 to 67 per cent in the early 1870s. By the late 1880s arrests for drunkenness, assault, and other forms of violence had declined sharply in both absolute and relative terms. These changes reflect the more rapid turn-around of vessels, particularly steam vessels, which decreased total time spent in port and opportunities for arrest for such petty crimes as drunkenness. But the changes reflect also general trends in British and colonial shipping: they reflect the sailor's increasing resort to bargaining, to litigation, and to withdrawal of labour as means of protecting his rights.

Why did sailors withdraw labour? In the absence of formal organization among sailors, and in the absence of many records that allow the sailor's voice to be heard, it is difficult to assess the reasons. The motives in Atlantic Canadian vessels were unlikely to be very different from those of sailors appearing in court in Canadian ports (discussed by Fingard) or in British ports. During the campaign against unseaworthy ships led by Plimsoll and others in the 1870s, the British government attempted to keep more detailed records on vessels alleged to be unseaworthy and on sailors who refused duty in merchant vessels. For most of the sailors committed to prison in the 1870s for refusing to proceed to sea from a port in the United Kingdom there exists a brief statement of the reasons for refusing to work. Table 18 summarizes these reasons for sailors convicted in 1870, 1871, and 1872 (excluding the large number of cases where the reason was not given). The stated reasons may conceal the real reasons, of course, and shipowners often protested that "unprincipled seamen" used unseaworthiness "as an excuse for being relieved from their engagements, more especially in cases where they have received a payment of wages in advance, or where they have thought they could improve their position."[18]

Concern over unseaworthy ships had preceded Plimsoll by many decades, of course. Since 1855 law officers of the crown had ad-

TABLE 18

Reasons for Refusal to Proceed in Vessels Leaving British Ports, 1870-2

Reason Given by Sailors	No.	%
Vessel unseaworthy/leaky	284	36.5
Vessel overladen	24	3.1
Vessel under-manned	57	7.3
Inadequate provisions	52	6.7
Gear or pumps not working	6	0.8
Inadequate crew accommodations	51	6.6
Wages or advance too low	11	1.4
Other complaint about vessel or work conditions	22	2.8
Did not like master/master violent	48	6.2
Did not like mate/mate violent/dispute with mate	34	4.4
Did not like crew	6	0.8
Refusal to act as scabs	11	1.4
Drunk at the time	69	8.9
Arrived late	39	5.0
Personal illness	23	3.0
Illness in family	4	0.5
Unexplained desertion/other	37	4.7

Source: "Return of the Crews of Merchant Ships, which have been committed to Prison in the Years 1870, 1871 and 1872 for Refusing to Proceed to Sea," British Parliamentary Papers, 1873, vol. LIX, 245ff. Nationality of sailors is not given, but probably most were British.

vised the Board of Trade that sailors did have the right to refuse to serve in unseaworthy vessels. This left the onus of proof on the sailors themselves, but from 1864, if not before, British magistrates were advised to order surveys of vessels where allegations had been made. This encouraged sailors in their resort to litigation or to consular authority in foreign ports. Possibly the opportunity of better wages in other vessels or of spending an advance were reasons more common than sailors would admit in court. But this does not mean that allegations of unseaworthiness may be dismissed as spurious. In 1877 the Board of Trade ordered over 200 vessels to be detained because they were overladen. In the mid-1870s over 2,000 sailors in British vessels died each year; one estimate suggests that 36,000 seamen perished between 1872 and 1884.[19]

If sailors frequently complained about unseaworthy vessels, they had reason to do so.[20] As Table 18 suggests, most convictions followed from sailors' complaints about their vessels or working conditions: almost two-thirds fall into this category. Another 13 per cent of refusals to work followed from complaints about the master, mate, or crew of a vessel (in one vessel the crew refused to work when it discovered the previous crew on board, on strike for higher wages). In a small minority of cases, conviction followed from the vices commonly attributed to seamen in the British and colonial merchant marine: drunkenness and dilatoriness. The sailor's refusal to work was part of a struggle for control over working conditions. The struggle to improve working conditions at sea was not merely a campaign by humanitarian reformers at the parliamentary level.

It is possible to focus on the vessels of Atlantic Canada, but to do so the historian must use the official logs for those vessels, even though the logs do not allow the precision of statistical analysis. An extensive survey of these logs suggests that the pattern reflected in Table 18 was repeated in Canadian vessels: refusal to work and refusal to obey orders were the most common reasons for entries in logs relating to misdemeanours by sailors.[21] Most disputes resulted from apparent attempts by owners to minimize operating costs and concerned manning of the vessel, hours of work, victualling, cargo-handling, or seaworthiness. Statutory regulations in these areas were usually voluntary – matters of custom – rather than compulsory. Working conditions were governed by a contract, and the sailor could refuse to sign the contract, but he had no right to bargain formally over its content. This situation ensured that customary practice, and practices that sailors now claimed as tradition, would collide with the interests of owners determined to minimize costs.

Undermanning was a common cost-cutting tactic. Protests occurred as a result, both during and at the beginning of a voyage. There was no statutory regulation of the minimum number of men required in a vessel, although an act of 1835 (5 and 6 William IV, cap 19) had specified a minimum number of apprentices to be carried in vessels of different tonnages. Various recommendations about proper manning levels followed, as well as humanitarian outcry that served to legitimize protest by seamen. And there was legal compulsion in cases where an undermanned vessel was judged to be unseaworthy because of the undermanning.[22] In Tinby Roads, South Wales, on 5 December 1866, an AB named George Harris refused to proceed to sea on the grounds that the vessel was short one man; a magistrate found in his favour and the master hired another seaman.[23]

Outside the United Kingdom, faced with a ruthless master, the crew might not so easily win its case. In July 1871 the *Beau Monde*, a vessel owned by the Moran family of Saint Martin's, New Brunswick, was lying in Honolulu. Seven ABs refused to man the windlass to heave the anchor: "They said there was not sufficient men on board" and they went into the forecastle. The master, a Scotsman named John W. Ross, stated in the official log that the vessel was fully manned: "The Ship has got her full number of crew 24 all tole & one passenger." The crew list indicated that only 20 crew members were employed in a three-masted ship of 1,047 registered tons. And on this same day the chief mate, an Englishman with previous experience in the *Beau Monde*, was discharged and advised the crew not to proceed in the vessel.

But Ross would not be delayed: together with his mates and petty officers and the passenger, he raised the anchor and made sail. The crew members went on deck to find the vessel under way. They said that "they would go to work if they got the pay for men that is short." The master declared that the matter would have to be settled in court on arrival in England. There is no report of a court case upon arrival in Liverpool, and the master paid off the crew. But it had not been an easy passage, for the official log records several subsequent instances of refusal to work, as well as cases of scurvy. Compared to other ships of her size in the early 1870s, the *Beau Monde* had gone round the Horn short two ABs; the crew had not been able to do anything about it.[24]

Disputes over seaworthiness often occurred before the voyage began but could also occur at sea. When a vessel was damaged at sea the master often had a difficult choice to make: should he proceed to his intended destination or put into the nearest port for repairs? Proceeding with the voyage often required repairs at sea, extra work for the crew, long hours at the pumps, and increased risk. While seeking to avoid the loss of cargo or vessel, the master was under great pressure to complete the voyage as quickly as possible. Often he would decide to proceed, but his decision required the co-operation of his crew, which did not have the same interest in a speedy passage.

In 1871 the barque *Newcastle* of Windsor was five days from Greenock bound for New Orleans when she met a gale and sprung a leak. On 20 April the master reported that he had found no less than seven feet of water in the hold, and the crew manned the pumps for 16 hours. Eventually the men reduced the water to three feet eight inches, but "when turning all hands to pump ship, the[y] refused to proceed any further unless I hove up to England." The master went into the hold, found the source of the leak, but could not "get at it" to make repairs. In these circumstances the crew had its way, and the master returned to port in Britain.[25]

A similar problem occurred on board the *Pomona* of Saint John when she went aground in fog in the St Lawrence in 1868. The crew managed to get the vessel off the rocks after eight days of heavy work but refused to work unless the master put back to Quebec for repairs. In such circumstances refusing to work could result in lengthy bargaining, and in the *Pomona* bargaining continued for four days. The master argued that they could not reach Quebec because the vessel would not beat to windward. The crew argued for the nearest port, and finally they agreed on St John's, Newfoundland.[26] In this case, several circumstances had led to bargaining and consensus: the mutual recognition of danger, a degree of mutual respect, and the recognition that both sides had power with which to back up any threats.

More often, however, the complaint of unseaworthiness would lead to a court decision or to a confrontation at sea. On leaving Montevideo in 1869 the *Alexander* of Saint John struck a reef. The men refused to proceed unless the vessel were surveyed, and they struck work for 24 hours. The master judged that it was safe to proceed and that repairs could not be effected in Montevideo. He was supported by his mates. He put the three "ringleaders" in irons and so persuaded the rest of the crew to set sail.[27]

The log books suggest that disputes over hours of work were very frequent in Atlantic Canadian vessels. Here the conflict between custom and the interests of owners was very clear. Canadian vessels followed the pattern of watch above and watch below. Neither the official logs nor the crew articles made formal note of a common violation of this tradition in Canadian vessels: no afternoon watch below. Masters who ordered both watches on deck in the afternoon often heard the following response: "Seamen refused to come on deck to assist in setting up Rigging and various other jobs of work to secure the Rigging told the mate they would not stop on deck in the afternoon."[28]

By the 1870s crews serving in ocean-going vessels appear to have lost the battle over afternoon watch, and most would expect work in that watch, but there were still occasional protests and references to past custom. In the *John Barbour* of Saint John, sailing from Montreal to Montevideo in 1873, the master attempted to begin the morning work 10 minutes before custom allowed. At 5:50 a.m. he "ordered the watch to muster buckets to wash decks down." The sailors "murmured" and replied that "it was not 4 Bells (6 o'clock)." The master chose to make an example of one sailor, whom he put in irons. Later the same watch challenged the master on behalf of its colleague and cited the custom of afternoon watch below. At half past noon on 4 January, with drawn sheath knives in their hands, the men "refused to do any more work until W. Lewis was released and that they should not be kept up in the afternoon watch." The master went "to considerable trouble" (meaning, likely, that a fight ensued or that he employed a revolver) and "got them driven into the forecastle & confined them there without food until they were willing to go to their duty." The men did not return to work until noon of 7 January: they had been without food for three days. William Lewis held out for five days and then returned to work.[29]

Disputes also occurred over work on Sunday and other holidays. Here, too, custom collided with the impatience of masters determined to lay on sail or to see port times reduced. Tradition held that on Sunday necessary work about the sails and rigging would be done but that other tasks about the vessel would not occur. In vessels where David Perley Crowe was master, for instance, "the men were free to sleep, to mend or wash clothing, to engage in games or to spend the time as they saw fit."[30] But when in 1867 the master of the *David G. Fleming* of Saint John wanted to move his vessel from its anchorage into the inner harbour at Aden, his crew refused to proceed "as it was Sunday." Before the consul the master argued that "it was absolutely necessary to move the ship as she was lying in a dangerous position." Such an argument was well calculated to impress a British consul, and even tradition obliged that work be done on Sunday if a vessel were at risk. If the deckhands denied that the vessel was in danger, the consul would heed the master's judgment. The men were ordered to work, their only alternative being a jail sentence.[31]

Where the dispute could not so easily be referred to a consul or magistrate, the crew might win the dispute. On the *Peter Maxwell* of Saint John, in mid-Atlantic bound for Saint John, George Sulis ordered his crew to stitch the fore sail, which had been split in heavy weather. The crew refused this task on the grounds that it was Sunday. Sulis argued not only the need for safety but the need for speed: "It was impossible to get the Ship to the Westward without canvass." The crew was not persuaded, and the first mate and a boy stitched the sail.[32]

Very often it appears that the religious convictions of masters encouraged them toward traditional Sunday observance. But at least one Nova Scotia master, M.P. McElhinney of Windsor, took Sunday observance too far. He insisted not only that all crew members attend his "Divine Service" on Sundays but that washing clothes was a violation of the sabbath. He fined men who commited this offence, and we do not know whose will prevailed in the subsequent conflict.[33] There were few formal holidays in this industry, but Christmas Day was usually observed by the avoidance of non-essential work. When Thomas Trefry tried to insist that his crew wash decks on Christmas Day, all refused. Since his vessel was in port, Trefry had an option: he could and did hire shore workers to do the work and charged the cost to his seven ABs.[34]

Disputes also occurred over the hours of work in port, again because tradition often contradicted the needs of the master and because the practice of cargo-handling varied from one port to another. In Atlantic Canada sailors were gradually replaced in major ports by shore workers, but in many ports throughout the world sailors took a major part in the tasks of loading and discharging cargo.[35] Sailors were required to do such work, and the laws about refusing work or disobeying the command of the master would apply. But there was considerable room for interpretation and dispute.

At many ports work proceeded from 6 a.m. to 6 p.m. Dispute often arose in ports where such hours were not observed, and where (as in South American guano ports) lighters carrying cargo might come alongside in the evening. In July 1870 the *Tasmanian* of Saint John was loading guano in the Guanape Islands when the crew struck: "The whole of the crew refused to take in about a ton of Guano because it was 6 o'clock. I told them 6 oclock had nothing to do with them when there was cargo alongside. I explained to them of the risk and value of it but they still refused to work Ephraim Waters and Israel Francis being ringleaders."[36] Waters and Francis were taken to the consul who told them "they must take the Guano in whenever it came alongside." The men appear to have returned to work, under the threat of being put in irons. In August 1865, the crew of the ship *Zambesi* of Saint John struck work in the Chincha Islands for the same reason. The master, John Cameron, argued that "there are no regular hours at Chinchas" and put six ABs in irons when they continued to refuse work. A British consul came on board to hear the men's complaint: he stated that "the rules of the port were to work at all hours that Cargo could be got"; the men insisted that they would not work before 6 a.m. or after 6 p.m. The consul ordered them "into confinement with bread and water for food until such time as they should turn too." Within five days the men had returned to work, but three weeks later they all struck again, refusing to sail the vessel from Callao. Only after further visits to the consul (we do not know what occurred at this time) did the vessel proceed.[37] Disputes over loading after 6 p.m. also occurred in American cotton ports and in the West Indies.[38]

Attempts to economize in the provision of food led to confrontations in which the resistance of workers had a clear purpose. Complaints about grub were inevitably more common on longer voyages, when vessels were more likely to run short of provisions, or when food was spoiled and bread was stale. Disputes over victuals were also frequent because by the 1860s crew articles stated the amount that the crew was promised on a daily or weekly basis, and so the crew had prior knowledge and a clear basis for argument if the scale were violated.

Disputes over victualling often involved threats and violence, and here violence was clearly directed toward the improvement of conditions of service. Only a few days out of Liverpool, Charles Curry, master of the *Juno* of Windsor, found himself faced by an enraged crew which had discovered that, faced with a long voyage to Rio de Janeiro, the bread was already stale. "The remainder of the crew came aft and threatened to take our lives. I then went on deck and told them I would give them better bread," but the problem was not solved. On the next day the crew "armed themselves with belaying pins and clubs," and the master forced the men back toward the forecastle by brandishing his revolver. Upon arrival in Rio the crew demanded to see the British consul, and when the master refused to allow more than two of them ashore, most deserted.[39]

Sometimes complaints over victualling were resolved in favour of the crew, when the quantity promised in the crew list had not been given, or when the quality was so bad that the food was inedible. In Rangoon on 18 September 1872, a British consul examined samples of biscuit from the ship *S. Vaughan* after six ABs had refused duty. "The samples produced and admitted by the Master and officer to be the ships' bread were decidedly bad." The master agreed to remove all stale bread from the vessel and was ordered to pay the crew "compensation for the number of days during which it was issued to them."[40] At other times the crew of a badly provisioned vessel had no option but jail or desertion. When Edward Baxter, master of the Saint John ship *Ann Gray*, ordered his vessel under way from the Clyde to Saint John via Belfast, his 12 ABs and one OS refused to proceed on the grounds that "they wanted to be better fed" and that "the stove would not keep the forecastle warm at sea" because of inadequate fuel (the date was 1 December). All these deckhands were sent to jail for six weeks, and Baxter hired another crew, all of whose members deserted in Belfast. A third crew took the vessel to Saint John and promptly deserted.[41]

In theory sailors knew in advance what food they would receive. In practice, however, they did not know what stores the vessel carried. The list of provisions may be deceptive. Underneath the scale of provisions on the front of most crew lists were the words "Equivalent substitutes at Master's option" – which left the matter open to interpretation. Samuel Hughes, master of the *William Carvill*, sailing in 1869 from Liverpool to Rangoon, agreed to provide something less than the Board of Trade–recommended scale of 1868, but nevertheless a fairly common diet: 1½ pounds of beef or pork daily; a pound of bread a day; 1½ pounds of flour weekly; peas three times a week; and sugar, coffee, water, and lime juice. It is very unlikely that the crew received even this minimal diet, because after six months at sea five men, including the cook, had scurvy.[42] In a letter accompanying his official log, the master blamed the scurvy on "bad Aden water" and the refusal of the men to drink fresh rain water at sea.

When victualling was clearly inferior, crews might obtain some relief by appealing to a magistrate or consul, but neither the likelihood of redress nor the penalties imposed constituted an effective deterrent. The ship *Athenais* of Saint John set sail for Callao from Aden on 29 August 1866. She was so badly provisioned that on arrival in Callao on 10 December most crew members, including the first mate, were suffering from scurvy. The consul ordered a doctor to investigate, and the doctor ordered 12 seamen and the first mate into hospital. On 17 December the consul advised the master, William Birch, that his vessel would not be given clearance until a full investigation had been carried out.

A naval court inquiry into the causes of scurvy found "the Beef and Pork has been of very inferior quality, and the Lime Juice quite useless as an anti-scorbutic, which we consider to have been the sole causes of the sickness of the crew and consequently we deem the owners of the ship highly reprehensible and adjudge them to pay the hospital expenses, as well as the expenses for the surveying of the proceedings." The court stated further that the master "has shown a culpable want of attention to his crew while sick, and who we consider highly to blame for leaving Aden knowing the inferior quality of the Provisions with so small a supply of livestock." After this reprimand the vessel was allowed to sail, which she did on 19 December. Birch had been delayed only a few days. On his next voyage we find Birch making his own silent protest: he recorded in his official log what food was issued to the crew on almost every day of the voyage.[43]

There is evidence that seamen in Canadian vessels were sometimes ordered to perform work not normally associated with their ranks. Many disputes arose in such circumstances, when interpretations of custom differed. In the *Beau Monde*, passing through the Red Sea in 1868, the mate ordered both the cook and the steward to assist in reefing the fore topsail. The cook refused on the grounds that, since it was noon, he was "going to make the men's dinner." The master attempted to resolve the dispute by putting the cook in irons: he clearly expected that the cook must assist in working the sails at any time of day. After two days in irons the cook returned to his galley, but he had not forgotten his disagreement with the master and he refused to do any extra work. A few weeks later he served the master pea soup "quite covered on the top with small flies and a quantity of large maggots," and the master gave up the struggle, noting in his log that "acts of dirtiness are of frequent occurrence with the Cook."[44]

Sailors were sticklers for routine, and they could use the ship's routine as grounds for "working to rule." Isaac Doane, master of the *Gertrude* of Saint John, discovered an entire crew of "sea lawyers" after he refused to give them coffee at 6:30 a.m., when they were accustomed to it. "They all made answer and said they would not work half so hard as they had done." The protest continued with the crew protesting about late breakfasts and refusing to work unless breakfast were served promptly at 6 a.m.[45]

Crew articles, as they became more detailed and comprehensive, could also serve as the basis of working to rule. In December 1869 the *William Carvill* of Saint John was at sea from Moulmein to Liverpool when the crew demanded that butter and bread be weighed out individually to each man, instead of being weighed out once for the whole watch before the men divided it among each other. The dispute arose not between deckhands but from conditions in the ship: several crew members had previously refused to work and had requested their discharge in Moulmein, which the master denied them. When the master refused to order that butter be weighed individually, the crew refused to take it. On 1 January the master "sent to the men three bottles of wine being new year's day," but they returned [it] saying it was not on the articles." On 2 January the men were served a half-pound of rice each (presumably in lieu of potatoes), but "they returned it saying it was on the articles only as a *substitute*. They were offered Preserved Potatoes they also refused to take them." On 11 January the men were demanding individual weighing of their quarter-ounce of tea, their bread, their three ounces of molasses, and their lime juice and sugar. On 19 January Thomas Clarke, AB, "refused to have his sugar saying it was too much weight saying the Steward wanted to Rob the owners." Other ABs refused their lime juice and sugar on the same grounds. The sarcastic defence of the owner's interest was a pointed rebuke of master and officers.[46]

Sailors knew that the master was the servant of shipowners, and they understood that by contract they were doing no more than selling labour power in return for wages. The universal use of a formal contract legitimized sailors' protests, and this was what so infuriated masters and owners: the sale of labour power by contract had legitimized informal bargaining over all conditions of employment. Now the sailor raised issues that masters thought trivial or picayune. The master of a New Brunswick barque, shortly after leaving Saint John, discovered that his starboard watch "refused to work, on a/c of the bread, it is good but the fellows having seen some of the fresh, are not content till they get some of it." Later in the same voyage, "the men all came aft and requested molasses in their Barley soup, & said the beef & bread was bad, the infernal scoundrels all they want is to get some hold of us."[47]

Such complaints were not a simple response to hunger nor even a defence of established custom. First one watch, and then an entire crew, were claiming a right grounded in their view of natural justice and a "moral economy of provision."[48] The presence of fresh bread, only a few days from port, proved that it was possible to provide fresh bread; therefore nothing inferior was acceptable. The uncontrollable fury of sailors in particular instances suggests not a simple, unreasoning response to deprivation, but rather a sense of moral outrage at the violation of assumed rights. In 1873 the master of a Saint John ship infringed upon his second mate's right to spend more shore leave as he chose, and the second mate responded in violent rage, attacking the master with his fists and with a boathook: "I found the 2nd mate in a Rum Shop drinking and a good deal the worse for liquor, I called him out and told him I wondered at him drinking that way, and he said what I drink I pay for, I dont want you or any other Buger to pay for my drink I suppose I can come and drink as well as you ... On the way to the ship he was very impudent, saying it was all my fault, I did not know the way to handle men, I told him I would treat him as he deserved, he said ... you starve gutted animal, you can only give me the law and no more."[49] It was not only drink but also pride and moral outrage that moved this sailor to violence.

In the last half of the nineteenth century it was possible to charge masters with assault and to obtain convictions. There were definable limits to the use of punitive force, and sailors took advantage of this fact. On many occasions crews acted together to attempt to remove one of their fellows from irons when they felt an injustice had been done, or when the punishment caused the victim to become ill. Moral outrage against an excess of force often led to further violence, as occurred in Aden in 1866 when the master of the *Henry* of Saint John was summoned before the magistrate on a charge of criminal violence against six of his seamen. When the magistrate dismissed the charge and the triumphant master ordered the men back to the ship, the six plaintiffs were so enraged at the failure of justice that they attacked and thrashed the master in the court-room, whereupon they were sentenced to three months in prison.[50] Violent as they often were, seamen were moved by a moral consensus that law and contractual obligations seemed to sanction: "You can give me the law and no more."

How effective were seamen in this primitive bargaining process? It is impossible to know precisely how many court actions resulted in decisions favourable to sailors, but the evidence of the official logs suggests that where sailors refused duty they rarely won their case. Most disputes were settled at sea, however, where withdrawal of labour could be a potent weapon. Provided a vessel were not in danger, the crew could cease work at less cost to itself than to the master, and of course master and officers were always outnumbered.

Nevertheless, master and officers always possessed superior power, even at sea. The master was usually the only person in a vessel who possessed firearms. Occasionally one reads of able seamen with firearms, and in one very leaky New Brunswick vessel in 1855 a crew demanded extra food for extra work, and, according to the master, "they are firing pistols ocationaly to intimidate and force ther demands."[51] Seamen usually possessed only sheath-knives; masters kept pistols and sometimes shotguns in their cabins. Rarely was a master confronted by an entire crew at the same time, and well before violence was threatened a cautious master attempted to isolate "ringleaders" from the rest in order to divide and weaken his opponents. If all else failed, the power to withdraw food would usually force men into submission. Faced with such powers even a united crew had difficulty in winning concessions from a determined master.

The crew of the *Brenda* of Halifax was overpowered even by a weak master in 1869. George Tilley appears to have had frequent troubles with his crews: on his previous voyage the entire crew refused to work until Tilley replaced the steward (the men believed that the steward was trying to poison them); and on that voyage

Tilley's wife had been assaulted by the second mate.[52] Now, on 28 March 1869, Tilley's crew refused to work. The *Brenda* was lying at the South-West Pass, near the mouth of the Mississippi, and Tilley had given orders to heave the anchor and set sail for Pensacola. The crew first objected to setting sail on a Sunday. But there were other issues at stake, for on the next day the crew had still not touched the anchors and was insisting on a survey of the vessel, believing it to be unseaworthy. The master answered that no surveyors were available in South-West Pass; the men would have to sail to Pensacola before a survey could be made.

The crew continued to refuse work, but the master still had options open to him. First he threatened to put the spokesmen for the crew in irons; the men, "cursing and using the most fearful language," went toward the forecastle. The master went to his cabin and took out his revolver; thus equipped, and accompanied by his two officers and bosun, he went toward the forecastle. Having identified two men as "ringleaders," he called them out. The two men came out of the forecastle with knives in hand and dared the master to shoot them. The master hesitated, thinking that "if I went to any stringent measures there might be trouble."

At this point Tilley ordered the cook and the steward to give no food to the crew. At 5 p.m. on the 29th, having had no food all day, the men were in a mood to negotiate. They offered to sail to Pensacola if the master would discharge them there. The master, "having to make any kind of promise to get the anchors hove up," agreed to let the consul in Pensacola settle the matter. By this combination of force, withdrawal of food, and the promised intervention of the consul, the master had his way. The men were fed, and the vessel proceeded to Pensacola. There, on 5 April, a surveyor appointed by the consul declared the vessel to be "fit for any service." By 9 April, ten seamen, having failed to win their case, had deserted.[53]

The master possessed other means by which to enforce work-discipline at sea. He was physically removed from the crew, and he could use this distance to separate the men from each other and to exercise his authority over each man separately. The master remained on the poop or in his cabin: if he chose to speak directly to a seaman, it was always on his terms, following a summons to come aft. And every sailor had his "trick at the wheel," when he stood for hours, alone with the master on the poop. There, while his eyes passed from compass to vessel to the sea, the sailor could see the master standing a few feet away, a silent figure of authority. One did not speak to him, except to acknowledge an order. The master said nothing, unless the vessel were off course, and then uttered whatever advice or insult he chose. One did not enter the master's cabin, except to receive a reprimand, to witness one's misdemeanours recorded in the log, or to receive medical treatment. Authority in the vessel was visible but remote, but the master could impress and even intimidate by his silent presence.

The final guarantee of the master's superior power at sea was his possession of nautical instruments and his knowledge of their use. The first mate might possess these things as well, but it was unlikely that any other person in the vessel did so. There are remarkably few stories that tell of a master who had so lost all his other powers that his knowledge was his only remaining weapon. In a British ship, the *Berwickshire*, sailing from London to India, the master used his knowledge to overpower a crew – and the story, or others like it, would have travelled through forecastles around the world, among the many yarns of masters and men. The master wanted normal work on Sunday; the crew went to work, grumbling; a violent "bucko" mate set off a brawl, and a united crew forced the master and mates to hide in the master's cabin. The bosun took charge of the deck, "but having no nautical instruments at his command it was not long before the crew were out of their reckoning ... Recognizing their helplessness they commenced to parley with the skipper and eventually they offered to release him and the other officers if he would let bygones be bygones. To this he agreed." In Bombay the master summoned the police and charged his crew with mutiny.[54] For a few hours the crew thought that it had control of the vessel, but the illusion was short-lived. Such was the power that the art and science of navigation had bestowed on the master of large sailing ships.

Against the formidable powers of the master the crew did have means of bargaining and of protection, as we have seen. It also possessed rights under common law, and men could bring charges of assault against master and officers. Convicting a master of assault usually required proof that the use of force had been unprovoked and that the crew had committed no prior violation of disciplinary provisions in the Merchant Shipping Acts. If a master were convicted, the penalty was usually a fine (in Aden in 1866 the master of a Saint John vessel was convicted of assault on members of his crew and fined 30 shillings). In Hong Kong in 1894 the master of a Halifax vessel was convicted of murdering a crew member, and there were other cases where British masters were convicted of murder.[55] The sentences were usually light, however. Certainly the possibility of charging a master with assault did little to alter the balance of power in a ship.

Official logs and court records can give the misleading impression that violence was unusually chronic in sailing vessels. But there is no way to know whether violence and corporal punishment were more common at sea than in mines and factories. Masters and foremen on land were not required by law to record all disciplinary actions. And even official logs themselves suggest that the incidence of violence should not be exaggerated. Most entries in the logs relate to non-violent incidents, to illness, to accidents, or to damage to vessel or cargo. Most pages in most official logs are blank – silent testimony to the fact that nothing occurred to disturb the routine of work at sea.

But even if violence were infrequent, conflict was endemic. The power of the master, and the stringent legal framework governing work at sea, were designed in part to contain that conflict. One measure of that conflict is the frequency with which men sought to escape from their workplace. Although the crew of the *Brenda* was overpowered by the master in 1869, and took the vessel to Pensacola as he wished, it did have an option apart from further submission. It could, and did, leave the vessel, withdrawing labour permanently from that employer.

Taking leave of a vessel was not the same as taking leave of other workplaces: here the manner of one's going was far more a matter for decision by both employer and employee, and the process was governed by statutory law. One did not simply pick up one's tools, or give notice, and leave. The sailor signed a contract to serve in particular places and for specified periods of time. To leave without permission of the master, and before the terms of the contract were fulfilled, was desertion – an offence punishable by the forfeit of wages earned and 12 weeks' imprisonment. Desertion was at one level an expression of discontent, and it was inherently an act of conflict between employer and employee. For sailors, as for workers in other industries characterized by isolation and high turn-over rates, quitting was a "demonstration of freedom and independence of the employer."[56] In the smaller sailing vessels of Atlantic Canada, making short coastal runs or passages to Britain and back, such expressions of discontent were relatively rare. By the later nineteenth century they were very common.

The master's stated reasons for the departure of his crew are not a perfect guide to motives or circumstances. There were many reasons for leaving vessels, and the crew lists miss some. Very often, as log books make clear, a mutually agreed discharge conceals dissatisfaction on both sides. Any analysis of reasons for leaving a vessel based on entries in crew agreements is likely to underestimate the number of escapes or discharges resulting from discontent. The entry "failed to join" offers no guide to the reasons for not joining, which may have nothing to do with the vessel.

There were ways to leave a ship at sea, and one suspects that these were not always reported accurately. Sailors sometimes threatened to jump overboard, and occasionally they carried out the threat.[57] Suicide was rare in sailing vessels, but it may be underreported. The main problem with the reporting of discharges in the crew lists is that the entries were made by the master and so reflect his interpretation of events. Leaving a vessel was an act defined by laws that the sailor did not write. If sailors had given their reasons for leaving a vessel, the record would look very different. But the crew agreements remain an indispensable guide, if not to the motives of sailors, to relations between the sailor and authority upon departure.

For virtually all who signed crew agreements in our four fleets there is an entry under "Date, Place, and Cause of Leaving this Ship." Almost half (49.4 per cent) were discharged by mutual consent at the end of the voyage. Only a very small number (1.9 per cent) remained with the vessel at the end of the voyage, and most of these were officers. There were other reasons that make no formal statement of conflict with authority: sailors were discharged by mutual consent during voyages (10.3 per cent); were discharged because of illness (1.0 per cent); died at sea (0.8 per cent); or were discharged because the vessel was sold, wrecked, or condemned, or because the voyage was abandoned (1.1 per cent). In a majority of cases, therefore, sailors left vessels without placing themselves in conflict with law or authority. What is surprising is the number of departures that involved conflict because the sailor was departing before the terms of his contract were fulfilled. About 35.5 per cent of departures fell into this broad category. They included desertion (25.4 per cent), either before or during a voyage; failure to join (9.3 per cent); discharge before sailing (0.3 per cent); discharge by court order or into jail (0.4 per cent); and discharge following demotion or refusal to work (0.1 per cent).

Departures involving conflict or discontent increased over time. Desertions were slightly under 20 per cent of all discharges in the 1860s. By the years 1879 to 1890 desertions had risen to 28.7 per cent in all four fleets. The proportion failing to join increased from less than 6 per cent in the 1860s to 11 per cent in the 1880s. In the same decades the proportion remaining at the end of the voyage fell, and so did the proportion discharged by mutual consent at the end of the voyage. The pattern is the same in all four fleets. There is no more telling measure of the increase of conflict in the workplace than this: by the 1880s two in every five sailors ran afoul of both their masters and the law in the course of the average voyage by the manner of their leaving their ships, and their departure made them liable to prison sentences. In the 1860s the proportion had been one in four; in the 1840s, at least in the vessels of Atlantic Canada, much lower.

Sailors had many opportunities to leave before their voyage was completed, and many personal, economic, and other factors could persuade a man to leave his ship. It is possible, however, to say something about the conditions in which desertion occurred and in which it increased. The timing of the increase in desertion affords a first indication of those conditions. Graph 11 plots the proportion of desertions and failure to join on an annual basis for the Saint John fleet, in those years for which data are adequate. The desertion rate was already high in the 1860s, but the upward trend is slight before 1877. The proportion of desertions then rose: it was higher in the mid-1880s than ever before, and higher again in the late 1890s. A comparison with Graph 10 – the freight rate indices – suggests an interesting coincidence. The desertion rate increased when freight rates fell, and there is a strong negative correlation (the coefficient is − 0.81) between the two series. The coincidence is unlikely to be accidental, for there is other evidence to suggest that desertion was a response to the pressure on wages and other cost-cutting measures that followed from declining rates of return.

GRAPH 11

Discharge Reasons by Year, Saint John Fleet, 1863–1910

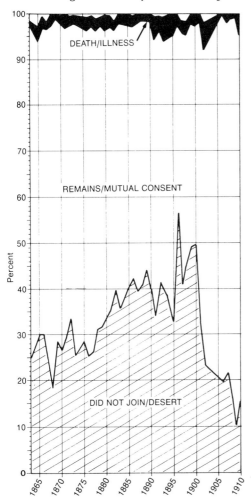

Source: Crew Agreements for Saint John-registered vessels, MHA.
Note: These figures are percentages of all stated reasons for leaving ships or for terminating the crew agreement.

Those who deserted were usually in the lower ranks and hired at the lowest rates of pay. Table 19 indicates the percentages of discharge reasons by rank. This table is based on discharges of sailors in four fleets, but it matters little which fleet we choose, and in

TABLE 19

Discharge Reasons (%) by Rank, Four Fleets, 1863-1914

Discharge Reason	Officer	Petty Officer	AB	OS	Other*
Did not join/desert	8.0	15.1	41.5	36.4	20.9
Dishonourable discharge	0.2	0.2	0.5	0.3	0.2
By mutual consent	83.7	79.1	54.3	58.0	69.3
Remains with vessel	5.0	2.7	1.0	2.2	6.9
Death/illness	1.5	1.7	1.8	2.1	1.8
Other	1.6	1.2	0.9	1.0	0.9

Source: Crew Lists, MHA.

* Other includes boys and apprentices and a number of engineers and trimmers in the handful of steamers in the sample.

most of the analysis that follows the Saint John crew file will be used. Very few officers failed to join or deserted, but a large proportion of ABs and OSs ended their service in a vessel before a voyage began or by deserting during the voyage. Most of the increase in desertion rates over time was accounted for by the increasing propensity of ABs to desert and, to a lesser extent, by the increase in deckhands as a proportion of the total labour force.

Desertion rates increased across time for all sailors, whatever their rank, so there were certainly many other factors at work. The longer the voyage, in space and time, the greater the proportion of the crew that deserted. A longer voyage offered more opportunities to desert and increased the likelihood of disputes over victualling and other working conditions. It also increased the likelihood of arrival in ports where labour was relatively scarce, and where the wage differential between those in the ship and those on shore, or in other ships, would tempt men to desert. Many other conditions of work and of conflict accompanied the longer voyage and increased the frequency of desertion. But time was certainly a factor in the process, for it was relatively easy to sign on for a West Indian passage and know that whatever the conditions might be, and whatever disputes might develop, one would have to endure them for only a few weeks before obtaining one's discharge.

TABLE 20

Discharge Reasons by Trade Route (%), Four Fleets, 1863-1914

Trade	Did Not Join/ Deserted	Remained at End	Discharge by Mutual Consent
West Indies	23.7	3.3	69.4
Europe/Britain	9.2	4.9	84.3
East Coast			
North America	26.2	6.6	60.9
North Atlantic	37.0	2.3	59.2
South America	34.5	0.7	60.7
Pacific/Far East	37.1	0.7	58.6

Source: Crew Lists, MHA.

Table 20 offers a comparison between discharges in a few broad types of voyage. The first three routes involved coastal or short-distance voyages; the next three were longer voyages and trans-oceanic passages. On the longer voyages, more than a third of sailors signing on deserted during the voyage or failed to join. Following a long voyage the crew was very unlikely to remain with the same vessel. The proportion of voyages in the latter categories increased by the 1880s and 1890s and these longer voyages were one important condition of increasing conflict and desertion. One reason for the fall in desertion rates after 1896 (see Graph 11) was that voyage duration declined and the proportion of shorter coastal voyages increased again, as the large ocean-going sailing vessels went off registry more quickly than did smaller vessels.

Frequency of desertion also increased with the size of vessels. So did the number of "dishonourable" discharges. In the Saint John fleet, as in the others, a small proportion of crews in our sample served in vessels under 250 tons. But in those that did, no sailor received a "dishonourable" discharge (meaning discharge into jail, discharge following demotion, and the like), and only 12.5 per cent failed to join or deserted. In vessels of 500 tons and more no less than 31.3 per cent failed to join or deserted (see also Table 21, limited to North Atlantic voyages in the 1880s). Illness and death were much more frequent in large vessels than in smaller ones (in small vessels 1.1 per cent of those signing crew lists left through ill-ness or death; in vessels over 500 tons, 2.5 per cent). There is a con-nection, of course, between size of vessel and length of voyage; but the larger vessel was also the workplace in which the older pater-nalism and localism had weakened or disappeared. In larger vessels fewer sailors were associated with the master or the vessel by past experience, family connection, language, or the ties of a common homeland.

Certain factors having to do with the personal characteristics of sailors do not help to explain the rise in desertion rates. Those born in certain places were more likely to desert than to be discharged by mutual consent. Europeans, Scandinavians, and Americans deserted more often than did those born in British North America or Britain.[58] But this fact is unhelpful: a larger proportion of Cana-dians and British held officer rank, where desertion was least likely; and a larger proportion of Europeans and Scandinavians served in the 1880s and 1890s, when desertion rates had risen for all nationalities. The nationality of the sailor offers no guide to his behaviour on leaving a vessel.[59] There is no source that allows a statistical measure of the relationship between nationality and mis-demeanours during work at sea, but no national group was unusually prone to "dishonourable" discharge, and a relationship between nationality and conflict with authority at sea seems unlikely.

Did the increasing average age of deckhands have anything to do with desertion? It is possible that older sailors may have engaged more readily in conflict when freight rates fell and owners and masters demanded more of both vessels and men. But age explains little: older sailors were slightly less likely to desert, and less likely to receive "dishonourable" discharges, than were sailors in their twenties.[60] Did literacy contribute to the desertion rates, by pro-viding a better-educated and more litigious labour force, which was more likely to enter into disputes with masters? There is in fact no statistical relationship between literacy and reason for discharges, when we look at particular ranks and time periods.[61] Literate seamen were neither more nor less likely than the others to desert to to receive "dishonourable" discharges.

Desertion was a consequence not of the personal characteristics of the sailor but of the relationship between worker and employer and

TABLE 21

Desertions, North Atlantic Voyages, Saint John Fleet, 1880s

Tonnage Class	% of Starting Crew Members Who Desert
100–249 tons	15.0
250–499 tons	19.9
500–999 tons	36.7
1,000–1,499 tons	36.1
1,500 + tons	44.1

Source: Saint John Crew Lists, MHA.

between worker and workplace. The worker was pressured to leave his vessel by conditions on board, or he was tempted to desert by the prospect of better opportunities on shore or in other vessels. In any particular instance, desertion was likely to result from some combination of these "push" and "pull" factors. Certain masters seem to have had an unusual number of deserters, and there is evidence to suggest that masters from British North America were more likely to experience a high rate of desertion and of dishonourable discharges. In the 1880s, for instance, almost 31 per cent of the crews hired by masters residing in Nova Scotia or New Brunswick deserted. Where the master of a Saint John vessel stated his residence to be the United Kingdom, his desertion rate was only 21.6 per cent.

More impressive evidence follows if one asks this question: if there was a high rate of desertion from a vessel, what were the chances that the master was from Nova Scotia or New Brunswick? The probability was, in fact, very high. Of those masters in the Saint John file who experienced a desertion rate of 30 per cent or more among their crews, over 90 per cent resided in Nova Scotia or New Brunswick. Of those masters who experienced a low desertion rate (less than 20 per cent) a large proportion (42 per cent) gave as their residence a place outside British North America. Even more striking is the evidence that masters residing in British North America were more likely to discharge their crews into jail: in the period from 1879 to 1890, sailors working for a Canadian master were more than four times as likely to receive a "dishonourable" discharge as were sailors working for a master who resided in Britain.[62]

Part of the reason for the differences noted here is that Canadian masters frequented those places and trade routes where desertion was likely, for reasons that had nothing to do with the master himself. But there were other reasons for the higher desertion rate among "Bluenose" masters: the reputation for harsh discipline, imposed as much by force as by law, was not entirely undeserved. Canadian owners and masters were determined to cut costs in their industry. They tended to sail their vessels with fewer men than did British owners and masters, for instance.[63] There can be little doubt that the high desertion rate was in part the result of the cost-cutting pressures imposed by British North American owners and masters, and the conflict that often resulted.

One other condition helps to explain the rising desertion rate: the growing disparity between wage levels in a vessel and wage levels elsewhere. To some extent this was a long-standing cause of desertion: wages for sailors signing on in British and European ports had long since been lower than wages in North American ports. To the sailor who signed on in Britain for a few pounds a month, the knowledge that wage levels in his North American port of call were several times as high was a strong temptation to desert. By the last decades of the nineteenth century the disparity between wages in sailing ships and wages on land had increased. And there was now another difference: steamers were also hiring crews, and they offered higher wages for deckhands than did sailing vessels, particularly on the western side of the Atlantic. Sterling wages paid to ABs in sailing vessels did not increase; after the 1870s they declined slightly. By the 1880s and 1890s a larger number of sailors were entering ports on the western coasts of North America, where the labour market for sailors was small and wages tended to be very high in relative terms. Falling rates of return in the sailing ship industry increased conflict between employer and employee by encouraging the sailor to desert in search of better opportunities.

There is a relationship between the reason for leaving a vessel and the port where the sailor left. Ports in Canada and the United States accounted for only 23.4 per cent of all discharges from vessels in the Saint John fleet. But the majority of departures in those North American ports were desertions. The result is that Canadian and US ports accounted for no less than 64.4 per cent of

TABLE 22

North American High-Desertion Ports, 1863–1914

Port	Desertions as % of All Man-entrances	Average AB Wages ($) from the Port
New York	49.0	23.11
San Francisco	45.8	21.25
Baltimore	39.0	23.12
Portland, Ore.	39.0	31.50
Saint John	37.6	21.49
Portland, Me.	37.5	21.35
Philadelphia	35.2	25.27
New Orleans	31.9	22.03
Boston	30.9	21.29
Port Townshend, Wash.	30.3	25.00
Pensacola	29.4	17.79
Charleston, SC	27.5	25.41
All US ports	33.0	23.18
Quebec City	21.2	18.00
Liverpool AB sterling wage		14.87

Source: Saint John Crew Lists, MHA.

all desertions.[64] The increase in the overall desertion rate resulted partly from the fact that by the 1880s a larger proportion of sailors was entering North American ports. Even more important, of all crews leaving in North American ports by the 1880s, a larger proportion left by deserting. Thus, in the 1860s, 59.9 per cent of departures in North America were desertions; by the 1880s, this proportion had risen to 70 per cent.

Table 22 lists the major desertion ports in North America. The propensity to desert in a port must be measured by reference to the total number of desertion opportunities, or the number of man-entrances into port. No less than a third of man-entrances into US ports resulted in desertion (the only other region near to this rate was Australia, with 30 per cent).[65] On an average passage from Britain or Europe to New York, the master could expect to lose almost half his crew.

Table 22 suggests something of the experience of the able seaman who signed on for the return voyage from Liverpool to the United States. He might earn £3 a month from Liverpool. He arrived in the United States to find that unskilled general labourers on shore were earning more than he was. If the AB from Liverpool could desert and find a berth in another vessel putting out from the American port, his monthly wages could increase by 40 per cent or by as much as 110 per cent.

Such wage disparities may appear to shift the emphasis from the vessel itself to alternative opportunities on land. But "push" factors remain important in the explanation of desertion rates. One of every three desertions occurred outside North America. One in every five occurred in continental Europe, the West Indies, South America, Africa, India, or Asia, where local opportunities were less likely to be attractive. And even where high American wage levels played a part, it was the contrast between wage levels in most vessels and wage levels outside the vessel that created the incentive to desert.

We can see the "push" factor of low wages operating very clearly to encourage desertion: desertion occurred where wages were significantly below average. In this analysis, only able seamen's wages are included; all wages are converted to dollars (at $4.86 per pound sterling). In the Saint John fleet, the average monthly wage for the AB who remained in a vessel at the end of the voyage was $19.56. The average wage for the AB who received an "honourable" discharge was $18.59. But the average wages for ABs who deserted was only $15.83. The average wage for those receiving a "dishonourable" discharge was even lower ($15.10). Analysis of variance confirms that these averages are significantly different.[66]

The effect of low wages was particularly dramatic among sailors who left vessels in North American ports. Table 23 compares by levels of wages ABs who left in selected North American ports (Quebec City, New York, Philadelphia, Baltimore, New Orleans, and San Francisco). Where wage levels were low (less than $12.99 or the sterling equivalent) over 81 per cent of those leaving were deserters. Ninety-six per cent of all desertions were accounted for by those in the lowest wage category.[67]

Desertion was an illegal action that resulted in part from differential wage levels. It was a form of conflict originating within

TABLE 23

Wage Levels and Discharges of ABs Entering Selected North American
Ports, 1863–1914

AB Monthly Wages	% of Crew Remaining Or Receiving Honourable Discharge	% of Crew Deserting	% of Crew Leaving for Other Reason*
$12.99 or less	17.6	81.5	0.9
$13.00–$14.99	11.4	52.3	36.4
$15.00–$16.99	54.7	41.1	4.2
$17.00 or more	75.2	18.1	6.7

Source: Saint John Crew Lists, MHA.

* Did not join, discharge before sailing, discharged into jail, and other "dishonourable" discharge.

the capitalist labour market and within the wage relationship between labour and employer. For the sailor it was nothing more than a means of self-improvement and a form of bargaining, although the sailor did not use such words. Wages were low and conditions poor in one place; desertion might offer a remedy. As a bargaining tactic, desertion affected wage levels, not only for individual deserters but throughout the industry. Where the destination of a vessel was a known high-desertion port or area, the master often paid higher wages to his ABs. Thus if a vessel were sailing for the United States and paying sterling wages, average wages would be 8 per cent higher than if the destination were the United Kingdom, and 10 per cent higher than if the destination were Africa, India, or Asia.

A more refined analysis requires that we look at departures from specific ports and in specific time periods. Such analysis confirms that masters were persuaded to offer higher wages when sailing to high-desertion areas. If we look at wages for ABs hired in Liverpool in 1872 and 1873, there is a significant difference between mean wages by the intended destination of the vessel. The mean wage where the destination was British North America was slightly under £4. Where the destination was the United States, the average was about £3-17-0. But where the destination was any other part of the world, the average wage was about £3-3-0.[68] There was a difference here of more than 20 per cent between average wages to North America and average wages to other places.

These higher wages were certainly not offered because of a shortage of sailors wishing to travel the passage to North America. There is instead evidence that masters could be more selective in their choice of crew on these routes. Harris Barnes of Halifax states in his "Reminiscence" that in 1863 he could not find work at all in a vessel from Liverpool to North America: "The end of all was I did as many others had to do, I paid my passage to New York in one of the large packet ships about ready to sail."[69] In 1884, Cephas Pearl of Tancook, Nova Scotia, signed on a vessel in Liverpool for Boston: he used an alias – "George Smith" of London – because, he said, if you hailed from "America" the master would not hire you, for fear you would jump ship in the United States.[70] Masters tried to select their crews carefully, and there was no shortage of sailors willing to make the Atlantic crossing. The higher wages must therefore be an inducement of another sort: either an attempt to reduce the wage disparity upon arrival in North America or an inducement designed to allow greater selectivity in the choice of men.

There is other evidence that masters were compelled to respond to the threat of desertion. Trying to locate and apprehend deserters was difficult and costly. Prevention was a better cure, and so masters attempted to place restrictions on crews sailing for high-desertion ports. The most common restriction was the denial of shore leave at a foreign port, or the denial of any advance of wages in a foreign port, or both of these restrictions together. The former was applied more often as time passed, until, by the 1890s, 79 per cent of Saint John vessels sailed with this restriction applied to the crew.

Even before workers were organized and before the term *strike* was known, withdrawing labour was commonplace as a means of protection and as a bargaining tactic. Its frequency is suggested not simply by the ratio of desertions to port-entrances, but even more by the ratio of desertion to time worked. We know for each sailor the number of days worked in each vessel, and for entire fleets the total man-years worked by crews between 1863 and the early

1900s. For the Saint John fleet there were, over this period, 0.6 desertions per man-year worked (the rate went up from 0.44 in the 1860s to 0.81 in the 1890s): sailors deserted on average once for every year and eight months worked. This form of withdrawal was certainly more frequent than any other. It was also much more frequent than the rare "dishonourable" discharge. In the Saint John fleet there were only 1.7 "dishonourable" discharges for every hundred man-years worked.

Conflict with authority was endemic in sailing vessels, but violent confrontations were less frequent than official records and the reminiscences of sailors might suggest. Conflict took the form of non-violent litigation and withdrawal of labour, and increased when the state sought to protect capital invested in shipping by extensive regulatory measures relating to the labour supply and work-discipline at sea. Sailors sought to use the law to their advantage and to use the vessel's dependence on their labour as a means of bargaining with their masters. When bargaining was impossible they withdrew their labour by desertion, and desertion itself became part of the bargaining process.

To the struggle with employers and with authority sailors brought the capacity for adaptation and survival of men who were literate, migratory, self-reliant, and tenacious in defence of assumed rights. They were not enfeebled and brutalized by their workplace, but they had learned, as James Doane Coffin put it, "to be content with what you have and use all the means of getting more."[71] From their mutual dependence on each other and on the skills necessary for work and survival, they learned a simple moral creed which informed their view of social norms and obligations in the workplace:

So when one has proved his friendship
Cling to him who clings to you
Those who stand amid the tempest
Firm as when the skies are blue
Will be friends while life endureth
Cling to those who cling to you[72]

And in the recurring conflict with their employers, they believed what John Froude of Twillingate had learned in his seafaring career – that human ingenuity and the lottery of good fortune were greater than the power of the state:

all things eant done

By mite but by prvdence which is
Present with us all as we travell threw the
Changing scens of life oer land and sea[73]

CHAPTER SEVEN

Capital, Labour, and Wages

Sailing ships were pre-industrial craft, but this does not mean that technological change was arrested. In many other types of work, pre-industrial technology could survive for decades beside a new industrial technology and be influenced by it: in cotton, after all, hand looms remained in use long after power looms had appeared. Handloom weavers did not immediately abandon their craft, but they were subject to declining conditions and increasing exploitation. Deckhands in the age of sail saw many technological refinements that allowed their craft to survive. Those refinements were part of the owners' ongoing struggle to wrest productivity gains from capital invested in shipping and to decrease their dependence on labour.

The sailing ship industry became more capital-intensive in the last half of the nineteenth century, and the change was constant and impressive. There is more than one way to express the ratio of capital to labour, but in this industry the ratio of men to tonnage makes sense because we know both tonnage and numbers of men exactly – there is no need to use estimates or approximations of reality. Also, tonnage is an approximate measure of carrying capacity. At the simplest level, product in this industry was the moving of carrying capacity across water, and so any increase in tonnage per man, or any decline in the man-ton ratio, represents a potential increase in output per man (this potential will be realized, of course, only if the hull remains filled with cargo and if freight rates remain stable). An alternative is to measure the real value of capital employed, compare this with the cost of labour employed, and observe change in these two variables over time.

Such estimates are possible, but they add little information to the ratio of tonnage to men, since both the dollar value of wooden-hulled tonnage and average wages per man traced similar paths over time, increasing slightly in the early 1870s and declining slowly from the early 1870s to the end of the century.

Graph 12 shows the man-ton ratio for vessels in the Saint John fleet between 1863 and 1899. The ratio was 2.7 men per hundred tons in 1863 (the master is included in all calculations of the man-ton ratio). This represents a considerable change from the 1840s, when the Yarmouth fleet had required four men for every hundred tons. The ratio was 15 per cent lower than the figure (3.14) for all British vessels engaged in transatlantic trades to and from Liverpool in 1853.[1] More remarkable, however, by the end of the century the ratio had fallen by almost half, to around 1.45 men for every hundred tons. The decline was almost continuous, at an annual rate of 1.8 per cent to 1899. In other fleets the ratios were very similar, and the rate of change was slightly faster (2.4 per cent per year to 1899 for Yarmouth; 2.1 per cent a year for Halifax).[2]

What accounts for this change in labour requirement? There is no simple answer, and the question takes the historian beyond quantifiable measures and into a realm of work experience that we may never fully recover. Part of the change is easy to explain. Sailors were required to perform a number of manual tasks in order to propel a vessel and to keep her in good running order. In general, the bigger the vessel, the more men required: the larger vessel had more working parts, more deck space, a larger sail area, and so on. But the relation between vessel size and number of men was not linear: as vessels increased in size, the increments in labour became smaller. This was not a peculiarity of sailing vessels, and in Canadian sailing vessels the phenomenon is easily explained: most ocean-going vessels had only three masts and a limited number of sails; it was possible to increase hull size under these masts and sails, without increasing proportionately the total labour required. Thus a 500-ton barque might have three masts and 15 or 16 separate pieces of canvas in its sail plan; it might require 12 or 13 men. But a 1,000-ton barque had the same number of masts, had only a few more sails, and it could be worked with only a few additional men. Thus the increasing average tonnage of vessels in Canadian fleets explains part of the savings in labour effected in

GRAPH 12

Man-Ton Ratios, Saint John Fleet, 1863–1900

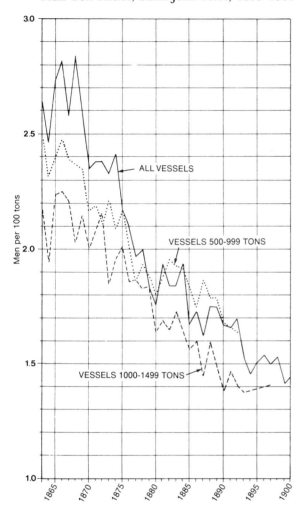

Source: Saint John Crew Agreements, MHA.

Note: Ratios are for men per 100 tons.

the last decades of the century. The mean tonnage of vessels clearing port in the Saint John crew list sample increased by 40 per cent from the 1860s to the 1890s, and this change accounts for a significant portion of the decline in man-ton ratios in the fleet.

But this is only the beginning of the story. Graph 12 also includes man-ton ratios for vessels within particular tonnage classes. Ratios were usually lower in the larger tonnage class, as we should expect. But there was a considerable change in the man-ton ratio within each tonnage class: little of this shift can be explained by change in mean tonnage of vessels. It is possible to observe the alterations in manning levels in individual vessels: by looking at vessels individually, rather than in the aggregate, we remove the effect of changes in tonnage on the man-ton ratio. The *Tasmanian* of Saint John, a vessel of 1,136 registered tons, survived for over 28 years on the Saint John registry.[3] In the early 1860s she sailed with 25 to 30 men (a man-ton ratio of 2.2 to 2.6 men per hundred tons). Toward the end of her career, in 1889, she was being worked by 16 or 17 men. Here was a dramatic change in the labour requirement: a drop of 40 per cent. If the *Tasmanian* had merely fallen into the hands of an unusually ruthless master in 1889 we should need to inquire no further. But her experience was not unique or even very unusual. Most Saint John vessels that survived more than a few years carried fewer men as time passed. Of all vessels in the Saint John file for which crew records have been entered onto computer tape, and for which there are voyage records in six years or more, two-thirds experienced a measurable saving in labour during their careers. The average change for all such vessels, including even those that experienced no decline in manning levels, was 8 per cent; many vessels (23 per cent) had lost at least 20 per cent of their men.[4]

It is possible to estimate the proportion of the total decline in manning levels caused by factors other than tonnage change. This has been done by two methods, for two fleets. All vessels represented in the Halifax crew list file for which there are 10 or more voyages were selected. For these vessels, annual average changes in man-ton ratios were estimated from regression equations of the form $\log Y = a + bt$. The estimated rate of change was weighted by the number of voyages for each vessel, and the resulting annual change in the labour-capital ratio was -0.57 per cent.[5] This figure is small, but it was 28 per cent of the average annual change for all vessels. This is the proportion of the change in man-ton ratios that cannot be explained by increasing average tonnage.

A much more laborious exercise was applied to the Saint John fleet: for all vessels in the crew list file for which crew records were entered, the percentage change in the man-ton ratio from one year to the next was calculated. The average annual change for all 1,068 cases was − 0.48 per cent, or more than 7 per cent over the lifetime of the average vessel. Since the average annual change in man-ton ratios for the entire fleet was minus 1.8 per cent, we may infer that about 27 per cent of the overall change in man-ton ratios was caused by factors other than tonnage change (this result is very close to the estimate of 28 per cent for the Halifax fleet). We must still explain this change, for it represented a very large potential gain in labour productivity. We must seek to understand how the *Tasmanian* - and vessels like her - could lose 10 men from a crew of 27 and still carry her cargoes across the Atlantic.

The change in manning levels was not accomplished by sailing more slowly and cautiously. With fewer men in the forecastle this might have been a common response among masters: they might not risk putting on full canvas in heavy weather and leaving it there with a crew that was too small to take in sail quickly. Caution and delay might be the necessary conditions for such severe losses in manpower. In fact delays did not occur: the evidence that passage times on major routes decreased from the 1860s to the 1880s is substantial and conclusive.[6] There were certainly many reasons for shorter sailing times, and increasing hull size was probably a factor, since the top speed of a displacement hull is related to the square root of the length of the ship (thus the very long steel windjammers of the early twentieth century were theoretically capable of higher speeds than the smaller wooden clippers of the 1850s and 1860s).[7] Other changes, such as wider knowledge of prevailing winds and better charts, must have helped masters make quicker passages. Certainly it is unlikely that masters were exercising greater caution, or forgoing their interest in quick passages, in the interest of savings in wage costs.

Did fewer men mean greater risks, therefore, and more losses at sea? Perhaps the condition and the price for undermanning were more wear and tear, more frequent repairs, and more tonnage lost at sea. It is impossible to know whether repairs were more frequent as time passed. We can, however, measure loss rates, and there the evidence is conclusive: there was no significant increase, even as man-ton ratios fell. The first measure of loss rates is a simple percentage: the proportion of all newly registered vessels that ended their careers in a marine disaster. By this measure, loss rates did increase, but the measure is misleading. After the 1860s fewer

TABLE 24

Marine Disasters, Saint John Fleet, 1860-99

Decade	Tonnage Lost at Sea (Annual Average)	% of Tonnage on Registry*
1860-9	5,773	6.3
1870-9	8,407	4.9
1880-9	9,184	4.9
1890-9	5,357	6.2

Source: Board of Trade series 107/108 vessel registries for Saint John.

* These are decennial averages of annual percentages. Tonnage on registry includes only vessels of 250 tons or more and excludes all vessels transferred within three years of first registration.

vessels were being transferred to British registry or sold to foreigners. Since a larger proportion of tonnage was remaining on local registry, for this reason alone a larger proportion would be subject to marine disaster as time passed. It is also possible that an ageing fleet was more likely to experience losses, as older and over-worked hulls became vulnerable to waterlogging and leaks.

The most sensitive measure of loss rates is the proportion of vessels in service lost in each year. For the Saint John fleet this figure increased from an annual average of 3.6 per cent in the 1860s to 4.3 per cent in the 1880s. Given that vessels on registry in the 1860s included a larger proportion of young vessels about to be transferred to Britain or elsewhere, it is surprising that the increase in loss rate was not even greater by the 1880s. If we exclude from the calculation all vessels transferred rapidly from the registry to ownership elsewhere, we have a better measure of the loss rate in the fleet actually retained in local hands. The results (Table 24) suggest a decline in losses after the 1860s. Only in the 1890s did the loss rate return to the level of the 1860s. A similar analysis for the Yarmouth fleet produced a similar result.[8]

The mean service life of vessels continued to increase even as man-ton ratios fell, whatever the reason for registry closure. Thus the average age of vessels suffering a marine disaster increased by 28 per cent from the 1860s to the 1880s (from 10 years to 12.8 years).[9] Of course undermanning may still have contributed to the loss rate, and losses might have been fewer if vessels had carried more men. Such considerations do not weaken the conclusion that a remarkable decline in manning levels was accompanied by no significant increase in depreciation or loss rates. Behind any changes occurring in the ageing craft of Atlantic Canada lay a dramatic accomplishment in the manual art of seafaring.

Much of this accomplishment was the result of changes in the technology, the combination of rope and canvas and spars to which men applied their labour. One means of saving labour had long been well known: by cutting the number and size of square sails in a vessel, one reduced the total amount of labour required. Square sail was difficult to trim, and reefing, setting, or furling sail usually required several men to climb aloft.

But how did one reduce square sail without losing propulsive power and seaworthiness? The best compromise proved to be the barque – the vessel that had fore and aft sail, rather than square sail, on the mizzen mast. Whereas a ship in the 1870s might have 15 separate square sails, many barques carried only 10. The additional fore and aft sails in the barque could be worked from the deck by a few men. A considerable saving in labour was thereby achieved, with only a small sacrifice in total sail area. The vessel owners of Atlantic Canada were likely to have known all of this. Certainly the Moran family of Liverpool and Saint John knew, and by the 1870s it was converting a few of its ships to barques. Referring to the *Prince Leopold* (1,397 tons), Robert Moran wrote in 1876: "The mizzen mast in the latter is quite rotten, and as we are refitting the rigging she will be converted to a barque at considerable saving in the working. The *Beau Monde* sails better and is more cheaply handled since made into a barque."[10] A letter a few months later refers to the conversion of another vessel, the *Tribune* (1,122 tons), and to one master's estimate that such conversion to the barque rig would save £500 in a few years.[11]

The Morans' experience with *Beau Monde* was not unique. As Table 25 indicates, there was a considerable difference between the labour requirement in barques and that in ships, particularly in vessels above 900 tons. These data come from Saint John vessels where crews have been analysed, and there are two possible objections to the results. First, there is no attempt here to control for trade route or for time period. Perhaps the manning levels in barques were low because the barques were over-represented in the

TABLE 25

Number of Men by Tonnage Class and Rig, Saint John Fleet, 1863–1914

Tonnage Range	Ship	Barque	% Difference	No. of Cases (Ship/ Barque)
700–799	13.6	11.5	− 15.4	35/160
800–899	12.6	13.2	+ 4.8	14/143
900–999	18.5	14.2	− 23.2	70/99
1,000–1,099	18.5	13.7	− 25.9	132/17
1,100–1,199	20.1	14.1	− 29.9	117/113
1,200–1,299	21.6	13.7	− 36.6	59/45

Source: Saint John Crew Lists, MHA.

1880s and 1890s, when man-ton ratios had fallen for reasons having nothing to do with rig. This problem is easily solved: if we look only at vessels in North Atlantic trade routes in the 1870s, or vessels in the North Atlantic in the 1880s, significant differences between the two rigs remain.[12] In the 1870s the differences are very close to those in Table 25, and the deviation around the mean is sufficiently low to indicate that the difference between the means for the two rigs is significant.

Second, crew agreements do not always state the vessel's rig. Information on the rig of vessels must come from vessel registries, and so we cannot always be certain that the ships in the sample really were ships for the whole of their lifetimes. This problem may have weakened earlier analysis, but not the results in Table 25.[13] The surest way to remove the effect of any re-rigging is to analyse vessels at the beginning of their careers, when the registry information on rig is most likely to be accurate. If we include only the first three voyages of every vessel, the results reported in Table 25 remain much the same.[14] The differences between ships and barques were real, and the gradual shift away from the ship helps to explain the decline in man-ton ratios reported in Graph 12. In the 1860s, less than a third of all voyages in the Saint John file were by barques; over a half were by ships. By the 1880s over 56 per cent of voyages were accounted for by vessels that were barques at the time of their registry – there were probably more barques, in fact, for we do not know how many ships had been re-rigged.

Two factors explain most of the change in the labour-capital ratio described in Graph 12: the growth in the average tonnage of three-masted vessels and the shift toward the barque rig. But still our story is not complete. Even if we look only at vessels of the same tonnage and the same rig, sailing in the same trade routes, we still see a decline in manning levels over time. Consider the barques of Saint John: if we take only voyages by barques in the North Atlantic, break down tonnages into 100-ton ranges, and calculate the percentage change in number of men in the 1870s and the 1880s, we find a decline in the number of men in almost all tonnage classes. Weighting the percentage changes by the number of cases in each tonnage class yields an estimate of change in manning levels of 8.3 per cent. In other words, the average barque sailed with 8 per cent fewer men in the 1880s, compared to the 1870s – and this drop had nothing to do with changes in tonnage or major alterations in sail plan.

There were other changes in the sail plan and rigging of vessels in the later nineteenth century. Perhaps most important for the labour in a vessel was the increasing use of double topsails. The topsail was no mere adjunct to the mainsail (or course) below it. It was more likely to be the principal sail in a ship. Almost as large as the course, it was often the first sail to be set and the last to be taken in. Raising and lowering this sail to and from its yard were heavy work for several men, often performed in poor weather.

Dividing the topsail into two sails was a major change in nineteenth-century sailing ships. The invention was not the work of one or even two men, but it is usually associated with two American ship masters, Robert Forbes in 1841 and Frederick Howes in 1853. Howes's prototype suggests the intent behind the idea of double topsails. His first change was to fit a light spar across the middle of the old single topsail. To shorten sail quickly, this spar remained fixed, the halliards were let go, and the upper half of the sail fell forward, in front of the lower half of the sail, where it was becalmed. Shortening sail could thus be done very quickly, from the deck. Much of the heavy manual labour associated with reefing had been saved. A small change in sail technology had saved both labour and the time required to shorten sail in heavy weather. In subsequent modifications it was more common to have two separate sails: the yard of the lower topsail was fixed to the mast, whereas the yard of the upper topsail could be raised and lowered.

A related invention was roller reefing gear, introduced by Henry Cunningham in 1850. Although less popular than the double topsail system, Cunningham's gear reveals again the purpose of reducing the number of reef-points and reducing the heavy labour involved in reefing. In roller reefing the yard rotated as it was lowered and the sail was wrapped around the yard. Roller reefing was less popular than double topsails because roller reefing gear had more parts that could become jammed or frozen and because it was too easy for the sail to roll unevenly around the yard. Both changes, however, pointed in the same direction: it was now possible to reduce the ship to close-reefed topsails or to take in a sail with fewer men, none of whom had to leave the deck. The success of double topsails was such that doubling the topgallants was also attempted in some vessels.[15]

The timing of these changes in sail plan in Canadian vessels is not known as precisely as we might wish. Certainly the brigantine *Herbert Huntington* of Yarmouth carried double topsails when she was built in 1856.[16] Surviving paintings and builders' plans suggest that the double topsail was increasingly common in the 1860s and standard in new vessels by the 1870s. David R. MacGregor believes that double topsail patents were adopted more quickly in Canada than in Britain.[17] The barque *Talisman*, built at Beaver River, Nova Scotia, in 1872, carried both double topsails and double topgallants.

Another labour-saving economy was the disappearance of studdingsails (pronounced "stunsails") after the 1860s: it required several men to set or take in these sails, and other changes in sail plan more than compensated for the removal of the studdingsails. Masters were also discovering that it was possible to eliminate certain sails without losing driving power: studdingsails, and sometimes square sails on the mizzen mast, might reduce the effectiveness of other sails by blanketting them. Masters knew that using all sails in a vessel might increase the vessel's heeling and increase leeway (meaning that the vessel was pushed sideways). As early as 1850 the supercargo of the barque *Susan* of Saint John noted that his vessel "goes along as fast with topsails and courses as she does with all sails set, for the more you put on the worse she steers, which is a great detriment to her onward progress."[19] These changes in sail plan and sail technology help to explain the savings in labour that occurred from the 1850s to the 1870s.

Other technical changes appeared in the 1880s and 1890s. These include the donkey engine, to assist mainly in the handling of cargo, but also in weighing anchor. There were 89 donkeymen hired in the vessels of Saint John for which crew have been analysed; since most were hired in later decades, this would suggest that the engines were present in more than 10 per cent of all voyages after 1880, but there may have been even more such engines, since the donkey engine could be present without a donkeyman, its operation the responsibility of the ABs or others.

Other changes included the use of hoisting engines to assist in working some of the sails, but such engines were more often introduced after the turn of the century. The canvas windmill pump replaced the hand-driven pump in some vessels and allowed much of the pumping of water from the bilges to be done by the power of wind. Wire standing rigging eased the task of setting up the rigging (removing the slack from the shrouds and stays).

It is also possible that the quality of both rope and blocks was improving with time. Canadian owners and builders tended to purchase these items from local manufacturers or suppliers or from American sources. Contemporaries commented on the superior quality of American gear, compared to British: "In our British way of life at sea, whenever there was a difficult way of doing a thing, you did it the difficult way ... [American ships] had blocks – beautiful – they were machined. You could take a sheave out of one of our blocks and you'd find instead of running in a vertical plane it would probably be like that – you know, absolutely cocked-eyed, and so on, but not in those [Americans] nor in a German ship. And their cordage! Their lovely cordage compared with ours, you know."[20] Canadian vessels may have carried larger blocks than did British: this would have eased the task of hauling up yards. American and Canadian cotton sail tended to be light and of high quality, but it was prone to mildew and difficult to handle when wet. Changes in sail-cloth probably did not save labour, but one authority insisted that lighter spars did contribute.[21]

These changes in the technology of wood, wind, and sail account for a large part of the savings in labour effected in the last decades of the nineteenth century. But there was more than technological change here. The same vessels sometimes carried fewer men than at other times. It is unlikely that changes in technology or in trade route explain the difference. Much of the difference was accounted for by the men themselves. The decline in man-ton ratios must also be understood at another level, apart from the change in machinery: it was the result of influences in relations between owners, masters, and employees. The constant orders from managing owners to minimize operating costs had their effect: masters sailed with fewer men over time.

Changes in technology helped them to do this, but so also did their workers. Sailors were older, on average, by the 1880s and 1890s, as were masters. There is an inverse correlation between the number of men in a vessel and the average age of the crew, when tonnage is constant. That is, the older the crew, the smaller the crew. There may be no causal connection here, because crews were ageing and man-ton ratios falling simultaneously, perhaps for other reasons. But even when we look at vessels of the same size, in the same period, man-ton ratios were lower where crews were older.[22] Age, in this industry, was a surrogate for experience: by the 1880s and 1890s owners could rely on the experience and skills of men who had been to sea many times before. And the man who had been to sea for many years had been "all the while accumulating first-hand knowledge of the conditions obtaining over all those seas he traversed, learning by experience the weather-signs and all the grammar of the language that the ocean speaks to its intimate friends."[23]

The "Bluenose" master was worthy of his reputation for making unusual demands upon his men. Whatever the size of his vessel, and wherever he might sail, the Canadian master expected fewer men to do the work. This is one of those few areas where birthplace appears to make a measurable difference. A selection of the relevant data is presented in Table 26. Nova Scotian and other Canadian masters sailed with fewer men than British masters of Saint John-registered vessels. Only among 1,000-ton vessels in the 1890s did British masters carry fewer men than did their North American colleagues. As the percentages in the last column indicate, the differences could be quite substantial, and they remain when we look at specific periods. Whatever the nationality, the

TABLE 26

Man-Ton Ratios, Saint John Fleet, 1863–1914

| Tonnage Class | Years | Birthplace of Masters | | | % Difference: Britain–NS |
		Nova Scotia	Other BNA	Britain	
500–999	1863–1914	2.00	1.99	2.18	+ 9.0
	1860s	2.28	2.41	2.61	+ 14.5
	1890s	1.72	1.53	2.14	+ 24.4
1,000–1,499	1863–1914	1.65	1.78	1.99	+ 20.6
	1860s	2.06	2.19	2.18	+ 5.8
	1890s	1.36	1.44	1.32	2.9
1,500 and more	1863–1914	1.21	1.07	1.47	+ 21.5
	1870s	1.58	1.73	1.65	+ 4.4
	1890s	1.38	1.48	1.54	+ 11.6

Source: Saint John Crew Lists, MHA.

man-ton ratio fell between 1860 and 1890, but in most decades and most tonnage classes the Canadian master sailed with fewer men. Birthplace explains nothing by itself, of course. Behind the statistics lie the expectations of the "Bluenose" master and the long experience of trading to and from "high-wage" ports. He expected the machinery to do the work and subjected labour inputs to the strictest economy.

These expectations originated also with the managing owners of Nova Scotia and New Brunswick. The fear that the Board of Trade in London might impose a manning scale on all British vessels prompted them to speak out against such regulation and to defend their own practices. Following meetings of shipowners in Saint John in the mid-1890s, William Smith, Canada's deputy minister of marine and fisheries, presented the shipowners' case to Britain's Parliamentary Select Committee on Manning.[24] Smith insisted that "the work of the crews is now much less laborious than in the old style of ship." There were donkey engines in many vessels, and "amongst the different appliances now in use may be mentioned the patent windlass, steering gear, pumps, power capstans, patent sheaves, double top-gallant yards, etc."

This explanation clearly struck the committee members as a recommendation for legalized undermanning. The Saint John owners proposed a manning scale 10 to 26 per cent lower than that which the committee eventually recommended for vessels between 800 and 1,600 tons. The Canadian view was that manning levels should be left to owners and masters, since manpower needs varied from one vessel to another. Even if a "fair" manning scale were enacted into law, "they would rather be left alone." Master and machinery did the work, and safety required no legislative interference. Smith made clear, however, that cost was the underlying concern of those whom he represented: "It is all they can do now, to run their ships, and if there is any more expense – the Board of Trade seems to be a great dread – they are afraid of the Board of Trade more than anything else."

These attitudes are reflected in the lower man-ton ratios for Canadian-resident managing owners, compared to the manning levels for managing owners resident in Britain. The Saint John fleet offers an opportunity for comparison, since about a quarter of the voyages for which crews have been analysed were managed by owners residing outside Canada. In all tonnage classes, and in most decades, the Canadian-resident managing owners operated with fewer men than did those outside Canada.[25]

A more interesting comparison can be made with sailing vessels registered in the United Kingdom, thanks to the sampling of all non-Canadian crew lists from 1860 to 1899, a project initiated by David Alexander in 1979. The sample of all British crew lists contains 1,092 voyages by sailing vessels for which all crew information was analysed; the total number of crew members in the sample was 22,022. The comparison between British and Canadian sailing vessels is startling, although Canadian managing owners and masters in the late nineteenth century would not have been surprised.

The comparison in Table 27 is between the British vessels and Yarmouth-registered vessels, controlling for both tonnage class and decade. Choosing the Yarmouth fleet heightens the contrast, for a glance at Table 26 reveals that the Yarmouth manning levels were slightly lower even than those of Nova Scotian masters in the Saint John fleet. In every tonnage class and every decade Yarmouth vessels sailed with fewer men than British vessels, and the difference was often substantial. By the 1890s the Yarmouth vessel of

TABLE 27

Man-Ton Ratios in Sailing Vessels of Britain and of Yarmouth, 1860-99

Decade	250–499 Tons		500–999 Tons		1,000–1,499 Tons		1,500 + Tons	
	Yarmouth	Britain	Yarmouth	Britain	Yarmouth	Britain	Yarmouth	Britain
1860s	2.95	3.98	2.16	3.04	1.73	2.52	–	–
1870s	2.82	3.81	1.83	2.68	1.56	2.19	1.38	2.76
1880s	2.41	3.06	1.63	2.48	1.42	2.02	1.21	2.78
1890s	2.30	2.78	1.49	2.16	1.30	2.00	1.16	–

Sources: Yarmouth Crew Lists and 1 per cent sample of British Empire Crew Lists, MHA. The numbers of cases in these tonnage classes were 1,940 voyages for Yarmouth vessels and 763 for British vessels.

1,200 tons sailed with 15 or 16 men, including the master. A British vessel of the same tonnage carried 24 men. Canadian vessels carried few if any boys or apprentices, whereas the British vessel often carried several, and these would be counted in the crew. All hands in the Canadian vessel were therefore "effectives" – so argued William Smith before the Select Committee on Manning.[26] But there was much more to the difference than this. Canadian managing owners adapted the technology and expected their employees, both masters and men, to co-operate.

The workers in this industry did not benefit from whatever gains in productivity occurred in their ships. Shipowners not only reduced the size of their labour force; they also held average wages remarkably constant through the last decades of the century. It matters little which of the four major fleets we choose here: Graphs 13 and 14 are based on the fleets for which the crew sample is largest (the Saint John sample contains 54,147 crew records; the Windsor sample, 56,061). A minority of sailors were paid in dollars, but the trend is similar for ABs paid in sterling and those paid in dollars: after the peak in the early 1870s, which coincided with a peak in freight rates, average wages were kept well below that peak, and dollar wages declined particularly sharply till 1900. Dollar wages were always higher than wages paid in sterling, and with the increase in vessel departures from US ports after the 1860s an increasing proportion of crews was being paid dollar wages.

GRAPH 13

Monthly Wages of ABs, Saint John Fleet, 1863–1903

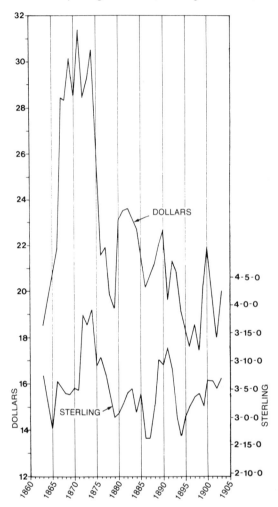

Source: Saint John Crew Agreements, MHA.
Note: A pound sterling is assumed to be worth $4.86.

Given this fact, it is remarkable that overall wage payments remained so flat. In Graph 14 the average for each rank is weighted
by the number receiving wages in each currency: in spite of the increasing importance of dollar wages, the average wage for ABs and
OSs fell after the early 1870s. The wage per man, including all

GRAPH 14

Average Monthly Wages of All Crew Members by Rank, Windsor Fleet, 1863–1904

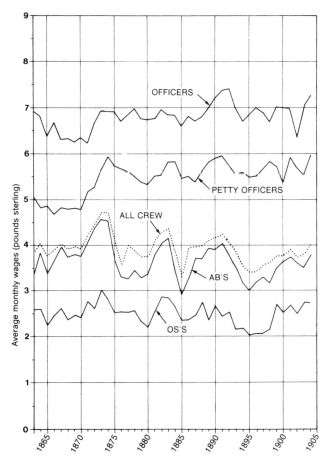

Source: Windsor Crew Agreements, MHA.

Note: Officers include first, second, and third mates. Petty officers include bosun, carpenter, sailmaker, cook, and steward. In the average for each rank, dollars are converted to sterling at $4.86 and weighted by the number of sailors receiving such wages. The average for all crew members is weighted by the number at each rank. Sailors in steamers are excluded.

crew, fell by almost 10 per cent from the 1870s to the 1890s. The index for all crew is weighted by the number of crew at each rank: one reason for the overall decline in average wages was that the proportion of crew at the lower ranks increased over time. The decline in average AB wages, and the increasing proportion of ABs, together account in large part for the overall fall in wages in the fleet. Real wages did not decline much, if at all, because of the effect of deflation in these decades. But wages in sailing ships were lower than wages in most landward industries, particularly in North America. And shipowners were using the labour market to their advantage, employing increasing numbers of European and Scandinavian sailors in a successful effort to keep wage costs as low as possible. "How do you propose to keep up the mercantile marine and the historical British sailor?" the Saint John shipowners were asked. They replied: "Well, we can now get foreigners, and in many cases they are cheaper."[27]

Sailors did not benefit from the productivity gains to which they contributed. It is possible to show the gains that employers made, by estimating the growth of total output in the industry and comparing this to the growth of all labour inputs. The first step toward measuring the growth of output in this industry is to estimate vessel-days at sea. The vessel itself is not a useful unit of analysis, and so the next step is to multiply vessel-days by the average tonnage of vessels in the fleet. The result (Graph 15) is ton-months at sea in each year, for all vessels in the Saint John fleet for which crew lists survive. The annual data closely follow annual totals of ocean-going tonnage on registry in Saint John, but the estimate of ton-months takes into account increasing average voyage duration and shorter port times in the later years.

This trend should be compared with two others that measure labour inputs and labour costs. Total man-months is a measure of total labour inputs based on tonnage at sea and the known man-ton ratios for the Saint John fleet. Total wages paid is an estimate of the total wage bill, derived from the product of man-months worked and average monthly wages for the fleet. The effect of changes in man-ton ratios and average wages was critically important: tonnage at sea, with potential to earn revenue, increased more rapidly than did total wages until 1881, and the difference is a measure of the potential gain in labour productivity in the fleet.

Table 28 presents annual growth rates based on the data in Graph 15. The first period (1863–73) is chosen to coincide with peaks in freight rates. In this period, tonnage at sea grew rapidly, as did tonnage on registry in the port of Saint John. In the bottom row tonnage at sea is adjusted by an index of freight rates. Since

GRAPH 15

Tonnage at Sea, Labour Inputs, and Total Wage Payments, Saint John
Fleet, 1863-1900

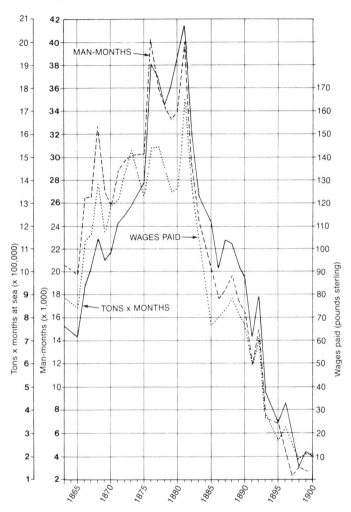

Source: Saint John Crew Agreements, MHA.

output is a function of carrying capacity and freight rates, this last
estimate must be an approximation of the growth in gross output,
assuming no significant change in the ratio of ballast to cargo.
Although average wages increased to a peak in 1873, growth in
output exceeded growth of labour inputs by 3 per cent a year, and

TABLE 28

Annual Growth Rates (%) of Tonnage at Sea and Labour Inputs, Saint John Fleet, 1863-99

	1863–73	1863–81	1881–99
Ton-months	+ 5.3	+ 6.5	− 12.6
Man-months	+ 3.3	+ 3.5	− 13.9
Total wage costs	+ 5.1	+ 3.5	− 14.7
Ton months adjusted by freight rate index	+ 6.3	+ 4.9	− 14.1

Source: Saint John Crew Lists, MHA.

Note: All growth rates are estimated from regression equations of the form log $Y = a + bt$. The Matthews sailing ship freight index is used to 1881, the Isserlis index thereafter.

output growth exceeded growth in wage costs by 1.2 per cent a year. There was almost certainly significant growth in labour productivity in this period, in terms of output per unit of labour employed. Extending the analysis from 1863 to 1881 confirms the point: in the late 1870s average wages as well as man-ton ratios fell. Tonnage at sea grew much more quickly than did total wages paid – by this admittedly crude measure, labour productivity increased by 1.4 per cent a year.[28]

Any gains depended, of course, on whether or not tonnage at sea was in fact earning revenue by carrying cargoes. While the ratio of ballast to cargo was increasing in North Atlantic passages by sailing vessels in later decades, Canadian shipowners reacted by shifting tonnage into other trades. It is impossible to measure the cargo-ballast ratio precisely, but there was probably some increase in ballast throughout the fleet. Nevertheless, total wage costs declined more rapidly than did tonnage at sea after 1881; thus labour productivity gains may have continued, although they were certainly very small, if they existed at all. It is very surprising, however, to find no evidence for a precipitous decline in labour productivity in the 1880s and 1890s.

Behind the statistics lie remarkable changes in the work and the experience of seafaring. Fewer men, who worked after 1873 for lower wages, sailed more tonnage across oceans. The result was the survival of the sailing ship industry. The steep decline in freight rates forced many out of the industry. For those shipowners who remained, there were still profits to be made. Rates of return on capital had been high in the early 1870s; for many vessels and many owners, rates of return remained positive even in the 1880s.[29] Such returns existed in part because between 1863 and 1900 there was a significant difference between growth in total wages paid and growth in total tonnage sailed (ton-months in Table 28).

Those who prospered least from this industry were the diminishing number of older "hands" in the forecastle, the men and women who agreed to serve in the Bluenose vessel in spite of its reputation. Although technological changes explain much of the savings in labour costs from which owners benefited, they do not tell the whole story. One part of Frederick William Wallace's account rings true, for all his condescension toward the men of the forecastle: "No sailor could ship on a B.N.A. vessel and expect an easy time of it."[30] The owner was niggardly, and the master, the trustee of a substantial investment of capital, had a vested interest in a clean vessel, a speedy passage, and no claims upon insurers. Canadian vessels increasingly sailed without insurance, and the master stood between profit and disaster.

There was no afternoon watch below, says Wallace, but constant demands to lay on sail even in poor weather, and the inevitable burden of repairs that followed. How did 16 men sail the same vessel that had once required 28? The sailor knew: "In those days there were so few members of a crew, whether boys or men, that one hand not pulling his weight ... I mean you'd have a ruddy broken leg they'd say you was swinging the ruddy lead you know, because you're not doin' your job, they're doin' it for you, and that's that."[31] Fewer men performed the same tasks, for smaller rewards, and thereby guaranteed the value of capital invested in wooden sailing vessels.

CHAPTER EIGHT

Home to the Sea

The wooden vessel was a place of work, and it was a small community of men and women living together at sea. The records of these seafaring workers are voluminous, but to the landsman a century later there remains a mystery, hidden behind the thousands of silent, blank pages of official logs and the laconic repetition of latitude and longitude in many thousands of ships' logs. We can no longer enter the sailors' communities or eat their food or see with their eyes, and so we cannot understand why these small communities of seafaring workers formed and reformed themselves, returning to face the risks of seafaring and exploitation by a craft in decline.

It is easy to understand why so many returned to the safety and the higher wages of landward occupations. We do not know why so many returned, by choice, to the sea. Still less do we understand the words that perhaps no other workplace could evoke from those who had served and suffered there: "I loved my ship. Maybe I could not then have said it. Today I know I did."[1] To understand these things we must look beyond capital and technology and see the workplace as a community, a place where there was more to human interaction than the social relations dictated by technology, production, or the ownership of capital, important as these were. This community held particular satisfactions for its members, as well as fear and hardship. There was much there that was mundane and cruel, but beside the profane we must also set the poetic, and because history is not only about the extraordinary, we must also record the ordinary humanity of seafaring people.

There is a great deal in the historical record to confirm the impression that "jack" was a simple-minded fellow, the victim of his own meagre talents and of unscrupulous landsmen, who returned to sea because he knew no escape. It is true that many sailors were loaded onto their vessels insensate with drink.[2] It may well be that many were conditioned to seafaring, in the same way that inmates of prisons may become conditioned to their place of confinement.

A former British apprentice remembered his shipmates in the forecastle:

Their refuge was the ship. They, in their way, were happy in a ship, very happy in a ship. Their bowels were used to the rubbish that we ate, but they were used to the grub in their way ... They had a routine of a kind which they were accustomed to ... They were just picked up by some moll and given a week or two to run their money out, and then back jack, go get a ship, and that's that ... At least their reasoning was not complicated, what reasoning they had. You see through a hard life they had come to accept the instruction "Up aloft there!" and up they went, very frequently to their deaths, but they saw no reason why they should not go. It was their life, there it is, and they had no other.[3]

While this description is undoubtedly true of many, and while it is the voice of a seaman, it is only part of the story. Although lacking the condescension of the shipowner, by itself this view masks the complexity of the seaman's responses to his place of work and says little of the positive satisfactions that seafaring could afford. There was more to this workplace than mindless routine and sullen acceptance of exploitation.

Most sailors returned to sea knowing full well the risks, the discomforts, and the hardships that awaited them. Only a small fraction of the workers in sailing vessels were on their first voyage, after all. And those who went to sea usually did so in cold sobriety. In 1885 the *Nautical Magazine* reported a survey of more than 6,700 sailors signing on in British ports over several years: reformers and marine officials had sought to discover how many sailors were sober and how many drunk when joining their ships. Ninety-six per cent of those joining were judged to be sober.[4] Whether sober or not, these sailors knew very well that their chosen workplace was very dangerous.

and as the great waves began
To roll over our ship it brought to
My mind the saying. the men that
Go down to the sea in ships and do
Their business in great waters they
See the dangers of the sea.
...
While landsmen on their beads of comfort
Fondly locked in beauties arms
Intertainments joy and pleasure
Free from Whild seas tempets storms[5]

Disasters at sea were widely reported in the nineteenth century, and there must have been few sailors who had never felt close to death at some time in their working lives. They did not know, as we do today, that mortality rates were declining in this industry in the last decades of the nineteenth century. The aggregate number of deaths was better known than the trend. In the British merchant marine in 1881, 3,278 seamen were killed in accidents, and these were one in 60 serving sailors.[6] One estimate suggests that the industrial accident rate was four times higher than in coal mining.[7] By 1896 the death rate had fallen to one in 117 serving sailors, largely because of the increasing proportion of sailors working in iron and steam. For those in sailing vessels the loss rate remained one in 60.

In Canadian vessels at least 0.8 per cent of those who signed crew agreements died during the voyage, and there is the possibility of some under-reporting here.[8] The average number of days worked per voyage by those who signed crew agreements was about 120 days; the lowest estimate of mortality would be one death for every 39 man-years at sea. Most who died at sea died by drowning, when their vessel was lost at sea or when they fell overboard.

But many sailors died of diseases contracted during long voyages to unfamiliar places. Table 29 shows the causes of death among the 12,408 seamen in British and colonial vessels between 1875 and 1877. Two-thirds of all deaths were the result of accidents. The most common accidental deaths were those resulting from the wreck or loss of the vessel, but almost as many deaths were caused by other accidents, and there were many of these, particularly in sailing vessels. In the four major fleets of Atlantic Canada 51 per

TABLE 29

Causes of Death of Sailors as Reported to the Board of Trade, 1875-7

Cause	Percentage of Total
Fevers (yellow fever, ague, smallpox, measles)	7.7
Diseases of the brain or nervous system (apoplexy, paralysis, epilepsy, etc)	2.5
Diseases of the heart or circulatory system	3.0
Diseases of the lungs (pneumonia, bronchitis, asthma)	5.0
Diseases of stomach, liver, or bowels (dysentery, cholera)	5.5
Diseases of urinary and genital organs	0.7
Diseases of skin or cellular tissue (ulcer, gangrene, abscess)	0.4
Rheumatism or rheumatic fever	0.3
Scurvy	0.2
Other diseases	1.8
Natural causes	0.8
Drowning by wreck of vessel	34.0
Drowning by accident other than wreck	24.9
Other accidental death	7.7
Homicide	0.5
Suicide	0.8
Unknown	4.2
Total	100
Number	12,408

Source: Return showing causes of death of British seamen reported to the Board of Trade, British Parliamentary Papers, 1878, vol. LXVII, 68.

cent of all deaths occurred when sailors fell overboard or were washed overboard in heavy seas. Sailors also died by falling from the rigging and striking the deck; less often they fell down a hatch, into the hold of the vessel. In a workplace with so many moving parts, operating in high winds, danger was part of the work itself: a loose rope or a torn sail could easily knock a man from the rigging in a high wind. But sailors also died of diseases: Table 29 suggests that in the mid-1870s 27 per cent died of diseases, many of which must have resulted directly from the nature or the location of their work. In Canadian sailing vessels the proportion who died of disease was probably about the same.[9] Homicide was rare, and it was less common than suicide.[10]

Disease attracted less attention than did shipwrecks as a cause of death among sailors, but seamen had heard stories of plague in distant ports or had faced the threat at first hand. Almost every year, vessels were delayed in South American ports by yellow fever or other diseases. In the spring of 1871 the brig *Daisy* of Yarmouth stood for two months off Buenos Aires, with the crew afraid to go on shore: "Throughout all the shipping is inactive and all business on shore is suspended on account of the dreadful plague that has been and is now reigning in the ill fated city ... I trust we may be preserved from the fever for the sake of Jesus who was crucified for us."[11] Disease also struck sailors in North American ports, and the sight of vessels in quarantine was common. In April 1884, for instance, 12 Canadian vessels were in quarantine in Pensacola harbour because of yellow fever.[12] The rumour of smallpox or the threat from one afflicted sailor could prompt entire crews to refuse work or to insist that a dying man be put in irons lest he endanger the rest of the crew.[13]

The fear of disease was different from fear of the sea, for there were no weapons against disease, and sailors knew that the contents of the master's medicine chest afforded little protection. They had a healthy disdain for lime juice as an anti-scorbutic, disliked its throat-rasping taste, and often refused this meagre concession to prevention of disease.[14] Whatever the causes of illness and death, sailors needed no Samuel Plimsoll to tell them of the risks of their occupation.

Sailors also knew the extremes of physical discomfort that must be endured in their small communities at sea. The commonplace experience is seldom recorded: for nights in succession men slept in wet clothes, on bare boards, having at most a bug-infested "donkey's breakfast" for a mattress. If the forecastle were a deckhouse, rarely was it watertight, but very often the cold was more tolerable than any warmth, for the heat of a stove would bring out the insects and cockroaches "in their thousands."[15] The inadequacy of the ship's victuals takes the daily experience of the seafarer beyond the comprehension of landsmen, for heavy physical labour was often not sustained by a relatively large caloric intake such as that enjoyed by some workers on land. Cephas Pearl of Tancook describes "our meals, which consists of hard bread, bootleg coffee, salt beef, and a greasy yellow broth called pea soup. Evenings we get a small taste of hash and soft bread but it's mighty small, I tell you. This is our diet, day after day."[16] The persistence of scurvy in merchant sailing vessels, even in the late nineteenth century, suggests a continuing problem of vitamin deficiency which lime juice did nothing to counteract. The vegetables served to sailors were often a discomfort in themselves: "Now these vegetables, god knows what they were. They were like, well, they ... they did look like bricks. And you just broke a lump off, you see, and threw it in the pan, and that was supposed to swell out as they do now. But you couldn't recognize these as vegetables, I assure you. The stuff used to float to the surface and stay there."[17] The diet was not supplemented either by grog or by beer, as it was in the navy and in many landward occupations.

Old seamen, long since retired to land, might easily take a perverse pride in the hardships and risks that they had known in their youth. But this does not help us to understand why they returned to sea when they were young men, to endure such conditions for $18 a month. It is not only the uncomprehending landsman a century later who wonders why workers should have chosen such a workplace. The question was also asked in that time and place, by seamen themselves. So strange was life at sea, to the novice seaman, and so different from the work he had known on land, that he too wondered at his choices.

Cephas Pearl, son of a lighthouse keeper, signed on a deep-sea sailing vessel for the first time in 1883. Pearl allows us to share the silent contemplation of his work. He had worked in schooners, and so he learned the deckhand's tasks quickly, even though he held the lowly rank of ordinary seaman. "As a seaman I fancy I'm getting along very well. I know every rope and know where to find them to. I take my wheel and look-out the same as the rest and with my watch-mates I get along all right."[18] But Pearl was a dreamer, and his mind wandered as he stood at the wheel: "I stand with both hands grasped firmly to the spokes of the wheel. I watch the compass and her head and steady her as she comes up and falls off, with a turn to ease her frequently to the plunging sea. But in fine weather I become careless, my mind wanders off to other regions, and the first thing I know the captain is shouting to know where I am going, I look at the compass, she is two points off, down goes the wheel with a swing and once more she is steady on her course."[19]

On lookout at night Pearl was by himself, struggling to keep awake, and "my mind will run on, all sorts of wild ideas." This is when he worried over the choices he had made: "Sometimes I will picture to myself the folly of going to sea. I know I could be comfortable at home were I to stay there." Part of the answer lay in a "passion to roam about and see strange countries," but Pearl knew that there was more to his choice than this, something that he had not words to describe. "There seems to be something so grand and strange about the sea, it is a something I cannot account for in spite of all the hardships and the suffering that has to be endured, there seems to be something which binds you to it, at least it seems so with me." This was not the nostalgia of an old man reminiscing upon his youth. Nor did Pearl go to sea because he lacked opportunities on land: he had been a blacksmith's apprentice and a fisherman but quit both occupations to sign on a deep-sea vessel.

John Butler of Yarmouth also thought about finding work on land: "I would give up the sea or go short voyages in a small vessel. I would like it better and try and get a nice little home of our own" (Butler was writing to his wife). But something prevented Butler from fulfilling this dream: "I often picture out something of the kind; but there, I am building castles in the air."[20]

There is a far more eloquent voice from the forecastle, who puzzled over the same question for many years. The fisherman from Newfoundland, John Froude, wrote and rewrote his "simple dirie" until it became an extended meditation upon the fate of the seafarer. He was a lean and hard man, "many times doing what I aught not to have done." He knocked down policemen in Brazil; he was "in a great row ang got locked up" in New York; when his shipmates "came to me with knives in Hand" on the deck of their vessel "I pulled out my revolver and fired at them ..."; in jail he found himself in the company of "rogues and Rascals which appeared to be very ny As bad as myself."[21]

John Froude was also a photographer. He recorded, in pictures and in words, his life at sea and the lives of his fellows. "I was made a free agent and nature took its course." Here was the heart of the mystery, for as free men "we sailed away for many days leaving our native soil and the old country far behind." "Why did I leave that whild sea coast ... To turn my back on home and friends."[22] Several voyages later he found work in England, and there

I had seen all the pleasures of life
And enjoyed all the comforts that
This world could afford
...
But after all the pleasures amusements
Enjments comforts money and Friends
There is yet something which I fail to
Understand that is I am anxious to
Leave here and cross on the other side
Of the great Atlantic[23]

And so he went to sea again. When eventually he returned to Newfoundland, he knew he was returning to the place where he "could
never git a Dollar to call my own"; there he remained at sea, in
coastal trading, and so "the mistery which I failed to understand is
yet Undesolved." Seventy-seven years old, when his seafaring days
were over, he still puzzled over that "strange content" of the man at
sea.[24]

   Froude's extended reverie, echoing the cadence and rhymes of
hymns and sea shanties, is in itself an answer to the dual mystery of
his return to the sea and his return to Newfoundland. In part his
answer was that of Cephas Pearl and many others: as a child he saw
the schooners sail to Lisbon and Pernambuco and Demerara, he
heard the yarns of sailors who had seen these places, and his
curiosity about "the wonders of the World" was never assuaged.
And once at sea, Froude found himself in a community of workers
who were sharing "the best of times that I ever had spent."[25] He saw
landsmen and envied none. His vessel was not a place of confinement, still less of misery, for all its terrors and hardships. Observing convicts at work in Africa the seaman said: "I feel glad that I
am free and enjoying life as best I can."[26] It was true that many
died at sea, while sweethearts, friends, and wives urged the sailor
to stay on land,

But this is all a notion
Bold Jack cant understand
While some die upon the ocean
And some die on the land[27]

The well-known risks of work at sea were no deterrent. Instead the
perils of life at sea could become a matter of pride to an adven-

turous and curious youth: " 'I'm going to sea in the merchant service, father,' I said. 'You'll find it a hard life, my son,' said he, and in his voice was a ring of pride that his son had chosen a hard life."[28]

Sailors knew that the "grub" at sea was woefully inadequate, but John Froude and his fellows in the forecastle did not rely on ship's stores alone. It is impossible to measure the actual food consumption of sailors from the victualling scales on crew agreements, or even from the complete inventory of ship's stores, where it exists. With patient ingenuity sailors supplemented their diet, and the search for food was part of their life together. The sailor was a fisherman: flying fish, tuna, cod, shark, turtles, bonito, and even dolphin found their way onto his plate.[29] William Miles Collins of Advocate Harbour, in the West Indies in 1885, caught a dolphin, and this "sport was continued at every favourable opportunity during the remainder of the passage." A year later, on a passage from Nova Scotia to England, Collins "caught sixteen codfish which with our little shark and nine porpoises caught on the passage makes a very good season of fishing for a merchantman."[30] There were birds at sea, and some could be caught and eaten. "We once ate an albatross, dear dear dear. And it was awful, it was awful, and I give the cook his due, he stewed it for hours and hours and hours."[31]

The easiest way to supplement diet was to buy food from dockside traders whenever the vessel put into port: oysters in Nova Scotia, salmon in the Pacific northwest, fruit in the tropics, and vegetables from street urchins in every major port. And with shore leave the first priority was never drink but food: "Bring me three servings of ham and eggs all at once on one plate, and bring the same for every one of us."[32] And often in the vessel itself there was more to eat than the cook might serve. Cases of tinned salmon shipped from British Columbia easily broke open during loading, and tins of salmon found their way into sea chests and under mattresses.[33] There were chickens in many vessels whose eggs never found their appointed destination on the plate of the master's wife. One starving boy supped happily on baby food intended for the master's child.[34] Seamen in the navy occasionally ate rats, well fed from the ship's biscuit and cheese. But merchant seamen in the later nineteenth century usually had better means of supplementing their diet.

The forecastle was forever damp and the work was dangerous, but labour in a sailing vessel was not unremitting. The vessel was a place of work – and of entertainment. John Froude wondered why he left the landsman's pleasures and amusements to go to sea, and he answered the question himself: time passes quickly at sea because it is spent "with a song A joke or a yarn or a play."[35] There were differences between entertainments on land and those at sea. At sea, audience and performers were one, and at sea work and entertainment often merged. This was no music hall entertainment, as it became on land, where the audience was the passive recipient of professional offerings. At sea men made their own entertainment. In the forecastle during watch below "the yarns go round and round and you are not counted a sailor if you can't keep your end up," Cephas Pearl tells us. "I now count myself as great an old shell as the general class, and when the yarn goes round of your adventures in marine life, why I tell of my trips to 'Frisco and different parts of the world that I have heard of, and as no person knows me or the difference, why it is hoisted in all right."[36]

Whether or not Pearl's yarns were "hoisted in," he points to one of the functions of the yarn in the small forecastle community: it was one way that men came to know each other, part of "the ritual of affirming ties with the brotherhood of men."[37] In the great barques and ships there might be no members of a watch who knew each other before signing on. The yarn was a story, a means of passing time with one's fellows in idle moments, and a casual introduction of oneself to those with whom one must work and live. In an indirect way the yarn answered a number of questions. Had the storyteller been to sea before? Was he a man of experience? Where had he been, and in what ships? Above all, since the yarn must reflect personal experience at some level, was the storyteller a real sailor or a mere lubber? As Joseph Conrad noted, the general conduct of ships and their handling could be discussed with delight and pleasure by men "who found in their work, not bread alone, but an outlet for the peculiarities of their temperament."[38]

John Froude's diary is, in this sense, a yarn, or a series of yarns. It is an oral recitation of personal experience that allows us to hear yarns, as his fellow ABs must have heard them from his lips. The story of his "great row" with the bunker boys in New York is a miniature epic, told in the perfect economy of language that comes only from frequent recitation. In a few minutes the speaker tells of two battles, the destruction of a bar-room, capture by police, the inmates of a New York jail, the quality of American justice, and the final victory and reconciliation of shipmates. The moral of the story – that sailors hold no malice – was for posterity, not for the forecastle, since the point was obvious to seamen.

Told in the forecastle, Froude's yarn carried a message about the storyteller himself: he had fought the worst of New York's bunker boys, and he would fire his revolver at his shipmates if they attacked him with knives. He had the nerve to compliment New York policemen on their skilful driving of the "black Mary":

> there came four
> Police and put me unboard the black Mary
> And drove me to the lockup when on my way
> There in joking I said boys I never
> Enjoy a decent ride only when I am
> Driving with you[39]

Here was a man of such self-possession and assurance that when the great row was over he would have a "jolly time" with the very man who had threatened to disembowel him with a sheath knife. Here was a seaman who could look after himself and whom one could trust. The yarn was an entertainment, but not simply an idle pastime.

Work and entertainment merged in the shanty, sung to co-ordinate and ease the labour of men heaving on capstan bars or pulling together on halyards. Shanties were of many types: the capstan shanty (*Shenandoah* was a capstan shanty) was designed to encourage the continuous effort necessary for heaving on capstan bars. In the halyard shanty the accent on particular words co-ordinated the work of several men hauling on one rope. *The Maid of Amsterdam* was a pumping shanty, sung by men at the back-breaking work of heaving the levers of pumps up and down and was timed to fit the downward movement of the pump wheel.[40]

> I put my hand upon her knee
> Sez she, 'Young man, yer rather free'
>
> A rovin', a rovin'
> Since rovin's bin me ru-i-in,

We'll go no more a-rovin',
With you, fair maid.

The shanty was a work song, and often it was a yarn it itself, a part
of the story of one's life at sea, and a way of coming to terms with
that life. In the shanties sailors expressed homesickness, the long-
ing for pleasures on shore, and the tribulations of work at sea. In
the shanty the sailor could complain or "growl" about his life
without fear of betraying weakness. A good shantyman could
improvise sly complaints about the behaviour of officers or the
quality of the victuals.[41] In the shanty the sailor might even lament
the act of going to sea:

Come, all ye bully sailormen, an' listen to me song.
O, I hope ye just will listen till I tell yiz what went wrong,
Take my advise don't drink strong rum, nor go sleepin' wid a whore,
But just get spliced, that's my advice, and go ter sea no more![42]

For men becalmed for weeks on the passage home, the song might
be a consolation. "The sailmaker came from the forecastle and
stood by the rail, staring at the bleak Diegos. His voice broke the
silence:

Good-bye and farewell to you, fair Spanish ladies;
Good-bye and farewell to you, ladies of Spain;
For we've received orders to sail for old England,
But we hope very soon we shall see you again."[43]

The song worked upon the spirit of the sailor and sustained weary
bodies: the chorus of voices, heard above the thunder of canvas
and wind, told the sailor that he was master of his domain.

Singing also occurred in the common leisure time, especially in
the dog watches, when all were likely to be on deck. "Dog watch is
generally passed in a lively way," Cephas Pearl tells us. "This is the
hours from 6 to 8 p.m. and they are always spent making merry
some way. Perhaps some good singer is entertaining the rest of the
watch with a song, or some person is telling an old salt story, or at
another time all hands will join in a game of euchre."[44] On certain
vessels, if one were lucky, there would be a musician or two, apart
from the shantyman. "Some of our crew are very good hands at the

violin and concertina, and scarcely an evening passed but there would be music and sport of some sort."[45]

In the dog watches most sailors did not sing shanties, which were usually sung only to accompany work. More often they sang ballads or love songs or popular songs. Sailors also sang hymns, in vessels where Robert Goudey or Mark McElhiney or other Bluenose masters insisted upon attendance at religious service on Sunday. On such occasions the chorus of baritones was accompanied by the voices of women, for the stewardess sang with the crew, and the master's wife stood nearby. There were few if any other workplaces where workers spent so much time singing.

But there was more to dog watch entertainment than singing and yarning. Men played cards or checkers or raced cockroaches. Often there were animals at sea: "What good times a cat on board a ship gets compared to a shore cat. A cat or a dog are nursed like children and often all hands are watching and laughing at a cat playing, what a shoreman would never condescend to notice, but our pleasures are so few that we make the most of everything however small." In the dog watches there were tests of strength, boxing, races up the rigging, and dancing. "And there was always someone carving or whittling some object," remembers John Congdon Crowe. "Barnacles have been made into match or toothpick holders. The webbed feet of albatross have been converted into odd but creditable purses. A shark's backbone is excellent material for a very presentable walking stick. Many articles made with various coloured twines and silk fabrics are quite ingenious and show the result of many hours of patient labour."[46]

In this community there were often women and children. Canadian shipowners were more willing than British owners to allow masters to take their wives and children to sea. The women were remote from the men in the forecastle, but they were still part of the little community at sea. In larger British vessels after the turn of the century a master's wife might have no contact with the crew at all: "She was entirely, entirely separated from the crew except for the singing of hymns on a Sunday night," says the apprentice E.L. Davies of Robert Goudey's wife. The same Mrs Goudey, interviewed many years later in her Yarmouth home, tells us that at sea she had nothing to do but knitting and embroidery and caring for her children.[47]

But decades earlier, in the smaller Canadian vessels of the nineteenth century, the master's wife was closer to the crew. She might
never leave the poop deck, but she was more often seen and heard,
and she might be acquainted with some of the men, if they came
from the same town or village in the Maritimes. When her husband went on shore, Annie Butler did not like to be left alone "sad
and lonely among a set of roughs. Oh I do not do not like it. If they
would not get angry and swear at each other it would not seem so
bad." But she was the centre of polite attention when she ventured
on deck: "I think I shall try it again sometime as I got treated so
well. The mate seemed very glad to have my company. The steward got my chair and brought me some coffee. The men are all
very respectful and polite to me."[48] Soon she was conversing with
the men, lending them a Bible, and sending them hot drinks when
they were ill.

The reactions of seamen to a master's wife and children are
seldom recorded, but one suspects that the gentlewoman among
them was more than a distant reminder of absent women. She may
have represented gentility and refinement; certainly she was to be
respected. In port in Japan in the 1890s John Congdon Crowe's
mother, with a baby in her arms, stood at the door of the cabin
and refused to allow an armed and angry sailor to enter in search
of the mate. Several days later the same sailor was at the wheel
when "Mother came up on deck carrying a folding deck chair. One
of the cardinal rules of the ship is that the steersman must never
leave his post. Mother had some difficulty opening the chair.
Leaving the wheel, Daley came on the run, took the chair from
Mother, forcefully opened it, and with a bow asked where she
wished it placed." Several weeks later the same seaman "came aft
carrying what might be described as a handbag ... It had been
made of twine in three colours: red, white and blue, woven in a
close mesh. The whole thing represented hours of patient, tedious
work ... He wanted Mother to accept it as a gift."[49]

Occasionally the women from the poop were more than remote
figures of respect, at least in Canadian vessels. Fally Cochran, the
17-year-old daughter of a New Brunswick master, kept a detailed
log of a voyage in 1860, in which she noted the vessel's position,
wind directions, log line readings, changes in sail, and the activities
of the crew. She had work to do, apart from mending her father's
shirts, and her work took her off the poop. We find her painting

the front of the poop, painting the capstan, and catching fish. She was also her father's medical assistant. When the mate's hand was crushed by a chain "I have bound it up with Frius Balsam & lint." A few days later "one of our men is laid up he complains of pain all through his body I have given him some medicine and hope he will be better soon."[50] Amelia Holder was only 14 when her father began to teach her navigation and the use of the log line; she also made signal flags for their vessel.[51]

Young Abigail Ryerson of Yarmouth, on her first voyage with her husband in 1847, did a variety of work on deck and in the cabin: she assisted the cook by baking bread, tarts, gingerbread, biscuits, and cakes. Much of her work, she says, was in "the necessary branches of housewifery," but she also observed closely and understood the work of the crew and assisted with navigation. "I am highly delighted with the idea of any practical branch of education."[52] It is no surprise to find that a master's wife could take charge of a vessel and run it herself. In 1894, with her husband in jail on a charge of manslaughter, Jane Crowe discharged a cargo, paid the bills, and took the *Selkirk* of Halifax from Hong Kong to Cebu.[53]

Nova Scotian masters often shared their work and their cares with their wives and sometimes admitted their debt. "I don't like to be beat," wrote John Butler to his wife. "You remember that. We have been *Shipmates*."[54] Abigail Ryerson referred to her husband as "our ship mate the Captain."[55] Even where the work of the wife was confined to the shipboard home and family and circumscribed by bourgeois social norms, it was work that a woman shipmate did with care and pride, and which a shipmaster sorely missed if his wife remained ashore.

For those who lived beyond the poop the master's family added to the variety of life at sea. There was an image of woman and of childhood before the male brotherhood of the forecastle. They saw only images, or momentary reflections of the whole, because they saw only what occurred on the poop. What they saw was very real, however, and it was only a few feet away. They might see children playing, a little girl skipping ("I skip a good deal now," wrote Amelia Holder in 1869), and a boy throwing his toys into the sea: "Willie has a mania for throwing things overboard," writes Alice Coalfleet in 1890. "He has thrown 3 hammers, 1 pair pinchers, his bow and arrow, a tin funnel, and clothes line."[56] The family at sea celebrated festive occasions, and Amelia Holder wondered "whether Santa Claus would visit us south of the line."[57]

Unseen below the poop deck, but still known to the sailors, were more important events, such as the one that Alice Coalfleet confided to her diary in 1887: "I retired at 7:30 trying to read but other matters require my attention – at 10 o'clock a little stranger makes his appearance – he is very welcome, a dear pretty little fellow, his little head covered with black hair – Dodd is doctor, nurse and everything else, washes and dresses the little one, lays him alongside of me, then stands and recites funny poetry to make me forget my pains."[58] A shipmaster had served as midwife, and as his workers took their turns at the wheel they might hear the crying of a baby below. In his *Poem of the Sea* Duncan Morris, of Advocate, Nova Scotia, remembered another such occasion:

I stood one day beside the wheel, the course was "full and by,"
When suddenly beneath my feet I heard an infant cry;
Then sauntered aft our Captain, grim, his face aglow with joy; Said he,
"our crew's once more complete; I've shipped an eight-pound boy."[59]

It is fruitless to speculate on the meaning of these images for seamen, because their responses are so rarely recorded. But in Canadian vessels, where women were so often present, there was another dimension to shipboard life, a small domestic pageant with the poop for a stage.

Even where women were present, the sailing ship was still predominantly a male community. Was seafaring an escape from domestic responsibility, and even at some deeper psychological level a release from the company of women and from the cares and compulsion of sexual relationships? Ask a deep-sea sailor the question and silence follows, or, in one case, the confession of a private rumination: "I have often wondered about this."[60]

At one level Bill Adams's memoir *Ships and Women*, one of the finest works about seafaring in the English language, is a meditation on the male adolescent relationship to a ship and to women, where the ship becomes a surrogate woman and the timid youth bestows upon *Silberhorn* the burden of emotions that he cannot give to women. A ship was female because she was the projection of those qualities that seafaring men associated with woman, however stereotypical those associations may have been. For many younger sailors going to sea was not only an escape from women, but the severing of family ties and an initiation to adulthood. It might even be a crude form of introduction to adult sexuality, through the yarns about women told by older seamen and the frequent opportunity for sexual encounters when the vessel put into port.[61] Seafaring could be an escape from women, into the genderless company of men, but it was also an initiation to manhood.

There is no need to postulate a biologically innate tendency toward male bonding in order to recognize the gregarious propensities of men and the satisfactions that male segregation can afford. Seafaring had the additional satisfaction that it took young men beyond the society of landsmen, into an exclusive brotherhood of Neptune's disciples, men who shared a "secret," like members of a secret society.[62] The knowledge of the sea, possessed only by a seaman, was his secret, and it separated him forever from the uninitiated landsman.

Seafaring had its own initiation rituals, which often followed and even included the repeated demonstration of the candidate's unworthiness. The boy, the apprentice, or the young ordinary seaman on his first voyage was hazed and ordered about by the able seamen, and "if we paid no heed they resorted to the methods of a gangster's enforcer, but always with good humour and even glee."[63] The miserable offender was then brought before Neptune's court, in a ritual that endured into the twentieth century in many British and Canadian vessels. It is remembered here by a Canadian who was at sea in the 1920s:

On crossing the Equator, second mate Sam Hort organized the initiation of newcomers to the realm of King Neptune. The old carpenter sat on a bench in a long gown with a trident hat painted red. Sam Hort as Neptune's priest wore a backwards souwester and oilskin. Neptune's nigger and Neptune's policeman attended in amazing costumes. We four Ordinary Seamen had been seized at noon and locked up with no dinner. When the court was ready we were taken out one by one and presented to Neptune with a resume of our characters which turned out to be deplorable. Several penances and punishments were awarded. We were made to eat rotten eggs, stood on our heads in a barrel of water, tarred from head to foot with Stockholm tar and whacked with policeman's sticks. The Captain and his wife watched from the poop. Next day they gave us each a certificate.[64]

The initiation, with its attendant punishments, demonstrated to the youngster that he had no protectors other than Neptune's company and that his dependence on his family and his ties with landsmen were broken. Hazing and punishment stimulated a desire for acceptance and strengthened the emotional bonds between initiates. Even if the initiation ceremony were absent, there must have been a moment for every young sailor when he knew that he had been accepted and that the suffering of the novice was over. "I still remember feeling a glow when one Able Seaman said to another in my presence, 'Did I see Snowy at the yardarm in that squall?' and a reply 'Usually the little bastard is last out of the forecastle when all hands are called ... Yes he was there ... Yardarms don't care who furls them nowadays'."[65]

The exclusive fellowship of seamen was reinforced by a shared language, an idiom of seamanship that had its own power and beauty. "Among my shipmates sexual images loomed large in their word pictures. These pictures were embellished – or, if the speaker lacked skill in language, degraded – by expletive. The expletive was usually used for emphasis, and talented men made it effective. The untalented were merely tiresome to listen to."[66] The sexual imagery was rooted in heterosexuality, although references to sexual perversion were common. Rarely did the relationship between men become sexual itself, although homosexuality may have been more common where young apprentices were commonly employed. The occasional references to homosexuality in British and Canadian vessels, and the reminiscences of former sailors, suggest that it did occur but that the prejudice against it was very strong. "Homosexuality was laughed about, but in no ship of my acquaintance did any such practice go on ... Many of us wondered whether homosexuality existed in reality."[67]

The bonds of fellowship were forged by the elements that governed life at sea. To the landsmen these elements might be terrifying, or merely cold and monotonous: "Sunday 24th. – The Holy sabbath. What a multitude of thoughts come crowding in on each one of us as we stood, gathered on the deck of our ship this morning and gazed on the lonely and solitary expanse of sea around us. No tolling of church bells, no chimes, no meeting of friends, nothing but a dreary and dull sameness of desolation."[68] The seaman looked upon the same northern waters, and, with very different ears, he heard

the strange sad moaning of thy waves
breaking upon the desolate strand
and whistling threwh the trembling spars
in ocean rhythm unknown on land
the moaning of the midnight gale
that swept the cordage of our barque
will long remain when other things
are lost forever in the dark[69]

The seaman worked in a place of infinite variety, and in his stoic and unromantic way he saw its beauties. In 1891, on board a vessel carrying oil to Yokohama, William Collins tried to describe a "fine day" at sea: "To say that this is a fine day does not convey any idea of the real conditions of the weather. The waning moon rose clear and distinct as if painted on canvas, but it would baffle the skill of the most clever artist to reproduce anything half as striking or sublime. The day continues throughout to be the most beautiful that the mind of man can conceive."[70]

The tropical sea was totally different from the northern waters which the Nova Scotian sailor first knew. In 1864 the young Harris Barnes entered the horse latitudes for the first time: "How beautiful the appearance of the tropical seas - folds of light, fleecy corona, sure sign of bright skies were ever-present, swarms of flying fish pursued by huge dolphins, and occasionally a hungry shark were observed sporting in the blue waves, that rolled ever onward in one direction, westward." The sailor also came to know the night sky, as did Harris Barnes: "A new firmament diffused its twinkling light above, a firmament altogether different from that those living at the 45th parallel are familiar with ... Often while serving my lonely trick at the helm at night I have watched for relief, when the hours appeared more than their usual length, by the setting of Orion or Taurus, or by some star of the first magnitude, such as Capella or Arcturus, Vega or Antares, but now for the first time I watched for the swing or cast of the Cross denoting the hour of midnight." Part of the sailor's secret knowledge was his uncommon familiarity with earthly and heavenly domains which landsmen never saw.

In their watery domain, seamen saw many things that only a few attempted to describe or explain. One such phenomenon was St Elmo's fire, an electrical discharge that takes place at the mastheads and yardarms of a ship under certain atmospheric conditions:

Now there was a wild cracking above as two of the topgallants were ripped apart. The sound of splitting canvas was like that of battering machine guns. What appeared to be flames ran along the lee-side of the deck seeming to lick up everything. They mounted the ropes and the rigging ... Then suddenly the wind and the rain stopped ... Then on the trucks of the three masts appeared a golden glow like a halo. The haloes became brighter and larger; then the same golden glow appeared at the Royal yard-arms, on the topgallant, and a golden ribbon crept down the backstays ... I watched this phenomenon scarcely breathing as it appeared on the head of a man standing in the rigging. He was knotting some broken ropes. The brilliant halo cast its light over the man's face making it look like the face of a corpse.[72]

The fires of night gave rise to many superstitions, and these too were part of the private knowledge of the seafaring community.

Sailors lived with the wind, and wind was "all our care and talk." And the wind, like the vessel herself, acquired a human character, as one British sailor remembered: "Up aloft in the trades, or somewhere, like that, or even when it is blowing like buggery, neither one nor the other, I mean up in the trades with a wind that is just like a girl's hand stroking your face and you are seeing those lovely little white horses you know, and you are driving through them, and the cumulous cloud above, you know, the broken cumulous cloud, that is beautiful, beautiful."[73] How can I love the cruel waves? asked John Froude. He could not love the sea, "yet in my heart I sing its praise," for the waves had "born me safe"and

I have seen them crowned with shining foam
and spangled with the fires of night
I have known dreatful in the dark
and tranquil in the morning light
go stand on yonder headland bold
and watch the bellows of my dream
behold their majesty and power
and you with me will feel the same[74]

Sailors were not church-going men, and they often bewildered the reformers in church missions, but sometimes they expressed their own form of piety, an animistic worship of the natural elements that governed their lives. "Oh, what a fit place for the meditating and contemplative mind to muse on the works of nature and of nature's god," wrote George Smith of Saint John in 1859.[75] John Froude saw "gods hand" in the waves, and throughout his life he knew that there was a power beyond the capacity of man to control or understand:

> he holds the future in his hand he knows my lot and disteny he rides upon the raging storm and plants his footsteps in the sea[76]

These were the thoughts of the most eloquent of sailors, those few men in the forecastle who put their yarns on paper. Not all sailors were diarists; those who were may not have been typical, but their words must not be dismissed for that reason. They reflect more closely than any other sources the experience of those who did not write, and even those who did not read. They tell us something of the ordinary experience that lies behind the blank pages of log books. They tell of the sight and the sound of the sea, as sailors saw and heard it.

And they tell us something else about the sea, so simple that it is easy to forget: the sailor was the only human being who worked and lived in a place that was in motion. The sea, said John Froude, has a rhythm unknown on land. Having returned to land, the sailor's first steps were awkward; and at first he might have difficulty sleeping. We may only speculate upon the psychological effects of a life spent in constant, but varying, rhythmic motion. It may have been one of the reasons why sleep came so easily, and so deeply, to men and women at sea. "I am positive," wrote one seafaring diarist, "that if I live to get home I shall have to get Julia's cradle and hire some person to rock me when I go to sleep, as the reaction from so much rocking at present to none at all could be injurious."[77]

Even in his sleep the sailor was so sensitive to motion that a sudden change in his movement could cause him to wake, Walter Runciman tells us.[78] The rhythm of the sailing vessel was totally different from that of the steamer, for engines and screw propellers changed the effect of the sea upon a hull. With his entire body in motion, the sailor lived with the primary element of music as part of his being. As he moved to the rhythm of the sea, his motion was accompanied by sounds – the waves slapping the hull, the rhythmic creaking of the hemp or manila ropes whose sound kept time with the rise and fall of the vessel, the creaking of the ship's joints in a swell.

The sailor was also the only human being who knew the total absence of motion and of sound: in a true calm at sea, the universe was still. In a prolonged calm, even the sailors themselves might fall silent and stop singing. In a world without sound and without motion, for days on end, the loss of their normal sensory existence could drive men close to madness. Sailors lived in their own world of sound and motion, and the loss of motion, as in a vessel in port, brought its own discomfort: "Now that we are at sea once more," said Cephas Pearl, "I feel myself again, for I would rather have a week at sea than a day in port, that is when I have to stay by the ship."[79]

Pearl's home was now a forecastle. The sailing ship did not separate work from home, as did the factory. In this very real way it reunited work and home for many (if not all) sailors: "I don't know that any circumstances come to my mind where the men out of the fo'c'sle were anything else but good-hearted. You see they were at home, that was the only home they knew."[80] And so the community of men at sea lived somewhat apart from the industrial societies that it served. The sailing ship, far more than its steam-powered contemporaries, represented an escape from land and from the social norms of landsmen. To this extent seafaring could impart the satisfaction of anti-authoritarian act: it was an escape from the authority of parents, from the dreary monotony of landward work, and from the direct influence of all landward institutions.

To some extent the escape was an illusion, for the ship had its own rigid codes and its state-enforced discipline. But sailors could still believe that, because they voluntarily accepted the authority of master and mate when they signed on, this was a self-imposed discipline and a self-chosen authority. Sailoring even offered a brief and perhaps illusory escape from wage slavery, for at sea cash had little value, except for the occasional purchases from the master's slop chest, and the sailor could say, "I don't want money and I don't need and I hadn't got money either. I never robbed a man in my life that I knew about or anybody else, my owners or anybody else. I don't want their things. It's foreign to me, to my entire nature, you see."[81] This is a paradox of the workplace at sea: a proto-factory with rigid codes and often harsh discipline, the ship was a conduit for the rebels and iconoclasts in "the Atlantic diaspora."[82] It was also a workplace hierarchy with a pervasive egalitarianism, "where sailors are comrades and brothers and friends while engaged as a loyal ships crew."[83]

The paradox points to the limits of working-class resistance in this proto-industrial community. Sailors protested the infringement of seafaring codes, but they did not reject the code itself. Seafaring could be "degrading," they knew, but "in spite of these injustices you feel you're one with the ship, she must go. Something gets you in these ships, you find yourself wrapped up, the same spirit as the master's, the ship's got to go and go as hard as you."[84]

The egalitarianism of shared work embraced even the master, if he were not excessively brutal, and the various satisfactions of communal life and work disarmed the rebel. Rarely did the seafarer own a share of the capital invested in his ship, but he and his fellows were in control of their great machine, and for sailors the product of labour was not money but the mastery of wind and sea which took them through the storm and safely back to land. This control was not an illusion, and it separates the sailing ship man from his successors. John Froude and his comrades were victims of exploitation but not of alienation: "I feel glad that I am free."[85] In his disdain for material accumulation, in his sturdy independence, and in his lofty indifference to the power of state and capital, the sailing ship man was rarely a rebel and rarely a trade unionist. He was more deeply conscious of his craft than of his class. He was a pre-industrial worker who survived for a long time the incursions of industrial capitalism.

CHAPTER NINE

An Industrial Workplace

Industrial capital went to sea in the form of iron hulls and steam engines. No longer did seafarers harness the power of wind and water with rope and canvas, collaborating with vast stores of energy that lay beyond their capacity to create or even to control. Now men drew energy from coal and steam, driving iron and steel through the resistance of wind and water. For many years steam-engines served as auxiliary means of propulsion in sailing vessels. For many years there were steam-engines in vessels with wooden hulls, and full suits of sail in vessels with iron hulls. Gradually, however, vessels having both iron hulls and steam power came to dominate the output of British shipyards: 1875 and 1876 were the last years in which the total tonnage of new sailing vessels built and first registered in the United Kingdom exceeded the tonnage of new iron-hulled steamers.[1] For many years thereafter sail-powered tonnage still dominated world shipping, whether the hulls were of iron or wood: in 1890 a majority of German tonnage was still powered by sail; as late as 1910 the majority of US and of Scandinavian tonnage was powered by sail.[2]

An industrial revolution in shipping occurred in Atlantic Canada, although more slowly than elsewhere. Shipowners in Atlantic Canada knew about the advantages of steam power and iron hulls, and they knew that sailing vessels were being replaced in many trades in the last half of the century. The possession of large sailing ship fleets did not deter investment in new technology, however. On the contrary, Atlantic Canadian shipowners had long since been applying labour-saving innovations in their ships. The pressure of falling returns in sailing ships encouraged many to invest in steamships for use in coastal and ocean trading. The port of Saint John saw many steamers and auxiliary steamers entered on her registry books: 93,300 tons were registered before 1915. A further 65,000 tons were registered in Yarmouth, Halifax, and Windsor. Most of these vessels were a small departure from the sailing vessels that they replaced. They were auxiliary steamers for use in general trading – "tramp" steamers which, like the sailing fleets, carried general cargoes to any destination rather than plying regular routes. Most carried full sails, and few had iron hulls. They were similar in tonnage and dimensions to barques and ships.

The shipping industry in Atlantic Canada certainly declined after 1880 – but not because wooden sailing ships were obsolete. It did not decline because regional investors lacked information about new technology or because they were reluctant to move capital into industrial production. There was no backward-looking caution or conservatism here; there was instead an economic environment and an investment calculus profoundly influenced by domestic landward opportunities and state policies. Maritime entrepreneurs would participate in Canadian industrialization but would do so by investing in landward industries and by trying to attract Canadian trade goods through their ports, to be shipped not only in their own hulls but in cheap non-Canadian tonnage hired in the international shipping market.[3]

Thus the steamships registered in Saint John were only 7.3 per cent of all new tonnage in the port between 1850 and 1914. A growing proportion of tonnage entering and clearing port was non-Canadian. The industrial transition occurred here, but the place of ownership or registry of vessels became less important than ever before, and to understand the transition we must look at vessels owned or registered in central Canada and in Britain. In the ports of Atlantic Canada the transition to industrial capital in shipping removed shipping further than ever before from the social formations of outport villages in the age of merchant capital. Seafaring in Atlantic Canada was part of an industrial process that transcended national and regional boundaries.

The industrial revolution was a reduction of labour relative to capital in the workplace, in terms of both quantity and control. There was an increase in the number of unskilled workers, but this was part of the overall reduction of labour and the concentration of control in the hands of a few trusted specialists. The process

TABLE 30

Average Monthly Wages of Sailors in Saint John Steamers and
Auxiliary Steamers, 1863-1914

Rank	Average Wage ($)	No. of Cases
Officer (first, second, or third mate)	43.89	223
Able seaman	19.26	761
Ordinary seaman	12.15	102
Chief engineer	71.10	97
Second engineer	59.07	91
Third engineer	38.96	91
Fourth engineer	24.80	93
Fireman	21.15	157
Fireman/trimmer	21.61	653
Trimmer	10.77	23

Source: Saint John Crew Lists, MHA.

began in the auxiliary steamer, where part of the responsibility for
propulsion passed from the mates and their watches on deck to the
chief engineer and his crew in the engine room. In the sailing
vessels of Atlantic Canada over 60 per cent of the crew consisted of
able seamen or ordinary seamen. In the auxiliary steamers in our
crew list sample from four major ports in Atlantic Canada, only a
third of the crews were ABs or OSs.[4] The ranks of petty officers had
been increased by the addition of a chief engineer, and almost half
of the crews consisted of specialist mechanics or new types of
worker: assistant engineers, firemen, trimmers, oilers or greasers,
and (where there were passengers) assistant stewards, storesmen,
pursers, and even the occasional surgeon.

The engineers and firemen changed the hierarchy of work and
the wage structure in shipping. In the auxiliary steamer it was
possible, if only for short periods of time, for the vessel to be propelled entirely without the labour of able seamen. The AB saw both
control and rewards shift to others, and a wage differential between the AB and petty officers appeared that was greater than any
in sailing vessels. Table 30 presents a summary of average sterling
wages, converted to dollar equivalents, for those employed in

steamers and auxiliary steamers registered in Saint John. Chief engineers earned considerably more than officers, and even more than chief mates. The chief engineer earned as much as many masters of sailing vessels. Even the fireman was earning more than the AB, although this differential had less to do with skill than with the extra rewards required to attract men into an exceptionally undesirable job.

There were many other steam-powered vessels owned and operated in Atlantic Canada in the late nineteenth and early twentieth centuries, apart from the cargo-carrying tramps registered in Saint John. Several companies operated coastal steamers in the region or on regular runs to the West Indies or the United States. In many of these vessels the industrial transition was more advanced than in the tramp steamers, and the deckhand was even less important. The Bowring steamer *Florizel*, for instance, was a seal hunter, a passenger liner, and a cargo carrier. Her 3,081 gross tons were powered by triple expansion engines, and she had a bunker capacity of 450 tons. In 1918 her crew of 61 included more waiters than deckhands. Her 10 seamen were only 16 per cent of the total, whereas in the engine room, under the supervision of the engineers, there were 15 firemen and trimmers.[5] In such a vessel there were three clear divisions to the labour force: the deck crew, under the supervision of the mates; the engine room, controlled by the chief engineer; and the service department, run by the chief steward.

By the end of the nineteenth century Canadian liner companies were employing even larger vessels from both Atlantic and Pacific ports. In these vessels the ratio of capital to labour was much greater than in the small tramp steamer, and the division of the workplace into separate departments, each with its own hierarchy, was even more clear. The Canadian Pacific Railway's *Empress of Japan*, an auxiliary steamer of 5,904 tons, carried sails, but ABs made up only 20 per cent of her crew.[6] Much more numerous were the employees in the engine room and the service workers. The vessel carried a chief engineer, second engineer, third engineer, junior third engineer, fourth engineer, and four assistant engineers, as well as firemen, trimmers, an electrician, and a boilermaker. Among the service and catering workers were the purser, assistant purser, chief steward, second steward, storekeeper, barkeeper, chef, baker, barber, steerage steward, steerage stewardess, and surgeon. Although the total number of employees might be between 90 and 100, the propulsion of the vessel was the work of two-thirds of these.

The ratio of capital to labour was higher in steamers where there were no passengers. In the *Empress of Montreal*, for instance, the man-ton ratio was usually below one man per hundred tons when she sailed without passengers in the early 1900s. The vessel usually carried only 12 ABs and a few deck boys, and the cattlemen outnumbered the deckhands. Cattlemen were a new type of unskilled worker in Canadian ships, having little skill and a relatively high desertion rate, and the AB did not consider them part of the crew at all. Cephas Pearl once worked in such a vessel: "We have," he said, "beside our crew, a number of men to look after the cattle, and a more cowardly and brutal set I never saw before."[7]

As Pearl's contempt for the cattlemen suggests, new social distinctions developed within the steamship. These distinctions were reflected in, and reinforced by, spatial segregation of workers, which was built into the structure of the ship. In cargo steamers the deckhands slept in the forecastle, still located in the nose of the ship. They were joined by the firemen, but often a partition separated seamen from firemen, with firemen on the port side and seamen to the starboard.[8] The accommodations for master, officers, and engineers had moved to midships, below the bridge and near to the chartroom and wireless telegraphy room.

There was among steamship men a saying that "oil and water don't mix," referring to the differences in social background and training that separated officers from engineers. Some large liner companies built this distinction into their ships, providing separate smokerooms and separate dining tables for officers and engineers.[9] Stewards' quarters were also located amidships, but stewards did not associate with officers, and even in American ships it was the custom "for each man to eat in the pantry of the class in which he works."[10] The ship was a social hierarchy of many fine distinctions, which served to reinforce discipline and to confirm the rewards of promotion.

The social distinctions of the steamship were those not of the outport village but of industrial society in general and of British steamships in particular. It is a minor paradox of Canadian history that even after Confederation Canadian merchant shipping remained closely tied to British shipping and British maritime law. The structure of subordination and superordination in Canadian steamships followed closely the pattern in British steamships.

Transatlantic connections extended from the ship itself to the crews and their training. Canadian steamships were often built in Britain; Canadian officers and masters learned their trade by studying British manuals; Canadian steamships employed Scottish engineers; and if the seaman from Atlantic Canada was to find a ship in a Canadian port, it was increasingly likely that the ship would be registered in Britain, although there were many Norwegian and other European vessels in Canadian ports at the end of the nineteenth century.

Even John Froude, the fisherman from Twillingate, worked a passage in a British "royal mail" steamer carrying 120 crew.[11] Sailors born in British North America were a small proportion of all those signing onto British vessels (under 2 per cent between 1860 and 1914), but they appeared in their hundreds every year.[12] Here they witnessed the industrial workplace in full development. To study the British steamship in this period is not a digression, therefore, but an essential recognition of the broader context in which the industrial workplace must be understood.

When Canadian sailors joined British tramp steamers in the last decades of the nineteenth century, more likely than not they found themselves in vessels of 1,500 tons or more, and many were in vessels of 3,000 tons or more. They were also in a relatively capital-intensive industry in which the ratio of labour to capital was rapidly changing (see Graph 16). By the 1880s British steamers were carrying fewer men per ton than were British sailing vessels, and by the late 1890s steamships were carrying 50 per cent fewer men per ton than sailing vessels.

In the industrial workplace labour was reduced, and it was subject to increasing division and specialization (Table 31). The deck crew, including officers, was now in the minority, and only 25.4 per cent employed in steam were ABs or OSs. The division of labour increased the proportion of those who had supervisory roles. Both the chief steward and the cook had supervisory roles, since both were likely to have assistants under them. Their assistants were usually men or boys, for despite the increase in catering and service jobs, so many of which were filled by women on land, seafaring remained a male-dominated occupation. Of every thousand workers

GRAPH 16

Man-Ton Ratios in British Sailing Vessels and Steamers, 1863–1913

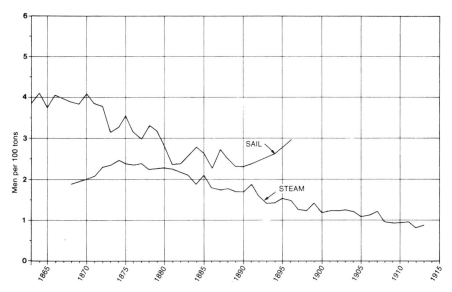

Source: Non-Canadian Crew Agreement Sample, MHA.

hired below the rank of master in British steamships, about seven were women. Sailing ship masters working for British shipowners were much more reluctant to hire women than were Canadian masters, and the prejudice seems to have continued among steamship masters.[13] On both sides of the Atlantic, however, steamships remained male-dominated workplaces, and the continuing exclusion of women to specific menial and subordinate roles, such as that of stewardess, was part of the structure of the industrial workplace.

Even if they remained in subordinate ranks, seafaring workers in steamships were likely to remain longer at sea than those in sailing ships. Seafaring was still a young man's occupation, but in steamships there were many older men, and almost half the crews were aged 30 or over (Table 32). Obviously there were advantages and comforts in steamships. The workplace allowed one to maintain a home and family on shore, and it was much less punishing to mind and body. Wages were often low, but steamship men had the advantages of regular food and the frequent return to port. On the western side of the Atlantic the seaman who found a berth in a

TABLE 31

Distribution of Sailors by Rank, British Sailing Vessels and
Steamers, 1863–1914

Rank	Sail (%)	Steam (%)
Officers and Deck Crew		
First mate	5.8	2.9
Second mate	2.3	2.7
Third mate	0.5	1.1
Fourth mate	0.02	0.5
Bosun	3.0	1.6
Bosun and mate	0.1	0.5
Carpenter	2.9	2.0
Sailmaker	0.9	0.01
AB	55.0	23.9
OS	9.4	1.5
Boy	1.7	0.7
Apprentice	6.9	0.1
Donkeyman	0.2	2.1
Quartermaster	0.7	1.1
Lascar	0.1	0.4
Others	1.6	3.8
Sub-total	91.1	44.9
Catering/Service		
Cook	2.6	2.8
Assistant cook	0.1	1.7
Cook/steward	2.7	0.3
Steward	2.2	3.6
Assistant steward	0.3	5.4
Stewardess	0.01	0.7
Cook and seaman	0.8	0
Steward and AB	0.05	0
Storeskeeper	0.01	0.3
Purser	0.03	0.5
Surgeon	0.07	0.5
Others	0	3.2
Sub-total	8.9	19.0

Table 31 (continued)

Rank	Sail (%)	Steam (%)
Engine Room		
Chief engineer		2.8
Second engineer		2.9
Third engineer		2.3
Fourth engineer		1.0
Fireman		18.1
Trimmer		4.5
Fireman and trimmer		2.9
AB and trimmer		0.7
Oiler/greaser		0.3
Others		0.6
Sub-total		36.1
Total		100
Number	22,022	58,432

Source: Non-Canadian Crew List Sample, MHA. The unit of analysis is the signature on the crew list. Thus the same person may appear more than once, and there may be more than one person at a particular rank on the same voyage.

coastal steamer held onto his job as long as he could, for he "had status, fun, food and money."[14]

In the British merchant marine and in Canadian coasters, workers returned more often to their birthplaces. This occurred in part because of the different origins of men in sail and men in steam. Foreign-born seamen were more common in sailing vessels than in steamers. British-born sailors came most often from places by the sea, but inland towns supplied a larger proportion of the labour force in sail than in steam (Map 11). The major ports (London, Liverpool, and Glasgow) supplied a larger proportion in steam (25 per cent) than in sail (15 per cent), and over a third of those employed in steam came from 10 port towns. Where the "limejuicer" in sail often travelled some distance from home before signing on, the steamship man signed on in the place of his birth and returned more easily to that birthplace.

The steamship man was away from land and home for shorter periods of time. Crew agreements stated the maximum term of ser-

TABLE 32

Age Distribution of Crew Members in British
Vessels, 1863-1914

Age	Sail (%)	Steam (%)
1-9	0.04	0.06
10-19	15.7	5.4
20-29	49.8	45.4
30-39	21.6	30.3
40-49	9.6	14.4
50-59	2.9	4.0
60+	0.3	0.5
Total	21,756	62,271
Missing	266	98

Source: Non-Canadian Crew List Sample, MHA.

vice for which crew members signed on: over 30 per cent of Canadian sailing ship agreements specified two years or more; British sailing ship masters usually anticipated shorter voyages, and only 24 per cent of their agreements specified two years or more. But steamers were much less demanding: only 14.3 per cent stated a term of two years or more. Even in tramp steamers sailors were likely to know how long each passage and each voyage would take. The average AB in sail served three times as many days in each voyage as did the AB in steam; between the 1870s and the early 1900s this disparity increased, as more sailing ships moved into long-distance trades (Table 33). The data point to a basic condition of life for workers in steamships: the workplace was unlikely to be the only home they knew, and the industrial workplace separated work from home.

With shorter passages and regular returns to land, sailors could leave a ship more easily. This does not mean that conflict ended. The retention rate remained remarkably low: very few sailors remained with their vessel at the end of a voyage. The desertion rate at first sight appears to be much lower in steam than in sail, but the comparisons in Table 34 do not take into account the length of voyages. In terms of man-years worked, the differences were slight,

MAP 11
Birthplaces of Sailors in British Sailing and Steam Vessels, 1863-1914

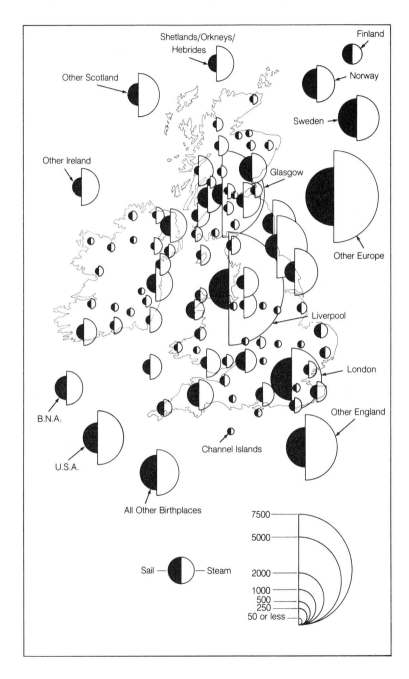

TABLE 33

Average Days of Service per Voyage by ABs in British Ships, 1860-1914

	Sail		Steam	
	Average	n	Average	n
1860s	164	3,687	49	220
1870s	138	3,453	61	2,286
1880s	162	2,379	51	4,746
1890s	171	1,746	51	3,723
1900-14	173	483	59	3,837

Source: Non-Canadian Crew List Sample, MHA.

and desertion rates were actually higher in British steamers than in British sailing vessels (0.6 desertions per man-year in steamers; 0.4 in sail).[15] Certainly the death rate was much lower in steamships: the data suggest a death rate of one in every 54 man-years worked in steamers, compared to one in 27 in sailing vessels.[16] Discharge by mutual consent was much more common at the end of a steamer voyage. The steamship was certainly a safer workplace. It was also a workplace in which much of the bargaining between employer and employee had been transferred to land, especially after the rise of seamen's trade unions.[17]

The sailor who went from sail to steam did not always find comfort and security in his new workplace. Although there was a compulsory victualling scale after 1906, the conditions of life and work in a tramp steamer could be as hard as in a sailing vessel. Only a minority of masters and seamen worked in the floating palaces of the Cunard and White Star lines. There was, of course, the compensation of higher wages in steamships. This advantage should not be exaggerated, however: the wages of most deckhands and engine room workers were still well below the wages of skilled workers in most landward occupations.

If there was any improvement in wage levels by the early 1900s, gains were eroded by inflation, and there was no improvement for most deckhands, firemen, trimmers, and catering workers. As Graph 17 indicates, wages for deck officers increased significantly by the early 1900s. Real wage gains were restricted largely to officers and engineers, while the wages of most others held constant

TABLE 34

Reasons for Leaving Vessels in Canadian and British Fleets, 1863-1914

Reason (%)	Four Canadian Fleets	British Sailing Vessels	British Steamers
Remains at end of voyage	1.9	5.6	3.3
Discharge by mutual consent at voyage end	49.4	57.9	79.3
Discharged before or during voyage	10.7	13.7	6.9
Did not join/deserts	34.7	16.0	9.1
Died	0.8	1.7	0.3
Discharged ill	1.0	1.2	0.6
Dishonourable discharge	0.4	0.5	0.1
Discharged because vessel wrecked, vessel in accident, or voyage terminated	1.1	3.3	0.3
Promoted	0.05	0.06	0
Other	0	0	0
Total	100	100	100
Number	180,938	22,016	62,324

Source: Crew Lists for vessels registered in Saint John, Yarmouth, Halifax, and Windsor, and Non-Canadian Crew List Sample, MHA.

or declined. Wage differentials widened, as ABs, OSs, firemen, and trimmers fell further behind petty officers, officers, and others in supervisory roles.[18] It is no surprise to find desertion in steamers concentrated among those in the low-wage ranks.[19]

The most important changes in the transition from sail to steam occurred in the division of labour as it was defined by rank. The reduction of labour was accompanied by an increasing division of labour, increasing specialization, and a narrowing of the range of tasks assigned to each rank. These changes were not the inevitable consequence of the technology itself; they were the outcome of existing social relations of production in sailing ships, modified

GRAPH 17

Average Wages of Sailors in British Ships, 1863–1908

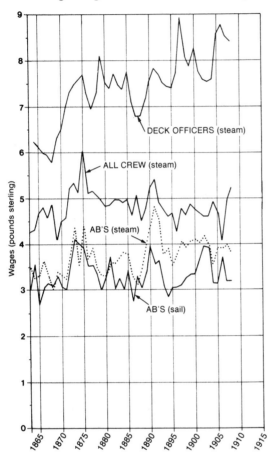

Source: Non-Canadian Crew Agreement Sample, MHA.

and adapted to the steamship technology. To the existing work-place hierarchy an engine room crew was added, while the labour of deckhands was reduced and redefined.

In this process there was no conscious effort by shipowners to "deskill" workers in order to reduce the dependence of capital on labour. The transition to iron, steel, and steam, followed by the transition to diesel power and other forms of propulsion, resulted from an ongoing search for a complex of advantages, including seaworthiness, greater longevity, increased average carrying capacity, and lower costs of purchase, maintenance, and operation.[20]

Yet there were relationships between capital and labour that descriptions of industrialization too often ignore. Technological changes in merchant shipping too often appear as the beneficial consequences of exogenous innovations in marine engineering. In fact the industrial transition, as Robin Craig has reminded us, was the result of an ongoing interaction between shipowners, marine engineers, naval architects, and shipbuilders.[21] The impetus for this collaboration came very much from the demands of shipowners and from competition between shipowners, which intensified in the last decades of the nineteenth century as freight rates and rates of return fell.

The marine engineer knew that "evolutionary changes" came from an "economical conflict" and from "the constant effort to effect economies of first cost and actual working."[22] "Ship design is of necessity a compromise the conflicting elements of which render it most difficult to arrive at a satisfactory solution of the problem. Broadly speaking, in the successful cargo carrier this compromise must be represented by a combination of the minimum initial cost and minimum cost of running and maintenance, with maximum carrying power and the requisite strength and stability."[23]

A conspicuous advantage of the iron or steel hull was that it reduced labour costs per unit of carrying capacity. But there were other advantages. The successful "compromise" embodied in the iron steamer was a solution that released the shipowner at many points from dependence on skilled labour. The disadvantage of the wooden sailing ship was that it gave responsibility for large units of capital to wage-paid employees. The wooden sailing ship was a short-lived asset whose very existence depended on the skills of the master, his officers, and his deckhands.

Atlantic Canadian shipowners were aware of this disadvantage; indeed, they were obsessed by it. They struggled either to control labour in sailing vessels or to replace it, because they knew that "every improvement tending to lessen labour adds so much to the money-earning qualities of the vessel."[24] The fledgling Canadian science of marine engineering inherited the problem of "labour costs": "In view of the increased cost of fuel and labour it will be necessary to improve the design not only of the ship itself but of everything connected with ocean transportation ... Manual labour must be superseded by mechanical appliances. Where manual labour cannot be dispensed with it should be supplied with such mechanical aids as will render it more effective."[25] When diesel engines and other internal combustion engines began to appear, they, too, carried the advantage that they replaced much of the labour in the engine room. The internal combustion engine was preferable, said one engineer, partly because "of the saving in wages of the engineer who is now one of the ordinary deck hands."[26]

Whatever the mode of propulsion, it was not simply the skilled workers who were displaced by machinery. The object was to lower the total dependence on labour, whether skilled or unskilled. Often the unskilled workers were of greater concern than the skilled because of the damage or delays that they might cause. As James Healey wrote in the 1930s: "Ships are valuable property with intricate machinery which can easily be damaged ... The destructive element among the crews on any fleet is so small as to be almost incalculable; but the shipowner is helpless against it. It is both the result and the cause of the social and economic chasm between seamen and shipowners."[27] The marine engineer knew that changes in modes of propulsion could reduce the "helpless" vulnerability of the shipowner: "The mere fact of doing away with the rougher class of labour on board ships would be a great advantage."[28]

The presence of expensive machinery meant that skill could not be displaced entirely, or responsibility and control removed, even from the deckhand. Certainly much of the contemporary literature on the subject would lead us to the opposite conclusion, however. Knowledgeable observers in the late nineteenth century repeated a simple "deskilling" argument: where sailhandling was reduced or gone altogether, where reefing was a "vanished art," and where steering was done by a few specialist quartermasters, then "you shall often find a man occupying an AB's position who is really only an unskilled labourer."[29] The deckhands "are little better than labourers," wrote Charles Booth; "in place of the splicing, bracing, setting and general manipulation of ropes and sails and other work of navigation, they are now chiefly occupied in cleaning, scrubbing, scouring, holystoning, polishing and painting the different parts of the ship."[30]

The able seamen himself agreed. Writing about his work in an auxiliary steamer in 1884, Cephas Pearl tells us that "work consists mostly of washing and scrubbing, and whoever can use a holystone can be an AB." At the conclusion of his memoir, Benjamin Doane of Barrington declared: "With the vanishing of sails, the sailor and his peculiar skill are obsolete, and the word 'sailor' is a figure of speech."[31] The contemporary opinion contains an important truth: the peculiar skills of the sailor were very largely those of sail-handling, and the craft of seafaring was disappearing. But this is only part of the story, and it does not necessarily follow that the AB's work was henceforth devoid of skill. If the AB had become an unskilled worker, why should his wages be higher in a steamship than in a sailing vessel (Graph 17)?

The premium earned by the AB in steamers suggests that the old "deskilling" argument should be qualified. With the disappearance of sails, certain types of skill were no longer required, and there was certainly a narrowing of the range of tasks that fell to the deckhands. But the AB was no mere scrubber of decks: he had become a tender of new types of machinery, and shipowners were prepared to pay a premium to hire experienced and reliable men. The knowledge required of "the efficient deckhand" remained extensive. He must know the names and functions of many parts of the ship, and a range of nautical terms. He must know how to splice both wire and fibre rope, how to stow cabin cable, how to secure anchors, how to rig a derrick, how to operate winches, and how to work other cargo-handling gear. He must know about the safe handling of hatch covers, lifeboats, and fire-fighting devices. The maintenance of increasingly complex cargo-handling machinery and other equipment was a large part of the deckhand's work, even if his work was supervised by the bosun or other specialists.[32] ABs shared only a small part of the conception and execution of tasks in a steamship, but they retained a degree of control and responsibility that placed them outside the ranks of the unskilled.

Shipowners paid a premium for experience and reliability, but ABs were now a minority of workers in a ship, and there were other means by which capital reduced its dependence on labour. The ship was more than ever divided between those in supervisory roles, responsible for the conception and execution of tasks, and un-skilled or semi-skilled labour. No work role is totally lacking in skill, but at least 40 per cent of those listed in Table 31 must be classed as unskilled. The fireman worked in a fiery hell, sometimes standing beside his boilers for four hours in each watch, shovelling coal, keeping his fires burning and keeping them "clean," and trying to keep his balance as the vessel pitched and rolled beneath him.[33] The trimmer was often a little further removed from the reverberating voice of the boiler, but he worked in the dusty, unventilated darkness of the bunkers, moving coal for the use of the firemen. This work required care, for failure to bunker correctly could lead to coal slides. But this was strenuous manual labour, characterized not so much by skill as by physical and mental strain and a variety of risks – from the inhalation of dust, from collapsing mountains of coal, and from fire or explosion. A man who had done this work once remarked that by comparison the coal-hewer in a mine had a gentleman's life.[34]

Within the ship there was no escape for the trimmer but through promotion, and promotion depended upon the chief engineer. If a trimmer were "reliable" and "sober" he could hope for promotion to fireman. The most fortunate of the firemen might be promoted to greaser or oiler, the man who cleaned the engine room and oiled the bearings. As the machinery increased in complexity the opportunity to reward the most reliable worker increased: a greaser might be placed in charge of a dynamo or a refrigerating machine. Further advance, to the rank of junior engineer, would require shore training. To the extent that the chief engineer controlled promotion, he held considerable powers of reward and punishment. And in such a workplace hierarchy, workers were often self-supervising: if a newcomer were "willing" and "fairly subservient" he would receive "tolerable treatment from the older members of the crew," but "if he is lazy or impertinent he will be glad when the ship docks."[35]

The work and status of the steward varied a great deal. In a tramp steamer, where there were no passengers, the steward was a general service worker responsible for stores, linen, cutlery, and for the upkeep of galley and cabins. In a passenger liner, the chief steward was more like the manager of a hotel, and he might have more men under his command than either the first officer or the chief engineer. Most of his workers were unskilled, and once again "promotion was the final reward for ability and faithfulness in lesser positions of trust."[36] One began as the steerage or third-class steward, and with promotion one ascended into the tourist class and then into the first-class compartments. The cook had his own assistants, and so the service sector was often divided into two sub-hierarchies, each with its own petty distinctions of status. All workers in service and catering were treated as social inferiors by officers and engineers.[37]

The division of labour in the industrial workplace narrowed both discretion and task range for all but the minority of officers and engineers at the top of the hierarchy. Less than a century before the *Empress* liners entered Canadian waters, most ships in eastern Canada could have been worked from port to port by their crews, without the supervision of officers, and most workers had some share in and some knowledge of most tasks in a vessel. Now, by the early years of the twentieth century, the indispensable range of knowledge and skill resided in the master, his officers, and the chief engineer. This separation of conception from execution, of knowledge from manual labour, was not a simple technological imperative. It did not occur because the knowledge required to work a ship was henceforth beyond the capacity of individuals to absorb. On the contrary, officers were required to have a very extensive knowledge of their ships and of navigation, machinery, and principles of management. Training schools for officers preached that officers should be able to perform any task that they may instruct others to perform.[38]

Skill was part of a structure of authority in which knowledge and social distance reinforced the powers of management. Nautical schools on both sides of the Atlantic taught future officers the essential connection between management and social class: "When a man reaches the quarterdeck he should have the 'quarterdeck face' and the bearings and manners of an officer and a gentleman."[39] The prospective officer learned that "we were better than any AB because we had access to skills of which he knew nothing ... This knowledge, we thought, gave us a merited superiority. Merit, however, appeared to be an insufficient mark of distinction for *social* distance was also encouraged."[40] Rank in the ship and social class overlapped because, as so often happened in the British merchant marine, officers were recruited from a different social class than deckhands, and even engineers came from a different section of the working class than deckhands.[41]

The distinctions of social class, and the habits of deference that they assumed, endured and were reinforced because of their function in the industrial workplace – they helped to enjoin obedience and to preserve the structure of authority. An officer in training should not spend too long in the forecastle, insisted the nautical schools, "because a man would have difficulty in becoming an impartial and efficient officer if there were a possibility of his meeting and associating with old shipmates who knew him as a former boon companion." The officer must have "the bearing and manners of a gentleman" so that "he will command the respect of unlicensed members of the crew."[42]

In officers' manuals the bearing and accent of the gentleman became the essentials of managerial expertise: "Your treatment of the man at the wheel should be typical of your treatment of the whole crew. Say nothing whatever to him except to give him orders. You may have a very kindly disposition, but if so, do not display it to the crew. It does not follow you should scowl or swear at them, that would be running to the other extreme. Give your orders in a voice that will make itself perfectly audible; see that you are promptly obeyed, and say nothing more. Stick to that, and you will find yourself respected by the men."[43] Here was a workplace of structural inequalities that had no need of the mediating influences of a "kindly disposition" or humane countenance. In its essentials, the relationship between ship's officer and merchant seaman was that of factory manager and factory worker.

A significant difference between landward and seaward workplaces was the extent to which the merchant marine borrowed from military models of discipline. "The work of the mate resolves itself more and more into generalship," and naval models of dress and behaviour were borrowed for industrial ends.[44] No longer were there masters, mates, and seamen. Now there were captains, officers, and ratings. In Canada the transfer of social and military distinctions into the seaborne workplace was not so easily accomplished, but it was attempted nonetheless. In the steamship the captain and his officers lived in their cabins below the bridge, and the only men they might share meals with would be the engineers. Officers might socialize with passengers; crew did not.

In coastal steamers and in liners, officers and men were distinguished from each other by their dress. In Bowring's coastal steamers, officers wore a blue uniform with quasi-military gold stripes and badges; every deckhand wore a blue guernsey.[45] In the West Indies steamers in the twentieth century captains and officers were encouraged to join the naval reserve, and if the captain and a sufficient number of his officers were in the naval reserve the merchant vessel was allowed to fly the naval reserve ensign. At sea, dinner for captain and officers was a full-dress affair, with uniform jackets, bow ties, and butterfly collars. Canadian National and Canadian Pacific steamships were "strange masculine bastions ruled by autocrats from ivory towers."[46] These were the social relations of the industrial workplace.

The sailor of the industrial age lived apart from the sea, protected from the waves and from their sound by caverns of iron and steel. Inside his place of work he might admire the power of the machine, and the engineer might cherish his engines, as Rudyard Kipling knew:

The crank-throws give the double-bass, the feed-pump sobs an' heaves,
An' now the main eccentrics start their quarrel on the sheaves:
Her time, her own appointed time, the rocking link-head bides,
Till – hear that note? – the rod's return whings glimmerin' through the
    guides.
They're all awa! True beat, full power, the clanging chorus goes
Clear to the tunnel where they sit, my purrin' dynamoes.[47]

To the fireman and the trimmer there was no purring note but a fiery roar, far louder than the sound of the sea. Far above, the deckhand heard neither the dynamoes nor the waves but felt instead the simple content of dry clothes and a warm berth. Alone in his office, the first officer worked at his bills of lading, while the master consulted his charts and his instruments. Both men looked forward, perhaps, to a full night's sleep, and to their return to port in a few weeks' time. With these workers and these landsmen, the industrial revolution went to sea.

Notes

INTRODUCTION

1 "Literacy among Canadian and Foreign Seamen, 1863-1899," in Rosemary Ommer and Gerald Panting, eds., *Working Men Who Got Wet* (St John's: MHG, 1980), 32. This paper was read by Gerald Panting at the Fourth Conference of the Atlantic Canada Shipping Project, held at Memorial University of Newfoundland in July 1980. David Alexander died the next day. He was seriously ill when he wrote the above paper, thought it disappointing and incomplete, and frequently used four-letter words when referring to it.

2 Frank T. Bullen, *The Men of the Merchant Service* (London: Smith, Elder, 1900), 254. Cf. A.H. Clark, *The Clipper Ship Era* (New York: G.P. Putnam, 1910), 127.

3 Particularly useful are Tony Lane, *Grey Dawn Breaking: British Merchant Seafarers in the Late Twentieth Century* (Manchester: Manchester University Press, 1986); Tony Lane, "Neither Officers Nor Gentlemen," *History Workshop Journal*, no. 19 (spring 1985); J.M.M. Hill, *The Seafaring Career* (London: Tavistock Institute, 1972); Conrad Dixon, "Pound and Pint: Diet in the Merchant Service," in Sarah Palmer and Glyndwr Williams, *Charted and Uncharted Waters* (London: NMM, 1981); Conrad Dixon, "Legislation and the Sailor's Lot, 1660-1914," in Paul Adam, ed., *Seamen in Society* (Bucharest: Commission internationale d'histoire maritime, 1980); A.G. Course, *The Merchant Navy: A Social History* (London: F. Muller, 1963); Michael Mason, Basil Greenhill, and Robin Craig, *The British Seafarer* (London: Hutcheson/BBC, 1980); Peter Fricke, *Seafarer and Community: Towards a Social Understanding of Seafaring* (London: Croom Helm, 1973); and, of course, Ralph Davis, *The Rise of the English Shipping Industry in the Seventeenth and Eigh-*

teenth Centuries (London: Macmillan, 1962). American sources are numerous, but see E.P. Hohman, *Seaman Ashore: A Study of the United Seamen's Service and of Merchant Seamen in Port* (New Haven: Yale University Press, 1952), and J.C. Healey, *Foc's'le and Glory-Hole: A Study of the Merchant Seaman and His Occupation* (New York: Oxford University Press, 1936).

4 Much of the literature on fishing is cited in Peter R. Sinclair, *From Traps to Draggers: Domestic Commodity Production in Northwest Newfoundland, 1850–1982* (St John's: Institute of Social and Economic Research, 1985); and see Raoul Andersen and Cato Wadel, eds., *North Atlantic Fishermen: Anthropological Essays on Modern Fishing* (St John's: Institute of Social and Economic Research, 1972); Christopher Moore, *Louisbourg Portraits: Life in an Eighteenth Century Garrison Town* (Toronto: Macmillan, 1982); B.A. Balcom, *History of the Lunenburg Fishing Industry* (Lunenburg: Lunenburg Marine Museum, 1977); Jean-Francois Brière, "The Safety of Navigation in the 18th Century French Cod Fisheries," *Acadiensis*, XVI, no. 2 (spring 1987), 85–94; Gilles Proulx, *Between France and New France: Life aboard the Tall Sailing Ships* (Toronto: Dundurn Press, 1984); J.S. Pritchard, "Ships, Men and Commerce: A Study of Maritime Activity in New France" (PhD thesis, University of Toronto, 1971). On mid-twentieth-century organizations see John Stanton, *Life and Death of a Union: The Canadian Seamen's Union* (Toronto: Steel Rail Educational Publishing, 1978); Jim Green, *Against the Tide: The Story of the Canadian Seamen's Union* (Toronto: Progress Books, 1986); William Kaplan, *Everything That Floats: Pat Sullivan, Hal Banks, and the Seamen's Unions of Canada* (Toronto: University of Toronto Press, 1987). On naval seafaring see the bibliography by O.A. Cooke, *The Canadian Military Experience, 1867–1983: A Bibliography* (Ottawa: Department of National Defence, 1984), 39–68. On sealing see Briton Cooper Busch, *The War against the Seals: A History of the North American Seal Fishery* (Kingston and Montreal: McGill-Queen's University Press, 1985), particularly its useful bibliography. On whaling see Benjamin Doane, *Following the Sea* (Halifax: NSM, 1987); W.A. Hagelund, *Whaler's No More: A History of Whaling on the West Coast* (Madeira Park, BC: Harbour Publishing, 1987).

5 Judith Fingard, *Jack in Port: Sailortowns of Eastern Canada* (Toronto: University of Toronto Press, 1982); Richard Rice, "Sailortown: Theory and Method in Ordinary People's History," *Acadiensis*, XIII, no. 1 (autumn 1983), 154–68.

6 John Harland and Mark Myers, *Seamanship in the Age of Sail: An Account of the Shiphandling of the Sailing Man-of-War 1600–1860, Based on Contemporary Sources* (London: Conway Maritime Press, 1984); Frederick William Wallace, *Wooden Ships and Iron Men* (London: Hodder and Stoughton, 1924); Stanley T. Spicer, *Masters of Sail: The Era of Square-Rigged Vessels in the Maritime Provinces* (Toronto: Ryerson Press, 1968); Claude K. Darrach, *From a Coastal Schooner's Log* (Halifax: NSM, 1979); Cassie Brown with Harold Horwood, *Death on the Ice* (Toronto: Doubleday, 1974); Cassie Brown, *A Winter's Tale: The Wreck of the Florizel* (Toronto: Doubleday, 1976). See also R.J. Cunningham and K.R. Mabee, *Tall Ships and Master Mariners* (St John's: Breakwater Books, 1985); Charles Armour and Thomas Lackey, *Sailing Ships of the Maritimes* (Toronto: McGraw-Hill Ryerson, 1975).

7 *On the High Seas: The Diary of Capt. John W. Froude* (St John's: Jesperson Press, 1983); see also Benjamin Doane, *Following the Sea* (Halifax: NSM, 1987).

8 I am citing chapter titles in Francis W. Grant, *Adventures at Sea* (Hantsport, NS: Lancelot Press, 1983).

9 This is most clear in the writings of Frederick William Wallace. But free of this condescension, and a very valuable work, is Frederick William Wallace, *Roving Fisherman: An Autobiography* (Gardenvale, Que.: Canadian Fisherman, 1955).

10 In this respect, the Canadian Nautical Research Society, its conferences, and its newsletter, *Argonauta*, perform a valuable service.

11 Morris Berman, "The Toolbox and the Playground: Present Comments on Future Historiography" (a talk given at the symposium of historians from Victoria and from Simon Fraser University, held at Qualicum, BC, Feb. 1987); cf. James M. Rhodes, *The Hitler Movement: A Modern Millenarian Revolution* (Stanford: Hoover Institution Press, 1980), 20.

12 Joseph Conrad, *The Mirror of the Sea* (London: Dent, 1923), 29.

13 Marcus Rediker, " 'Under the Banner of King Death': The Social World of Anglo-American Pirates, 1716 to 1726," *William and Mary Quarterly*, XXXVIII, no. 2 (April 1981), 201–27; and Rediker's book *Between the Devil and the Deep Blue Sea: Merchant Seamen, Pirates, and the Anglo-American Maritime World, 1700–1750* (Cambridge: Cambridge University Press, 1987).

14 Robert Schrank, ed., *Industrial Democracy At Sea: Authority and Democracy on a Norwegian Freighter* (Cambridge, Mass.: MIT Press, 1983).

15 The following discussion is indebted to Harry Braverman, *Labor and Monopoly Capital: The Degradation of Work in the Twentieth Century* (New York: Monthly Review Press, 1974); Charles More, *Skill and the English Working Class, 1870–1914* (London: Croom Helm, 1980); Alan Fox, *Beyond Contract: Work, Power and Trust Relations* (London: Faber and Faber, 1974); John Storey, *Managerial Prerogative and the Question of Control* (London: Routledge and Kegan Paul, 1983).

16 Fox, *Beyond Contract*, 19.

17 It is also possible that discretion may remain as a division of labour occurs and as task range narrows: see ibid., 208–9; and in the Canadian context Craig Heron and Robert Storey, eds., *On the Job: Confronting the Labour Process in Canada* (Kingston and Montreal: McGill-Queen's University Press, 1986).

18 Fox, *Beyond Contract*, 16–21.

19 Schrank, *Industrial Democracy at Sea*, 98–9.

20 Fingard, *Jack in Port*, 3. Judith Fingard raised this issue in her commentary on a paper that I presented to the Annual Meetings of the Canadian Historical Association in Winnipeg in 1986, and I am grateful for her well-directed questioning.

21 Marx, *Capital: A Critique of Political Economy* (Moscow: Foreign Languages Publishing House, 1957), vol. II, chap. 6, 149–51; see also L.R. Macdonald, "Merchants against Industry: An Idea and Its Origins," *Canadian Historical Review*, LVI, no. 3 (Sept. 1975), 268.

22 Occasionally British sailors are cited in what follows – if they worked in Canadian vessels or sailed under a Canadian master, or where they reflect a commonplace experience of work in sailing ships.

23 Michael R. Bouquet, *No Gallant Ship: Studies in Local and Maritime History* (London: Hollis & Carter, 1959), 163.

24 Bill Adams, "Ships and Women," in Bill Adams, *Ships and Memories* (Brighton: Teredo Books, 1975), 77.

CHAPTER ONE

1 In 1945, according to the census of that year, there were 758 fishing schooners or other auxiliary schooners in Newfoundland. In 1950 there were 120 schooners engaged in fishing in Canada: Canada, *Census*, 1951, vol. IX: Fisheries, Table 4.

2 On the pink or pinky schooner see H.F. Pullen, *Atlantic Schooners* (Fredericton: Brunswick Press, 1967), 14–15. The Cunard Line's

Lusitania of 31,500 tons was built in 1906. In that year the average tonnage of steamers on Canadian registry was a mere 134 tons: Report of the Department of Marine, 1906, Canada *Sessional Papers*, 1906. Official figures on Canadian tonnage are summarized in Keith Matthews, "The Shipping Industry of Atlantic Canada: Themes and Problems," in Keith Matthews and Gerald Panting, eds., *Ships and Shipbuilding in the North Atlantic Region* (St John's: MHG, 1978), 1-18.

3 E.P. Hohman, *Seaman Ashore: A Study of the United Seaman's Service and of Merchant Seamen in Port* (New Haven: Yale University Press, 1952), 224.

4 Peter Linebaugh, "All the Atlantic Mountains Shook," *Labour/Le Travailleur*, 10 (autumn 1982), 107-8.

5 Joseph Conrad, *The Mirror of the Sea* (London: Dent, 1923), 30.

6 Alan Villiers, *Wild Ocean: The Story of the North Atlantic and the Men Who Sailed It* (New York: McGraw-Hill, 1957); Charles H. Cotter, *The Atlantic Ocean* (Glasgow: Brown, Son and Ferguson, 1974).

7 Meteorological Office, *Meteorology for Mariners* (London: H.M. Stationery Office, 1967), 92 (Figure 7.5).

8 Figures on temperature and precipitation are in H.B. Lackey, *Oceanography and Canadian Atlantic Waters* (Ottawa: Fisheries Research Board of Canada Bulletin 134, 1961); see also Alan Villiers, *Wild Ocean* (New York: McGraw-Hill, 1957).

9 The crew lists in the MHA do not include passages between British North American ports. Shipping intelligence columns in newspapers report most coastal and ocean-going clearances; however, locally owned or locally registered vessels cannot be identified easily, since the newspapers report only the names of masters and vessels and not port of registry.

10 From the Board of Trade series 98 crew lists for vessels registered in Saint John, Halifax, Yarmouth, and Charlottetown between 1846 and 1854. These crew lists are on microfilm in the MHA. Results appear also in Eric W. Sager and Gerald Panting, "Staple Economies and the Rise and Decline of the Shipping Industry in Atlantic Canada, 1820-1914," in Lewis R. Fischer and Gerald Panting, eds., *Change and Adaptation in Maritime History: The North Atlantic Fleets in the Nineteenth Century* (St John's: MHG, 1985), 12.

11 Sambro Light Duties, PANS, RG 31-105, vol. 2. Computer analysis of the vessel registries for Halifax suggests that there were about 15,000 tons on registry in Halifax in 1826, if we include only those vessels

having one or more owners resident in Halifax County upon first registry of the vessel. The Light Duties for 1826 record 17,049 tons entering Halifax, including only vessels reported to be owned in Halifax.

12 Of the 125,548 tons newly registered in Saint John in the 1820s, 60.6 per cent consisted of tonnage in vessels of 250 tons or more. These were larger vessels, rigged mainly as barques and ships, and designed mainly for the transatlantic passage carrying timber. Data are from the computer analysis of Board of Trade series 107 and 108 vessel registries for Saint John.

13 The nine ports for which vessel registries have been analysed were Saint John (1820-1914), Halifax (1820-1914), Miramichi (1828-1914), Yarmouth (1840-1914), Pictou (1840-1914), Windsor (1849-1914), Charlottetown (1820-1914), Sydney (1842-1914), and St John's (1820-1936).

14 The number of "coastways" and foreign clearances for each year between 1839 and 1844, distinguishing the country of ownership of vessels, is given in a return printed in the "Report of the Select Committee on Steam Communication with Great Britain," *Journals of the House of Assembly*, Newfoundland, 1845, Appendices. The average tonnage of these coastal clearances is assumed to be the average tonnage of vessels on registry in St John's, from the computer analysis of Board of Trade 107/108 vessel registries.

15 John W. Froude, *On the High Seas: The Diary of Capt. John W. Froude* (St John's: Jesperson Press, 1983), 18.

16 Ibid., 11.

17 Nicholas Smith, *Fifty Two Years at the Labrador Fishery* (London: A.H. Stockwell, 1936), cited in Peter Neary and Patrick O'Flaherty, *By Great Waters: A Newfoundland and Labrador Anthology* (Toronto: University of Toronto Press, 1974), 171-2.

18 Froude, *On the High Seas*, 8.

19 Norman Duncan, *The Way of the Sea* (New York, 1903), cited in Neary and O'Flaherty, *By Great Waters*, 122.

20 Frederick William Wallace, *Roving Fisherman: An Autobiography* (Gardenvale, Que.: Canadian Fisherman, 1955), 138.

21 On the sloop, see Charles Armour and Thomas Lackey, *Sailing Ships of the Maritimes* (Toronto: McGraw-Hill Ryerson, 1975), 26-7.

22 Chapelle notes that the crews of some Marblehead schooners lived aft, under the quarterdeck: Howard I. Chapelle, *The American Fishing Schooners 1825-1935* (New York: Norton, 1973), 36. On the evolu-

tion of the schooner, see also William A. Baker, *Sloops and Shallops* (Barre, Mass.: Barre Publishing, 1966); Howard I. Chapelle, *The History of the American Sailing Ships* (New York: W.W. Norton, 1935); Basil Greenhill, *The Merchant Schooners* (London: David and Charles, 1968); E. Keble Chatterton, *Fore and Aft* (London: Seeley, Service & Co., 1912); Joseph E. Garland, *Down to the Sea: The Fishing Schooners of Gloucester* (Boston: David R. Godine, 1983); Harry D. Roberts with Michael O. Nowlan, *The Newfoundland Fish Boxes: A Chronicle of the Fishery* (Fredericton: Brunswick Press, 1982).

23 See the illustrations in Roberts and Nowlan, *Newfoundland Fish Boxes*, 14, 22, 26, 40, 42, 47, 51, 52, 60, 61; and in Nicolas De Jong and Marven Moore, *Launched from Prince Edward Island* (Charlottetown: P.E.I. Heritage Foundation, 1981), 17, 21, 39, 51, 73, 75, 159.

24 Board of Trade series 107/108 vessel registries for Saint John, Halifax, Yarmouth, Charlottetown, Windsor, Pictou, Miramichi, and Sydney; and the registries for St John's.

25 J.B. Jukes, *Excursions in and about Newfoundland* (London, 1842), cited in Peter Neary and Patrick O'Flaherty, *By Great Waters: A Newfoundland Anthology* (Toronto: University of Toronto Press, 1974), 80-1. In 1838 Benjamin Doane sailed from Barrington in a schooner with no forecastle: Benjamin Doane, *Following the Sea* (Halifax: NSM, 1987), 8. Newly registered Yarmouth schooners were on average 49.3 feet in length, according to the registries, in the 1840s. By the 1880s new Yarmouth schooners were on average 64.9 feet in length. See David Alexander, "The Port of Yarmouth, Nova Scotia, 1840-1889," in Matthews and Panting, *Ships and Shipbuilding*, 82.

26 Wallace, *Roving Fisherman*, 20.

27 Garland, *Down to the Sea*, 109; Claude Darrach, *From a Coastal Schooner's Log* (Halifax: NSM, 1979), 5, 16, 47.

28 S.E. Shipp Diary, 20 August 1874, Provincial Archives of Newfoundland and Labrador. Shipp was in the *Rolling Wave*, a Miramichi-built brig of 153 tons. On the forecastle see Michael R. Bouquet, *No Gallant Ship: Studies in Maritime and Local History* (London: Hollis & Carter, 1959), 167; Basil Greenhill, *The Merchant Schooners* (NMM reprint, 1978), vol. I, 211-18.

29 F.W. Wallace, *Roving Fisherman* (Gardenvale, Que.: Canadian Fisherman, 1955), 84.

30 Shipp Diary, 21 Aug. 1874.

31 Diary of Cephas Pearl, PANS, RG 7, no. 14A, 1884.

32 Halyard winches appeared in American fishing schooners in the 1850s and 1860s: Chapelle, *American Fishing Schooners*, 668. On the windlass see ibid., 669–80; David R. MacGregor, *Merchant Sailing Ships, 1815–1850* (London: Conway Maritime Press, 1984), 47–9, 88–9.

33 Chapelle describes a 152-ton schooner, the *Columbia*, with 53 single blocks, 25 double blocks, and 2 triple blocks: Chapelle, *American Fishing Schooners*, 345–7.

34 The length-breadth ratio in small vessels registered in Saint John and Halifax declined from the 1850s to the 1880s. For vessels of both ports of 10–99 tons in the 1850s the ratio was 3.56; by the 1880s it was 3.07. For vessels of 100–249 tons the ratio was 4.05 in the 1850s and 3.50 in the 1880s. See also David Alexander, "The Port of Yarmouth," 82. Chapelle states that by 1920 the average Nova Scotia fishing schooner was larger than the Gloucester schooner, but with less proportionate depth: Chapelle, *American Fishing Schooners*, 263.

35 Wallace, *Roving Fisherman*, 120; Chapelle, *American Fishing Schooners*, 136–7.

36 Two larger Canadian schooners appear in Charles Armour and Thomas Lackey, *Sailing Ships of the Maritimes*, 202–7; see also W.J. Lewis Parker, "The Operation and Management of the Great New England Schooners," in Basil Greenhill, ed., *Problems of Ship Management and Operation 1870–1900* (Greenwich: NMM, 1972), 17–25.

37 There were 745 brigantines newly registered in Halifax between 1820 and 1914 - 11.5 per cent of all new registrations. There were 735 brigantines newly registered in St John's between 1820 and 1936 - 7.6 per cent of all new registrations.

38 Based on the analysis of MHA crew lists for 353 voyages by St John's-registered vessels between 1863 and 1899. In the 100–149-ton class there were 23 schooner voyages and 77 brigantine voyages.

39 Admiral Colville in 1761, cited in Pullen, *Atlantic Schooners*, 9.

40 MacGregor, *Merchant Sailing Ships*, 26.

41 St John's Crew Lists, MHA. There were 35 brigantine voyages and 26 brig voyages in the 150–199 tonnage class. In the 200–249-ton class brigantines carried 8.3 men ($n = 15$) while brigs carried 10.5 men ($n = 21$).

42 Halifax Crew Lists, MHA. In this class there were 66 brigantine voyages and 26 brig voyages.

43 Between 1820 and 1914 there were 616 brigs newly registered in Saint John, and 484 brigantines. In Halifax, by contrast, there were 745 newly registered brigantines between 1820 and 1914, and 513 brigs.

44 Other qualities conducive to speed were a high degree of sharpness in the hull as it entered the water; a minimum of roughness or foulness in the bottom; and a low ratio of vessel weight or displacement to the size of the rig. See Howard Chapelle, *The Search for Speed under Sail 1700–1855* (New York: W.W. Norton, 1967), 398ff.

45 Saint John and Halifax vessel registries. The length-breadth ratio in clippers was over 5, and in "extreme" clippers over 5.5; Donald McKay's *Lightning* had a ratio of 5.7 in registered dimensions. See ibid., 321–97.

46 MacGregor, *Merchant Sailing Ships*, 30; Armour and Lackey, *Sailing Ships*, 48-9.

47 In the Yarmouth fleet, for instance, almost 94 per cent of the newly registered schooners were under 100 tons; 83 per cent of brigantines were 100-249 tons; none of the barques was under 250 tons. David Alexander and Gerry Panting, "The Mercantile Fleet and Its Owners: Yarmouth, Nova Scotia, 1840-1889," *Acadiensis*, VII (spring 1978), 6, note 12.

48 David Williams analysed man-ton ratios for vessels in transatlantic trades to and from Liverpool in 1832 and 1853. In 1832 ships of 200-299 tons carried fewer men on average than did barques in the same class; ships in the 300-399-ton range also carried fewer men than barques. Williams, "Crew Size in Trans-Atlantic Trades in the Mid-Nineteenth Century," in Rosemary Ommer and Gerald Panting, eds., *Working Men Who Get Wet* (St John's: MHG, 1980), 14.

49 Crews were on average smaller in vessels on passages between British North America and Britain, compared to vessels of the same tonnage classes on passages between Britain and South America, Central America, or the West Indies. Ibid., 116-17.

50 In 1876 the total tonnage of clearances by schooners in coasting was 719,787 tons: Canada, *Sessional Papers*, 1877, vol. X, no. 1, 759.

51 In St John's between 1839 and 1844 the average number of entrances and clearances per month in the four months between December and March was 97; for the rest of the year, 319. From a return based on customs information and printed in Newfoundland, *Journals of the*

House of Assembly, 1845, Appendices, 264. In 1826-7 the *Nova Scotian* reported a monthly average of 52 entrances and clearances between December and March, compared to 102 for the rest of the year. The St John's figures are higher than those for Halifax because the *Nova Scotian* did not report all coastal clearances.

52 Froude, *On the High Seas,* 216.

CHAPTER TWO

1 Harry Braverman, *Labor and Monopoly Capital: The Degradation of Work in the Twentieth Century* (New York: Monthly Review Press, 1974), 109. On merchant capital and its relationship to labour see ibid., 61-3; Alan Fox, *Beyond Contract: Work, Power and Trust Relations* (London: Faber and Faber, 1974), 178-9; Sidney Pollard, *The Genesis of Modern Management: A Study of the Industrial Revolution in Britain* (Cambridge, Mass.: E. Arnold, 1965), 38. On merchant control and master-servant relations in Newfoundland see Steven D. Antler, "Colonial Exploitation and Economic Stagnation in Nineteenth Century Newfoundland" (unpublished PhD thesis, University of Connecticut, 1975), and Gerald M. Sider, *Culture and Class in Anthropology and History: A Newfoundland Illustration* (Cambridge: Cambridge University Press, 1986), especially 26-8, 35-6.

2 On master-servant relations and planters see Sider, *Culture and Class,* 47-55; C. Grant Head, *Eighteenth Century Newfoundland: A Geographer's Perspective* (Toronto: McClelland and Stewart, 1976), 141-3, 218-20; C.R. Fay, *Life and Labour in Newfoundland* (Toronto: University of Toronto Press, 1956), 19-20, 22-3, 44-5, 138-9; Shannon Ryan, *Fish Out of Water: The Newfoundland Saltfish Trade 1814–1914* (St John's: Breakwater Books, 1986), 47, 61-2.

3 Steven D. Antler, "Colonial Exploitation," 80-8; Antler, "The Capitalist Underdevelopment of Nineteenth Century Newfoundland," in Robert J. Brym and R. James Sacouman, *Underdevelopment and Social Movements in Atlantic Canada* (Toronto: New Hogtown Press, 1979), 191-4; Ryan, *Fish Out of Water,* 61-2; Sider, *Culture and Class,* 47-58. On the truck system see Rosemary Ommer, " 'All the Fish of the Post': Resource Property Rights and Development in a Nineteenth Century Inshore Fishery," *Acadiensis,* IX, no. 2 (spring 1981), 107-23.

4 From the computer files created from the vessel registries for St John's, 1820-1936 (total number of registries: 12,592). The registries

used were the Board of Trade series 107 and 108 colonial ship registries (to 1890). From 1890 on, port copies of registries were used:
these are on microfilm in the Provincial Archives of Newfoundland
and Labrador, St John's, and in the National Archives of Canada,
Ottawa; registry books containing registries not yet closed are held by
Canada Customs, Sir Humphrey Gilbert Building, St John's.

5 From the computer files created from vessel registries for Halifax,
1820-1914, and Yarmouth, 1840-1914. Registries used were Board of
Trade series 107 and 108 ship registries, microfilm of port copies of
registries after 1890, and registry books held by Canada Customs,
Halifax.

6 Victor Butler, *Sposin' I Dies in D' Dory* (St John's: Jesperson Printing,
1977), 67.

7 Ibid., 48-51.

8 Andrew Herman, "Conceptualizing Control: Domination and Hegemony in the Capitalist Labor Process," *The Insurgent Sociologist*,
vol. II, no. 3 (fall 1982), 10-11. The distinction originates with Marx
in *Capital*, vol. I (New York: Vintage, 1976), 949-1065.

9 The contract of Bartholomew McGrath and John Nowlan, 1840,
cited in Sider, *Culture and Class*, 48; R.H. Bonnycastle, *Newfoundland in 1842* (London: H. Colburn, 1842), vol. II, 215-6.

10 Fox, *Beyond Contract*, 185.

11 Sider, *Culture and Class*, 48.

12 Christopher Hill, *Society and Puritanism in Pre-Revolutionary
England* (London: Secker and Warburg, 1964), 460; see also Ralph
Davis, *The Rise of the English Shipping Industry in the Seventeenth
and Eighteenth Centuries* (London: Macmillan, 1962), 116-21.

13 In Nova Scotia "the unit of production was a two-fold domestic type
involving the inshore fisherman and his family": L. Gene Barrett,
"Underdevelopment and Social Movements in the Nova Scotia Fishing Industry to 1938," in Brym and Sacouman, *Underdevelopment
and Social Movements*, 128-9. The quotation is from Sider, *Culture
and Class*, 28.

14 James C. Faris, *Cat Harbour: A Newfoundland Fishing Settlement* (St
John's: Institute of Social and Economic Research, 1972), 104. On
kinship relationships in fishing see Thomas F. Nemec, "I Fish with My
Brother: The Structure and Behaviour of Agnatic-Based Fishing
Crews in a Newfoundland Irish Outport," in R.R. Andersen and C.
Wadel, eds., *North Atlantic Fishermen* (St John's: Institute of Social
and Economic Research, 1972), 9-34; Geoffrey Stiles, "Labor

Recruitment and the Family Crew in Newfoundland," in R.R. Andersen, ed., *North Atlantic Maritime Cultures* (The Hague: Mouton, 1979), 189–208; Peter R. Sinclair, *From Traps to Draggers: Domestic Commodity Production in Northwest Newfoundland 1850– 1982* (St John's: Institute of Social and Economic Research, 1982), 14–30, 43–51; Roch Samson, *Fishermen and Merchants in 19th Century Gaspé* (Ottawa: Parks Canada, 1984), 50–1.

15 F.W. Wallace, "Life on the Grand Banks," *National Geographic*, XL, no. 1 (July 1921), 11; see also Wallace, *Roving Fisherman: An Autobiography* (Gardenvale, Que.: Canadian Fisherman, 1955), 26–7.

16 Joseph E. Garland, *Down to the Sea: The Fishing Schooners of Gloucester* (Boston: David R. Godine, 1983), 109.

17 Judith Fingard, *Jack in Port: Sailortowns of Eastern Canada* (Toronto: University of Toronto Press, 1982), 161.

18 On the share system see B.A. Balcom, *History of the Lunenburg Fishing Industry* (Lunenburg: Lunenburg Marine Museum, 1977), 28; Wallace, *Roving Fisherman*, 34–6; and the testimony of Michael Carney, A.N. Whitman, and W.C. Boak in *Royal Commission on the Relations of Capital and Labor in Canada*, 1889, vol. V, 136–42.

19 Wallace, *Roving Fisherman*, 35.

20 Butler, *Sposin' I Dies*, 68.

21 Canada, Department of Transport, Registers of Seamen Engaged at the Port of Saint John on Coastal Vessels 1883–1889, NBM. The first 30 Saint John–registered vessels in 1883 were sampled, and all crew for those vessels from early 1883 through the first half of 1884. The documents do not state whether it was birthplace or residence that was being recorded, but presumably sailors were stating their normal or family domicile.

22 Fingard, *Jack in Port*, 67 and 259 n 35.

23 Reminiscences of Harris Barnes, 1862–63, PANS, MG 108, no. 9.

24 Wallace, *Roving Fisherman*, 138.

25 The analysis that follows is from the original crew agreements for St John's-registered vessels between 1863 and 1899, MHA.

26 From the Board of Trade series 98 Crew Agreements for vessels registered in St John's, the first 20 vessels of less than 200 tons clearing St John's were sampled. Only 29 per cent of crew members were born in Newfoundland, but this was at the end of the great period of immigration from England and Ireland. No less than 90 per cent were born in Newfoundland or Britain, and most of the latter likely lived in Newfoundland.

27 Based on analysis of the Board of Trade series 98 Crew Lists for Yarmouth in 1846 and 1847, microfilm, MHA. Most (39) of the 50 voyages in the sample were between British North America and the British Isles.

28 On these connections see Gerry Panting, "Cradle of Enterprise: Yarmouth, Nova Scotia, 1840-1889," in Lewis R. Fischer and Eric W. Sager, eds., *The Enterprising Canadians: Entrepreneurs and Economic Development in Eastern Canada 1820–1914* (St John's: MHG, 1979), 255-71.

29 In ocean-going vessels after 1863 for which crew lists have been analysed, supercargoes appear very rarely. Of 182,616 signatures on crew lists for vessels of Saint John, Yarmouth, Halifax, and Windsor, only 20 were signatures of supercargoes.

30 On the distinction between trading vessels and general cargo vessels see John J.B. Hutchins, *The American Maritime Industries and Public Policy, 1789-1914* (Cambridge, Mass.: Harvard University Press, 1941), 239.

31 Board of Trade series 98 Crew Agareements. The voyage was from Yarmouth to the United Kingdom via Saint John.

32 On the problems of desertion in high-wage British North American ports see Fingard, *Jack in Port*, 141-53.

33 Victor Butler, *The Little Nord Easter: Reminiscences of a Placentia Bayman* (St John's: Memorial University, 1975), 111. Claude Darrach remembers hearty meals in coastal schooners in *From a Coastal Schooner's Log* (Halifax: NSM, 1979), 12, 23. Basil Greenhill states that food was generally better in schooners: *The Merchant Schooners* (London: NMM, 1978), vol. I, 216.

34 In the 191-ton brig *Pioneer*, built in Nova Scotia in 1856, the young Robert Thomas served as cook and was treated like a "slave": Aled Eames, ed., *Ship Master: The Life and Letters of Capt. Robert Thomas* (Denbigh: Gwynedd Archives Service, 1980), 34.

35 Conrad Dixon, "Pound and Pint: Diet in the Merchant Service 1750-1980," in Sarah Palmer and Glyndwr Williams, *Charted and Uncharted Waters* (London: NMM, 1981), 164-80. The 1868 Board of Trade scale was: 1 to 1½ lb. salt beef or pork daily; 1½ lb. fresh bread or ¾ lb. biscuit daily; 1 lb. fresh potatoes daily or dried vegetables weekly; 2 lb. flour weekly and ¾ pint peas weekly; 1 lb. sugar or 2 lb. molasses weekly; 1½ gallons water daily; and small quantities of currants or raisins, condiments, tea, coffee, and lime juice.

36 This would mean that illness was a cause of 0.4 per cent of all discharges, compared to 1 per cent of all discharges in the fleets of Saint John, Yarmouth, Halifax, and Windsor between 1863 and 1914.

37 These words appear on the crew agreements of the *Burman* of Yarmouth, 1846; the brig *Corfu* of Saint John, 1846; the *Argyle*, 253 tons, of Yarmouth, 1857. Board of Trade series 98 Crew Lists.

38 Of 486 discharges, 472 remained on board or received honourable discharges; nine deserted; two were discharged sick; and three died.

39 Darrach, *From a Coastal Schooner's Log*, x. On the close relations between master and sailor in earlier times, and on the participation of master and mate in work about the deck in small vessels in the 1840s, see Benjamin Doane, *Following the Sea* (Halifax: NSM, 1987), especially chapters 3-7.

40 Butler, *Sposin' I Dies*, 32.

41 The description that follows is from Garland, *Down to the Sea*, 69-70; and Darrach, *From a Coastal Schooner's Log*, 6-8.

42 Darrach, *From a Coastal Schooner's Log*, 8.

43 For a modern account of getting under way see Eric Hiscock, *Cruising under Sail*, 3rd ed., (Oxford: Oxford University Press, 1981), 229-33.

44 Garland, *Down to the Sea*, 45-7.

45 Wallace, *Roving Fisherman*, 54.

46 Garland, *Down to the Sea*, 74; Wallace, *Roving Fisherman*, 148.

47 Wallace, *Roving Fisherman*, 54.

48 The procedure is described in Darrach, *From a Coastal Schooner's Log*, 25.

49 George Whiteley, *Northern Seas Hardy Sailors* (New York: W.W. Norton, 1982), 32.

50 Ibid., 83-110; Feenie Ziner, *Bluenose, Queen of the Grand Banks* (Philadelphia: Chilton Book Co., 1970), 38-40. See also Andrew Horwood, *Newfoundland Ships and Men* (St John's: Macey's Publishing, 1971); G.J. Gillespie, *Bluenose Skipper* (Fredericton: Brunswick Press, 1955).

51 The procedure is described in Darrach, *From a Coastal Schooner's Log*, 90-103.

52 Joseph Conrad, *The Mirror of the Sea* (London: Dent, 1923), 23-33.

53 R.F. Sparkes, *The Winds Softly Sigh* (St John's: Breakwater Books, 1981), 40.

54 Ibid., 40-1.

55 J. Malcolm Green, "Autobiographical Memoir of a Deep-Water Apprentice," NMM, Accession no. 80/102.

56 Hiscock, *Cruising under Sail*, 364ff.

57 Fingard, *Jack in Port*, 63.

58 Butler, *Little Nord Easter*, 42, 47-8.

59 Ibid., 111.

60 All man-ton ratio calculations include the master. These ratios were somewhat lower than those for British vessels, at least in mid-century. In 1853 the ratio for schooners entering and clearing Liverpool was 5.93, according to David Williams, "Crew Size in Trans-Atlantic Trades in the Mid-Nineteenth Century," in Rosemary Ommer and Gerald Panting, eds., *Working Men Who Got Wet* (St John's: MHG, 1980), Table 5, p. 118.

61 The collection of crew agreements for St John's-registered vessels from 1863 to 1899 suggests that small vessels were often used in trans-atlantic passages. The 200-ton brigantine might carry coal, iron, or a general cargo from Britain to St John's. Such a vessel might carry 320 tons of coal at 13 shillings per ton; see an example in Greenhill, *The Merchant Schooners*, vol. I, 238, and for coal rates see Sarah Palmer, "The British Coal Export Trade, 1850-1913," in David Alexander and Rosemary Ommer, eds., *Volumes Not Values: Canadian Sailing Ships and World Trades* (St John's: MHG, 1979), 343-4. Gross earnings would be £208 sterling. If the vessel carried nine men and the master earned £12 a month, the mate £7, and the rest £3 each on average, and if other operating costs and depreciation were three times the wage bill, net returns from such a passage might be from £40 to £50, or five shillings per ton.

For the 1,000-ton barque with a coal cargo the calculation was very different: 1,500 tons of coal at 13 shillings would yield £975, but the wage bill was proportionately smaller – perhaps £80 for a 30-day passage. Even if other costs were four times the wage bill, the net returns would be £575, or over 11 shillings per ton.

The barque *N.B. Lewis*, of 1,328 tons, carried 2,082 tons of coal from Penarth to Rio in 1888. Her total wage costs were $452 monthly (about £93), and her total operating costs, including wages, were slightly more than £4,000 a year on average between 1886 and 1893. See Clement W. Crowell, *Novascotiaman* (Halifax: NSM, 1979), 379-85.

62 The fate of a fish exporting schooner owner, faced with steam competition, is revealed in the exchanges between Alfred Jones and other MPs in Canada's House of Commons *Debates*, 14 June 1887, 991ff.

63 Of all sailing tonnage entering Newfoundland ports in 1892, 1893,

and 1894, 6.8 per cent entered in ballast. By 1899, 1900, and 1901, 31.1 per cent was entering in ballast. Calculated from annual tables entitled "Number, Tonnage, and Crews of Sailing Vessels Entered at Ports in Newfoundland," Newfoundland Customs Returns, *Journals of the House of Assembly*, 1893-5, 1900-2, Appendices.

64 Beet sugar production represented 53 per cent of world sugar supply by 1884, and the price received for Cuban sugar fell: see Eric Williams, *From Columbus to Castro: The History of the Caribbean, 1492–1969* (London: Deutsch, 1970), 361-79; Louis A. Perez, *Cuba between Empires, 1878-1902* (Pittsburgh: University of Pittsburgh, 1983), 18-19. See also Ryan, *Fish Out of Water*, 233-5.

65 While entries in ballast were increasing on most routes, the problem by the end of the century was to find return cargoes from the West Indies, Brazil, and the United States. By 1899/1901 the proportion of sailing tonnage entering Newfoundland in ballast was 11 per cent from British colonies, 41 per cent from the United States, and 100 per cent from Brazil. Customs Returns, Newfoundland, *Journals of the House of Assembly*, 1900-2.

66 Substantial net migration from Newfoundland occurred from 1884, and possibly between 1874 and 1884: David Alexander, "Newfoundland's Traditional Economy and Development to 1934," *Acadiensis*, V, no. 2 (spring 1976), 63; Patricia Thornton, "Some Preliminary Comments on the Extent and Consequences of Out-Migration from the Atlantic Region, 1870-1920," in Lewis R. Fischer and Eric W. Sager, *Merchant Shipping and Economic Development in Atlantic Canada* (St John's: MHG, 1982), 217.

67 *On the High Seas: The Diary of John Froude* (St John's: Jesperson Press, 1983), 15.

68 From returns of vessels clearing Newfoundland ports in Newfoundland, *Journals of the House of Assembly*, Appendices. In the early 1870s the ratio to the United States was between 5 and 6. In 1876 the ratio jumped to 9.4.

69 Crew agreements for vessels registered in St John's 1863-99, MHG. In the Saint John-registered fleet, 0.5 per cent of all crew positions (excluding masters) were filled by Newfoundland-born sailors in 1863-78; by 1891-1912 the proportion was the same. In the three major Nova Scotia fleets – Yarmouth, Halifax, and Windsor – the proportion of Newfoundlanders was 0.6 per cent 1863-78 and 0.6 per cent 1891-1912.

70 "Report of the Select Committee to Inquire into Shipwrecks of

Timber Ships," *Parliamentary Papers*, 1839, vol. IX, 227, 241, 245, 248, 267.

71 Butler, *Sposin' I Dies*, 73.

72 The story is told in Garland, *Down to the Sea*, 80.

73 "Select Committee [on] Shipwrecks," *Parliamentary Papers*, 1839, vol. IX, 232.

74 Froude, *On the High Seas*, 15.

75 Sparkes, *The Winds Softly Sigh*, 46.

76 Conrad, *The Mirror of the Sea*, 7.

CHAPTER THREE

1 "Tramps and Ladies" is the title of chapter 6 of Michael Mason, Basil Greenhill, and Robin Craig, *The British Seafarer* (London: Hutcheson/BBC, 1980). This work is not one of romantic nostalgia.

2 Alan Villiers, *Voyaging with the Wind: An Introduction to Sailing Large Square-Rigged Ships* (London: NMM, 1975), 47-8.

3 A.W. Kirkaldy, *British Shipping: Its History, Organization, and Importance* (Newton Abbot: David and Charles Reprints, 1970), 36-7; Peter N. Davies, "The Development of the Liner Trades," in Keith Matthews and Gerald Panting, eds., *Ships and Shipbuilding in the North Atlantic Region* (St John's: MHG, 1978), 179-80; C.E. Fayle, *A Short History of the World's Shipping Industry* (London: Dial Press, 1933), 239; David R. MacGregor, *Merchant Sailing Ships 1850-1875* (London: Conway Maritime Press, 1984), 13-14, 20.

4 B.R. Mitchell and P. Deane, *Abstract of British Historical Statistics* (Cambridge: Cambridge University Press, 1962), Transport 3, 223.

5 For descriptions of shipyards see Stanley T. Spicer, *Masters of Sail* (Toronto: Ryerson Press, 1968), 115-45. John Russell's shipyard in Miramichi had accommodations for 50 men in 1849 (ibid., 117). According to the Canadian census of 1871 there were on average 17.5 employees per establishment in New Brunswick shipyards. There were fewer men on average in most other industrial establishments. See Peter D. McClelland, "The New Brunswick Economy in the Nineteenth Century" (unpublished PhD thesis, Harvard University, 1966), Table XLIX, 183.

6 Board of Trade Series 107/108 vessel registries; David Alexander, "The Port of Yarmouth, Nova Scotia, 1840-1889," in Matthews and Panting, *Ships and Shipbuilding*, 82.

7 Alexander, "The Port of Yarmouth," 83.

8 From SPSS systems files based on Saint John and Halifax vessel registries, MHA.

9 Official figures were not always overestimates of tonnage actually on registry and in service. Our recalculations of both Charlottetown and St John's tonnage in service for several years in the nineteenth century suggest that the registrar may have been underestimating tonnage on registry.

10 Port times ranged usually from 20 to 35 days. Passage times across the Atlantic were usually 45–60 days westbound and 30–45 days eastbound. In the four-month period May through August a vessel undertaking a voyage from the British Isles to the United States and back was likely to be in port for 20 to 30 per cent of the time. Vessels were more likely to be in port for repairs, or for lack of cargo, in winter. For passage times and port times see Lewis R. Fischer, "The Great Mud Hole Fleet: The Voyages and Productivity of the Sailing Vessels of Saint John, 1863-1912," in David Alexander and Rosemary Ommer, eds., *Volumes Not Values* (St John's: MHG, 1979), 136–42.

11 The total number employed in forest industries in both provinces, according to the census, was 18,234 in 1870: see S.A. Saunders, *The Economic History of the Maritime Provinces* (Fredericton: Acadiensis Press, 1984), 137.

12 The number of shipyard workers is necessarily an estimate, but the census of 1871 records 2,204 employed in Nova Scotia shipyards and 1,481 in New Brunswick yards (Saunders, *Economic History*, 137). Prince Edward Island produced about 40 per cent of the shipping tonnage of New Brunswick in 1870, so we may estimate employment in its yards at 600, yielding a total of about 4,285 shipyard workers in the three provinces. My estimate of mid-summer employment in shipping, excluding Newfoundland vessels, is between 12,733 and 15,184.

13 Of 8,737 departures by vessels of Saint John in the Saint John crew list sample, departures were more frequent in mid-summer than in winter: an average of 853 a month from June to September and 595 from December to March.

14 From the SPSS systems files on owners of the four ports, taken from Board of Trade series 107/108 colonial ship registries. On ownership see also David Alexander and Gerry Panting, "The Mercantile Fleet and Its Owners: Yarmouth, Nova Scotia, 1840-1889," *Acadiensis*, VII, 2 (spring 1978), 3-28; Richard Rice, "The Wrights of Saint John:

A Study in Shipbuilding and Shipping in the Maritimes, 1839-1855," in D.S. Macmillan, ed., *Canadian Business History: Selected Studies* (Toronto: McClelland and Stewart, 1972); A. Gregg Finley, "The Morans of St. Martins, N.B., 1850-1880: Toward an Understanding of Family Participation in Maritime Enterprise," in Lewis R. Fischer and Eric W. Sager, eds., *The Enterprising Canadians: Entrepreneurs and Economic Development in Eastern Canada, 1820-1914* (St John's: MHG, 1979); Clement W. Crowell, *Novascotiaman* (Halifax: NSM, 1979).

15 William Roche to Captain Hore, brig *Kate*, 13 July 1837, in William Roche Sr. Account Book and Letter Book, PANS. Equally valuable correspondence with masters can be found in the Ward Papers, NBM, and in the Duncan Letterbooks, PAPEI.

16 Roche to Captain Hore, 5 Nov. 1837, in Roche Letterbook, PANS.

17 Roche to Captain Hore, 18 June 1838, in Roche Letterbook, PANS.

18 "Report of the Select Committee on the Causes of the Present Depression," House of Commons *Journals*, vol. X (1876), Appendix No. 3, 173.

19 Maurice Dobb, *Studies in the Development of Capitalism* (London: Routledge and Kegan Paul, 1946), 266-7.

20 Harry Braverman, *Labor and Monopoly Capital* (New York: Monthly Review Press, 1974), 258.

21 John Ward and Sons to Captain John Lawrence, barque *Clarence*, 17 Aug. 1840, Ward Papers packet 3, NBM.

22 Ward and Sons to James Tibbett of Quebec, 1 June 1843, Ward Papers packet 3, NBM.

23 "They were men of the same type," writes Clement W. Crowell, *Novascotiaman*, 26.

24 William Stevenson to James Peake, 4 Dec. 1843, Peake Papers, no. 641, PAPEI.

25 Robert Quirk to Captain T. Richards, 2 March 1882, Duncan Letterbooks, vol. 362, PAPEI.

26 G.D. Urquhart, ed., *Dues and Charges on Shipping in Foreign Ports* (London, 1872); A.A. Mocatta, M.J. Mustill, and S.C. Body, *Scrutton on Charter Parties and Bills of Lading*, 18th ed., (London: Sweet and Maxwell, 1974); Frank T. Bullen, *Men of the Merchant Service* (London: Smith, Elder, 1900) 53-62; Crowell, *Novascotiaman*.

27 The best source is R.W. Stevens, *On the Stowage of Ships and Their Cargoes*, 6th ed., (London: Longmans, 1873).

28 W.E. May, *History of Marine Navigation* (Henley on Thames: Foulis, 1973); Peter Kemp, "Chartmaking," in *The Oxford Companion to Ships and the Sea* (London: Oxford University Press, 1976), 155-61.

29 W.H. Rosser, *A Self-Instructor in Navigation and Nautical Astronomy* (London, 1863). This volume was widely used for local marine board examinations.

30 John Harland and Mark Myers, *Seamanship in the Age of Sail* (Annapolis, Md.: Naval Institute Press, 1985), 63-4.

31 Ibid., 63-4.

32 Carrying full sail also affected steering. In 1850 the barque *Susan* "goes along as fast with top sails and courses as she does with all set, for the more you put on the worse she steers which is a great detriment to her onward progress." Journal of James N. Smith, 1850, shelf A96, NBM.

33 Harland and Myers, *Seamanship in the Age of Sail*, especially chap. 12-18.

34 James Duncan to Captain Richard Welch, 21 Aug. 1873, Duncan Letterbooks, PAPEI.

35 W.S. Lindsay, *History of Merchant Shipping and Ancient Commerce* (New York: AMS Press, 1965), vol. III, 287-321.

36 Aled Eames, *Ship Master* (Denbigh: Gwynned Archives Services, 1980), 118. See also *Journal of the Margaret Rait 1840-1844; Captain James Doan Coffin* (Hantsport, NS: Lancelot Press, 1984).

37 Journal of Captain I.B. Morris, 1878, in Maritime Museum of the Atlantic, Halifax.

38 Maritime historians have yet to absorb David F. Noble, *America by Design: Science, Technology and the Rise of Corporate Capitalism* (New York: Knopf, 1977), and *Forces of Production: A Social History of Industrial Automation* (New York: Knopf, 1984). But see Ralph Davis, *The Rise of the English Shipping Industry in the Seventeenth and Eighteenth Centuries* (London: Macmillan, 1962), chap. 6, 7, and 8.

39 Harland and Myers, *Seamanship*, 92.

40 Much of the description that follows is from *Specification of a Barque* (Dumbarton, 1885), a printed description of the *Bowman B. Law*, a British-built iron barque of 1,359 tons ordered by William Law and Co. of Yarmouth. An account of the vessel is in Eric J. Ruff, "Specifications of a Barque" (paper presented to the American Society for Oceanic History, Halifax, 1980). Because of her iron hull, the vessel was unlike most others in fleets of the Maritimes, but she does show

how far removed the sailing vessel of the 1880s could be from its ancestors at the beginning of the century and from its contemporaries in coasting.

41 Joseph Conrad, *The Mirror of the Sea* (London: Dent, 1923), 6.

42 *Specification of a Barque*, 8-9.

43 Ibid., 27.

44 Conrad, *Mirror of the Sea*, 17.

45 In the four major fleets for which crew members have been analysed, 2.5 per cent of the 13,271 mates (first, second, or third mate) were illiterate; of 8,427 first mates, 67 (0.8 per cent) were illiterate.

46 Bullen, *Men of the Merchant Service*, 111; see also F.W. Wallace, *Wooden Ships and Iron Men* (London: Hodder and Stoughton, 1924), 174-81.

47 Wallace, *Wooden Ships and Iron Men*, 181.

48 Of 4,097 second mates in four fleets, 197 were illiterate, not including those coded as signing with difficulty.

49 Compare this with Wallace, *Wooden Ships and Iron Men*, 180, where he says that the Bluenose second mate was "usually a mere youth." Those having second-mate rank were even older by the 1890s; after 1890, 79 per cent of second mates in the Saint John fleet were 30 or over.

50 Bullen, *Men of the Merchant Service*, 137-8.

51 Matthews and Panting, *Ships and Shipbuilding*, 230.

52 Lindsay, *History of Merchant Shipping*, vol. III, 492. On state intervention see also Oliver MacDonagh, *A Pattern of Government Growth 1800-1860* (London: MacGibbon & Kee, 1961); Neville Upham, *The Load Line – A Hallmark of Safety* (London: NMM, 1978); David Masters, *The Plimsoll Mark* (London: Cassell and Co., 1955); David M. Williams, "State Regulation of Merchant Shipping 1839-1914: The Bulk Carrying Trades," in Sarah Palmer and Glyndwr Williams, *Charted and Uncharted Waters* (London: NMM, 1981), 55-80; Conrad Dixon, "Legislation and the Sailor's Lot," in Paul Adam, ed., *Seamen in Society: Proceedings of the International Commission on Maritime History* (Bucharest: Commission internationale d'histoire maritime, 1980), vol. III, 96-103.

53 "Report of the Select Committee appointed to inquire into the causes of shipwrecks," (British) *Parliamentary Papers*, 1836, vol. XVII, 373; Jane H. Wilde, "The Creation of the Marine Department of the Board of Trade," *Journal of Transport History*, II, no. 4 (Nov. 1956), 194.

54 Wilde, "Creation of the Marine Department," 195-6.

55 Lindsay, *History of Merchant Shipping*, vol. III, 297-9; Clifford Jeans, "The First Statutory Qualifications for Seafarers," *Transport History*, VI, no. 3 (Nov. 1973), 248-67.

56 Hansard, *Parliamentary Debates*, 3rd series, CVIII, 11 Feb. 1850, 668, 671; see also CVII, 1849, 224-5.

57 Mercantile Marine Act, 1850: 13 & 14 Vic., cap 93.

58 Ibid.; see also Rosser, *A Self-Instructor*, 6-7.

59 Fourth Annual Report of the Department of Marine and Fisheries, in Canada, *Sessional Papers*, 1871, vol. V, 46.

60 On British influence on Canadian shipping laws see Ted L. McDorman, "The Development of Shipping Laws and Policy in Canada: An Historical Examination of the British Influence" (unpublished master of laws thesis, Dalhousie University, 1982).

61 Fourth Annual Report, Marine and Fisheries, 46-9; *Sessional Papers*, 1872, Appendix no. 34.

62 Ibid.; and see Wallace, *Wooden Ships and Iron Men*, 171.

63 Canada, *Sessional Papers*, 1872, no. 5, Appendix 34.

64 "Report of the Chairman of Board of Examiners of Masters and Mates," Canada, *Sessional Papers*, 1873, no. 4, Appendix 12.

65 Canada, *Sessional Papers*, 1885, no. 9, Appendix no. 3.

66 Conrad Dixon, "Legislation and the Sailor's Lot, 1660-1914," in Adam, ed., *Seamen in Society*, vol. III, 98.

67 Lindsay, *History of Merchant Shipping*, vol. III, 45-8. Although Lindsay was sceptical about the consular reports, he concluded that, even allowing for exaggeration, "there is too much reason for believing that the character of British ships and the conduct of British crews were then greatly inferior to those of other nations."

68 There are, therefore, many pages of excerpts from merchant shipping acts in the log books contained with crew lists in the MHA.

69 Lindsay, *History of Merchant Shipping*, vol. III, 497.

70 Ibid., vol. III, 471; Merchant Seaman's Act, 7 & 8 Vic. cap 112; 8 & 9 Vic. cap 116.

71 Dixon, "Legislation," 98; A.G. Course, *The Merchant Navy: A Social History* (London: Frederich Muller, 1963), 214-39.

72 Lindsay, *History of Merchant Shipping*, vol. III, 473.

73 Ibid., 473-4, 496-7.

74 George W. Murray, master of the *J.L. Wickwire* of Windsor, Official No. 52098, Philadelphia to Antwerp, 1869-70, MHA.

75 Wallace, *Wooden Ships and Iron Men*, 165-6.

76 Lindsay, *History of Merchant Shipping*, vol. III, 497.

77 Bullen, *Men of the Merchant Service*, 40.

78 Wallace, *Wooden Ships and Iron Men*, 165-6.

79 Erving Goffman, "On the Characteristics of Total Institutions," in *Asylums: Essays on the Social Situation of Mental Patients and Other Inmates* (Garden City, NY: Anchor Books, 1961), 3-124. Goffman includes merchant ships among total institutions.

CHAPTER FOUR

1 Samuel Leech, c. 1812, cited in Michael Mason, Basil Greenhill, and Robin Craig, *The British Seafarer* (London: Hutcheson/BBC, 1980), chap. 2. Marx used the words "living appendage" in discussing the subordination of labour: see Andrew Herman, "Conceptualization and Control: Domination and Hegemony in the Capitalist Labor Process," *The Insurgent Sociologist*, II, no. 3 (fall 1982), 11.

2 Alan Fox, *Beyond Contract: Work, Power and Trust Relations* (London: Faber and Faber, 1974), 185-6.

3 P. Selznick, *Law, Society and Industrial Justice* (New York: Russell Sage Foundation, 1969), 135; cited in Fox, *Beyond Contract*, 188.

4 J.R. Commons, *Legal Foundations of Capitalism* (New York: Macmillan, 1924), 285.

5 By division of labour is meant the differentiation of work into a number of separate tasks, each allocated to a person who proceeds to specialize in those tasks. Obviously the result maybe a specialist whose work nevertheless embodies both task range and high degrees of discretion. On ambiguities in the division of labour concept see Fox, *Beyond Contract*, 208-9; and see Harry Braverman, *Labor and Monopoly Capital* (New York: Monthly Review Press, 1974), 75-83.

6 The unit of analysis, here as elsewhere, is the signatory of the crew list. There were fewer than 2,177 separate individuals in the sample, since sailors often remained in their vessel for more than one voyage.

7 Frank T. Bullen, *The Men of the Merchant Service* (London: Smith, Elder, 1900), 212.

8 Ibid., 159-60.

9 Cf. Charles More, *Skill and the English Working Class 1870-1914* (London: Croom Helm, 1980), 190-1.

10 Bullen, *Men of the Merchant Service*, 153; F.W. Wallace, *Wooden Ships and Iron Men* (London: Hodder and Stoughton, 1924), 182-3.

11 Bullen, *Men of the Merchant Service*, 171-9.

12 Ibid., 183-6.

13 Wallace, *Wooden Ships*, 183-6.

14 On watches see *On the High Seas: The Diary of Capt. John W. Froude* (St John's: Jesperson Press, 1983), 87-8; R.J. Cornewall-Jones, *The British Merchant Service* (London: S. Low, Marston, 1898), 296; Bullen, *Men of the Merchant Service*, 263-7.

15 Wallace, *Wooden Ships*, 190; Bullen, *Men of the Merchant Service*, 268.

16 By 1889 he was in a steamer that had "about 120 seamen unbord": *On the High Seas*, 45.

17 Saint John Crew List files, MHA. Records for 8,737 voyages by vessels in this fleet were coded; for 2,061 voyages (23.6 per cent) all crew were coded. The average number of men at voyage start, excluding the master, was 14.4 (standard deviation = 6.8).

18 A vessel having such dimensions might be 1,000 tons under the deck; a registered ton was meant to approximate 100 cubic feet.

19 The ship *Oliver Lange*, 1,236 tons, built in Saint John in 1853, carried a foremast of 134 feet from deck to truck, a main mast of 140 feet, and a mizzen mast of 110 feet. Total mast and spar dimensions were over 1,000 feet. See Charles Armour and Thomas Lackey, *Sailing Ships of the Maritimes* (Toronto: McGraw-Hill Ryerson, 1975), 64.

20 The 652-ton *Eva*, built 1865-6, included iron and copper worth $3,750 and chains and anchor worth $932; total costs excluding labour were $18,330. The ship *Arizona*, 1,302 tons, built 1868-9, included $4,934 for iron and copper, and $1,390 for chains and anchor; total costs excluding labour were $29,332. This did not include iron in rigging and outfit. Expenditures are given in T.E. Millidge Papers, Shipyard Ledger, NBM, and in Peter D. McClelland, "The New Brunswick Economy in the Nineteenth Century" (PhD thesis, Harvard, 1966), 191.

21 Frank Killam was questioned by the Select Committee on the Causes of the Present Depression (1876): House of Commons *Journals*, vol. X, 1876, Appendix 3, 166. Killam also estimated that 30 to 60 tons of mineral salt would be used in building such a ship.

22 David R. MacGregor, *Merchant Sailing Ships 1815-1850* (London: Conway Maritime Press, 1984), 150-1; Stanley Spicer, *Masters of Sail* (Toronto: Ryerson Press, 1968), 35; Wallace, *Wooden Ships*, 157.

23 In the 1870s, 3½-inch hemp rope weighed 2 pounds 13 ounces per fathom and had a "breaking strain" of 3.06 tons; wire rigging of 2½

inches weighed 5 pounds 8 ounces per fathom and had a breaking strain of 6 tons. The substitute for 3½-inch hemp might be 1½-inch wire, however, and this weighed only 2 pounds per fathom. See Charles Burney, *Young Seaman's Manual and Rigger's Guide* (London: Trubner and Co., 1877), 523-5.

24 On the windlass see MacGregor, *Merchant Sailing Ships 1815-1850*, 46-7, 88-9; and David R. MacGregor, *Merchant Sailing Ships 1850–1875* (London: Conway Maritime Press, 1984), 116, 129. There is an illustration of the Emerson windlass in a brochure of J. Snelling & Co. of New York, entitled *Ship, Steamboat and Yacht Fixtures*, to be found in Jonathan Steele Papers, MS-2-70, Dalhousie University Archives. Canadian shipowners were receiving information on ship fittings from both British and American sources.

25 John Harland and Mark Myers, *Seamanship in the Age of Sail* (Annapolis, Md.: Naval Institute Press, 1984), 232-4.

26 *Specification of a Barque* (Dumbarton, 1885); Eric J. Ruff, "Specifications of a Barque" (paper presented to the American Society for Oceanic History, Halifax, 1980).

27 A complete account of 50,095 passages between ports appears in Eric W. Sager and Gerry Panting, "Staple Economies and the Rise and Decline of the Shipping Industry in Atlantic Canada, 1820-1914," in Lewis R. Fischer and Gerald Panting, eds., *Change and Adaptation in Maritime History: The North Atlantic Fleets in the Nineteenth Century* (St John's: MHG, 1985), 24.

28 G.S. Graham, "The Ascendancy of the Sailing Ship, 1850-1885," *Economic History Review*, IX, no. 1 (1956-7), 75-88.

29 Breaking down vessel-days, or voyage duration in days, by trade route for the Windsor fleet yields the following proportions for the period 1890-1912: North Atlantic: 22.7 per cent; South American (east and west): 38.8 per cent; other: 38.5 per cent.

30 These averages are for Saint John vessels in the Saint John Crew List file, MHA. The deviation around the mean was always very high. For vessels under 250 tons the average voyage was 113.9 days ($n = 551$; standard deviation = 76.8). For vessels of 250-499 tons the average was 142.6 days ($n = 1,664$; standard deviation = 100.5). For vessels of 500-999 tons the mean was 148.5 days ($n = 3,738$; standard deviation = 118.0). For vessels of 1,000-1,499 tons the mean was 224.0 days ($n = 2,204$; deviation = 186.1). For vessels over 1,500 tons the mean was 263.9 days ($n = 578$; deviation = 218.9), rising to 304 days in the 1890s.

31 Lewis R. Fischer, "The Great Mud Hole Fleet: The Voyages and Productivity of the Sailing Vessels of Saint John, 1863-1912," in David
Alexander and Rosemary Ommer, eds., *Volumes Not Values: Canadian Sailing Ships and World Trades* (St John's: MHG, 1979), 135.

32 *On the High Seas*, 78.

33 There are many dictionaries of nautical language. See, for instance,
A.G. Course, *A Dictionary of Nautical Terms* (London: Arco Publi-
cations, 1962); C.W.T. Layton, *Dictionary of Nautical Words and
Terms* (Glasgow: Brown, Son and Ferguson, 1955); and the dictionaries listed in Harland and Myers, *Seamanship in the Age of Sail*,
314-5.

34 *On the High Seas*, 92.

35 The best short description of rigging and sails is Harland and Myers,
Seamanship in the Age of Sail, chap. 2. See also Alan Villiers, *The
Way of a Ship* (New York: Scribner, 1953), chap. 5 and 6; Harold A.
Underhill, *Masting and Rigging: The Clipper Ship and Ocean Car-
rier* (Glasgow: Brown, Son and Ferguson, 1946); Harold A. Under-
hill, *Sailing Ship Rigs and Rigging* (Glasgow: Brown, Son and
Ferguson, 1955).

36 Harland and Myers, *Seamanship*, 124. On reefing see ibid., 137-54.
The *S.L. Tilley*, a 785-ton ship built at Saint John in 1856, is portrayed with three reef-bands on the fore and mizzen topsails, double
topsails on the main (with a single reef-band on the upper topsail),
and single reef-bands on the courses. A painting of the *St. George*, a
ship built in Tynemouth, NB, in 1836, indicates four reef-bands on
the main and fore topsails and two reef-bands on the courses. See the
illustrations in Armour and Lackey, *Sailing Ships*, 35, 37, 41, 53,
56, 63, 69, *passim*; in later paintings the number of reef-bands
diminishes.

37 R.H. Dana, *Two Years before the Mast* (New York: World Publishing, 1946), 100-1.

38 Bent G. Sivertz, of Nanoose Bay, BC, interviewed by the author in
January 1987. Sivertz worked 1922-32 in sailing vessels, including
lumber carriers, mainly in the Pacific Ocean. The work he describes
was commonplace in square-rigged vessels of the late nineteenth and
early twentieth centuries.

39 Swigging is described in Eric Hiscock, *Cruising under Sail*, 3rd ed.,
(Oxford: Oxford University Press, 1981), 102.

40 Bill Adams, *Ships and Memories* (Brighton: Teredo Books, 1975),
329. Freeing ports were the square ports in the bulwarks that allowed
seawater shipped on deck to run over the sides.

41 Sivertz interview.

42 E.L. Davies, interviewed by Campbell McMurray, Oral History collection, NMM.

43 Benjamin Doane, *Following the Sea* (Halifax: Nova Scotia Museum, 1987), 194.

44 Sivertz interview.

45 On steering see Harland and Myers, *Seamanship*, 174-80.

46 On splicing and marling spike seamanship see Clifford W. Ashley, *The Ashley Book of Knots* (New York: Doubleday, Doran, 1944).

47 Ken Attiwill, *Horizon* (London: n.d.), 40; the author was employed in a Finnish vessel in the early 20th century.

48 Bullen, *Men of the Merchant Service*, 178.

49 Demotions recorded in the collection of official logs in the MHA are too numerous to list. In the collection of official logs in the NBM is the log of *Highlands* of Saint John (Official No. 88255) for 1899-1900. Several ABs were demoted to OS at $10 a month. Among those demoted were men with experience at sea: "Read the above over to W. Hanigan, he admits he is not a sailor but is a fireman." One was demoted to boy from AB because he "knows nothing about seamanship whatever, he says he came out from England on a steamer as trimmer, I disrate him to Boy at 30/-."

50 Basil Greenhill, *The Merchant Schooners*, reprint (London: NMM 1978), vol. I, 197.

CHAPTER FIVE

1 Boswell, *Life of Johnson* (London: Modern Library, 1935), 585; cited in David Alexander, "Literacy among Canadian and Foreign Seamen, 1863-1899," in Rosemay Ommer and Gerald Panting, eds., *Working Men Who Got Wet* (St John's: MHG, 1980), 3.

2 See, for instance, "Report of the Select Committee to Inquire into the Manning of British Ships," *British Parliamentary Papers*, 1896, vol. XL, 13.

3 Frank T. Bullen, *The Men of the Merchant Service* (London: Smith, Elder, 1900), 72.

4 F.W. Wallace, *Wooden Ships and Iron Men* (London: Hodder and Stoughton, 1924), 177.

5 Peter Bailey, " 'Will the Real Bill Banks Please Stand UP?' A Role Analysis of Victorian Working Class Respectability," *Journal of Social History*, XII (spring 1979), 336-53; "Alley Sloper's Half-holiday:

Comic Art in the 1880s," *History Workshop Journal,* XVI (autumn 1983), 4–31.

6 *On the High Seas: The Diary of Capt. John W. Froude* (St John's: Jesperson Press, 1983), 26.

7 Diary of Cephas Pearl, 1882, PANS, RG 7 no. 14A.

8 Aled Eames, *Ship Master* (Denbigh: Gwynedd Archives Service, 1980), 31.

9 Stanley Spicer, *Masters of Sail* (Toronto: Ryerson, 1968), 226; see also Jessie L. Beattie, *The Log Line: The Adventure of a Great Sailing Captain* (Toronto: McClelland and Stewart, 1972), 20.

10 Gareth Stedman Jones, *Outcast London* (Harmondsworth: Penguin Books, 1976), 76; Charles Booth, *Life and Labour of the People of London* (London: Macmillan, 1903), second series, vol. III, 363.

11 Elaine Bernard, *The Long Distance Feeling: A History of the Tele-communications Workers Union* (Vancouver: New Star Books, 1982), 13; Alan A. Brookes, "Outmigration from the Maritime Provinces, 1860–1900: Some Preliminary Considerations," in P.A. Buckner and David Frank, *The Acadiensis Reader: Volume Two: Atlantic Canada after Confederation* (Fredericton: Acadiensis Press, 1985), 54–5.

12 Spicer, *Masters of Sail*, 183.

13 Benjamin Doane, *Following the Sea* (Halifax: NSM, 1987), especially chap. 1–4.

14 All quantitative data in this chapter are from computer files created from the crew lists for vessels registered in Saint John, Yarmouth, Halifax, and Windsor, MHA. Voyage data for all crew lists were coded, and the resulting files are likely to contain information on over 60 per cent of voyages for each of four fleets. For Halifax, Yarmouth, and Windsor all crew members for every second vessel were entered and analysed; for Saint John, all crew for every fourth vessel. The files contain 22,811 crew records for the Halifax fleet, 49,642 for Yarmouth, 56,061 for Windsor, and 54,147 for Saint John. The resulting samples are sufficiently large that generalizations can be made without fear of statistical error.

For the methods of data entry see Lewis R. Fischer and Eric W. Sager, "An Approach to the Quantitative Analysis of British Shipping Records," *Business History,* XXII, no. 2 (July 1980), 135–51; Rosemary Ommer, Lewis R. Fischer, and Eric W. Sager, "The Data Base of the Atlantic Canada Shipping Project," in Lewis R. Fischer and Eric W. Sager, eds., *Merchant Shipping and Economic Development in Atlantic Canada* (St John's: MHG, 1982), 306.

15 For most of this period, colonial vessels were included with British vessels in entrances and clearances to and from major ports. See Sarah Palmer, "The British Shipping Industry 1850-1914," in Lewis R. Fischer and Gerald E. Panting, *Change and Adaptation in Maritime History: The North Atlantic Fleets in the Nineteenth Century* (St John's: MHG, 1985), Table 7, pp. 102-3; D.H. Aldcroft, ed., *The Development of British Industry and Foreign Competition, 1875-1914* (London: G. Allen and Unwin, 1968), 362-3.

16 In the Saint John fleet, with registry of each sailor's last ship and place of joining ship aggregated into broad regions or countries, Cramer's $V = 0.24$; lambda with last ship dependent $= 0.17$.

17 In 1860 British North America possessed 547,000 tons, or 4.1 per cent of world tonnage; in 1870 Canada possessed about a million tons, or 5.9 per cent; in 1880 Canada possessed 1.3 million tons, or 6.5 per cent. Sarah Palmer, "The British Shipping Industry," 90; Keith Matthews, "The Shipping Industry of Atlantic Canada: Themes and Problems," in Keith Matthews and Gerald Panting, eds., *Ships and Shipbuilding in the North Atlantic Region* (St John's: MHG, 1978), 9-18.

18 With registry of last ship and birthplace aggregated into eight regions or nationalities (New Brunswick, Nova Scotia, other British North America, British Isles, United States, Europe, and Scandinavia), Cramer's $V = 0.24$, and lambda with birthplace dependent $= 0.09$.

19 The best instance of close working relations between managing owner and masters is Lewis and Gullison, recorded in Clement Crowell, *Novascotiaman* (Halifax: NSM, 1979).

20 Bullen, *Men of the Merchant Service*, 26.

21 Crowell, *Novascotiaman*, 158.

22 Alexander, "Literacy among Canadian and Foreign Seamen," 7.

23 The category is titled "mariners" in 1871 and 1881 and "sailors" in 1891. For New Brunswick the totals were 2,094 in 1871, 2,058 in 1881, and 1,512 in 1891; for Nova Scotia 7,864 in 1871, 7,401 in 1881, and 5,425 in 1891. Obviously no estimate of the sailor population can be precise, but these figures suggest a trend at least. See "Occupations of the People," Canada *Census*, 1871, 1881, 1891. Total tonnage on registry in both provinces increased by slightly over 30 per cent from 1871 to 1881. Between 1881 and 1891 total tonnage on registry declined in Nova Scotia by about 17 per cent and in New Brunswick by about 42 per cent.

24 Rosemary Ommer, " 'Composed of All Nationalities': The Crews of

Windsor Vessels, 1862–1899," in Ommer and Panting, *Working Men Who Got Wet*, 207–9.

25 This is the "one percent" sample of all non-Canadian crew lists 1863–99 in the MHA. The total number of crew members on the 1,092 sailing ship voyages where they were coded was 22,022. For 92.7 per cent of these the sailor's birthplace is known. See also chap. 9 n 12.

26 In the Yarmouth fleet, for instance, two-thirds of non–Nova Scotian masters went to sea with crews more than 80 per cent non–Nova Scotian by birth. Many fewer Nova Scotian masters sailed with such largely non-native crews. Alternatively, where the crew consisted of a relatively high proportion of Nova Scotians (30 per cent or more), the master was almost certain to be Nova Scotian.

27 *Hannah Morris* of Windsor, Official No. 57179, Liverpool-Philadelphia-Liverpool, 1869, MHA.

28 *Africana* of Saint John, Official No. 37160, January 1863, MHA.

29 "Report of the Select Committee to Inquire into the Manning of British Ships," *Parliamentary Papers*, 1896, vol. XL, 1–13.

30 *Nautical Magazine*, June 1887, 487.

31 Only 0.3 per cent of all Europeans hired in the four fleets terminated their service through a "dishonourable" discharge (discharge into jail, discharge following demotion, and the like). The rate for those born in British North America was also 0.3 per cent, and for those born in Britain, 0.5 per cent. In the Saint John file, reason for discharge was aggregated into six categories (did not join, remained at end, honourable discharge, dishonourable discharge, desertion, and others): selecting only ABs, the relations between reason discharged and birthplace is weak in all three periods (in each period Cramer's $V = 0.06$). For 1863–78, desertion rates ranged from a low of 30 per cent for British-born to a high of 39.4 per cent for US-born, with rates for Canadian-born at 33.1 per cent, Europeans at 34.2 per cent, and Scandinavians at 36.5 per cent. For 1879–90, desertion rates for Canadian-born ABs fell to 24.9 per cent, but rates for Europeans (33.3 per cent) and Scandinavians (37.9 per cent) changed little. For 1891–1914, the rates for Canadian-born went up (30.2 per cent), while the rates for Europeans (33.7 per cent) and Scandinavians (33.0 per cent) again changed only slightly. The proportion of ABs receiving "dishonourable" discharges, over the whole period 1863–1912, was 0.9 per cent; Europeans (0.8 per cent) and Scandinavians (0.5 per cent) were below the overall average.

32 In the 1878–90 period, of all Scandanavians and other Europeans signed on in Saint John vessels, 42.8 per cent signed on for voyages to

South America, the Pacific, or the Far East; of all British North America-born crew, 33.2 per cent signed on for such longer voyages. For 1891–1912, the proportion of each group signing on for such voyages were: Scandinavians, 61.7 per cent; other Europeans, 60.7 per cent; British North America-born, 55.5 per cent.

33 Various comparisons can be made. Comparing nominal AB wages for ABs hired in Norwegian ports for service in ocean-going vessels (and most of these ABs were presumably Norwegian-born) with Canadian-born ABs in either the four Canadian fleets or British vessels suggests the following. In the 1860s ABs hired in Norway earned $9.91 a month ($n = 11,130$), whereas Canadian-born ABs earned $19.13 ($n = 1,634$). In the 1870s ABs hired in Norway earned $11.17 ($n = 18,748$), whereas Canadians earned $18.64 ($n = 4,877$). In the 1880s ABs hired in Norway earned $10.77 ($n = 17,152$), whereas Canadians earned $17.97 ($n = 3,890$). In the 1890s ABs hired in Norway earned $12.22 ($n = 19,260$), whereas Canadians earned $17.76 ($n = 1,103$). Norwegian currency and sterling are converted to dollars merely for ease of analysis and comparison. See Lewis R. Fischer, "How Heavy Was Jack Tar's Purse?: Comparative Wages in the Canadian and Norwegian Merchant Marines, 1863–1900" (paper presented to the Canadian Historical Association Annual Meetings, Winnipeg, 1986), Tables 3 and 6. See also Lewis R. Fischer and Helge W. Nordvik, "From Namsos to Halden: Myths and Realities in the History of Norwegian Seamen's Wages, 1850–1914," *Scandinavian Economic History Review*, XXXV, no. 1 (1987), 41–63. When adjusted for inflation, wages of deckhands may not have declined, and the advantage to Norwegian shipowners from lower wages should not be exaggerated.

34 All sterling wages were converted to dollars at $4.86. The average wage of all ABs in the Saint John fleet who were paid a monthly wage was $16.33. The average for those hired in European ports was $14.43. The average for those hired in ports in England was $14.89. The average AB wage for North Atlantic voyages, where payment was in sterling, was $16.85. The average for voyages to either coast of South America, the East Indies, East Asia, or the Pacific was $15.81. The average for voyages to India or Australia was $15.47.

35 Judith Fingard, *Jack in Port* (Toronto: University of Toronto Press, 1982), 45–6.

36 In the Saint John file, where ABs were paid in monthly dollar wages, the coefficient of variation for the mean wage was no less than 61 per cent.

37 See chap. 7; deflation, however, probably meant that real wages remained fairly constant.

38 Average turn-around for the 1860s was 31.4 days ($n = 809$); for the 1880s, 26.7 ($n = 2,011$); for the 1890s, 29.1 ($n = 524$). See also Lewis R. Fischer, "The Great Mud Hole Fleet," in Alexander and Ommer, *Volumes Not Values*, 138–41.

39 Again these figures are from the Saint John file. Results for the other three fleets are similar.

40 Bullen, *Men of the Merchant Service*, 235.

41 Ibid., 225.

42 Ibid., 255.

43 David Alexander, "Literacy among Canadian and Foreign Seamen," 6.

44 The exact figures are as follows, for 169,852 sailors in four major fleets (there were 12,809 missing cases, or 7.0 per cent of the total): signed clearly - 103,968 (61.2 per cent); signed with difficulty - 25,510 (15.0 per cent); signed with X - 40,374 (23.8 per cent).

45 From the sample of non-Canadian crew lists in the MHA. In sailing vessels the figures are: signed clearly, 66.0 per cent; signs with difficulty, 12.1 per cent; signs with X, 21.9 per cent (total number was 17,853, with 4,169 missing cases). In steamers, 71.5 per cent signed clearly, 7.3 per cent with difficulty, and 21.2 per cent with X (total number of cases 60,883, with 1,486 missing).

46 Alexander, "Literacy among Canadian and Foreign Seamen," 19–21.

47 Ibid., 17.

48 A more satisfactory comparison, between workers in the same age cohorts in different industries or countries at the same time, is difficult to find. Harvey Graff's information on workers employed by the Hawkesbury Lumber Co. in the Ottawa Valley offers an interesting comparison, because literacy is measured by ability to sign, and the time period is appropriate (1889–1903). Only 64 per cent of the skilled workers in this firm were literate. The high rate of illiteracy may reflect traditional illiteracy rates in the Ottawa Valley. Harvey Graff, *The Literacy Myth: Literacy and Social Structure in the Nineteenth Century City* (New York: Academic Press, 1979).

49 Froude, *On the High Seas*, 132.

50 Graff, *The Literacy Myth*, xviii.

51 There is a parallel discussion in Trevor Lummis, *Occupation and Society: The East Anglian Fishermen 1880–1914* (Cambridge: Cambridge University Press, 1985), 164–5, and Paul Thompson, Tony

Wailey, and Trevor Lummis, *Living the Fishing* (London: Routledge and Kegan Paul, 1983), 92.

52 Froude, *On the High Seas*, 183.

53 Benjamin Doane, *Following the Sea* (Halifax: NSM, 1987), 8.

54 *David* of Saint John, Liverpool-Moulmein, 1872–3, Official No. 6121, MHA.

55 *Magnet*, Patrick Keating, master, Official No. 30030, MHA.

CHAPTER SIX

1 Judith Fingard, *Jack in Port: Sailortowns of Eastern Canada* (Toronto: University of Toronto Press, 1982), 187–93.

2 Between 1863 and 1914 529 sailors departed from Saint John vessels of 250 tons and less; of these, none departed because of "dishonourable" discharge (discharge into jail, discharge following demotion, discharge because of refusal to proceed, and the like); only 8.1 per cent deserted. Of sailors leaving vessels of 250–499 tons, 0.5 per cent were "dishonourably" discharged and 18.4 per cent deserted. Of sailors leaving vessels of 500–999 tons, 0.5 per cent were "dishonourably" discharged and 26.8 per cent deserted. Of sailors leaving vessels of 1,000 tons and more, 0.7 per cent were "dishonourably" discharged and 21.2 deserted. The proportion of ABs who were "dishonourably" discharged changed little from one decade to the next and actually declined in the 1890s. This analysis is from the Saint John Crew List File, which contains 54,147 cases.

3 Diary of Annie Butler, 3 April and 12 April 1871, in the brig *Daisy* of Yarmouth. This diary is held by Mr. Raymond Simpson of Merigomish.

4 Letter of 5 March 1872 from James Duncan to Captain Murchison, Duncan Letterbook, PAPEI.

5 Clement Crowell, *Novascotiaman* (Halifax: NSM, 1979), 153.

6 James Kelso of Glasgow to L.C. Owen, 28 April 1874, Owen Letterbooks, PAPEI.

7 Robert Quirk to R.M.C. Stumbles, 5 May 1881, Duncan Letterbooks, vol. 362, PAPEI.

8 Robert Quirk to R.M.C. Stumbles, 23 March 1881, Duncan Letterbooks, vol. 362, PAPEI.

9 W.H. Moran to James H. Moran, 10 August 1871, Moran Papers, NBM.

10 "Action against a Yarmouth Captain," *Yarmouth Times*, 25 June 1884.

11 Fingard, *Jack in Port*, 140. In 1854 the inspector of prisons in the Southern and Western districts reported to the Home Office in London that nine of every twelve prisoners were sailors who had refused to continue their voyages: Tony Lane, " 'Philosophical Anarchists': British Merchant Seamen and Their Attitudes to Authority," typescript of a paper published in French in *Enragés*, (Paris), No. 11–12 (1983–4), 6–7.

12 *J.L. Wickwire* of Windsor, Official No. 52098, 1869–70, MHA.

13 Samlet av Svein Molaug, *Sjofolk Forteller: Hverdagshistorier fra seilskutetiden* (Oslo, 1977), 33. The translation is that of Capt. W.J. Lewis Parker, USCG (Ret), to whom I am grateful for this reference.

14 Fingard, *Jack in Port*, 140 and passim.

15 Reports of the Chief Constable, Quebec River Police, Canada *Sessional Papers*, 1871, no. 5; 1872, no. 5; 1873, no. 8; 1874, no. 4; 1875, no. 5.

16 Reports of the Montreal Harbour Police; Reports of the Chief Constable, Quebec Harbour Police, Canada *Sessional Papers*. The Montreal Harbour Police were disbanded in 1889 and the Quebec Harbour Police in 1893; see Fingard, *Jack in Port*, 30–2.

17 Fingard, *Jack in Port*, 140.

18 W.S. Lindsay, *History of Merchant Shipping and Ancient Commerce* (New York: AMS Press, 1965), vol. III, 472.

19 Returns of causes of deaths of seamen, *British Parliamentary Papers*, 1873, vol. LIX, p. 221; 1874, vol. LX, p. 219; 1875, vol. LXVIII, p. 331; 1876, vol. LXVI, p. 157; 1877, vol. LXXIV, p. 213. In 1873–4, 506 lives were lost on or near British coasts, and 4,034 on the high seas and abroad; of the latter, 1,440 were passengers. See Neville Upham, *The Load Line – A Hallmark of Safety* (Greenwich: NMM, 1978), viii–ix; A.G. Course, *The Merchant Navy: A Social History* (London: F. Mullen, 1963), 245, 247.

20 Samuel Plimsoll, MP, *Our Seamen: An Appeal* (London, 1873).

21 When crew lists were coded, an entry was made to record the presence of an interesting official log. The following section is based on the reading of several hundred official logs for vessels registered in Saint John, Yarmouth, Windsor, and Halifax, MHA.

22 Lindsay, *History of Merchant Shipping*, vol. III, 472–3.

23 Barque *Suffolk* of Glasgow, Official Number 46210, 1866–7, MHA.

24 *Beau Monde* of Saint John, Official No. 35237, 1870–2, MHA.

25 *Newcastle* of Windsor, Official No. 52087, 1871, MHA.

26 *Pomona* of Saint John, E.T. Irvine, master, Official No. 35051, 1868, MHA.

27 *Alexander* of Saint John, Henry Stinchcomb, master, Official No. 1421, 1869, MHA.

28 *Gertrude* of Saint John, I.W. Doane, master, Official No. 35178, 1870-1, MHA.

29 *John Barbour* of Saint John, Robert H.A. Ivey, master, Official No. 34742, 1872-3, MHA.

30 John Congdon Crowe, *In the Days of the Windjammers* (Toronto: Ryerson, 1959), 104.

31 *David G. Fleming* of Saint John, Robert Sully, master, Official No. 24197, 1866-8, MHA. A similar case occurred in the *War Spirit* of Saint John, Official No. 10900, in Pensacola on 29 March 1871.

32 *Peter Maxwell* of Saint John, Official No. 34938, 20 March 1870, MHA.

33 *David McNutt* of Windsor, Official No. 48436, 1868-9, MHA.

34 *Salus* of Halifax, Official No. 48137, In Savannah, 25 Dec. 1867, MHA.

35 Judith Fingard, "The Decline of the Sailor as a Ship Labourer in 19th Century Timber Ports," *Labour/Le Travailleur*, II (1977), 35-53.

36 *Tasmanian* of Saint John, Official No. 35076, July 1870, MHA.

37 *Zambesi* of Saint John, Official No. 35207, 1865-6, MHA.

38 On 2 December 1870, the crew of the *Maud* of Saint John, loading bales of cotton in Savannah, quit work at 6 p.m., leaving four bales of cotton on the wharf. It appears that the master hired others to load the remaining bales (*Maud*, Official No. 41890, 1870-1). In Belize on 24 January 1874 Henry Taylor ordered the crew of the *Fair and Easy* of Windsor to "take in some logs of mahogany that were chafing against the ship." The crew refused on the grounds that it was 9 p.m., and the sailors were sent to jail until the vessel sailed (*Fair and Easy*, Official No. 61487, 1873-4, MHA).

39 *Juno* of Windsor, Official No. 48477, 1873, MHA.

40 *S. Vaughan* of Windsor, Official No. 61466, 1872, MHA.

41 *Ann Gray* of Saint John, Official No. 34844, 1867-8, MHA.

42 *William Carvill* of Saint John, Official No. 35168, 1869-70, MHA.

43 *Athenais* of Saint John, Official No. 35141, 1868-9, MHA.

44 *Beau Monde* of Saint John, James Linskill, master, Official No. 35237, Nov.-Dec. 1867, MHA.

45 *Gertrude* of Saint John, Official No. 35178, 1868-9, MHA. For

another instance of "sogering" or working to rule see Richard Henry Dana, *Two Years before the Mast* (New York: World Publishing Co., 1946), 87.

46 *William Carvill* of Saint John, Hugh Seeds, master, Official No. 35168, 1869-70, MHA.

47 Journal of James N. Smith (supercargo), in the Barque *Susan*, 9 May and 15 July 1850, NBM.

48 E.P. Thompson, "The Moral Economy of the English Crowd in the Eighteenth Century," *Past & Present*, no. 50 (Feb. 1971), 136.

49 *Tasmanian* of Saint John, George B. Willis, master, Official No. 35076, 1872-3, MHA.

50 *Henry* of Saint John, A. Van Norden, master, Official No. 34891, 1866-7, MHA.

51 *Perekop*, Simon Graham, master, quoted in R.J. Cunningham and K.R. Mabee, *Tall Ships and Master Mariners* (St John's: Breakwater, 1985), 95. John Froude fired a revolver during a fight on deck in the 1890s: *On the High Seas: The Diary of Capt. John W. Froude* (St John's: Jesperson, 1983), 68. William Henry Sulis of Saint John, master of the *Africana*, kept both a revolver and "1 Double Bar Gun" in his cabin: *Africana* of Saint John, Official No. 37160, 1868-9, MHA. John Spain, master of the *Favourite* of Saint John, also carried both revolver and double-barrelled shotgun and allowed his carpenter to use and to fire the latter during a confrontation with an AB in July 1863 (*Favourite*, Official No. 2332, 1863, MHA).

52 *Brenda* of Halifax, Official No. 42385, 1867-8, from Cardiff to Madras, MHA.

53 *Brenda* of Halifax, Official No. 42385, 1868-9, MHA.

54 James Evans, *Recollections: or Incidents Culled from the Lives of Some of Our Seafaring Men* (Berwick-on-Tweed, 1908), 74-5.

55 *David G. Fleming* Robert Sulley, master, Official No. 24197, 1866-8. James Crowe, master of the *Selkirk* of Halifax, was arrested and convicted of murder, but a petition to the governor was successful after further evidence was heard, and Crowe was released. The story is told in letters from Crowe and from his wife to Martin Dickie, in Martin Dickie Papers, PANS, MG 7, vol. 93. The master and first mate of the British vessel *Lady Douglas* were convicted of murdering a seaman in 1887. The death penalty was commuted to five years' imprisonment for the master and 18 months for the mate: *Nautical Magazine* (Aug. 1887), 617. See also the trial of a master and mate who beat a 13-

year-old boy to death with a boat-hook in 1847. The defence argued that the "punishment administered to the deceased was the usual and ordinary mode of treating skulkers on ships, however rough it might appear to landsmen." The master was convicted of manslaughter and sentenced to two years in prison: Aled Eames, *Ships and Seamen of Anglesey* (Llangefori: Anglesey Antiquarian Society, 1973), 387.

56 A.J.M. Sykes, "Navvies: Their Work Attitudes," *Sociology*, III (1969), 26; Richard A. Rajala, "The Rude Science: Technology and Management in the West Coast Logging Industry 1890-1930" (unpublished MA thesis, University of Victoria, 1986); Edmund Bradwin, *The Bunkhouse Man* (Toronto: University of Toronto Press, 1972), 58-60, 74.

57 A Greek sailor repeatedly threatened to jump from the *Gertrude* of Saint John, Official No. 35178, 1865-6, MHA. The cook in the *Margaret Rait* jumped overboard after being beaten by the third mate and master: Captain James Doane Coffin, *Journal of the Margaret Rait 1840-1844* (Hantsport, NS: Lancelot Press, 1984), 26-7.

58 The proportion in the Saint John sample who deserted (excluding those who did not join), including all ranks and all cases after 1863, was as follows: Nova Scotians - 15.3 per cent; New Brunswickers - 15.0 per cent; English - 19.1 per cent; Scots - 16.5 per cent; Welsh - 18.4 per cent; Irish - 21.1 per cent; Scandinavians - 31.2 per cent; Germans - 29.7 per cent; French - 23.4 per cent; other Europeans - 28.1 per cent; Americans - 25.5 per cent.

59 Including only ABs signed on between 1891 and 1912, Canadian-born sailors were more likely to desert than others, but again the statistical relationship is weak: 47.2 per cent of British North America-born ABs deserted or failed to join in this period, compared to 41.1 per cent of Scandinavian ABs, 43.9 per cent of other Europeans, and 47.6 per cent of Americans.

60 In the Saint John fleet, 25.5 per cent of sailors aged 20-29 deserted; 0.8 per cent were discharged "dishonourably." Of those aged 35 or over, only 17.4 per cent deserted; 0.5 per cent were discharged "dishonourably." Selecting only ABs produces comparable differences.

61 In the Saint John fleet, selecting ABs only, the cross-tabulation of reason for discharge with literacy produces Cramer's $V = 0.02$. Of all ABs who were literate, 29.5 per cent deserted; of illiterate ABs, 27.7 per cent. Literate Canadians in the Yarmouth fleet were somewhat more likely to receive discharges by mutual consent or to remain with

the vessel: see David Alexander, "Literacy among Canadian and Foreign Seamen," in Rosemary Ommer and Gerald Panting, eds., *Working Men Who Got Wet* (St John's: MHG, 1980), 27.

62 Of crew members hired by masters who gave their residence as a place in British North America, 0.36 per cent were given "dishonourable" discharges; of those hired by masters residing in Britain, 0.08 per cent received "dishonourable" discharges.

63 See chapt. 7.

64 If we aggregate reason for discharge into four categories (remains with the vessel, discharge by mutual consent, dishonourable discharge, and desertion) and if we aggregate place of discharge into five regions, the cross-tabulation of reason with place yields Cramer's $V = 0.52$; lambda with reason dependent $= 0.33$. The relationship strengthens if we include only ABs: lambda with reasons dependent $= 0.45$.

65 Lewis R. Fischer, "A Dereliction of Duty: The Problem of Desertion in Nineteenth Century Sailing Vessels," in Ommer and Panting, *Working Men Who Got Wet*, 58.

66 The Scheffe multiple range test denotes means significantly different at the 0.05 confidence level. For AB wages broken down by four aggregated discharge reasons, discharge by mutual consent and remains were significantly different from desertion and "dishonourable" discharge.

67 Chi square $= 1218.4$ with 6 degrees of freedom; Cramer's $V = 0.36$.

68 The calculations were done in dollar equivalents, and the results were: \$19.26 where the destination was British North America; \$18.68 where the destination was the United States; \$15.46 where the destination was other.

69 Reminiscences of Harris Barnes, PANS, MG 108, no. 9.

70 Diary of Cephas Pearl, Feb. 1884, PANS, RG 7, no. 14A.

71 *Journal of the Margaret Rait 1840–1844* (Hantsport, NS, 1984), 48.

72 *On the High Seas*, 168.

73 Ibid., 122.

CHAPTER SEVEN

1 David Williams, "Crew Size in Trans-Atlantic Trades in the Mid-Nineteenth Century," in Rosemary Ommer and Gerald Panting, eds., *Working Men Who Got Wet* (St John's: MHG, 1980), 121.

2 In the Yarmouth fleet, for instance, the ratio was 2.65 men per 100 tons in 1863-5; it fell to 1.37 men per 100 tons in 1895-9. See Eric W. Sager, "Labour Productivity in the Shipping Fleets of Halifax and Yarmouth, Nova Scotia, 1863-1900," in Ommer and Panting, *Working Men Who Got Wet*, 159.

3 *Tasmanian* of Saint John, Official No. 35076, MHA.

4 In the Saint John SPSS Labour File with voyage as unit of analysis there are 2,061 voyages by 238 vessels. Most of these vessels had voyages that began in six different years.

5 See Sager, "Labour Productivity," 163.

6 Passage times are analysed in Eric W. Sager, "Sources of Productivity Change in the Halifax Ocean Fleet, 1863-1900," in David Alexander and Rosemary Ommer, eds., *Volumes Not Values: Canadian Sailing Ships and World Trades* (St John's: MHG, 1979), 93-116; and Lewis R. Fischer, "The Great Mud Hole Fleet: The Voyages and Productivity of the Sailing Vessels of Saint John, 1863-1912," ibid., 117-55.

7 John Harland and Mark Myers, *Seamanship in the Age of Sail* (Annapolis: Naval Institute Press, 1984), 46.

8 David Alexander and Gerry Panting, "The Mercantile Fleet and Its Owners: Yarmouth, Nova Scotia," *Acadiensis*, VII, no. 2 (spring 1978), 15.

9 From the analysis of vessels registered in Saint John, Miramichi, Halifax, Yarmouth, Windsor, and Pictou. "Vessel life" is the difference between date lost and date built, and "decades" refers to decade in which the vessel was built. The average for the 1860s is based on 1,060 cases; for the 1880s, 449 cases.

10 R.G. Moran to James H. Moran, 12 Sept. 1876, Moran Papers, NBM.

11 R.G. Moran to James H. Moran, 12 December 1876, Moran Papers, NBM. The ship *Lennie* of Yarmouth was converted to a barque in 1879: Charles Armour and Thomas Lackey, *Sailing Ships of the Maritimes* (Toronto: McGraw-Hill Ryerson, 1975), 116.

12 If we look only at ships and barques sailing in the 1870s, and only in North Atlantic trades, barques required fewer men in all classes above 900 tons. For vessels from 900 to 999 tons, barques carried 15.0 men ($n = 46$) and ships 19.7 ($n = 21$); from 1,000 to 1,099 tons, barques carried 13.6 men ($n = 7$) and ships 18.0 ($n = 30$); from 1,100 to 1,199 tons barques carried 15.6 men ($n = 8$) and ships 16.6 ($n = 17$). In North Atlantic trades in the 1880s, barques of 900 to 999 tons carried 13.0 men ($n = 30$) and ships 16.3 men ($n = 4$);

from 1,000 to 1,099 tons, barques carried 11.7 men ($n = 3$) and ships 16.0 men ($n = 20$); from 1,100 to 1,199 tons, barques carried 14.3 men ($n = 19$) and ships 16.4 men ($n = 14$).

13 The reference here is to Sager, "Labour Productivity," 165, where the difference between barques and ships was not so clear. It may be that many Yarmouth and Halifax ships were re-rigged as barques, and parts of the analysis of rig in this earlier essay should be treated with scepticism.

14 The percentage difference between barque and ship for each tonnage range (to be compared with column 3 in Table 25) is as follows: for vessels of 700–799 tons, − 28.2 per cent; for vessels of 800–899 tons, + 8.5 per cent; for vessels of 900–999 tons, − 24.3 per cent; for vessels of 1,000–1,099 tons, − 28.4 per cent; for vessels of 1,100–1,199 tons, − 26.9 per cent; for vessels of 1,200–1,299 tons, − 37.6 per cent. The breakdown of men by rig yields an F statistic of 99.1 (significance = 0.000) and an Eta^2 of 0.51.

15 Frederick William Wallace, *Wooden Ships and Iron Men* (London: Hodder & Stoughton, 1924), 154–5; Stanley Spicer, *Masters of Sail* (Toronto: Ryerson, 1968), 34–5; Armour and Lackey, *Sailing Ships of the Maritimes*, 49, 118; David R. MacGregor, *Merchant Sailing Ships 1850–1875* (London: Conway Maritime Press, 1984), 37–8, 46, 118; Harland and Myers, *Seamanship in the Age of Sail*, 137–8.

16 Wallace, *Wooden Ships and Iron Men*, 155.

17 MacGregor, *Merchant Sailing Ships 1850–1875*, 79.

18 Armour and Lackey, *Sailing Ships*, 118–9.

19 Journal of James N. Smith, barque Susan, 1850, in NBM, shelf A96.

20 E.L. Davies, interviewed by Campbell McMurray, in the Oral History collection, NMM.

21 See the exchange between Craig and Jannasch in Ommer and Panting, *Working Men Who Got Wet*, 185. Not much is known about Canadian sailcloth, but in North America cotton was cheaper, and increasingly sail was purchased from local producers, such as the Yarmouth Duck and Yarn Co. European flax sails were easier to handle, especially when wet, and the later Laeisz "Flying P" vessels carried flax only. In the nineteenth century there had been an improvement in the design and cut of American cotton sails. I am grateful to Niels Jannasch for this information. See also Alan Villiers, *The Way of a Ship* (London: White Lion, 1974), 26. William Smith of New Brunswick, Canada's deputy minister of marine and fisheries, said that

spars became lighter in the later decades of the nineteenth century: Report of the Select Committee to Inquire into the Manning of British Ships, British *Parliamentary Papers*, 1896, vol. XL, 615.

22 Sager, "Labor Productivity," 173-4.

23 Frank T. Bullen, *The Men of the Merchant Service* (London: Smith, Elder, 1900), 32.

24 Report of the Select Committee to Inquire into the Manning of British Ships, British *Parliamentary Papers*, 1896, vol. XL, 615ff.

25 In vessels of 500-999 tons the British North America-resident owners' vessels had a man-ton ratio of 2.00 and the other owners' vessels had a ratio 10.5 per cent higher; in this class there was no difference in the 1860s, but a larger difference in the 1870s and 1880s. Among vessels in the 1,000 1,499-ton class, British North American owners had a ratio overall of 1.09 men per 100 tons, compared to 1.58 for other owners, but the difference was marked only in the 1890s, when we control for time.

26 British *Parliamentary Papers*, 1896, vol. XL, 615-6.

27 William Smith, reporting his conversation with Saint John shipowners to the Select Committee on Manning, in ibid., 618.

28 Using a slightly different method of estimating output growth, a similar result was obtained for the Yarmouth fleet in Sager, "Labour Productivity," 180.

29 Eric W. Sager and Lewis R. Fischer, "The Pursuit of Profits: An Analysis of the Returns from the Shipping Industry of Atlantic Canada, 1850-1900," paper presented to the Atlantic Canada Studies Conference, 1983.

30 Wallace, *Wooden Ships and Iron Men*, 189-90.

31 E.L. Davies interview.

CHAPTER EIGHT

1 Bill Adams, "Ships and Women," in *Ships and Memories* (Brighton: Teredo Books, 1975), 77.

2 "My firm and many of the large steamship owners in Liverpool are compelled to send their ships into the river and lie at anchor for twenty-four hours to let the crews become sober," reported a Liverpool owner, W.J. Lamport, in 1873: "Preliminary Report of the Royal Commission on Unseaworthy Ships," British *Parliamentary Papers*, 1873, vol. XXXVI, 549, question 5607.

3 E.L. Davies, interviewed by Campbell McMurray, in the Oral History collection, NMM.

4 From a survey reported in the *Nautical Magazine* (Oct. 1885), 996. The survey was taken in one port, and the numbers shipped were: 1,094 in February 1871, 2,001 in November 1873, 2,872 in January 1882, and 792 in December 1884.

5 *On the High Seas: The Diary of Capt. John W. Froude* (St John's: Jesperson, 1983), 80.

6 *Nautical Magazine* (Dec. 1887), 977-99; (Feb. 1896), 106. See also Report of the Royal Commission on the Loss of Life at Sea, British *Parliamentary Papers*, 1887. The total employed in British ships in 1881 was 186,719; total accidental deaths, 3,278. By 1896 the total employed in sail was 58,537 and in steam 159,257; accidental deaths were 974 in sail and 885 in steam.

7 F.J. Lindop, "A History of Seaman's Trade Unionism to 1909," (MPhil thesis, University of London, 1971), 30.

8 There is usually a list of crew members even where the vessel was lost at sea, but vessels lost at sea may still be under-represented in the crew list archive. Further, those who died after being discharged due to illness may not always be counted. Of 180,932 who signed crew lists and for whom reason for leaving the vessel is known, 1,444 died. Another 1,769 were discharged because of illness.

9 Only 18.8 per cent died of known or reported diseases, but another 20 per cent died for reasons either unreported or unspecified in data entry, and a large proportion of the latter were probably deaths resulting from disease.

10 In 1893, 27 Europeans and 14 Asians, employed as firemen or trimmers on passages in the tropics, committed suicide in British vessels. In 1894 the numbers were 30 Europeans and 19 Asians. *Nautical Magazine* (April, 1896), 390.

11 Diary of Annie Butler, 14 April 1871, in the brig *Daisy* of Yarmouth. This diary is held by Mr. Raymond Simpson of Merigomish.

12 Frederick William Wallace, *In the Wake of the Windships* (Toronto: Musson Book Co., 1927), 67.

13 This occurred when a sailor in the *Harmonides* of Saint John had smallpox: *Harmonides*, ON 35245, 1871, MHA.

14 It is well known that lime juice is a relatively ineffective anti-scorbutic: Ivan M. Sharman, "Vitamin Requirements of the Human Body," in J. Watt, E.J. Freeman, and W.F. Bynum, *Starving Sailors; the Influence of Nutrition upon Naval and Maritime History* (Green-

wich: NMM, 1981), 24; Conrad Dixon, "Pound and Pint: Diet in the Merchant Service 1750-1980," in Sarah Palmer and Glyndwr Williams, eds., *Charted and Uncharted Waters* (Greenwich: NMM, 1981), 168.

15 Ewan MacColl and Peggy Seeger, eds., *Shellback: Reminiscences of Ben Bright, Mariner*, History Workshop Pamphlets series (Oxford n.d.), 20; E.L. Davies interview.

16 Cephas Pearl Diary, PANS, RG 7, no. 14A.

17 E.L. Davies interview.

18 Cephas Pearl Diary, 1884. He was in the *Flora B. Stafford*, 1,352 tons, as an OS.

19 Ibid.

20 John Butler to Annie Butler, 8 April 1872, written the day before their first son was born; the letters of John Butler are in the possession of Mr. Raymond Simpson of Merigomish.

21 *On the High Seas*, 2, 27, 70-2.

22 Ibid., 24, 50.

23 Ibid., 97.

24 Ibid., 215.

25 Ibid., 209.

26 Ibid., 46.

27 Ibid., 82.

28 Adams, "Ships and Women," 30.

29 See, for instance, Capt. James Doane Coffin, *Journal of the Margaret Rait 1840-1844* (Hantsport, NS, 1984), 37, 59; Adams, *Ships and Memories*, 92-3, 96, passim; Aled Eames, *Ship Master* (Denbigh: Gwynned Archives Service, 1980), 41, 136; Reminiscences of Harris Barnes, PANS, MG 108, no. 9 (1864).

30 Diary and Log Books of Capt. William Miles Collins, PANS, MG 7, vol. 115, diary number 1, 24 Feb. 1885, 29 May 1886.

31 Davies interview. See the chapter "Birds at Sea" in Jessie L. Beattie, *The Log Line: The Adventures of a Great Sailing Captain* (Toronto: McClelland and Stewart, 1972), 52-60. Benjamin Doane also describes the experience of eating sea-birds in his *Following the Sea* (Halifax: NSM, 1987), 83-4.

32 Adams, *Ships and Memories*, 80.

33 Ibid., 92-3.

34 E.L. Davies interview.

35 *On the High Seas*, 66.

36 Cephas Pearl Diary, 1884.

37 Yukio Mishima, *The Sailor Who Fell from Grace with the Sea* (Harmondsworth: Penguin Books, 1970), 14.

38 Conrad, *The Mirror of the Sea* (London: Dent, 1923), 31.

39 *On the High Seas*, 70-2.

40 Stan Hugill, *Shanties from the Seven Seas* (London: Routledge & Kegan Paul, 1961), 45-6.

41 Ibid., 32.

42 Ibid., 583.

43 Bill Adams, "Singers of the Sea," in *Ships and Memories*, 314-15.

44 Cephas Pearl Diary, 1883-4, in the *Flora B. Stafford*.

45 Ibid., 1884, in the *Trinidad*, 1,228 tons.

46 Eames, *Ship Master*, 135; John Congdon Crowe, *In the Days of the Windjammers* (Toronto: Ryerson, 1959), 127. See also Beattie, *Log Line*, 120-31, 163.

47 Goudey's wife appears briefly in the CBC radio program "Days of Sail," in the CBC Sound Archives, Toronto. E.L. Davies sailed under Goudey and remembers Goudey's wife with her children on the poop and singing hymns with the crew on Sunday (E.L. Davies interview).

48 Annie Butler Diary, 9 Jan. and 16 March 1871, in the brig *Daisy* of Yarmouth.

49 John Congdon Crowe, *In the Days of the Windjammers*, 58-62.

50 Fally Cochran Log (catalogued as "Log of the Ship Alabama"), by Fally Cochran, born St Martin's, NB, 1 Jan. 1843, NBM.

51 Journal of Amelia Holder (born 1855) in the brigantine *Mina*, 11 Dec. and 23 Dec. 1869 and 18 Jan. 1870, NBM.

52 Journal of Abigail Ryerson of Yarmouth, in the ship *Nova Scotian*, 1847-8. This diary is possessed by Mr. and Mrs. Ivor L. Jefferies of Saint John, who kindly donated a copy of their transcript of the document to the author and to the NBM.

53 Jane E. Crowe to Martin Dickie, 18 July 1844, in Dickie Papers, PANS, MG 7, vol. 93. See also Stanley T. Spicer, *Sails of Fundy: The Schooners and Square-riggers of the Parrsboro Shore* (Hantsport, NS: Lancelot Press, 1984), for the story of a woman seaman.

54 John K. Butler to Annie Butler, 13 Dec. 1872.

55 Journal of Abigail Ryerson, 2 Sept. 1847.

56 Diary of Alice Coalfleet in the barque *Plymouth*, 13 Oct. 1890. This diary is in Dalhousie University Archives.

57 Journal of Amelia Holder, 25 Dec. 1870.

58 Diary of Alice Coalfleet, 18 July 1887.

59 Spicer, *Sails of Fundy*, 120.

60 Bent G. Sivertz, interviewed by the author in Nanoose Bay, BC, in January 1987. Sivertz served in sailing vessels in the Pacific in the 1920s.

61 "In almost every ship's forecastle ... conversation is devoted mainly to discussions on three universal subjects: women, liquor, and venereal disease," writes Ken Attiwill in *Horizon* (London, n.d.), 58.

62 Cf. Lionel Tiger, *Men in Groups* (New York: Vintage, 1970), 167ff.

63 Bent G. Sivertz, "The 1922-23 Voyage of the Five-Masted Barquentine *Forest Friend*," unpublished paper presented to the Thermopylae Club of Victoria, 1981, 8.

64 Ibid., 12.

65 Ibid., 16-17.

66 Bent G. Sivertz, in a letter to the author, 8 Dec. 1986.

67 Ibid.

68 S.E. Shipp Diary, 24 Aug. 1874, Provincial Archives of Newfoundland and Labrador.

69 *On the High Seas*, 215.

70 Diary of William Collins, 2 April 1891.

71 Reminiscences of Harris Barnes (in the brig *Gondolier*, 1864).

72 Beattie, *The Log Line*, 41-2.

73 E.L. Davies interview.

74 *On the High Seas*, 218-19.

75 Journal of George F. Smith, in brigantine *Brisk* of Saint John, 27 Nov. 1859, NBM..

76 *On the High Seas*, 24, 219.

77 Journal of George F. Smith, 27 Nov. 1859, NBM.

78 Walter Runciman, cited in Michael Mason, Basil Greenhill, and Robin Craig, *The British Seafarer* (London: Hutcheson/BBC, 1980), chap. 2.

79 Cephas Pearl Diary, 1884.

80 E.L. Davies interview.

81 Ibid.

82 Peter Linebaugh, "All the Atlantic Mountains Shook," *Labour/Le Travailleur*, 10 (autumn 1982), 101-6.

83 *On the High Seas*, 209.

84 Sidney Riggs, cited in Mason, Greenhill, and Craig, *The British Seafarer*, chap. 6.

85 *On the High Seas*, 46.

CHAPTER NINE

1 See B.R. Mitchell and P. Deane, *Abstract of British Historical Statistics* (Cambridge: Cambridge University Press, 1962), 223.

2 Sarah Palmer, "The British Shipping Industry 1850-1914," in Lewis R. Fischer and Gerald Panting, eds., *Change and Adaptation in Maritime History* (St John's: MHG, 1985), 94.

3 See Eric W. Sager and Gerry Panting, "Staple Economies and the Rise and Decline of the Shipping Industry in Atlantic Canada, 1820-1914," in Fischer and Panting, *Change and Adaptation*, 1-45; and Eric W. Sager and Lewis R. Fischer, *Shipping and Shipbuilding in Atlantic Canada* (Ottawa: Canadian Historical Association, 1986).

4 The total number of sailors in steamers for which crew lists were coded was 4,428.

5 Cassie Brown, *A Winter's Tale: The Wreck of the Florizel* (Toronto: Doubleday, 1976), 265-70.

6 The log book of the *Empress of Japan* is one of several logs of CPR vessels in the NMM.

7 Cephas Pearl Diary, PANS, 1884.

8 J.C. Healey, *Foc's'le and Glory Hole: A Study of the Merchant Seaman and His Occupation* (New York: Oxford University Press, 1936), 48.

9 Tony Lane, "Neither Officers nor Gentlemen," *History Workshop Journal*, no. 19 (spring 1985), 129. See also H.C. McMurray, "Technology and Social Change at Sea: The Status and Position on Board of the Ship's Engineer," in Rosemary Ommer and Gerald Panting, eds., *Working Men Who Got Wet* (St John's: MHG, 1980), 37-50.

10 Ibid., 50.

11 *On the High Seas: The Diary of Capt. John W. Froude* (St John's: Jesperson Press, 1983), 45.

12 Based on a stratified random sample of non-Canadian vessels in the crew list collection, MHA. This sample, begun by David Alexander, was weighted to include vessels from each decade in proportion to the total number of vessels on British registry in each decade between 1860 and 1910. All crew information for every fifth vessel was coded; this yielded 84,391 crew records, of which 62,369, or 74 per cent, are records of sailors employed in steamers or auxiliary steamers. Most of the voyages for sailing vessels occurred in the 1860s and 1870s, since sailing tonnage declined quickly in relative importance, but voyage

starts by steamers are distributed across four decades. The sample includes complete crew information for 2,782 voyages by British vessels (1,690 of these were voyages by steamers or auxiliary steamers). The sample, sometimes referred to as the "one percent sample," in fact includes less than 1 per cent of sailors hired in British ships in these decades, but the sample is sufficiently large to allow certain cautious generalizations about the labour force.

The 2,782 voyages for which crew members were coded suggest that voyage patterns of steamers were quite different from patterns for sailing vessels. Most voyages, for sail or for steam, began in the United Kingdom. British home trades are almost completely absent from the sample, and liner companies are under-represented; the focus is on tramp steamers. Steamers and auxiliary steamers were employed most often in North Atlantic passages to and from Canada and the United States (23.6 per cent of voyages), on passages to or from the Mediterranean (13.4 per cent), on Black Sea voyages (10.9 per cent), on Baltic voyages (8.3 per cent), or on other, Europe-Britain voyages (13.7 per cent). Sailing vessels were employed much less often on the North Atlantic passage and more often outside the North Atlantic (voyages to the West Indies, Africa, the Indian Ocean, the East Indies, South America, Australia, and elsewhere in the Pacific were over 40 per cent of the voyages).

13 Of the 22,022 workers hired in non-Canadian sailing vessels, likely only three or four were women (there were a few more where the name does not make clear the sex of the worker). Women workers in sailing ships were viewed as a North American curiosity. In 1896 the *Nautical Magazine* remarked with surprise on the presence of women mates in the US merchant marine: *Nautical Magazine* (July 1896), 582.

14 Harry Bruce, *Lifeline: The Story of the Atlantic Ferries and Coastal Boats* (Toronto: Macmillan, 1977), 43-4.

15 The average time served per sailor per voyage in steam (all ranks below master) was 59 days in steam ($n = 21,970$). The desertion rate in the four Canadian fleets was 0.7 per man-year.

16 The death rates must be accepted as tentative rather than exact measures, because some deaths may have been unreported. The death rate in British sailing vessels seems much higher than in Canadian sailing vessels, but when the rates are adjusted for man-years at sea the difference is not so great.

17 On the rise of trade unions see Havelock Wilson, *My Stormy Voyage through Life* (London, 1925); Norman McCord, "Early Seamen's Unions in North East England," in Paul Adam, ed., *Seamen in Society* (Bucharest: Commission internationale d'histoire maritime, 1980), vol. III, 88-95.

18 In the early 1860s the average petty officer in a steamer was earning 75 per cent more than the average AB; by the early 1900s the difference was 100 per cent.

19 Almost 71 per cent of desertions were accounted for by those who were not officers, petty officers, ABs or OSs: this residual category, 55 per cent of all crews, consists mainly of firemen, trimmers, other engine room assistants, apprentices, and the catering staff under the cook or steward. A further 25 per cent of desertions were by ABs or OSs.

20 S.J.P. Thearle, "The Evolution of the Modern Cargo Steamer," *Transactions of the Institution of Naval Architects*, XLIX (1907), 100. See also Robin Craig, *The Ship: Steam Tramps and Cargo Liners* (London: NMM, 1980), 32.

21 Craig, *Steam Tramps and Cargo Liners*. The influence of the ship-owner and his demands is evident in the *Transactions of the Institution of Naval Architects*.

22 Thearle, "Evolution," 100.

23 Maxwell Ballard, "Notes on a New Design of Merchant Vessel," *Transactions of the Institution of Naval Architects*, LIII (1911), 300.

24 From a newspaper account of the launching of the Saint John vessel *Harry Troop*, contained in J.V. Troop Scrapbook, shelf 38, NBM.

25 A.W. Robinson, "Economy in Ocean Transportation," *Journal of the Engineering Institute of Canada* (Feb. 1919), 105, 106.

26 Linton Hope, "The Application of the Internal Combustion Engine to Fishing and Commercial Vessels," *Transactions of the Institution of Naval Architects*, LII (1910), 126.

27 Healey, *Foc's'le and Glory-Hole*, 165.

28 John List discussing a paper by I. Knudsen, "Results of Trials of the Diesel-Engined Sea-Going Vessel *Selandia*," *Transactions of the Institution of Naval Architects*, LIV (1912), 78.

29 Frank T. Bullen, *The Men of the Merchant Service* (London: Smith, Elder, 1900), 258; cf. William Morris Barnes, *Rolling Home* (London: Cassell and Co., 1931), 40-1.

30 Charles Booth, *Life and Labour of the People in London*, 2nd series, vol. III (New York: AMS Press, 1970), 361.

31 Cephas Pearl Diary, PANS. Benjamin Doane, *Following the Sea* (Halifax: NSM, 1987), 234.

32 See, for instance, C.H. Wright, *The Efficient Deck Hand*, 3rd ed. (Liverpool: James Laver, 1975); Capt. D. Wilson-Barker, *Things a Sailor Needs to Know* (London: C. Griffin, 1918). I am indebted to Tony Lane for his comments on this subject.

33 Healey, *Foc's'le and Glory-Hole*, 27.

34 Ibid., 26; Bullen, *The Men of the Merchant Service*, 324.

35 Healey, *Foc's'le and Glory-Hole*, 19, 28.

36 *Ibid*, 33.

37 *Ibid.*, 33–6; Bullen, *The Men of the Merchant Service*, 180–7.

38 Tony Lane, "Neither Officers nor Gentlemen," *History Workshop Journal*, no. 19 (spring 1985), 1936.

39 *Marine Journal* (21 May 1921), cited in Healey, *Foc's'le and Glory-Hole*, 32.

40 Lane, "Neither Officers nor Gentlemen," 136.

41 Ibid., 129.

42 Healey, *Foc's'le and Glory-Hole*, 40.

43 *Practical Hints to Young Officers in the Merchant Marine* (Glasgow, 1907), cited in Lane, "Neither Officers nor Gentlemen," 137.

44 Bullen, *The Men of the Merchant Service*, 84.

45 R.F. Sparkes, *The Winds Softly Sigh* (St John's: Breakwater Books, 1981), 46.

46 Felicity Harrington, *The Lady Boats: The Life and Times of Canada's West Indies Merchant Fleet* (Halifax: Dalhousie University, Canadian Marine Transportation Centre, 1980), 18–19.

47 Rudyard Kipling, "M'Andrew's Hymn" (1893), in *Rudyard Kipling's Verse* (London: Hodder and Stoughton, 1919), vol. I, 165.

Index

Able seaman. *See* Sailors: Skill

Accidents, 131, 224-6. *See also* Death rates

Adams, Bill, 12, 237

Alexander, David, 3, 158, 159, 214

Apprenticeship, 52, 134, 136, 157, 173, 215

Authority, 5-7, 49, 99-103, 114, 153, 164-200, 243, 263-4. *See also* Sailors: and relations with masters

Barnes, Harris, 50, 198, 240

Barque, 33, 36-8, 42, 76, 77, 79, 90, 104, 114-17, 207-9

Barquentine, 33, 42

Baxter, Edward, 179

Berman, Morris, 5

Birch, William, 180

Blackburn, Howard, 72

Blanketing, 86

Bluenose, 26

Booth, Charles, 138, 260

Bosun, 8, 9

Bowman B. Law, 90-2

Bowring and Co., 248, 264

Brig, 29, 33, 34-5, 36-7, 42, 51, 52

Brigantine, 31-3, 34, 35, 42, 51, 52, 69

British (non-Canadian) crew lists, 151-2, 214-15

Brittain, George, 162

Brown, Cassie, 4

Bullen, Frank, 93, 102, 111, 134, 157

Butler, Annie, 166, 235

Butler, John, 166-7, 228, 236

Cameron, John, 178

Canadian Pacific Railway Co., 248, 265

Cann, Lyman, 52

Cann, Thomas B., 52

Cattlemen, 249

Certificates of competence and of service, 84, 92, 94-8

Charter parties, 83, 96

Coastal shipping, 15-16, 21-45, 47, 49-52, 56, 60-4, 66-73, 77-8, 97, 118, 187, 190

Cochran, Fally, 235-6

Coffin, James Doane, 199

Collins, William Miles, 230, 240

Conrad, Joseph, 6, 15, 63, 73, 92, 231

Cooks, 56, 107, 112. *See also* Petty officers

Craft, craftsmen, 10-12, 14-15, 44, 61, 85, 135, 201, 244. *See also*

Sailhandling; Skill

Craig, Robin, 259

Crimps, 4, 141

Crowe, David Perley, 176

Crowe, Jane, 236

Crowe, John Congdon, 234, 235

Cunningham, Henry, 210

Curry, Charles, 178

Dana, Richard Henry, 127

Davies, E.L., 234

Darrach, Claude, 4

Death rates and risk, 131, 171, 187, 189, 191, 223-6, 229

Demurrage, 83

Department of Marine and Fisheries (Canada), 97

Desertion, 56, 57-8, 99, 101-2, 154-5, 166, 168-9, 172, 186-98; in steamships, 254-7

Discretion content, 8-9, 80-1, 105, 106-10, 111, 114, 129-31, 263-5

Division of labour, 9, 15, 28, 74, 88-9, 105, 106-10, 122, 246-53, 257-8

Dixon, Conrad, 99

Doane, Benjamin, 130-1, 138, 261

Doane, Isaac, 181

Donkey engines, 211, 213

Double topsails, 209-10
Duncan, James, 167
Dunnage, 84
Durkee, Amasa, 52
Durkee, Lyman J., 52

Emerson windlass, 116
Engineering (marine),
    258-60
Engineers, 247-9, 256, 265

Fingard, Judith, 4, 155,
    164, 169, 172
Firearms, 176, 179, 183,
    228, 232
Firemen, 247-9, 253, 262
Fishing, fishermen, 3,
    15-16, 24, 28-9, 31, 33,
    44-7, 48-9, 51, 56, 62-3,
    66, 70-1, 73, 137, 162,
    230; and cod trade,
    68-71; and sailors as
    fishermen, 230
Forbes, Robert, 209
Forecastle, 28, 29, 30-1,
    89, 101, 179, 184, 226,
    231-2, 243, 249
Fox, Alan, 8-9
Fraternalism, 48-54, 58-9,
    65-6, 72-3
Freight rates, 69-70, 75,
    79, 164-5, 166, 167,
    188, 201
Froud, John W., xviii, 4,
    24, 43, 71, 73, 114,
    122-3, 125, 137, 138,
    161, 199-200, 228-32,
    241, 242, 244, 250

Goffman, Erving, 103
Goudey, Aaron, 52
Goudey, Robert, 234
Grand Banks, 16, 18, 24,
    42, 48, 62-3, 71
Great Britain, 20, 22, 23,
    25, 45, 51, 53, 71,
    151-2, 250-65
Guano, 178
Gulf Stream, 16
Gullison, Benjamin, 82,
    145
Gullison, Frank, 82

Halifax, NS, Halifax vessels,
    13, 16, 20-2, 24, 25, 27,
    34-7, 42, 49, 63, 76, 79,
    96, 97, 117-19, 142-3,
    150-1, 161, 202, 204, 246
Harland, John, 4
Harris, George, 174
Hatch coamings, 90
Hatfield, Jacob K., 153
Healey, James, 260
Hill, Christopher, 47
Hohman, E.P., 14
Holder, Amelia, 236
Homosexuality, 239
Howes, Frederick, 209
Hughes, Samuel, 179

Industrial capital,
    industrialization, 4, 9,
    10-11, 13-15, 35, 38,
    72-3, 74-5, 103, 104-5,
    115-21, 164, 244, 245-65
Industrial democracy, 6,
    7-8, 12
Initiation rituals, 238-9

Jukes, J.B., 29

Killam, Frank, 80-1, 115
Killam, George, 52
Kipling, Rudyard, 265
Knowledge, 91, 93, 94-5,
    108, 122-7, 131-4, 185,
    205, 212, 263-5. See also
    Skill: and discretion
    content

Labouchere, Henry, 95
Labour markets, 4, 139-57,
    194-5
Labrador, 47, 48
Labrador Current, 16-17,
    18
Law, mercantile, 4, 83-4,
    86, 93-103, 164, 168-9,
    171-3, 188 passim, 250.
    See also Merchant
    Shipping Act of 1854
Lewis, Henry, 82
Lewis, N.B., 82
Lindsay, W.S., 93, 100-1
Linebaugh, Peter, 14

Liquor, and sobriety, 58,
    73, 82, 91, 99, 182, 223,
    227
Literacy, 92, 95, 157-63,
    192, 199
London, Jack, 158

McElhinney, M.P., 177,
    234
MacGregor, David R., 210
Maintenance and repairs,
    60, 73, 110-11, 133-4,
    261
Man-ton ratios and
    manning, 34, 37-8,
    67-8, 71, 72, 78, 110,
    115, 194, 201-21, 249,
    250-1
Management, 79, 80-3,
    86-103, 110, 134, 212,
    214, 263-4. See also
    Authority
Manson, Thomas, 162
Maritime history, 3-12
Marx, Karl, 10
Masters, 81-91, 96-8; ages
    of, 144; birthplaces of,
    142-3, 212-13; cabins of,
    90-2; and certificates,
    94-8; experience of, 144;
    loneliness of, 87; and
    navigation, 84-5, 91;
    relations with owners, 52,
    54, 67, 72, 79-88, 166-7,
    201, 246; relations with
    sailors, 80, 86-103,
    104-5, 168-200, 212-21;
    retention rates, 144-5;
    work of, 58-60 passim,
    81-5
Mates. See Officers
Matthews, Keith, 165
Maury, Matthew Fontaine,
    85
Merchant capital, mer-
    chants, 7, 13, 44-6, 66,
    78-88, 102, 166-7, 246;
    and fishermen, 44-52;
    relations with masters,
    52, 54, 67, 72, 79-88,
    166-7, 201, 246; and
    supercargo, 54

Merchant Marine Act of 1850, 94-5
Merchant Shipping Act of 1854, 96-101
Miramichi, 38
Mitchell, Peter, 96-7
Montreal Harbour Police, 170-3
Moran, Robert, 207
Moran, W.H., 167, 174
Morris, Duncan, 237
Morris, I.B., 87
Morris, John W., 152
Moule, John, 163
Murray, George, 168

Nautical Almanac, 84
Nautical astronomy, 84
Navigation Acts, 94
New Brunswick, 37, 38, 50, 53, 78, 96, 139, 143, 145-6, 197, 213
Newfoundland, 17, 18, 21, 23, 24, 26, 29, 34, 35, 39, 40, 44-8, 51-3, 62, 67-73, 106-7, 229
North Atlantic Ocean, 16-20, 118-19, 120-1
Nova Scotia, 16-18, 20, 22-5, 37, 44, 48, 50-1, 53, 70, 78, 96, 139, 143, 145-6, 192, 213, 230

Officers, 7, 65, 89, 91-2, 94-8, 106-7, 109, 110, 134-5, 145-9, 157, 190, 217, 247, 249, 256-7, 263-5
Ommer, Rosemary, 148-9
Owners, ownership, 45-6, 78-9, 166-7. See also Merchant capital

Pacific Ocean, 119-20
Parker, John P., 4
Paternalism, 44, 47, 48, 51-3, 56, 72-3, 79, 102, 104-5, 106, 164, 192
Pearl, Cephas, 198, 226-8, 229, 231, 243, 249, 261
Petty officers, 89, 106-7, 108, 109, 110-13, 134,

147, 180-1, 190, 217, 247-9, 250-1, 256-7
Pictou, 37
Pirates, 7
Planters, 44-6, 47
Plimsoll, Samuel, 101, 169, 226
Prince Edward Island, 39, 53
Professionalization, 74, 93-103

Quebec Harbour Police, 170-3
Quirk, Robert, 82-3, 167

Reefing, 126-7
Respectability, 137, 162
Rice, Richard, 4
Rigging, 27, 31-7, 60, 64, 75, 115-16, 122-3, 132, 211. See also Sailing ships
Roche, William, 80
Royal Navy, 88-9
Runciman, Walter, 242
Ryerson, Abigail, 236
Ryerson, George, 52, 167
Ryerson, John K., 52

Sailcloth, 211
Sailhandling, 24, 27-8, 32-5, 58-65, 80, 85-6, 122-33, 207, 260-1. See also Sailing ships
Sailing ships: and competition with steamships, 13-14, 74, 245-6; construction of, 26, 35; deck loads, 72; evolution of, in Atlantic Canada, 15-16, 26-43; historical writing on, 3-5; increased hull size, 75-6; and iron in, 35, 42, 75-6, 115-16; length-breadth ratios, 35, 76; maintenance of, 60, 73; rise of ocean fleets, 75-9; and sailhandling, 24, 27-8, 32-5, 58-65, 80, 85-6, 122-33, 207,

260-1; and sailing speeds, 205; and sails of, 24, 26-9, 32-7, 115, 122-33; and shipwrecks, 72, 205-6; and tonnage ranges, 21, 29, 34, 37, 40, 75-8, 202-3, 208; traders and general cargo carriers, 54; and unseaworthiness, 170-3, 174-6, 184; voyage duration, 121, 253-6; voyage patterns of, 19-25, 37, 51, 117-21, 191, 196, 312-13. See also Barque; Barquentine; Brig; Brigantine; Schooner; Ship rig; Sloop
Sailmaking, 111-12
Sailors: ages of, 51, 53-5, 56, 138-9, 146, 148, 153-4, 192, 212; bargaining by, 173-86, 196-8; and birthplaces, 51, 53, 71, 78, 140-1, 142-4, 147-55, 161-2, 192, 250, 253-5; community and class, 137, 162, 222, 244; and desertion, 56-8, 99, 101-2, 154-5, 166, 168-9, 172, 186-98, 254-7; discharges, 57-8, 186-99, 257; entertainments, of, 231-4; and firearms, 163, 176, 179, 183, 228, 232; and forecastle, 28, 29, 30-1, 89, 101, 179, 184, 226, 231-2, 243, 249; and fraternalism, 48-54, 58-9, 65-6; historical writing on, 3-6; illnesses of, 57, 187, 189, 191, 224-6; and labour contracts, 56, 105-6; language of, 26, 54, 64, 74, 148, 151, 153, 162, 164, 239; and literacy, 92, 157-63, 192, 199; and migration, 11, 71,

149, 161; and occupational pluralism, 73, 138-9; productivity of labour, 218-20; ranks of, 107, 250-1; reasons for going to sea, 137-8, 227; and relations with masters, 5-6, 29-30, 44-5, 47, 48, 49-50, 54-6, 58-9, 63-4, 65-6, 72-3, 80, 86-105, 134-5, 164-200, 196-8, 212-21; and religion, 241-2; reputation of, 3, 136-7; residences, 50-1; retention rates, 139-41, 254; risk of death, 131, 171, 187, 189, 191, 223-6, 229, 256-7; and sailhandling, 24, 27-8, 32-5, 58-65, 80, 85-6, 89, 122-33, 207, 260-1; total employment, 77-8; and wages, 49, 54-5, 66-7, 69-72, 75, 99, 106, 155-7, 171, 188-9, 194-8, 205, 214-21, 243, 247-8, 256-8; and watches, 89, 113-14, 175-6, 221, 233-4; and withdrawal of labour, 99-100, 169-73, 183-6, 187, 198-9; women, 51, 234-8, 250-1; work in port, 177-8; work on land, 138-9, 160-1; working environment, 16-26; working to rule, 181-2; yarns 231-3. *See also* Skill
St Elmo's fire, 240-1
Saint John, NB, Saint John vessels, 20, 21, 29, 36-8, 50, 51, 76, 79, 93, 96, 97, 108, 111, 117-19, 120, 140-3, 145, 150-1, 156, 159, 161, 182, 188-9, 192-7, 202-3, 204-6, 215-18, 246, 248
St John's, Nfld, 13, 21, 23, 24, 40, 42, 51, 77

Schooner, 13-15, 26, 28, 29, 31-5, 41-2, 45-6, 48, 49, 51, 52, 58-63, 67, 70-2, 73, 79, 91, 108, 110, 117, 162, 227
Scurvy, 57, 174, 179-80, 227
Sealing, 3, 29, 33, 62-3
Seasonality, 16-18, 42-3, 122
Select Committee on Shipwrecks (1836), 94
Shallop, 27-8
Shanties, 153, 232-3
Ship rig, 33, 36-8, 42, 114, 207-9
Shipbuilding, 75-6, 78, 88
Shipping offices, 101, 141
Sider, Gerald, 48
Skill: of able seaman, 114-15, 122-35, 260-2; of bosun, 110-11; in bracing the yards, 127-9; of carpenter, 111; of cook, 112; definitions of, 8-9; and deskilling, 246, 258-61; and discretion content, 8-9, 46, 48, 73, 105-10, 114, 129-31, 263-5; of engineer, 262; of fireman, 262; and knowledge, 8, 46, 58-66, 83-6, 122-7, 131-4, 185, 205, 212, 263-5; of master, 60-4, 81-7, 96-8; of mates, 91-2, 95-6; and navigation, 59-61, 63-6; of ordinary seaman, 134; and ropework, 133; in sailhandling, 58-66, 122-31, 260-1; of sailmaker, 111-12; in steamships, 258-65; in steering, 64-5, 131-2; and task range, 7-8, 9, 73, 106, 108, 110, 129, 131-4; and technical language, 64; of trimmer, 262; and wages, 55

Sloop, 27, 34, 42
Slop chest, 243
Smith, George, 242
Smith, William, 213-15
Spicer, George, 138
Spicer, Stanley, 4
Spiral bracing, 85-6
Staple trades, 15, 44, 66-70
Steamships, 7-8, 13, 40, 68-70, 118, 146, 157-8, 194, 245
Stewards, stewardesses, 106-7, 109, 112, 250-2. *See also* Petty officers
Stowage, 83-4
Sugar trade, 69-70
Suicide, 187, 225-6
Sulis, George, 177
Sunday observance, 100, 176-7
Supercargo, 79-80

Task range, 7-8, 9, 73, 106, 108, 110, 129, 131-4
Technology: and authority, 88-9; sailing ships, 4, 5, 8, 11, 13-14, 15-16, 26-9, 32-7, 104-5, 201, 209-11, 213, 222; and sails, 31-4, 207-13; in schooners, 67-8; steamships, 7-8, 13, 74-5, 157-8, 245; use of iron, 31, 35, 42, 75-6, 115-16
Telegraph, 80, 82, 166
Timber trade, 35, 37, 52, 72, 78
Trade unions, 3, 244
Trefry, Thomas, 177
Truck system, 45, 49

Undermanning, 173-4. *See also* Man-ton ratios

Victualling, 29, 56-7, 58, 89, 101, 112, 114, 178-83, 184, 190, 223, 226-7, 230, 233, 256

Violence, 3, 100, 168,
171-2, 176, 178, 182-6,
199, 228, 232
Voyage patterns, 19-25,
37, 51, 118-19, 191, 196,
254, 312-13

Wages, 75, 99, 106, 155-7,
171, 188-9, 194-8, 205,
214-21, 243, 247-8,
256-8

Wallace, Frederick
William, 4, 6, 102, 136,
137, 142, 153, 221
Ward, John, and Sons,
81-2
West Indies, 15, 20-5, 28,
45, 51, 52, 70, 121, 178,
248, 265
Whaling, 3
Windsor, NS, Windsor
vessels, 37, 76, 79, 96,

102, 117-19, 120, 142-3,
150-1, 215-17, 246
Wire rigging, 116-17, 211
Women, 51, 139, 184, 230,
234-8, 250-1

Yarmouth, NS, Yarmouth
vessels, 37, 52-7, 76, 79,
82, 94, 96, 117-19,
142-3, 145, 150-1, 202,
206, 214-15, 246